Small States:
Economic Review & Basic Statistics

Annual Series: Fourteenth Volume, Spring 2010

COMMONWEALTH SECRETARIAT

Commonwealth Secretariat
Marlborough House
Pall Mall
London SW1Y 5HX
United Kingdom

Published by the Commonwealth Secretariat
Designed by Wayzgoose
Cover design by kc gan designs
Printed by Hobbs the Printers Ltd, Totton, Hampshire

Wherever possible, the Commonwealth Secretariat uses paper sourced from sustainable forests or from sources that minimise a destructive impact on the environment.

Cover photo credit: Rebecca Nduku

Copies of this publication can be obtained from:

Publications Section
Commonwealth Secretariat
Marlborough House
Pall Mall
London SW1Y 5HX
United Kingdom
Tel: +44 (0)20 7747 6342
Fax: +44 (0)20 7839 9081
Email: *publications@commonwealth.int*
Website: *www.thecommonwealth.org/publications*

ISBN 978-1-84929-016-6 (paperback)
ISBN 978-1-84859-065-6 (downloadable e-book)
ISSN 1359-7507

Foreword

This is the fourteenth issue of this annual publication, which was previously published under the title *Basic Statistical Data on Selected Countries* (*with populations of less than 5 million*). It is intended as an essential reference for economists and policy-makers in small states (countries with populations of 1.5 million or less) and for their development partners. It also provides a useful resource for analysts from research and academic institutions. As in the previous issue, the publication is in two parts.

Part I provides an analysis of economic trends in small states in 2008 and three research articles. The analysis of economic trends focuses on the economic environment faced by small states, their external performance and key development issues facing policy-makers. The articles focus on international trade in services. The article by Dirk Willem te Velde looks at trade in knowledge-based services and how this can assist small states to grow their economies after the global economic and financial crisis. The article by Estella Aryada highlights the prospects for small states exporting health and wellness services, and the article by Chanda Chella looks at pro-poor tourism intervention through linkages between agriculture and tourism.

Part II contains 54 statistical tables covering all small states, as well as countries which at the end of 2007 had populations of 5 million or less. The inclusion of countries with populations above the small states population threshold of 1.5 million is for comparison purposes. Fifteen countries with populations of 5 million or less are included for the first time. They are: Albania, Armenia, Bosnia-Herzegovina, Georgia, Latvia, Lebanon, Lithuania, Macedonia FYR, Moldova, Mongolia, Montenegro, Turkmenistan, Croatia, Oman and Slovenia. The countries are grouped into three categories on the basis of their 2007 per capita gross national income. These are: (a) low-income countries with per capita income of US$935 and below; (b) middle-income countries with per capita income of US$936–11,455; and (c) high-income countries with per capita income of US$11,456 or more. The tables are organised under three headings: economic indicators; social and demographic indicators; and other development indicators.

The publication is a unique source of information on small states. It has been prepared by Constance Vigilance, Economic Adviser; Faiz Sobhan, Economic Officer; Graham Banton, Tony Traub, Ibukunoluwa Ibitoye, Wonderful Khonje, Research Officers; and Andrew Armitage, Programme Assistant, all from the Commonwealth Secretariat's Economic Affairs Division. External reviews were done at various stages in the preparation of the publication by Dr Naren Prasad and Dr John L Roberts. The work was carried out under the supervision and guidance of Janet Strachan, Adviser and Head of Section (Small States, Environment and Economic Management).

Cyrus Rustomjee
Director, Economic Affairs Division
Commonwealth Secretariat

Contents

Tables

Economic indicators

Figures

Abbreviations and Acronyms

ACP	African, Caribbean and Pacific
ADB	Asian Development Bank
AGOA	African Growth and Opportunity Act
BSN	Buyer-seller network
CPA	Cotonou Partnership Agreements
CPI	Consumer Price Index
DAC	Development Assistance Committee
DSB	Dispute Settlement Body
EC	European Commission
EFTA	European Free Trade Association
EIU	Economic Intelligence Unit
EPA	Economic partnership agreement
FAO	Food and Agriculture Organization
FDI	Foreign direct investment
GATS	General Agreement on Trade in Services
GDP	Gross domestic product
GiG	Gambia is Good
GNI	Gross national income
HDI	Human Development Index
HIPC	Heavily indebted poor country
ICT	Information and communication technology
IFSC	International Financial Services Centre (Botswana)
ILO	International Labour Organization
IMF	International Monetary Fund
IT	Information technology
JCI	Joint Commission International
LDC	Least developed country
MDRI	Multilateral debt relief initiative
MERCOSUR	Mercado Común del Sur (Southern Common Market)
MNE	Multinational enterprise
ODI	Overseas Development Institute
OECS	Organisation of Eastern Caribbean States
PRS	Poverty reduction strategy
RERF	Revenue Equalization Reserve Fund (Kiribati)
SACU	Southern African Customs Union
SIDS	Small island developing state
SMEs	Small and medium enterprises
SMMEs	Small, micro and medium enterprises
ST-EP	Sustainable Tourism-Eliminating Poverty
TIDCA	Trade, Investment and Development Co-operation Agreement
UEA	United Arab Emirates
UNCTAD	United Nations Conference on Trade and Development
UNDP	United Nations Development Programme
UNWTO	United Nations World Tourism Organization
USA	United States of America
WEF	World Economic Forum

WTO	World Trade Organization
WTTC	World Tourism and Travel Council

PART I

Recent Economic Trends in Commonwealth Small States

1. Recent Economic Trends in Commonwealth Small States

Introduction

This chapter examines the economic performance of Commonwealth small states in 2008 with the aim of identifying the economic trends that show how these countries are coping in the global economy. In the first section, the three key macroeconomic variables, gross domestic product (GDP), inflation and employment, are analysed to determine the trends in these variables and the factors that influence their movement. The second section reviews the external performance of small states so as to gauge their relations with the rest of the world. Movements in the current account and inflows to small states in the form of development aid, foreign direct investment (FDI) and remittances are evaluated. The effects of these trends on the public debt and official international reserves are also assessed. The third section analyses how these economic trends have affected human development trends in small states. The final section highlights the key policy issues facing small states, including how to facilitate the operations of small and medium enterprises (SMEs) and the competitiveness of small states' economies compared with those of other countries.

Economic environment

Overall economic growth trends

In 2008, the real GDP of Commonwealth small states grew by 2.7 per cent, compared with 4.3 per cent in the previous year (Figure 1.1 and Table 1.1). The growth rate of small states in 2008 was below the average for the world and that for developing countries as a whole. This lower growth rate can be attributed to the effects of the food, fuel and financial crisis on the economies of small states. In 2008, the world economy grew by 3 per cent, while emerging markets and developing countries grew by an impressive 6.1 per cent, led by developing Asia (including China and India), which grew by 7.9 per cent. An assessment of growth within regional groups shows that all regions grew more slowly in 2008, compared with 2007. However, the 2008 growth rate was higher than the average rate between 1992 and 2001.

Sources of growth

African small states: International Monetary Fund (IMF), *African Economic Outlook* and Economic Intelligence Unit (EIU) data show that the economies of African small states grew at a slower rate in 2008 than in 2007. The contraction in the world economy due to the global economic and financial crisis, as well as higher prices for food and fuel, led to contraction in the mining, tourism, agriculture and manufacturing sectors in these countries.

Botswana's real GDP growth rate declined in 2008 compared with the previous year due to the contraction in the mining and agricultural sectors and to slower growth in manufacturing. The fall in global demand for diamonds had a serious impact on the country's mining sector. The real GDP growth rate in 2008 was 3.1 per cent, compared with 4.8 per cent in 2007. The economy of **The Gambia** grew by 6.1 per cent in 2008, a slight fall compared with 6.3 per cent growth in 2007. Agricultural production improved strongly in 2008, but the rate of growth of services and industrial production dropped sharply, increasing by only 6.8 per cent and 0.7 per cent respectively in 2008. The Gambian economy is dominated by services, mainly from tourism and transit activities. Services accounted for 60.5 per cent of GDP in 2008. **Lesotho**'s economy contracted in 2008 as a result of the global financial and economic crisis, as well as high inflation caused by volatile food and fuel prices. The economic growth rate was estimated at 4.5 per cent in 2008, compared with 2.4 per cent in 2007. The **Mauritian** economy grew by 4.2 per cent in 2008 as a result of external shocks from the reduction in the preferential price of the country's sugar exports to European markets, high food and fuel prices, and the global financial crisis. **Mauritius** grew by 5.4 per cent in 2007. **Namibia**'s real GDP growth rate declined in 2008 compared with 2007 owing to the sharp fall in most mineral commodity prices. Real GDP grew by 3.3 per cent in 2008, compared with 5.5 per cent in 2007. The **Seychelles** economy contracted by 0.9 per cent in 2008, compared with 11.5 per cent growth in the

Figure 1.1. Real GDP growth rates, 2002–2008

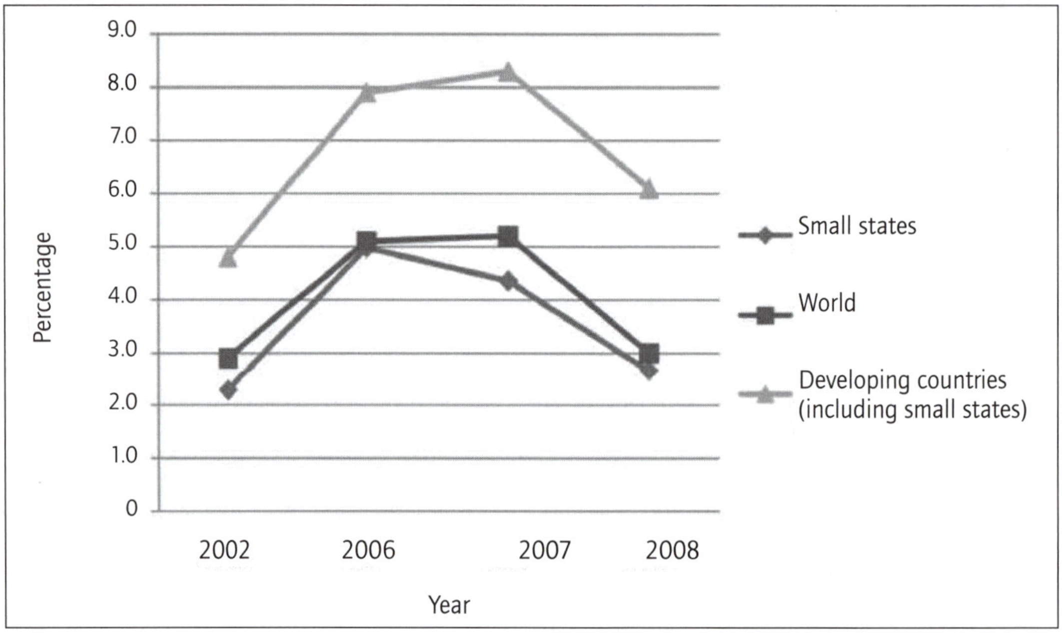

Source: IMF, *World Economic Outlook*, April 2010

previous year, as the tourism sector slowed due to reduced demand from the European markets as a result of recession in many European countries. **Swaziland**'s real GDP growth rate was estimated at 2.4 per cent in 2008, reflecting the impact of a slowdown in global growth on the country's manufacturing sector. Real GDP grew by 3.5 per cent in 2007.

Asia-Pacific small states: According to IMF, EIU and Asian Development Bank (ADB) data, the economies of countries in the Asia-Pacific region experienced lower growth rates or a contraction of their economies in 2008. As in other regions, the contraction in the world economy due to the global economic and financial crisis, together with higher

Table 1.1. Real GDP growth rates, 1992–2008

	Real annual average growth of GDP (%)				
	Average 1992–2001	2002	2006	2007	2008
Small states	**–**	**2.28**	**4.98**	**4.36**	**2.66**
African small states	4.31	2.37	5.76	5.63	3.24
Asia-Pacific small states	–	2.60	4.75	3.71	3.08
Caribbean small states	3.03	1.81	5.57	3.65	1.47
Mediterranean small states	–	2.35	3.85	4.45	2.85
World	**3.20**	**2.90**	**5.10**	**5.20**	**3.00**
Advanced economies	2.80	1.70	3.00	2.80	0.50
Other emerging markets and developing countries (including small states)	3.80	4.80	7.90	8.30	6.10
Regional groups					
Africa	2.80	7.40	6.50	6.90	5.50
Central and Eastern Europe	2.60	4.40	6.50	5.50	3.00
Commonwealth of Independent States	–	5.20	8.50	8.60	5.50
Developing Asia	7.30	6.90	9.80	10.60	7.90
Middle East and North Africa	3.40	3.80	5.70	5.60	5.10
Western hemisphere	3.00	0.50	5.60	5.80	4.30

Source: IMF, *World Economic Outlook*, April 2010

prices for food and fuel, had a negative effect on the economies of Asia-Pacific small states.

Brunei Darussalam's GDP contracted by 1.9 per cent in 2008 as a result of a decline in oil and gas production, as ageing oil and gas fields led to stoppages in production for maintenance and upgrading. In October 2008, the authorities guaranteed all bank deposits in order to insulate the Sultanate from the global financial turmoil. In 2007, Brunei Darussalam recorded a 0.2 per cent real GDP growth rate. The **Fijian** economy contracted by 0.1 per cent in 2008, following a contraction of 0.5 per cent in 2007. This occurred despite an increase in visitor arrivals and a general turnaround in the tourism sector, and increases in gold and mineral water production. Erosion in trade preferences affected growth in the manufacturing sector and sugar production declined as a result of bad weather. The economy of **Kiribati** contracted by 1.1 per cent in 2008, compared with 0.4 per cent growth in 2007. Approximately half of the national income of Kiribati comes from external sources, predominantly fishing licence fees, seafarer remittances, development assistance and revenue from the country's Revenue Equalization Reserve Fund (RERF). Government expenditure is also a major source of GDP growth. The growth rate of the **Maldives** economy fell in 2008 because of a slowdown in tourism, which accounts for a third of GDP. Real GDP grew by 6.3 per cent in 2008, compared with 7.2 per cent in 2007, as tourism sector value added grew by only 2.9 per cent in 2008, compared with 9.4 per cent in the previous year. **Nauru**'s economy grew by an estimated 1 per cent in fiscal year 2008 (end June 2008) as a result of increased exports of phosphate. In 2007, the economy contracted by 27.3 per cent. **Papua New Guinea**'s real GDP grew by 6.7 per cent in 2008, compared with 7.2 per cent in 2007, the highest GDP growth for over a decade. Growth in 2008 was based on a 9.2 per cent growth in services, 7.8 per cent growth in industry and 5 per cent growth in agriculture. **Samoa**'s economy grew by 0.3 per cent in 2008, as a result of a 5.7 per cent contraction in manufacturing, as the automotive parts assembly plant cut exports because of the global economic downturn. In addition, construction contracted by 7.3 per cent and tourism receipts fell by 7.6 per cent. In contrast, the Samoan economy expanded by 6 per cent in 2007. The growth perspective provided by the ADB differs from that of the IMF, which reports that Samoa's real GDP grew by 5 per cent in 2008, compared with 2.3 per cent in 2007. The economy of **Solomon Islands** grew by 7.3 per cent in 2008 as a consequence of growth in the copra, cocoa and fish sectors, although there was a significant decline in logging. In 2007, the economy grew by 10.7 per cent as a result of the high rate of growth in logging. **Tonga**'s economy grew by an estimated 0.8 per cent in fiscal year 2008 (end June 2008), due to reconstruction following the 2006 unrest, new tourism building projects and expansion in the transport and communications sub-sector as a result of increased competition in telecommunications. This compared with economic growth of only 0.4 per cent in fiscal year 2007, as a result of civil unrest. **Tuvalu**'s economy grew by 1.5 per cent in 2008 on account of a 9.8 per cent increase in government spending on public sector wages, goods and services, and grants and subsidies. The economy grew by 2.5 per cent in 2007. **Vanuatu**'s GDP grew by 6.3 per cent in 2008, compared with 6.7 per cent the previous year. Growth in 2008 was driven by property development and tourism, with visitor arrivals increasing by 13.3 per cent in the 12 months to September 2008.

Caribbean small states: The IMF and EIU data indicate that the global financial and economic crisis had a serious impact on the economic growth of most small states in the Caribbean, as most sectors experienced a contraction in economic activity. Of the 12 Caribbean small states, only three – Belize, Dominica, and St Kitts and Nevis – experienced higher growth rates than in the previous year.

The economy of **Antigua and Barbuda** grew by 1.8 per cent in 2008, compared with 6.5 per cent in the previous year. The economy of **The Bahamas** contracted by 1.7 per cent in 2008, due to the decline in the tourism sector, as the global financial crisis affected demand from the country's largest tourist market, the USA. This compares with a growth rate of 0.7 per cent in 2007. Economic activity slowed in **Barbados** in 2008, due mainly to a contraction in the tourism and construction sectors by 1 per cent and 3.1 per cent respectively and weak growth in the non-traded sector of only 1.2 per cent. As a result, real GDP grew by 0.2 per cent in 2008, compared with 3.4 per cent in the previous year. The

Table 1.2. Real GDP growth rates of Commonwealth small states, 1992–2008

	Real annual average growth of GDP (%)				
	Average 1992–2001	2002	2006	2007	2008
African small states	**4.3**	**2.4**	**5.8**	**5.6**	**3.2**
Botswana	5.4	9.0	5.1	4.8	3.1
Gambia, The	4.6	-3.2	6.5	6.3	6.1
Lesotho	4.2	1.1	6.5	2.4	4.5
Mauritius	5.6	1.9	3.9	5.4	4.2
Namibia	3.5	4.8	7.1	5.5	3.3
Seychelles	4.0	1.2	8.3	11.5	0.9
Swaziland	2.9	1.8	2.9	3.5	2.4
Asia-Pacific small states	**–**	**2.6**	**4.8**	**3.7**	**3.1**
Brunei Darussalam	2.2	3.9	4.4	0.2	-1.9
Fiji Islands	3.1	3.2	1.9	-0.5	-0.1
Kiribati	4.0	6.1	1.9	0.4	-1.1
Maldives	7.1	6.5	18.0	7.2	6.3
Papua New Guinea	3.6	2.0	2.3	7.2	6.7
Samoa	4.0	6.2	2.2	2.3	5.0
Solomon Islands	1.1	-2.8	6.9	10.7	7.3
Tonga	1.2	3.1	-0.3	0.4	0.8
Tuvalu	–	2.0	3.0	2.5	1.5
Vanuatu	2.7	-4.2	7.2	6.7	6.3
Caribbean small states	**3.0**	**1.8**	**5.6**	**3.7**	**1.5**
Antigua & Barbuda	3.3	2.0	12.9	6.5	1.8
Bahamas, The	2.7	2.6	4.3	0.7	-1.7
Barbados	1.1	0.7	3.2	3.4	0.2
Belize	5.4	5.1	4.7	1.2	3.8
Dominica	1.5	-5.1	4.8	2.5	3.2
Grenada	3.8	1.6	-2.3	4.9	2.2
Guyana	4.5	1.1	5.1	7.0	2.0
Jamaica	0.5	1.0	2.7	1.5	-0.9
St Kitts & Nevis	4.3	1.0	5.5	2.0	4.6
St Lucia	1.7	0.6	4.8	1.5	0.7
St Vincent & the Grenadines	2.9	3.2	7.6	8.0	-0.6
Trinidad & Tobago	4.6	7.9	13.5	4.6	2.3
Mediterranean small states	**–**	**2.4**	**3.9**	**4.5**	**2.9**
Cyprus	4.8	2.1	4.1	5.1	3.6
Malta	–	2.6	3.6	3.8	2.1

Source: IMF, *World Economic Outlook*, April 2010

Belize economy expanded by 3.8 per cent in 2008, compared with 1.2 per cent in the previous year, due to increased capital investment in the energy sector. The economy of **Dominica** grew by 3.2 per cent in 2008, compared with 2.5 per cent in the previous year. This was mainly due to reconstruction and recovery from the hurricanes which affected the island. Real GDP growth declined in **Grenada** in 2008, as the economy grew by only 2.2 per cent, compared with 4.9 per cent in 2007. The fall was the result of declines in the tourism and construction sectors due to the global economic downturn. **Guyana**'s real GDP grew by 2 per cent in 2008, compared with 7 per cent in the previous year. The decline in GDP growth resulted from contractions in the sugar sector (15.1%), forestry sector (15.2%) and manufacturing (2%). Growth was led by financial services (12%), transport and communication (9.9%), construction (8.5%) and mining and quarrying (6.1%). The **Jamaican** economy contracted by 0.9 per cent in 2008, compared with a 1.5 per cent growth in the previous year. Annual real GDP growth in Jamaica has averaged only 1 per cent since 1991. GDP was affected by declines in the tourism, mining and agricultural sectors, particularly during the second half of 2008. The economy of **St Kitts and Nevis** grew by 4.6 per cent in 2008, compared with 2 per cent in the previous year, as a result of the damage suffered as a result of hurricane Omar in October 2008 and the decline in the tourism sector caused by the global financial crisis. **St Lucia**'s economy grew by 0.7 per cent in 2008, compared with 1.5 per cent in the previous year because of slowing construction and tourism activity and a fall in banana exports after the hurricane. Growth in **St Vincent and the Grenadines** declined significantly in 2008 compared with the previous year, as a result of weakened activities in the tourism and agricultural sectors due mainly to declining visitor arrivals and a disease affecting the banana crop. The economy contracted by 0.6 per cent in 2008, compared with 8 per cent growth in 2007. As a result of weaker growth in the energy sector in the second half of 2008, economic growth in **Trinidad and Tobago** decelerated in 2008, compared with the previous year. Real GDP grew by 2.35 per cent in 2008, compared with 4.6 per cent in 2007.

Mediterranean small states: Commonwealth small states that are members of the EU were also negatively affected by the global financial crisis. They grew more slowly in 2008 than in the previous year.

EIU and IMF data show that the **Cypriot** economy grew by an estimated 3.6 per cent in 2008, compared with 5.1 per cent in 2007. Economic growth in 2008 was driven by rapid growth in bank lending, which was fuelled by higher demand for undeveloped land before the expected imposition of value-added tax and an increase in car purchases as a result of a tax cut. Economic activity in **Malta** slowed in 2008 compared with 2007 due to the global financial crisis. Government expenditure supported consumption, as investment and exports fell. Malta's economy grew by 2.1 per cent in 2008, compared with 3.8 per cent in the previous year.

Inflation

The data available from the IMF, EIU, Asian Development Bank and *African Economic Outlook* show that small states experienced higher average inflation in 2008 than in 2007 as the rise in international prices for food and fuel passed through to local economies. An examination of regional trends (Figure 1.2) shows that African small states experienced the highest average inflation rate, while inflation was lowest in Asia-Pacific small states.

African small states: With the exception of **The Gambia**, which saw a decline in inflation, higher food and fuel prices resulted in price increases in African small states. As shown in Table 1.3, these

Figure 1.2. Inflation trends in Commonwealth small states, 2000–2008

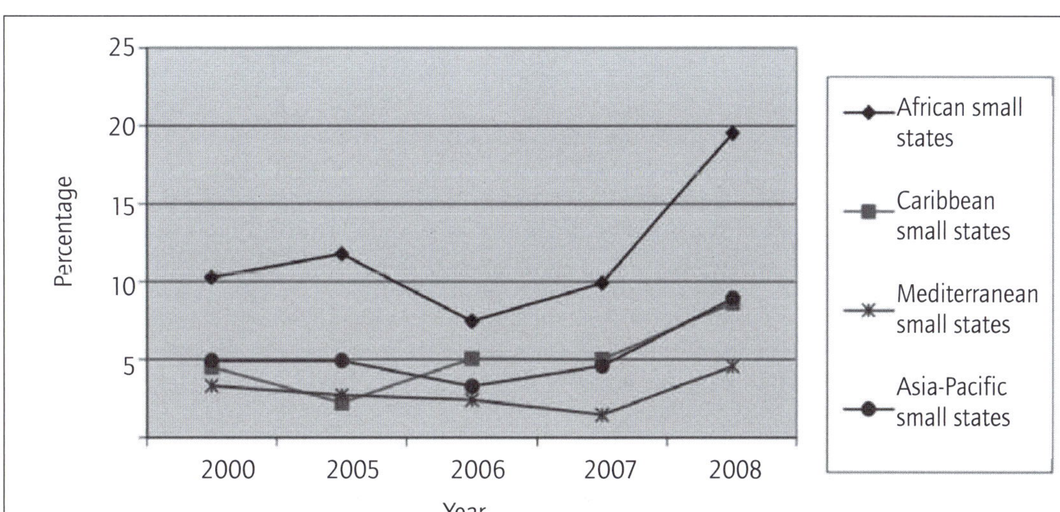

Source: IMF, *World Economic Outlook*, April 2010

inflation rates ranged from 4.5 per cent in The Gambia to 37 per cent in **Seychelles**. The Gambia's inflation rate was also affected by tight monetary policy and the depreciation of the currency. In addition to the effect of the increases in food and fuel prices, inflation rates in **Namibia** and **Swaziland** were influenced by developments in South Africa. The impact of currency devaluation, tax rises and cuts in subsidies also affected consumer prices in Seychelles.

Asia-Pacific small states: As in other small states, inflation in Asia-Pacific small states was affected by the rise in food and fuel prices.

Inflation in **Brunei Darussalam** averaged 2.7 per cent in 2008, higher than the 0.3 per cent recorded in 2007. Food, which makes up 29 per cent of the consumer price basket, was the primary contributor, reflecting higher international prices. The currency board arrangement and government subsidies have contributed to low inflation rates. Inflation averaged 7.8 per cent in **Fiji Islands** in 2008, compared with 4.8 per cent in 2007. The higher 2008 inflation rate resulted from increases in the prices of food and fuel. Inflation in **Kiribati** averaged 11 per cent in 2008, compared with 4.2 per cent in 2007. This increase occurred despite government subsidies to cushion the effect of the rise in the world price of fuel and rice. Inflation in **Maldives** averaged 12.3

Table 1.3. Inflation rates in Commonwealth small states, 1992–2008

	Average 1992–2001	2002	2006	2007	2008
African small states	**10.3**	**11.8**	**7 .5**	**9.9**	**19.5**
Botswana	10.0	8.0	11.6	7.1	12.6
Gambia, The	3.8	8.6	2.1	5.4	4.5
Lesotho	9.5	12.5	6.1	8.0	10.7
Mauritius	6.8	6.5	9.0	8.8	9.7
Namibia	9.7	11.3	5.1	6.7	10.0
Seychelles	2.7	0.2	–1.9	5.3	37.0
Swaziland	8.8	11.7	5.3	8.2	13.1
Asia-Pacific small states	**4.9**	**4.9**	**3.3**	**4.6**	**8.9**
Brunei Darussalam	1.9	–2.3	0.2	0.3	2.7
Fiji Islands	3.2	0.8	2.5	4.8	7.8
Kiribati	3.1	3.2	–1.5	4.2	11.0
Maldives	5.9	0.9	3.5	7.4	12.3
Papua New Guinea	9.7	11.8	2.4	0.9	10.8
Samoa	3.9	7.4	3.2	4.5	6.2
Solomon Islands	9.6	9.5	11.1	7.7	17.4
Tonga	4.0	10.8	6 .0	7.5	7.3
Vanuatu	2.8	2.0	2.0	3.9	4.8
Caribbean small states	**4.5**	**2.2**	**5.0**	**5.0**	**8.6**
Antigua & Barbuda	2.4	2.4	1.8	1.4	5.3
Bahamas, The	2.0	2.2	1.8	2.5	4.5
Barbados	2.5	–1.2	7.3	4.0	8.1
Belize	1.6	2.2	4.2	2.3	6.4
Dominica	1.7	0.1	2.6	3.2	6.4
Grenada	2.1	1.1	4.2	3.9	8.0
Guyana	8.9	5.4	6.7	12.2	8.1
Jamaica	19.3	7.0	8.5	9.3	22.0
St Kitts & Nevis	3.1	2.1	8.5	4.5	5.4
St Lucia	3.1	–0.3	3.6	1.9	7.2
St Vincent & the Grenadines	2.0	1.3	3.0	6.9	10.1
Trinidad & Tobago	5.3	4.2	8.3	7.9	12.1
Mediterranean small states	**3.3**	**2.7**	**2.4**	**1.5**	**4.6**
Cyprus	3.5	2.8	2.2	2.2	4.4
Malta	3.1	2.6	2.6	0.7	4.7

Source: IMF, *World Economic Outlook*, April 2010

per cent in 2008, compared with 7.4 per cent in the previous year, as a result of increases in the international prices of food, fuel and construction materials. In line with Australia, **Nauru**'s inflation rate averaged 4.5 per cent in fiscal year 2008 (end June 2008), compared with 2.9 per cent in 2007. The country imports 60 per cent of its goods and services from Australia and uses the Australian currency as legal tender. Inflation in **Papua New Guinea** averaged 10.8 per cent in 2008, compared with 0.9 per cent in 2007. This rise was the result of strong growth in money supply and credit, higher costs of fuel, transport and food staples, and increased government spending. Inflation averaged 6.2 per cent in **Samoa** in 2008, driven by rising food and fuel prices propelled by global price increases, higher costs of agricultural inputs and reduction in the supply of locally grown food. Inflation in 2007 was 4.5 per cent. Inflation in **Solomon Islands** averaged 17.4 per cent in 2008 as a result of the high prices of fuel and other imported items. This rate is more than double the 7.7 per cent inflation rate of 2007. **Tonga**'s inflation rate of 7.3 per cent for fiscal year 2008 (end June 2008) was driven by higher food, fuel, transport and electricity costs. The Australian dollar is legal tender in **Tuvalu** and consequently inflation is closely in line with that of Australia. In 2008, inflation was above the rate in Australia because of Tuvalu's sensitivity to higher fuel and transportation costs. Inflation averaged 4.8 per cent in **Vanuatu** in 2008, compared with 3.9 per cent in the previous year. Higher inflation in 2008 was a result of increases in food and fuel prices.

Caribbean small states: With the exception of **Guyana**, the global surge in food and fuel prices produced a rise in average inflation in Caribbean small states (Table 1.3). Guyana is a major food producer and so did not suffer from the rise in global food prices. In addition, the Guyana Government reduced excise taxes to mitigate the effect of the increase in world oil prices. These developments, as well as the levelling of prices following the implementation of VAT in 2007, resulted in a decline in Guyana's average inflation rate in 2008 compared to the previous year. Inflation averaged 8.1 per cent in 2008, compared with 12.32 per cent in 2007. In addition, for countries with fixed exchange rates, such as the Eastern Caribbean islands, **Barbados** and **The Bahamas**, the depreciation of the US dollar against other currencies contributed to a rise in consumer prices. **Jamaica** experienced the highest increase, due to the impact of tropical storm Gustav, which compounded the effect of rises in food and fuel prices. As a result, Jamaica's average inflation rate in 2008 was more than double that of 2007. Inflation averaged 22 per cent in Jamaica in 2008, compared with 9.3 per cent in 2007. Flooding and pricing rigidities also contributed to **Trinidad and Tobago**'s higher inflation rate compared with the previous year.

Mediterranean small states: High global food and energy prices resulted in higher inflation rates in both **Cyprus** and **Malta**. Inflation rates in these countries are calculated using the EU harmonised measure which allows for comparison between the data of EU member states. Inflation averaged 4.4 per cent in 2008 in Cyprus, compared with 2.2 per cent in 2007. In Malta, inflation averaged 4.7 per cent in 2008, compared with 0.7 per cent in the previous year.

Employment

The International Labour Organization (ILO) reports that unemployment increased in 2008 to an estimated 6 per cent. As the global financial crisis escalated, the number of working poor, people in vulnerable employment and unemployed increased. The highest unemployment rate was in north Africa at 10.3 per cent, with east Asia recording the lowest rate of 3.8 per cent. The regions where most of the Commonwealth small states are located – south-east Asia and the Pacific, Latin America and sub-Saharan Africa – recorded unemployment rates of 5.7 per cent, 7.3 per cent and 7.9 per cent.

African small states: Employment data are unavailable for most African small states. However, with declining growth rates in many of these countries, it can be assumed that unemployment grew in the sectors that contracted. However, EIU data for **Mauritius** show that unemployment fell slightly in 2008 to 7.8 per cent, compared with 8.5 per cent in the previous year, as diversification programmes continued to have a positive effect on the economy.

Asia-Pacific small states: The economies of the small states in the Asia-Pacific region either contracted or experienced lower growth rates in 2008. It can therefore be assumed that in countries where employment data are unavailable, the sectors most affected by the economic downturn experienced a decline in employment. EIU, IMF and ADB data show that unemployment in **Brunei Darussalam** fell to 5,089 in the second half of 2008 from 7,000 in late 2007, as the government assisted low-skilled unemployed workers to find jobs. The majority of those employed in the private sector are foreign nationals, with Bruneians accounting for just 31 per cent of the workforce. This is partly because Bruneians prefer to work in the government sector. Unemployment in **Fiji Islands** rose to 8.5 per cent at end 2008 as a result of the country's lower economic growth rate. The Government of **Kiribati** provides two-thirds of all the country's employment. New phosphate contracts had a positive effect on employment rates in **Nauru** in 2008. However, jobs were lost as a result of the closure of the Australian Government refugee centre. In **Papua New Guinea**, employment in the formal private sector, which accounts for only a small percentage of the labour force, increased by 10 per cent in the 12 months to June 2008. Unemployment increased in **Samoa** as the biggest private sector employer cut jobs and tourism declined. In the first nine months of 2008, 3 per cent of formal jobs in Samoa were lost, mainly in the construction and manufacturing sectors. In **Vanuatu,** the Employment Act was revised in consultation with the business community. The country also benefited from the expansion of the New Zealand Recognised Seasonal Employer scheme, under which Vanuatu citizens can take up temporary jobs in New Zealand's fruit industry.

Caribbean small states: Employment data are unavailable for most Caribbean small states. As most of the small states in the region experienced lower growth or a contraction in economic activity in 2008, it can be assumed that the sectors affected by the downturn shed jobs. EIU data show that the annual labour force survey completed in May 2008 in **The Bahamas** registered an unemployment rate of 8.7 per cent in Nassau and 9 per cent in Grand Bahama. This rate was expected to increase during the remainder of 2008 as the tourism and construction sectors were increasingly affected by the global financial crisis. The unemployment rate in **Barbados** stood at 8.4 per cent at end September 2008, compared with 7.1 per cent a year earlier. Most job losses were in the construction and utilities sector. **Grenada**'s unemployment rate at end 2008 was 24 per cent, partly due to a halt in some tourism development projects. **Jamaica**'s unemployment rate reached 11 per cent at end 2008, up from 9.9 per cent at end 2007. **St Lucia** recorded a 16.8 per cent unemployment rate in 2008, as declining growth and exports affected employment in the tourism and banana sectors. The unemployment rate in **Trinidad and Tobago** increased slightly during 2008 to reach 5.5 per cent by the end of the year.

Mediterranean small states: EIU data show a mixed employment situation in the two Mediterranean small states. In **Cyprus**, unemployment increased to 16 per cent at end 2008, compared with 15 per cent at end 2007. In **Malta**, the unemployment rate declined to an estimated 5.8 per cent at end 2008, as against 6.2 per cent in the previous year. Falling unemployment was the result of a 3.1 per cent increase in the number of full-time jobs and some gains in part-time employment. Although employment in manufacturing and tourism fell, 90 per cent of net job creation came from the private sector.

External performance

International trade relations

Despite the drafting of new modalities on agricultural and non-agricultural trade, there was very little progress in 2008 towards the conclusion of the Doha Trade Round. The World Trade Organization (WTO) reports that 35 new regional trade agreements were signed in 2008. The Dispute Settlement Body (DSB) of the WTO established three panels to adjudicate five new cases in 2008; this was the lowest number of panels since the inception of the adjudication system in 1995. One of these proceedings was the case brought by the EU against the USA and Canada. The aid for trade initiative focused on three areas in 2008: improving the monitoring of aid for trade flows and activities; accelerating the implementation of regional and national projects to build greater trade capacity; and strengthening developing country ownership of aid for trade schemes.

The Southern African Customs Union (SACU) concluded negotiations on three trade agreements in 2008; implementation will be finalised in 2009. The SACU-European Free Trade Association Free (EFTA) trade agreement came into effect on 1 May

2008. The countries involved are SACU members Botswana, Lesotho, Namibia, South Africa and Swaziland, and EFTA members Iceland, Liechtenstein, Norway and Switzerland. The objectives of the agreement include the liberalisation of trade in goods; increasing investment opportunities; and promoting adequate and effective protection of intellectual property rights.

The other two SACU agreements were the preferential trade agreement between SACU and Mercado Común del Sur (MERCOSUR), where negotiations were concluded in 2008 with signing scheduled for 2009. The members of MERCOSUR are Argentina, Brazil, Paraguay and Uruguay, with Bolivia, Chile, Colombia, Ecuador and Peru as associate members. Venezuela, although it is not a full member, has a signed membership agreement. In addition, a Trade, Investment and Development Co-operation Agreement (TIDCA) between SACU and the USA was signed in July 2008.

In the Caribbean, the CARIFORUM bloc (CARICOM plus the Dominican Republic) signed an economic partnership agreement (EPA) with the EU. The WTO-compatible EPA provides for the free movement of goods and services, and contains provisions covering investment protection, government procurement and intellectual property rights.

Current account balances

Commonwealth small states that are exporters of primary commodities experienced a favourable trading environment in 2008. As shown in Table 1.5, Botswana, Brunei Darussalam, Lesotho, Namibia, Papua New Guinea and Trinidad and Tobago achieved current account surpluses. These six small states are rich in natural resources and are exporters of petroleum and mining products. In addition to the decline in surpluses for several of the six countries mentioned above, most of the remaining small states experienced an increase in their current account deficit compared with the previous year. These developments indicate that small states are experiencing a deterioration in their relationship with the rest of the world, exporting less and receiving lower inflows and transfers from abroad. Brunei Darussalam, followed by Trinidad and Tobago, had the best external performance among small states (Table 1.5), while Seychelles and Maldives experienced current account deficits above 40 per cent of GDP.

African small states: Data from the EIU, IMF and *African Economic Outlook* show that the current account of all the African small states deteriorated in 2008.

US imports from Africa increased by 27.8 per cent in 2008 to US$86.1 billion. US$66.3 billion, or 77 per cent of these imports, were under the African Growth and Opportunity Act (AGOA). The increase in overall US imports can be attributed to the 31.9 per cent increase in crude oil imports. AGOA imports in 2008 were 29.8 per cent higher than in 2007. Fuel imports accounted for 92.3 per cent of overall AGOA imports. The remaining US$5.1 billion was 51.2 per cent higher than in the previous

Table 1.4. US Imports from Commonwealth small states (US$'000, customs value)

	Total 2007	Total 2008	AGOA including GSP 2007	AGOA including GSP 2008
Botswana	187,453	218,845	31,635	15,907
Gambia, The	148	641	36	–
Lesotho	443,018	379,617	3 74,098	338,940
Mauritius	187,020	1 19,906	176,189	101,742
Namibia	219,743	3 1,695	301,235	3,366
Seychelles	10,332	–	5 ,376	–
Swaziland	147,963	141,410	133,877	125,566

Source: United States International Trade Commission, available at http://reportweb.usitc.gov/africa/by.country.jsp, accessed May 2010

year. This increase can be attributed to a 224 per cent rise in imports of transportation equipment, 58.8 per cent increase in minerals and metals imports and 38.7 increase in chemical-related imports. However, imports of textiles and apparel and of agricultural products declined by 10.4 per cent and 7.9 per cent respectively. As shown in Table 1.4, the Commonwealth small states that benefit from AGOA saw a 43 per cent decline in their AGOA exports to the USA and a 25 per cent overall fall in US exports. This decline was partly due to the decline in the textile and apparel sector.

Botswana's current account surplus was estimated at 4.9 per cent of GDP in 2008, compared to 15.4 per cent in 2007, as diamond export revenues fell due to weak global demand and falling prices. **The Gambia**'s current account deficit widened in 2008 to 16 per cent of GDP, compared with 12.3 per cent of GDP in 2007, reflecting higher imports and the deepening global downturn, which cut exports, tourism receipts, remittances and FDI flows. **Lesotho**'s current account surplus is estimated at 9.6 per cent of GDP for 2008, compared with 14.1 per cent of GDP for 2007. Despite strong diamond and textiles exports, import growth outpaced export gains, leading to a rise in the overall trade deficit. SACU transfers to Lesotho amounted to 36.6 per cent of GDP in 2008. **Mauritius** recorded a current deficit of 10.4 per cent of GDP in 2008, compared with 5.6 per cent in the previous year, as the trade deficit rose by 40 per cent. **Namibia**'s current account surplus fell in 2008 compared with the previous year, reflecting mainly a 24.8 per cent increase in imports driven by high oil prices, as well as by substantial imports for mineral exploration and public infrastructure projects. **Namibia**'s trade deficit for 2008 amounted to US$234 million or 2 per cent of GDP, compared

Table 1.5. Current account balances (percentage of GDP)

	2005	2006	2007	2008
Brunei Darussalam	52.8	56.3	50.9	57.9
Trinidad & Tobago	22.5	39.6	25.7	33.8
Papua New Guinea	6.1	8.0	3.3	10.0
Lesotho	-7.9	4.7	14.1	9.6
Botswana	15.2	17.2	15.4	4.9
Namibia	4.7	13.8	9.1	2.7
Kiribati	-18.5	-2.9	-1.0	-0.6
Swaziland	-4.1	-7.4	0.7	-4.1
Malta	-8.8	-9.2	-6.2	-5.4
Vanuatu	-8.4	-5.3	-6.9	-5.9
Samoa	-9.6	-11.1	-15.9	-6.2
Belize	-13.6	-2.1	-4.0	-10.1
Mauritius	-5.2	-9.4	-5.6	-10.4
Barbados	-13.1	-8.4	-5.4	-10.5
Tonga	-5.2	-8.2	-8.8	-11.6
Guyana	-10.1	-13.1	-11.1	-13.2
Bahamas, The	-9.6	-18.9	-17.5	-15.4
Gambia, The	-18.5	-13.4	-12.3	-16.0
Solomon Islands	-7.0	-1.6	-8.2	-16.4
Cyprus	-5.9	-7.0	-11.7	-17.7
Fiji Islands	-9.9	-18.7	-13.6	-17.9
Jamaica	-9.6	-9.9	-16.3	-18.1
Antigua & Barbuda	-18.8	-31.6	-32.9	-28.9
St Lucia	-17.1	-30.2	-31.3	-30.7
Dominica	-26.0	-15.7	-25.0	-31.8
St Kitts & Nevis	-18.3	-20.4	-24.1	-34.3
St Vincent & the Grenadines	-22.3	-24.0	-34.6	-37.3
Grenada	-31.3	-33.2	-43.2	-38.7
Seychelles	-19.7	-13.9	-20.8	-44.7
Maldives	-36.4	-33.0	-41.5	-51.4

Source: IMF, *World Economic Outlook*, April 2010

with US$693 million, or 9.3 per cent of GDP, in 2007. **Seychelles**' current account deficit remained very high in 2008 at 44.7 per cent of GDP, owing to a steep rise in the trade deficit, as imports outpaced exports and tourism earnings were subdued. **Swaziland**'s current account surplus was US$28.2 million, or 4.1 per cent of GDP, in 2008, compared with 0.7 per cent of GDP in 2007. The higher surplus resulted from a surge in net current transfers, supplemented by growth in export earnings.

Asia-Pacific small states: IMF, EIU and Asian Development Bank data show that with the exception of Brunei Darussalam, Kiribati, Papua New Guinea and Samoa, the current account position of Asia-Pacific small states deteriorated in 2008 due to higher imports and declining export growth.

The current account surplus of **Brunei Darussalam** increased in 2008 compared with the previous year, due to higher prices for fuel and slower growth in imports. The country recorded a surplus of 57.9 per cent of GDP in 2008, compared with 50.9 per cent of GDP in 2007. The current account deficit of **Fiji Islands** widened in 2008 to about 17.9 per cent of GDP compared with 13.6 per cent in 2007, as imports rose 26.2 per cent, outpacing export growth of 23.1 per cent. The market value of **Kiribati** Revenue Equalisation Reserve Fund fell 20 per cent in 2008 as a result of the general slump in global financial markets. In addition, the revenue from fishing licences dropped by 22 per cent in the 2005–2007 period compared with 2002–2004, as a result of governance shortcomings that put the commercial viability of fish stocks at risk. **Maldives**' current account deficit widened in 2008 to 51.4 per cent of GDP, mainly as a result of the 26 per cent increase in imports. **Nauru**'s external position is determined primarily by the phosphate industry. In 2008, both export volumes and prices of phosphate rose. Australia is the biggest importer of phosphate from Nauru. **Papua New Guinea** recorded a current account surplus of US$228 million, or 10 per cent of GDP, at end 2008. This compares with a surplus of 3.3 per cent of GDP at end 2007. The higher 2008 surplus was mainly the result of increased revenues from the export of minerals. **Samoa**'s current account deficit improved in 2008 due to increases in export receipts and lower import payments. **Solomon Islands** recorded a current account deficit of 16.4 per cent of GDP at end 2008 compared with 8.2 per cent of GDP at end 2007. The higher 2008 deficit resulted mainly from a significant decline in logging. **Tonga**'s current account deficit deteriorated slightly in 2008 to reach 11.6 per cent of GDP by the end of the year. This higher deficit was due to increased imports. **Tuvalu** produces almost no merchandise exports. Export revenues in 2008 were mainly from fishing licences and fees from the .tv domain. While revenue from fishing licences increased by 18.7 per cent in 2008, fees from .tv remained flat. The value of the Tuvalu Trust Fund, which mainly invests in offshore markets, fell sharply in 2008 as a result of the global financial crisis. Consequently, there were no transfers from the fund to government revenue. **Vanuatu**'s current account deficit was estimated at 5.9 per cent of GDP in 2008, compared with 6.9 per cent in 2007. The increase in earnings from merchandise exports and tourism, and from official grants was offset by a 42 per cent increase in the cost of imports

Caribbean small states: The global financial and economic crisis and the rising prices of imports had a negative impact on the external position of Caribbean small states.

Antigua and Barbuda experienced a 5.9 per cent increase in its current account deficit in 2008, compared with the previous year. Its current account deficit amounted to US$425.5 million in 2008, compared with US$401.7 million in 2007. **The Bahamas**' current account deficit declined in 2008, due to lower construction-related imports and higher retained earnings. The current account deficit stood at 15.4 per cent of GDP at end 2008, compared with 17.5 per cent in 2007. **Barbados**' current account deficit widened in 2008 due to surging import spending and lower tourism receipts. The current account deficit was 10.5 per cent of GDP in 2008, compared with 5.4 per cent in 2007. **Belize**'s current account deficit widened in 2008 compared with the previous year, due to increased imports associated with FDI inflows in the construction and energy sectors, grant-related public investment and higher prices of imported food and fuel products. The current account deficit was 10.1 per cent of GDP in 2008, compared with 4 per cent in 2007. **Dominica** recorded a current account deficit of 31.8 per cent of GDP in 2008, compared with 25 per cent in 2007. This reflected higher reconstruction-related imports and lower exports following the hurricanes. **Grenada**'s current account deficit declined in 2008 compared with the previous year, as a result of a slowdown in economic activity. The country's current account deficit was US$36.4 million in 2008, compared with US$37.3 million in 2007. **Guyana**'s current account deficit increased in 2008 as a result of the decline in export receipts and the higher cost of fuel imports. The current account deficit was 13.2 per cent of GDP in 2008, compared with 11.1 per in the previous year. **Jamaica**'s current account deficit widened in 2008, partly due to the trade deficit caused by the higher cost of oil imports and weak prices for mining exports. This was offset by a surplus from tourism services and a current transfer surplus led by remittances. The current account deficit was 18.1 per cent of GDP in 2008, as against 16.3 per cent in 2007. **St Kitts and Nevis** saw a decline in its current account deficit, reflecting fewer imports and a decline in tourism receipts. The country recorded a current account deficit of 34.3 per cent of GDP in 2008, compared with 24.1 per cent in the previous year. **St Lucia**'s current account deficit declined compared with the previous year, due to an increase in exports of bananas and alcoholic beverages. A current account deficit of 30.7 per cent of GDP was recorded in 2008, compared with 31.3 per cent in 2007. **St Vincent and the Grenadines** recorded a current account deficit of 37.3 per cent of GDP in 2008, compared with 34.6 per cent of GDP in 2007. The increased current account deficit resulted from lower banana exports which outweighed the fall in imports caused by the global economic crisis and the slowdown in economic activity within the country. **Trinidad and Tobago** recorded a 2008 current account surplus of 33.8 per cent of GDP, compared with 25.7 in 2007. The improved surplus reflected a large trade surplus (22.7% of GDP), led by strong exports of natural gas, which offset a 30 per cent surge in imports, mainly of consumer goods and low current account transfers.

Mediterranean small states: Declining exports and higher prices for imports led to higher deficits in Cyprus and Malta. **Cyprus**'s current account deficit was estimated at 17.7 per cent of GDP at end 2008, compared with 11.7 per cent of GDP at end 2007. **Malta**'s current account deficit declined to around 5.4 per cent of GDP in 2008.

Inflows to small states

Foreign direct investment: UNCTAD reports that FDI flows declined by 14 per cent in 2008 as a result of the deepening global financial and economic crisis. FDI fell from a historic high of US$1,979 billion in 2007 to US$1,697 billion in 2008. The decline occurred mainly in developed countries, where the global crisis started, mostly due to the 39 per cent decline in cross border mergers and acquisitions sales. On the other hand, FDI continued to increase in developing and transition economies. By region, Africa showed the highest increase in FDI flows (27%), followed by south, east and south-east Asia (17%), west Asia (16%) and Latin America and the Caribbean (13%). Most of the US$88 billion received by Africa and the US$144 million received by Latin America and the Caribbean in 2008 was invested in natural resources industries. FDI inflows to small island developing states (SIDS) increased by 32 per cent in 2008, with investment focusing on a few countries. The World Bank balance of payments FDI inflows data show that Commonwealth small states received a total US$10.5 billion in FDI flows in 2008, compared with US$9.6 billion and US$9.1 billion in 2007 and 2006 respectively.

Development aid: The OECD reports that the 22 members of the Development Assistance Committee (DAC) increased development aid by 10.2 per cent in real terms to US$119.8 billion in 2008. This is the highest amount of aid given in one calendar year and represented 0.3 per cent of the combined gross national income (GNI) of members, well below the 0.7 per cent pledged at the 2002 Monterrey Conference. Only five countries, Denmark, Luxembourg, the Netherlands, Norway and Sweden, exceeded the 0.7 per cent of GNI target. The largest donors in 2008 were the USA, Germany, UK, France and Japan. Aid from the USA in 2008 amounted to US$26 billion, a 16.8 per cent increase in real terms, representing an ODA/GNI ratio of 0.18 per cent. Japan's net ODA was US$9.4 billion in 2008, 8.2 per cent higher than in the previous year and an ODA/GNI ratio of 0.18 per cent. Data on ODA from non-DAC members are largely unavailable. World Bank figures indicate that ODA (including that from DAC members) to low- and middle-income countries as a whole in 2008 was US$128.1 billion, 19.7 per cent higher than in the previous year (Figure 1.3). Small states shared 2 per

Figure 1.3. ODA to small states, 1990–2008

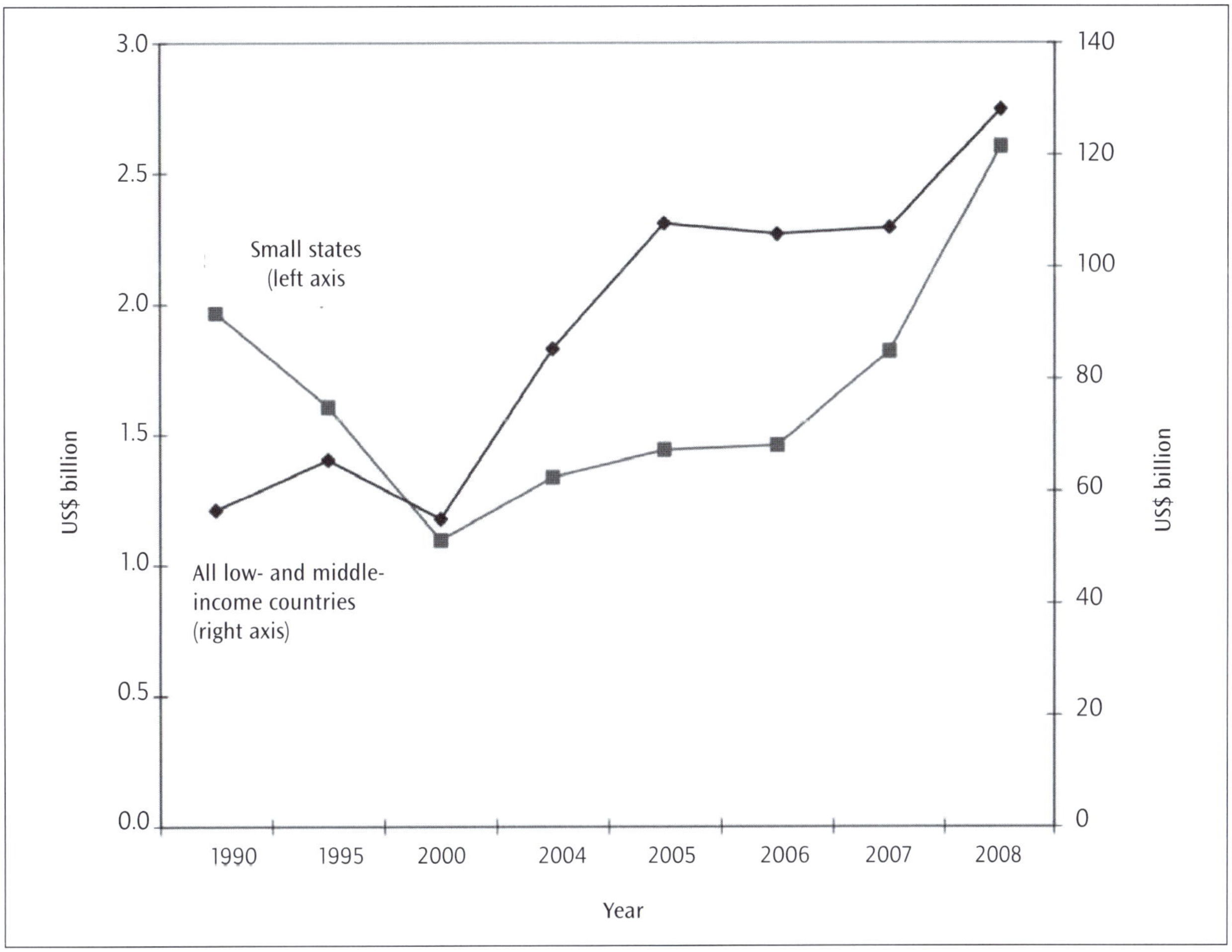

Source: World Bank, World Development Indicators, available at http://databank.worldbank.org, accessed May 2010

cent, or US$2.6 billion, of this aid – 43 per cent higher than in the previous year and the highest share of total ODA since 2000. As shown in Figure 1.4, African small states received the largest percentage of the aid.

Remittances: The World Bank revised downwards its remittances estimates for Seychelles. Data on remittances are captured from the balance of payments tables prepared by countries and reported by the IMF. This resulted in new overall estimates for remittances received by small states as a whole. Small states received US$4.5 billion in remittances in 2008, 1.9 per cent higher than the amount received in 2007 (Figure 1.5). Jamaica received 47.5 per cent of this total, followed by Lesotho (9.8%) and Guyana (6.2%). Remittances from Fijians abroad fell in 2008 as a result of a decline in offshore employment opportunities caused by the global economic slowdown, an end to the recruitment of Fijians by the British army and local currency appreciation. Remittances to Kiribati remained fairly stable in 2008 at around US$8 million, although their local currency value fluctuated. Remittances declined in Samoa as the increase in remittances from Australia and New Zealand was outweighed by a decline in remittances from the USA. Remittances to Tonga fell slightly in real terms, reflecting recession in the two main source countries – the USA and New Zealand.

Economic development issues

Public debt

Small states are among the most highly indebted countries in the world. Available data from the IMF, EIU, World Bank and ADB show that some small states have debt levels that are above the IMF 60 per cent solvency ratio of public debt to GDP.

Figure 1.4. Trends in ODA to small states by region, 1990–2008

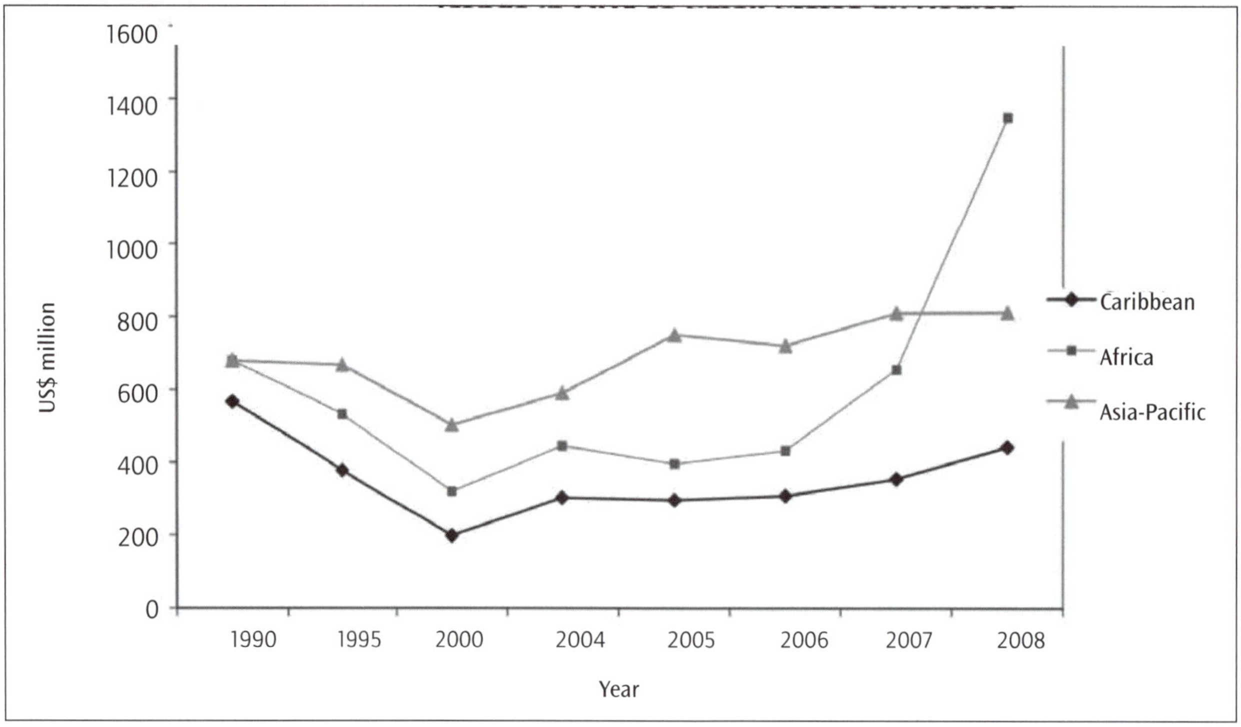

Source: World Bank, World Development Indicators, available at http://databank.worldbank.org, accessed May 2010

Figure 1.5. Total remittances to small states, 2006–2008

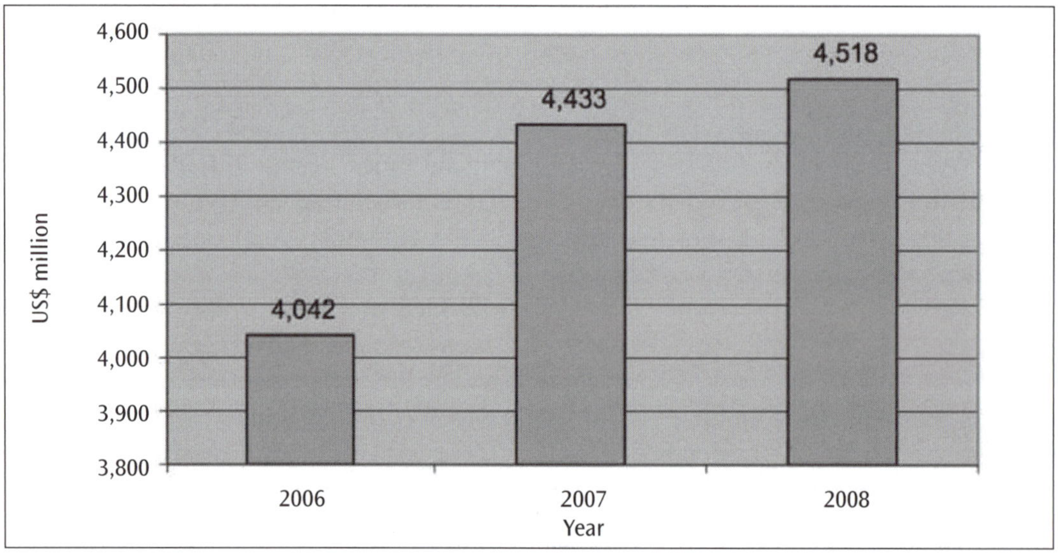

Source: World Bank, World Development Indicators, July 2009

African small states: Debt data for six of the seven African small states show that the debt of Lesotho, Mauritius and Namibia declined in 2008.

Botswana's external debt amounted to US$415 million at end 2008, compared with US$409 million at end 2007. **The Gambia**'s external debt amounted to US$311.4 million at end 2008, or 37.1 per cent of GDP. Despite receiving relief from the heavily indebted poor country (HIPC) initiative and the multilateral debt relief initiative (MDRI), The Gambia is at high risk of debt distress, since its

The debt crisis in Seychelles

Seychelles is experiencing an extreme balance of payments and debt crisis, with alarming implications for its economic development and hence the welfare of the population. By mid-2008, the country was facing huge macroeconomic imbalances and vulnerabilities resulting from enduring unsustainable macroeconomic policies, combined with the effects of the current global financial and economic crisis. These resulted in the near exhaustion of reserves and missed payments on public debt obligations. The level at which the exchange rate was pegged was not in line with economic fundamentals. This, combined with complex exchange rate restrictions and controls, has resulted in economic disruption, a parallel market for foreign exchange and insidious dollarisation of the economy. Seychelles approached the IMF for assistance in October 2008 and the Fund granted an emergency stand-by agreement in November 2008 subject to the implementation of a radical macroeconomic reform programme which includes:

- ***Exchange rate policy:*** Liberalisation of exchange rates, involving the elimination of all exchange restrictions and floating of the rupee;

- ***Fiscal policy:*** Contractionary fiscal policy, including a reduction in public employment, elimination of indirect subsidies and strengthening of a targeted social safety net;

- ***Monetary policy:*** Reform of policy framework to centre on liquidity management based on indirect instruments;

- ***Role of government:*** A reduction in the role of the state through further privatisation, better fiscal management and a review of the tax system. In addition to these measures, there needs to be a fundamental restructuring of public debt – a big reduction in debt obligations over the long term in line with repayment capacity – to ensure debt sustainability and to close external financing gaps.

The floatation of the exchange rate led to a sharp depreciation of the local currency by more than 100 per cent. As a result, inflation escalated by more than 60 per cent, aggregate demand declined sharply, cost of production increased due to doubling in the price of raw materials, some businesses have been faced with bankruptcies and the Seychelles Development Bank faced the risk of closure until a last minute rescue by the government.

The liberalisation of interest rates led to an increase in real rates (on treasury bills) from below 5 per cent in February 2008 to almost 10 per cent in January 2009, above the rates on lending and savings. This resulted in crowding out of domestic investment because the higher return on government bonds led to a diversion of investment by commercial banks and private individuals away from private sector investment into government securities.

The current climate is characterised by falling aggregate demand, low confidence, high interest rates, undervalued currency, hyper-inflation, low investment, rising unemployment, and rising levels of crime and social deprivation. The better global economic climate will boost tourism figures and FDI in 2010, which will lead to a recovery in real GDP growth from a forecast of –9.6 per cent in 2009 to 2.6 per cent in 2010. The IMF structural adjustment programme, though catastrophic in the current climate, is necessary for long-term growth and stability.

current debt-to-exports ratio is estimated at 135 per cent. **Lesotho**'s external debt levels have improved, dropping from 44.6 per cent of GDP in 2006 to an estimated 40.2 per cent in 2008, as the government has used its budget surplus to repay loans. **Mauritius**'s public debt has continued to decline, to 57.7 per cent of GDP in June 2008, compared with 63 per cent in June 2007. Mauritius has passed the Public Management Act 2008, which sets out strategic objectives that include the need to minimise the cost of the debt portfolio within an acceptable level of risk. **Namibia**'s external debt declined in 2008 by 20 per cent from US$1,003 million at end 2007 to US$798 million at end 2008. **Swaziland**'s external debt increased slightly in 2008 to reach US$546.3 million, compared with US$522.7 million in 2007.

Asia-Pacific small states: Where data are available, debt levels for the Asia-Pacific small states indicate that their public debt levels are sustainable and below the 60 per cent solvency threshold.

Fiji Islands' public debt remained at 48 per cent of GDP in 2008. The external debt of **Kiribati** fell to 9.1 per cent of GDP at end 2008. **Maldives**' public debt rose to around 57 per cent of GDP in 2008 from 40 per cent in 1999. The increased debt repayments by **Papua New Guinea**'s government lowered public debt to an estimated 29 per cent of GDP at end 2008. **Solomon Islands**' public debt continued to fall, to reach 31.8 per cent of GDP at end 2008, compared with 40.3 per cent at end 2007. **Tonga**'s external debt fell to 28.9 per cent of GDP in 2008, compared with 32.6 per cent in 2007. **Vanuatu**'s external public debt continued to decline to reach an estimated 18.5 per cent of GDP at end 2008.

Caribbean small states: The Caribbean small states are the most indebted small states, with most countries carrying debt above the 60 per cent of GDP ratio.

Antigua and Barbuda's public external debt increased in 2008 to reach 109.5 per cent by the end of the year. This figure is lower than the 158.4 per cent of GDP reached in 2004. **The Bahamas**' stock of external debt increased by 29.8 per cent in 2008 to reach US$383 million by the end of the year. **Barbados**' public debt rose to 77 per cent of GDP at end September 2008, due to increased borrowing to support countercyclical government expenditure. **Belize**'s public debt declined to 77.3 per cent of GDP at end 2008, compared with 88.6 per cent in the previous year. This fall was partly due to the implementation of a fiscal strategy aimed at cutting the debt ratio by about half by 2019. The stock of public external debt in **Dominica** increased by 1.3 per cent to reach US$217.4 million by the end of 2008. This level of debt is lower than the US$224.2 million recorded in 2004, reflecting the continued implementation of the debt-restructuring initiative.

Grenada's total public sector debt was 106.5 per cent of GDP at end 2008, compared with 112 per cent at the end of 2007. Nevertheless, the country remains in high debt distress due to lower GDP growth. **Guyana**'s public sector debt continued to decline following receipt of external debt relief. The country's debt to GDP ratio was 92.5 per cent at end 2008, compared with 94.2 per cent at the end of the previous year. **Jamaica**'s total external debt reached US$10.2 billion, a 5.1 per cent increase over the previous year. **St Kitts and Nevis**'s public sector debt ratio, one of the highest in the world, reached 177.6 per cent of GDP at end 2008, due to improved debt profiling. This is a significant decline from the 194.4 per cent of GDP recorded in 2004 and lower than the 2007 level of 181.7 per cent. However, interest payments on government debt, at 24 per cent of government spending in 2008, continue to crowd out social and development spending.

St Lucia's public sector debt continued to decline when compared with previous years, reaching 69.6 per cent of GDP at end 2008, mainly as a result of improved debt management in critical areas. **St Vincent and the Grenadines**' public sector debt was lower than in the previous four years, reaching 67.5 per cent of GDP at end 2008. The external debt of **Trinidad and Tobago** increased in 2008 by 13.8 per cent to reach US$3.3 billion by the end of the year.

Mediterranean small states: The debt of the EU small states, Cyprus and Malta, fell or remained unchanged in 2008. The government debt to GDP ratio fell sharply in **Cyprus**, from 60 per cent of GDP at end 2007 to an estimated 49 per cent at end 2008, reflecting the repayment of debt with maturing sinking funds. **Malta**'s government debt remained largely unchanged at an estimated 62.8 per cent of GDP.

Doing business in small states

The prosperity of small and medium enterprises is essential to the continuing development of small states. The World Bank's *Doing Business* 2009 report shows that the reforms implemented in 12 small states will have an effect on the ease with which SMEs can do business. The *Doing Business* report focuses on ten topics that measure the regulation and red tape relevant to the life cycle of a domestic small to medium-size firm. These topics are: starting a business; dealing with construction permits; employing workers; registering property; getting credit; protecting investors; paying taxes; trading across borders; enforcing contracts; and closing a business. *Doing Business* provides absolute indicators of each economy, as well as benchmarking that allows for comparison with other economies.

The 2007/2008 data in *Doing Business* show that the reforms implemented by Mauritius made it easier to start a business, register property and obtain credit. In Tonga, reforms made it easier to start a business and deal with construction permits. In Jamaica, it became easier to deal with construction permits and register a property, while in St Vincent and the Grenadines, it became easier to pay taxes and close a business. For some of the other small states, it became easier in at least one area covered by the *Doing Business* topic focus. It became easier to start a business in Lesotho and Namibia, obtain credit in Vanuatu and pay taxes in Antigua and Barbuda. Other countries had mixed results: in Botswana, it became easier to protect investors and trade across borders, but more difficult to pay taxes. Reforms implemented in Fiji Islands made it difficult to deal with construction permits and employ workers. In The Gambia in 2007/2008, it became more difficult for SMEs to employ workers.

When 26 small states are compared with 175 other countries in 2006 and 2007 and 178 countries in 2008 (Table 1.6), it emerges that with the exception of Tonga, St Kitts & Nevis, Grenada, Guyana and

Table 1.6. Small states' rankings on ease of doing business

2008 rank	2007 rank	2006 rank	Country
27	32	23	Mauritius
34	27	27	St Lucia
36	31	29	Fiji Islands
41	33	33	Antigua & Barbuda
43	42	39	Namibia
47	51	46	Tonga
51	48	44	Botswana
54	44	42	St Vincent & the Grenadines
59	56	51	Belize
60	53	49	Maldives
61	41	36	Samoa
62	58	54	Vanuatu
63	50	48	Jamaica
64	84	85	St Kitts & Nevis
67	59	55	Trinidad & Tobago
70	73	63	Grenada
73	60	58	Kiribati
77	72	65	Dominica
78	n/a	n/a	Brunei Darussalam
79	69	61	Solomon Islands
84	57	53	Papua New Guinea
90	84	83	Seychelles
95	76	67	Swaziland
104	136	133	Guyana
124	114	116	Lesotho
131	113	118	The Gambia

Source: World Bank, *Doing Business*, 2007 and 2008

Table 1.7. Global competitiveness of small states

Country	Overall index 2008–2009	Overall index 2007–2008	Basic requirements	Efficiency factors 2008–2009	Innovation factors
Brunei Darussalam	39	n/a	29	77	87
Cyprus	40	55	23	39	41
Barbados	47	50	33	56	51
Malta	52	56	40	44	56
Botswana	56	76	53	82	98
Mauritius	57	60	50	66	69
Namibia	80	89	48	93	104
Jamaica	86	78	97	75	72
Gambia, The	87	102	81	107	78
Trinidad & Tobago	92	84	65	80	79
Guyana	115	126	115	112	111
Lesotho	123	124	118	125	110

Source: World Economic Forum, www.weforum.org/en/initiatives/, accessed March 2010

Mauritius, it has generally become more difficult to do business in small states. With the exception of these five countries, small states have slipped down the rankings. Brunei Darussalam entered the rankings for the first time in 2008.

Competitiveness of small states

The World Economic Forum (WEF) global competitiveness index analyses the competitiveness of 12 Commonwealth small states. The WEF defines competitiveness as 'the set of institutions, policies, and factors that determine the level of productivity of a country'. The Competitiveness Index assesses countries in terms of basic requirements (institutions, infrastructure, macroeconomic stability, and health and primary education); efficiency enhancers (higher education and training, goods market efficiency, labour market efficiency, financial market sophistication, technological readiness and market size); and innovation and sophistication factors (business sophistication and innovation).

The assessment for 2008–2009 (see Table 1.7) shows that only 12 small states are included in the 134-country index. The highest ranking small state is Brunei Darussalam with an overall index ranking of 39. Compared with the previous assessment period of 2007–2008, the competitiveness of nine small states improved. Trinidad and Tobago and Jamaica showed declines in their competitiveness. A review of the sub-indexes show that small states tend to rank lower for efficiency and innovation. By regional standards, Barbados has been assessed as the most competitive country in the Caribbean. The country's relative macroeconomic weakness (114th) is counterbalanced by its institutional environment (20th), infrastructure (24th) and high quality primary education (5th) and higher (29th) education. Botswana has been assessed as the most competitive African country.

International reserves

The official international reserves of small states, as reported by the World Bank, declined by 17 per cent in 2008, as small states implemented measures to deal with the effects of the global economic and financial crisis and the rising cost of imports of food and fuel. With the exception of nine countries, all other small states experienced a decline in official international reserves. Total small state international reserves amounted to US$32.6 billion at end 2008, compared with US$39.2 billion at end 2007 (see Figure 1.6). The biggest gainer was Seychelles; as the country started to implement IMF reforms, official reserves increased by 56.6 per cent to reach US$63.8 million. Increases were also seen in Belize (up by 53.1 per cent to US$166.2 million), as the country started to benefit from increased investment in its natural resources. Namibia also benefited from increased investment in its natural resources; reserves increased by 44.3 per cent to reach US$1.3 billion, equivalent to 3.7 months of imports of goods and services. Papua New Guinea's

Figure 1.6. Official international reserves of small states, 2004–2008

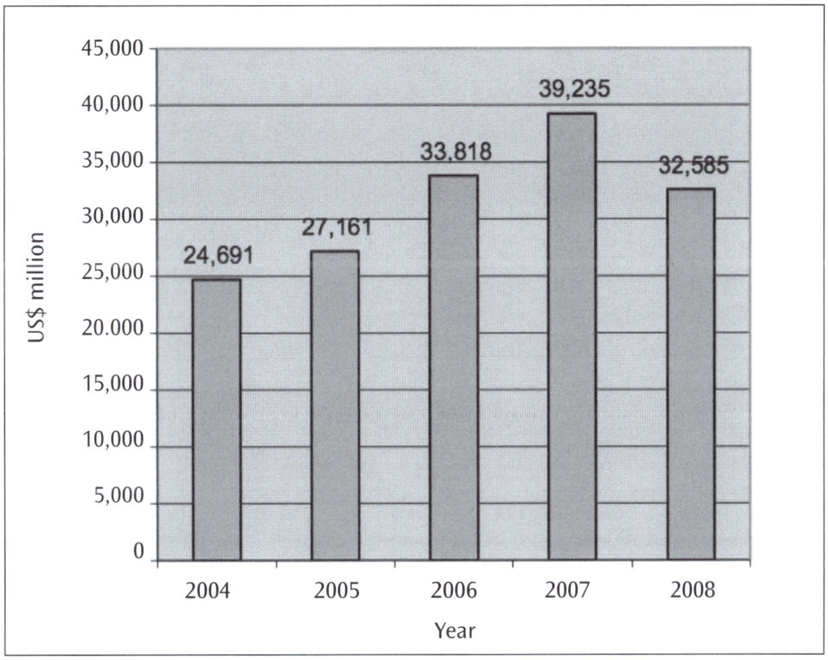

Source: World Bank, World Development Indicators, accessed May 2010

gross international reserves fell by 4.7 per cent to US$ billion by year end, equal to 11 months of imports. The decline of Barbados's gross international reserves by 12 per cent to US$738.5 million resulted in a decline in import cover from 4.4 months of imports in 2007 to 3.3 months of imports in 2008. The largest declines in reserves were experienced in Malta (90.2%), Cyprus (84.6%), Solomon Islands (24.8%) and Maldives (22%).

Human development indicators

Using the GNI per capita statistics as a measure, the prosperity of small states' inhabitants, with the exception of those in Kiribati, improved in 2008.

Table 1.8. Human development trends in small states

Very high HDI 2007 (rank)	High HDI 2007 (rank)	Medium HDI 2007 (rank)	Low HDI 2007 (rank)
1. Brunei Darussalam (30)	1. Antigua & Barbuda (47) ↑1	1. St Vincent & the Grenadines (91) ↑2	1. Gambia, The (168)
2. Cyprus (32)	2. Bahamas, The (52)	2. Belize (93) ↓3	
3. Barbados (37) ↑2	3. Seychelles (57)	3. Samoa (94) ↑2	
4. Malta (38) ↓3	4. St Kitts & Nevis (62) ↓2	4. Maldives (95) ↑2	
	5. Trinidad and Tobago (64) ↓2	5. Tonga (99) ↓5	
	6. St Lucia (69) ↓1	6. Jamaica (100) ↓8	
	7. Dominica (73) ↓2	7. Fiji Islands (108) ↓1	
	8. Grenada (74)	8. Guyana (114)	
	9. Mauritius (81)↓2	9. Botswana (125) ↑1	
		10. Vanuatu (126) ↓1	
		11. Namibia (128) ↑1	
		12. Solomon Islands (135)	
		13. Swaziland (142) ↓2	
		14. Papua New Guinea (148) ↓2	
		15. Lesotho (156) ↑1	

Note: ↑ or ↓ represents the number of places by which the country's HDI improved or declined between 2006 and 2007
Source: UN, *Human Development Report*, 2009

The 2009 *Human Development Report*, which presents Human Development Index (HDI) information for 2007, classifies countries into four categories, ranging from very high human development (HDI greater than 0.900), high human development (HDI greater than 0.800), medium human development (HDI greater than 0.500) and low human development (HDI less than 0.500). Under this measure (see Table 1.8), four Commonwealth small states were classified as countries with very high human development, nine as countries with high human development, 15 as countries with medium human development and one had low human development. Human resources data for Kiribati, Nauru and Tuvalu were unavailable. Commonwealth small states have generally performed well, out of a total of 182 countries.

The main social indicators show that with the exception of The Gambia, where life expectancy fell from 58.8 to 55.7 years, small states experienced an increase in their life expectancy and adult literacy rates between 2005 and 2007.

Key policy issues

Despite the challenges they are facing, small states are continuing to pursue their economic development objectives. Small states are concerned with implementing economic policies that diversify their economies, improve the public service, increase investment and private sector development, reduce poverty and increase growth rates.

African small states: Reports produced by the IMF, EIU and *African Economic Outlook* indicate that the small states in the African region are implementing various development plans to deal with the effects of the global economic and financial crisis, increase private sector development, diversify their economies, reduce poverty and improve the civil service.

The major policy issues in **Botswana** include private sector development and implementation of the national development plan. In 2008, the country's Commerce Confederation launched a new private sector development strategy with the aim of strengthening private sector participation in Botswana's economic development. In addition, in 2008 Botswana established six development hubs to promote and engage private sector participation. These hubs are in the areas of education, transportation, diamonds, innovation, health and agriculture. The country's seven-year 10th National Development plan focuses on economic diversification, job creation and poverty alleviation. The implementation of this plan was delayed because of the global financial crisis. The major policy issues in **The Gambia** include private sector development, promoting growth and reducing poverty, improving the civil service, especially with regard to formulating and implementing policy, transport infrastructure and improving the services offered by utilities. In order to cope with the effect of the global economic crisis on the economy of **Lesotho**, key policy issues include supporting domestic economic activity by stepping up public investment, implementing structural and institutional reforms, and improving the business climate and competitiveness. The key policy issue for **Mauritius** is diversification of the economy away from sugar, textiles, tourism and financial services. Vital to the diversification policy is an emphasis on education and infrastructure, particularly the development of a regional centre for information and communication technology (ICT). The main goals of **Namibia**'s third five-year National Development Plan are faster economic growth, reduced poverty and income inequality, increased private sector employment and faster land redistribution. The government also aims to change the procedures governing foreign investment in Namibia, as the current structure has failed to attract the expected level of investment. The major policy issue in **Seychelles** is the implementation of major economic reforms as mandated by the IMF. Reducing the role of the state while also facilitating the private sector are key requirements of this reform. In a boost to long-term prospects, the search for oil in Seychelles' extensive offshore waters is showing new promise. However, the lawlessness in Somali waters is spilling over into Seychelles through the impact of piracy on the fishing industry and cargo ships ferrying goods to Seychelles. **Swaziland**'s major policy issues include how to reconcile the large civil service with the need for economic reform. In addition, the country is seeking to make progress on privatisation, land reform and improving national infrastructure so as to attract more investment.

Asia-Pacific small states: Data from the EIU, IMF and Asian Development Bank show that the economic policy concerns of small states in the Asia-Pacific region include diversifying their economies, reducing poverty, increasing private investment, adapting and mitigating the effects of climate change, implementing capacity building programmes and ensuring macroeconomic stability.

Brunei Darussalam's major policy concern is the diversification of the country's economic base. This is especially important because the country's oil reserves are expected to last for approximately 20 years, while reserves of gas will last for approximately 30 years, according to the US Energy Information Agency. Diversification programmes include the construction of a methanol plant and investment in information and communication technology, a container port and a manufacturing hub. The main policy issues in **Fiji Islands** include the rising levels of poverty, as an estimated 25 per cent of the population has an income below a basic needs poverty line. In an effort to attract investment in export industries, the authorities are offering tax incentives. **Kiribati**, as a low-lying atoll nation, is vulnerable to the effects of global climate change. Major policy issues include putting in place adaptive measures such as water storage systems and drought resistant crops, reform of the civil service and public enterprises, finding new sources of revenue, and addressing rapid population growth and the need for technical training. The major policy issues in **Maldives** include addressing the shortage of skills and weak institutional capacity, maintaining public debt sustainability, advancing the role of the private sector and reducing income disparities between the capital, Malé, and the atolls. **Nauru**'s primary phosphate reserves are expected to last approximately five years and the country has started prospecting for secondary reserves that can last 20 years and provide exports worth A$1 billion. The key policy issues in the country include promoting performance-oriented public service, resolving high public debt and achieving good governance. **Papua New Guinea**'s policy concerns include improving public infrastructure, increasing the capacity of staff to plan and implement projects, increasing private sector participation in the economy and reducing the very high incidence of poverty. Key policy issues in **Samoa** include improvements in infrastructure, reform of state-owned enterprises and land reform to facilitate commercial use of land. The main policy concerns of **Solomon Islands** include slowing the depletion of foreign reserves, maintaining macroeconomic stability, addressing structural weakness that threaten the sustainability of growth and developing alternatives to logging. **Tonga**, though still experiencing the effects of the 2006 riots, expects to see the expansion of its tourism sector. External assistance from China, New Zealand and Australia will also boost the economy of the country. Remittances play a major role in Tonga and the country expects to benefit from the guest worker programmes of New Zealand and Australia. **Tuvalu**'s key policy issues include addressing the reduction in import duties required under the Pacific Island Country Trade Agreement, improving the tax system's efficiency and equity and widening income disparities, and coping with the vulnerability of the low-lying atoll country to climate change. In November 2008, tax and customs reforms, as well as a broad-based consumption tax, were approved. These initiatives were scheduled to take effect in 2009. The main economic policy concerns of **Vanuatu** include addressing the country's faltering export sector through measures including the trade reform proposals of the UN Development Programme, resuming its application for WTO membership and implementing the Pacific Island Countries Trade Agreement. The country is also concerned with implementing financial regulation and promoting the development of the tourist industry.

Caribbean small states: The small states of the Caribbean are concerned with ensuring macroeconomic stability, implementing diversification programmes and improving their competitiveness.

The major policy issues facing the six Commonwealth small states that are members of the Organisation of Eastern Caribbean States (OECS) and part of the Eastern Caribbean Currency Union – **Antigua and Barbuda**, **Dominica**, **Grenada**, **St Kitts and Nevis**, **St Lucia** and **St Vincent and the Grenadines** – include ensuring the resilience of the financial system, maintaining external stability and competitiveness, enhancing fiscal and debt sustainability and boosting crisis preparedness and capacity building. Policy concerns of **Dominica** include promoting private sector-led growth and lowering poverty and strengthening financial sector regulation. **Grenada**'s policy issues include restoring debt sustainability and improving the tax system. **St Kitts and Nevis** continued to pursue a number of policy measures, including civil service reform and strengthening its debt management capacity. Policy challenges facing **St Lucia** include implementing stronger and more proactive financial sector supervision and regulation in the light of recent financial sector difficulties.

Policy issues facing **The Bahamas** include rationalising public enterprises and pursuing privatisation, and diversifying the country's economic base. The major policy concerns facing **Barbados** include jumpstarting the economy following the economic slowdown, enhancing support for sensitive sectors, strengthening economic ties with non-traditional partners, and ensuring affordable housing and land for all Barbadians. **Belize**'s main policy concerns include strengthening oversight of its financial systems and implementing policies to strengthen fiscal sustainability, and pursuing reforms to reinvigorate growth, including developing a medium-term strategy for tourism and the agricultural sector. The main policy challenges facing **Guyana** include addressing competitiveness and implementation of governance reforms, particularly for procurement and financial monitoring. **Jamaica**'s policy concerns include reducing the debt-to-GDP ratio, invigorating GDP growth and improving the investment climate. **Trinidad and Tobago** is concerned about preserving macroeconomic stability and pursuing a viable diversification programme.

Mediterranean small states: The two EU Commonwealth small states are mainly concerned with maintaining macroeconomic stability in the face of the global economic and financial crisis.

The EIU data indicate that the main policy challenges in **Cyprus** include limiting the impact of the global financial crisis, coping with the fiscal challenges of an ageing population and boosting tourism and construction. **Malta**, like Cyprus, fully adopted the euro at the start of 2008. New policy challenges include returning the public finances to a more sustainable path in line with the European Commission (EC) guidelines. Other major policy challenges include coping with the impact of the global financial crisis, the privatisation programme and developing alternative energy sources.

Conclusion

In 2008, Commonwealth small states experienced slower growth than in previous years. Their growth rates have been lower than the world average and the average for emerging markets and developing countries as a whole. However, growth rates in small states were higher than in advanced economies, which were at the root of the current global economic crisis. The contraction in the world economy due to the global economic and financial crisis, as well as higher prices for food and fuel, led to contraction in the main sectors in 2008. The main economic sectors in small states include mining, tourism, petroleum, construction, agriculture and manufacturing.

Inflation was higher in 2008 as a result of the effect of the international rise in the prices of food and fuel. There was a decline in employment opportunities in most small states. The current account balances of most Commonwealth small states deteriorated in 2008, while inflows of FDI, ODA and remittances increased compared with 2007. The public debt of Africa, Asia-Pacific and Mediterranean small states was mostly within the solvency ratio of 60 per cent of GDP, while most Caribbean small states remain highly indebted.

With the exception of Guyana and Mauritius, it became more difficult to do business in small states in 2008. The competitiveness assessment shows that small states tend to rank lower on efficiency and innovation. Small states' international reserves fell by 17 per cent in 2008, as higher import prices, lower exports and the global financial crisis took effect.

Although social indicators have generally been of a high standard, the HDI rankings of many small states either remained the same or declined. Small states' policy-makers are concerned with implementing economic policies that diversify their economies, improve the public service, increase investment and private sector development, reduce poverty and increase growth. Despite these challenges, small states continue to pursue various options that will allow them to meet their economic development objectives and benefit from the global economy.

References

African Development Bank (2009). *African Economic Outlook*, 2008. Tunis, Tunisia: African Development Bank, available at www.africaneconomicoutlook.org

Asian Development Bank (2009). *Asian Development Outlook*, 2008. Manila: Asian Development Bank, available at www.adb.org

Economic Intelligence Unit (2009). *Country Reports 2009*, available at www.eiu.com

ILO (2009). *Global Employment Trends 2009*. Geneva: International Labour Organisation, available at www.ilo.org

IMF (2010). *World Economic Report*, April 2010. Washington, DC: International Monetary Fund, available at www.imf.org

IMF (2009). Article IV consultations for various countries. Washington, DC: International Monetary Fund, available at www.imf.org

UNCTAD (2009). *World Investment Report 2009: Transnational Corporations, Agricultural Production and Investment*. Geneva: United Nations Conference on Trade and Development, available at www.unctad.org

UNDP (2009). *Human Development Report 2009: Overcoming Barriers, Human Mobility and Development*. New York: United Nations Development Programme, available at hdr.undp.org/

United States International Trade Commission (2010). *Trade Data Reports*, available at http://reportweb.usitc.gov/africa

World Bank (2009). *Doing Business 2009*, available at www.doingbusiness.org

World Economic Forum (2010). *Global Competitiveness Report 2009–2010*, available at www.weforum.org/en/initiatives

2. Post-crisis Growth in Small States: The Role of Trade in Knowledge-based Services*

Dirk Willem te Velde[1]

Introduction

The global financial crisis has had an effect on all countries and small states are no exception (te Velde and Calí, 2010), although the effects vary markedly. However, some economic relationships still hold. As countries grow richer, their economic structures and institutions are transformed and the role of services becomes more important in their economies, especially in small states. The private sector drives much of this process, but government can support it. Indeed, a crucial choice for governments is whether they want to encourage this process and ensure that the right services are being promoted, or whether they stand aloof and slow down a necessary transformative processes towards a higher value added, high wage economy. It seems that trade in knowledge intensive services has also fared well in the current global financial crisis, contributing to growth that is resilient in the face of crisis.

This article argues that a whole range of policy measures are needed to promote the right type of services, including knowledge intensive service industries,[2] especially in a world that is increasingly globalised and competitive. Examples of small states and other countries that have successfully developed their services sectors show that *leadership*, i.e. a well-articulated approach from the higher echelons of government, which can support the entrepreneurial spirit of the private sector, is required to create a vision for the development of service sectors. This can support a *mindset* throughout the whole economy that is geared towards building a more globally competitive service-dependent economy, moving away from preference-dependent and protected sectors.

Engagement with the international economy in the area of trade in services is still important, and significant lessons can be learned from the experiences of successful small states and other developing countries. For example, Singapore and Mauritius would not have been able to develop their service sectors in the way that they have if they had not opened up to foreign tourists and to investment in ICT companies. On the other hand, not all engagement will automatically produce the desired outcomes, so a managed approach is important. International organisations can help by supporting a managed approach towards opening and assisting small states technically as well as financially to build the domestic capacity that can support a strong services sector. In this context it is important to consider the costs and benefits of services liberalisation and the way in which accompanying aid for trade measures in the WTO General Agreement on Trade in Services (GATS) and economic partnership agreement negotiations can help to enhance positive impacts and mitigate negative consequences.

Section 2 of this article discusses knowledge intensive services in small states and Section 3 considers the role of such services in promoting growth in small states. Section 4 provides a number of specific measures to enhance the services sector and Section 5 provides examples by sector. Section 6 presents conclusions.

---

*This article draws on M Qureshi and DW te Velde, *Growth Strategies for Small States in a Globalising World: The Role of Knowledge-based and Service Industries*, Commonwealth Secretariat (2008); and M Calí, K Ellis and DW te Velde, 'Services and Development: The Role of Regulation and Trade Liberalization', ODI Working Paper 298 (2008). Much of the detail is in these papers, while the article can be considered to be a summary review. The article also includes some evidence from larger countries to enrich the discussion. The author is grateful to Loretta Curtin for her support and would like to thank two anonymous referees for their excellent reviews. Contact: dw.tevelde@odi.org.uk

Knowledge-intensive services and small states: definitions and data

A number of knowledge-intensive services sectors are important for small states. Qureshi and te Velde (2008) suggest the following service sectors as sectors which have some current or potential capacity to export, which are somewhat competitive and respond to structural changes in import markets:

Tourism: Some parts of tourism services can be knowledge intensive and can be a step up the value added ladder from low value added activities to higher value added activities.

Financial services: Trading in financial services and back office support are often knowledge intensive. The offshore financial sector has contributed significantly to the exports and GDP of the Caribbean region.

Education services: Knowledge itself can be traded, e.g. there are many medical offshore schools in the Caribbean region (Brandon, 2003). Education services are also supplied through (temporary) movement of people.

Health services: The provision of health services is important for development.

Business IT services: The market for offshore services such as IT and other back-office operations is increasing rapidly worldwide. The Caribbean has entered the sector, exporting mainly to the USA.

Cultural services: Three types of cultural services are emerging in the Caribbean: music, street festivals, and film and video production.

Relatively little has been written about the services sector. This is because the sector is poorly defined and poorly covered by statistics. With this limitation in mind, data from the World Bank World Development Indicators show that the share of services in the world economy has recently increased as measured by the value added as a percentage of GDP.[3] Globally, over the period 1990–2005, the share of services in the economies of low-, middle- and high-income countries grew by 10 percentage points, to 50, 55 and 73 per cent, respectively. This implies that services contributed relatively more to growth; growth is extremely important for poverty reduction.

The services sector is also a major source of employment. Figure 2.1 shows that on average 52 per cent of the labour force in small states is engaged in the services sector. Its contribution to total employment is 35, 58 and 62 per cent in low-, middle- and high-income small states' economies, respectively.

Figure 2.1. Distribution of the labour force in services in small states (percentage)

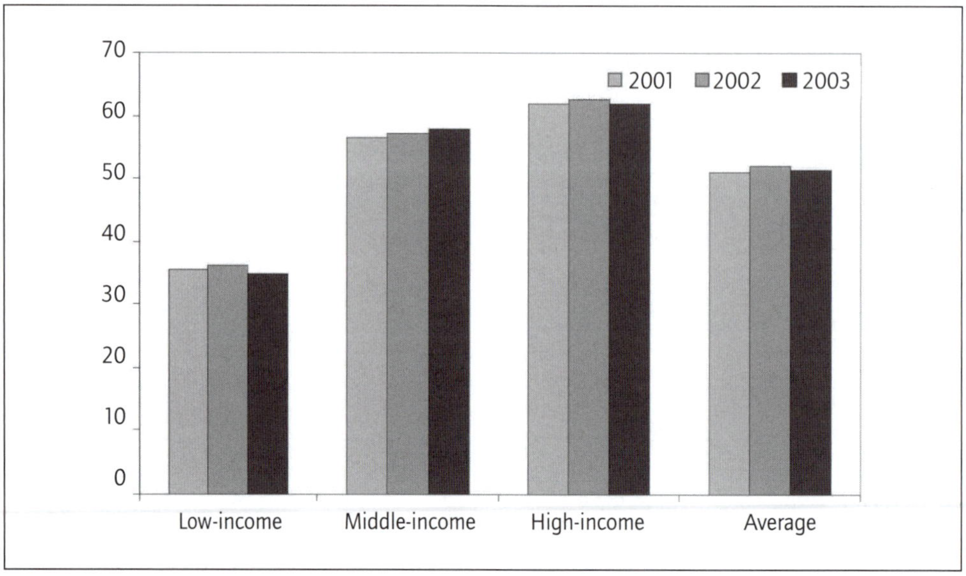

Source: Commonwealth Secretariat, *Small States Yearbook*, 2007

Figure 2.2. Share of services in total trade in goods and services (percentage)

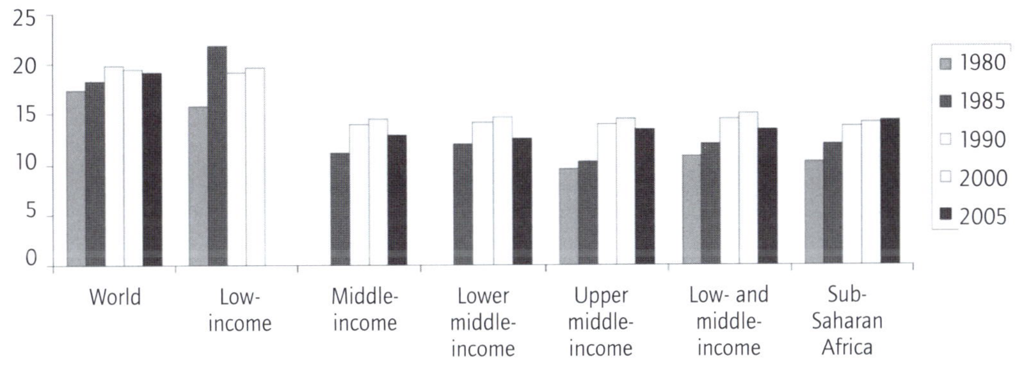

Source: World Bank, World Development Indicators, http://data.worldbank.org, accessed January 2010

Trade in services is increasingly important, but its importance varies by country. Figure 2.2 shows that the share of services has increased since 1980, now accounting for around 20 per cent (at least for those traded services that are measured in the balance of payments). The increase in the share has been faster in low-income countries and in sub-Saharan Africa.

Available balance of payments data capture only part of services supply, as discussed under trade negotiations. There are four different modes of supply of services: cross-border supply (Mode 1); services consumed abroad (Mode 2); services supplied via commercial presence abroad (Mode 3); and services supplied via temporary movements of labour (Mode 4).

Services data used to compute exports by mode are often based on proxies. For instance, Mode 3 exports of services are sometimes proxied by foreign direct investment. A better indicator would be sales of services by multinational enterprise (MNE) affiliates abroad, but such data are not always available. Similarly, Mode 4 exports of services should reflect sales by natural persons temporarily abroad, but this is proxied either by remittances (which may understate the true value, because sales may be higher than what is sent abroad, or overstate it, as remittances include permanent migrants) or by compensation of employees in subsidiaries of services MNEs. Neither of these are correct. Available data for small states tend to be poor, as their small size does not always allow for expensive data generating units.

The role of knowledge-based services in crisis-resilient growth in small states

The earlier literature identified private sector development, especially in the manufacturing sector, as one of the primary concerns in small economies (Winters and Martins, 2005; Briguglio *et al.*, 2005). This led Qureshi and te Velde (2008) to suggest that knowledge-based services are a useful way forward. Due to their small populations, the domestic market size is small in these countries. As a result, most of the firms in small states are small and medium enterprises with limited opportunities for reaping the benefits of economies of scale and investing in research and development. Hence, unit costs of production are higher as compared to larger economies. Also, many small states have a poor investment climate; this is particularly true for micro and very small states, as these face high utility costs (Winters and Martins, 2005, and below). Weak institutions, remoteness and lack of skilled labour or adequate human capital limits access to external capital and constrains industrial development. Of course some other countries, such as Singapore, are at the top of investment climate surveys,

Some small countries can also be characterised as having a lack of competition in product markets. This leads to a misallocation of resources, inefficiencies in production and no incentive for innovation. All these factors contribute to high unit production costs for firms in these countries. The high production costs are compounded by high transportation costs due to the remoteness, insularity or landlockedness of many small states. This implies that small states need to charge higher prices to stay in business or else accept lower returns on some part of their costs, compared with larger economies.

Winters and Martins (2005) support this view and find that business costs, particularly those for transport and labour, are significantly higher, especially in micro states. They argue that a small consignment size and poor infrastructure inflate the costs of trade and create strong economic disadvantages for these countries.

Both the small states agenda proposed in the Commonwealth/World Bank *Joint Task Force Report* (2000), and the review of this agenda (Briguglio *et al.*, 2006), identify serious challenges for development in small states due to their small size, remoteness and vulnerability. The review suggests that over the past few years the prospects for small states have deteriorated further due to preference erosion and the emergence of new competitors. It proposes that small states need to reposition themselves in the global economy and move into knowledge-based and other service industries.

Services generally affect development in several ways (Adlung, 2007; Qureshi and te Velde, 2008). Services can also be important for promoting inclusive growth. Although agriculture might be more effective in directly reducing poverty than other sectors, it is difficult to promote agriculture when other sectors have more promising growth prospects or when countries face preference erosion and competition from larger-scale producers (whilst increased domestic agriculture may reduce exposure to crises, it may not produce growth efficiently). Services already provide many jobs for the poor (from distribution to tourism); provide essential inputs into the investment climate (from transport to finance, electricity and telecommunications); and offer an opportunity to diversify and enjoy comparative and competitive advantages (from temporary migration to call centres).

Growth strategies in small states and other developing countries have in the past been based on agriculture and to some extent on manufacturing. A growth strategy based on knowledge-based services, where appropriate, would often imply a shift in thinking, as we argue in the conclusion of this article. A growth strategy based on developing services could be complemented by strategies which would also improve the contribution of agriculture to growth (in any case several agricultural outputs have a high knowledge content, e.g. sugar research, genetic engineering and horticulture). The promotion of services may also help sectors such as agriculture through direct and indirect linkages. For example, hotels and restaurants have large expenditures on food and drink, and buy local electronic goods, furniture and other manufactures.

There are also indirect effects. Of course there are leakages of the sector away from the country, but that is the case in other sectors as well, and there is little evidence to suggest that tourism is special. Econometric studies (Lejaragga and Walkenhorst, 2006) capture the dynamic effects of tourism on growth and suggest that growth can be tourism led, and that in some cases tourism contributes more to growth than other sectors. Matthijs and Subramanian (2007) also point to the dynamic effects of tourism. Increased air travel for tourism has reduced the cost of airfreight from African countries to Europe and provided new transport opportunities for small quantities of fresh products. Tourism also increases local demand for high quality fruit and vegetables and provides an outlet for produce that does not meet export standards. More generally, these studies argue that by positioning itself as a relatively close and attractive holiday destination, the gain for sub-Saharan Africa could not just be direct (in tourism services, hotels and restaurants), but also indirect: the fact that more direct flights arrive in African airports makes transport cheaper and export markets more readily accessible for African goods. This factor is very important for small and isolated countries.

For many developing countries, trade in services, especially tourism-related services, is already an important foreign exchange earner. Tourism is highly important for low- and middle-income small states due to their relatively less diversified services sector as compared with high-income states. A major challenge is to move up the value added ladder towards knowledge-intensive services. Generally, the higher the income levels in small countries, the more they are engaged in knowledge-based services.

For example, tourism typically accounts for over 50 per cent of the service exports of middle-income countries (for example Botswana, Mauritius, St Lucia and Vanuatu) and to a lesser extent for those of Singapore and United Arab Emirates (UAE). Singapore's service exports are skill intensive, including education, financial services and other professional business services, such as information and communication technology. UAE's major service sector is trade (external, wholesale and retail), which has developed due to excellent transport infrastructure facilities. However, the country is rapidly developing its financial, educational and tourism services sectors as well (Qureshi and te Velde, 2008).

The global financial crisis has opened up new roles for knowledge-based industries. The hospitality sector was set to register a decline of 8.8 per cent in 2009 due to the economic downturn in the main source markets, while tourist arrivals in Mauritius were expected to be around 835,000, lower than the 930,456 arrivals in 2008. Financial intermediation was set to grow at a lower rate. However, ICT proved to be one of the most resilient industries in the global crisis. The ICT sector continued to benefit from cost-saving measures around the globe, with growth rates in Mauritius of up to 10–12 per cent.

Borchert and Mattoo (2009) provide preliminary evidence of the resilience of services trade relative to goods trade. The drop in US services imports growth between October 2008 and April 2009 has been around four times smaller than the drop for goods imports. However, a wide variation of patterns emerges within the services categories. Transport, travel and financial services exports appear to be more affected by the global downturn, while other knowledge-intensive services have done better.

Markets for ICT products and services are expanding worldwide. While there have been decreases in some markets recently, in other sectors the crisis has led to new cost pressures, opening up new opportunities for low-cost locations. Thus, small states need to seize the new opportunities arising in the services sector, but they must also enhance productivity levels in existing services sectors by adopting appropriate policies and reforms relevant to their economies. Since international competition in services is growing, small states should focus on developing those services in which they can build up a competitive edge due to some locational advantage, e.g. tourism, education, or financial and legal services.

Measures to promote services and development

Several factors affect trade in services and the development of services sectors. The constraints to trade in services are complex and go beyond normal trade constraints. A policy-relevant approach distinguishes among three types of constraints (te Velde, 2006). These include:

- supply-side or domestic capacity constraints;
- domestic regulatory and institutional framework;
- external constraints (e.g. international rules and barriers relating to trade in services or pressures due to competition).

This approach provides an analytical lens on developing trade in services – trying to make sense of the various constraints. It delineates clear responsibilities for different actors in different sectors and ministries and other stakeholders. That said, trade in services, as a catalyst to promote economic diversification away from traditional sectors, involves a shift in thinking throughout the whole economy, involving different types of actions to overcome these constraints. For this, leadership or co-ordination from the top, which is also in tune with private sector needs, can be important. The examples of Mauritius and Singapore show that targeted initiatives can work in developing services sectors (Qureshi and te Velde, 2008). Targeted ideas introduced by government can help to attract the right people with integrity, intellect, energy, drive and application, who can find niche opportunities and then exploit them (Yew, 2000). Small countries may be at an advantage here, because they may have more flexibility in introducing changes than their larger peers.

Domestic regulatory frameworks

Appropriate regulation is crucial to benefiting from trade in services liberalisation. For some sectors, regulation is required for services to be traded. In other sectors, regulation is vital regardless of whether the sector is open to trade or not. Owing to the nature of services (which are commonly characterised by elements of natural monopoly and informational asymmetries), regulation is usually required to ensure that service markets work properly. However, regulation can also be unnecessarily burdensome and distorting, and may constitute a major barrier to services trade.

External constraints

Following Hoekman and Braga (1997), trade barriers can be grouped into the following categories:[4]

- Quotas (e.g. the number of flights on a route may be restricted);
- Local content and prohibitions (e.g. production activities and supplies may be restricted to nationals only);
- Price-based instruments (e.g. visa fees and entry/exit taxes or subsidies), which tend to hit small traders more than large-scale traders;
- Standards and accreditation requirements (e.g. non-recognition of degrees/certificates/diplomas obtained in foreign countries);
- Licensing and procurement requirements;
- Discriminatory access to distribution networks;
- No commitment on Mode 4 of supply of services.

There are other external constraints, such as external shocks or competition from third countries. WTO and EU trade negotiations could help to remove external barriers.

WTO GATS

WTO negotiations stalled in July 2008. The services negotiations did not progress well. Many countries did include new commitments as part of the Doha round which started in 2001. Other issues, such as agriculture, have generally been more important for developing countries.

But rules governing trade in services are an important way in which WTO membership could enhance trade performance through their potential effects on inward FDI. In 1995 the GATT/WTO included commitments on treatment of foreign providers of services in the GATS for the first time. Countries can commit to any of 155 sub-sectors and four modes. Mode 3 in particular relates to the conditions under which foreign firms have access to particular services sectors, and which conditions apply after their establishment.

There are three possible types of effects of the inclusion of a sector in a GATS schedule. First, countries can offer market access to foreign services providers, although in practice GATS commitments have gone little beyond existing liberalisation. Hence, GATS is hardly ever used as a liberalising tool. Second, the set of trade rules contained in GATS (especially Mode 3 on investment) provides for a transparent framework conducive to private sector activities, reducing uncertainty and encouraging investment. The third effect is signalling. Countries that make offers and requests to GATS are willing to seriously consider development of the services sectors, sending positive signals to potential investors.

Some empirical studies, such as te Velde and Nair (2006), suggest that trade negotiations, and GATS in particular, have been effective in attracting FDI in the tourism sector in the Caribbean. The statistical evidence suggests that those Caribbean countries that have more open and transparent rules also attracted more inward FDI, holding other factors (such as market size) constant. However, it should be added that investors generally see the commitment to trade rules as only one, minor, input into their investment decisions.

Economic partnership agreements

The Cotonou Partnership Agreements (CPA) contain a number of provisions on services. CPA Articles 41–43 deal with negotiations on trade in services, in particular Article 41.4, in which the EU and African, Caribbean and Pacific (ACP) countries agree to extend EPAs with the liberalisation of services in accordance with provisions of GATS. It should be noted that they do not oblige the ACP countries to conclude a trade in services component in any EPA. CPA Articles 41.2 and 41.3 provide for an affirmation of GATS commitments and crucially underline the need for special and differential treatment for ACP suppliers of services and the need to give sympathetic consideration to the ACP states' priorities for improvements in the European Commission (EC) schedule.

CPA Article 41.5 states that the EC shall support the ACP states' efforts to strengthen their capacity in the supply of services. Particular attention shall be paid to services related to labour, business, distribution, finance, tourism, culture, and construction and related engineering services with a view to enhancing their competitiveness and thereby increasing the value and the volume of their trade in goods and services. It does not state how this should be achieved.

Little progress has been made in actual services negotiations in EPA regions except for the Caribbean. Nonetheless, EPAs may lead to some real opportunities: better market access, better procedures for mutual recognition agreements, improved Mode 4 offers by the EC (te Velde, 2009), a request for more market access and health insurance portability, and for support measures to support the development of services sectors in the ACP.

Supply-side constraints

Supply-side constraints on export capacity which tend to apply to trade in services and goods include:

Human resources: Some services, such as professional business, financial and educational services, are skill intensive and require appropriately trained and qualified staff. However, most developing countries have a narrow range of tertiary education for providing such staff and many skilled people, whether they have been trained locally or abroad, migrate, which severely limits the availability of skilled and qualified human resources (although it can bring in resources via other routes).

Infrastructure: Low-income countries are typically characterised by a weak physical infrastructure (such as unpaved roads, underdeveloped ports, weak air connections, and unreliable electrification and water and sanitation systems) and poor information and communication technology. Poor infrastructural facilities restrict domestic, as well as foreign, investment in the economy.

Size: The limited size of the domestic markets of developing countries raises the need to increase market access to reap economies of scale. Some services have a minimum efficient scale that is greater than the size of the domestic market.

Information: A majority of exporters of services operate on a small scale and lack information on markets and regulations. In addition, they are unable to market their products, which may lead to a lack of information on the consumer's side as well. Services products are often 'experience' goods, where sales depend on a track record of international credibility and profile. It can take time to build up an international reputation and credibility, particularly because the fixed costs of establishing credibility are relatively high for small service providers.

Technology: Exporters in small states have limited access to (new) technology, which reduces their competitive edge.

Financial resources: Service providers, especially those operating on a small scale, face constraints in accessing financial resources, corrupt practices, weak banking systems, and unreliable monetary policies, exchange rates and exchange control.

Promoting knowledge-based services in small states

Tourism

Tourism is the biggest export service sector in many small states. Global tourism receipts have more than doubled in the past 15 years (World Tourism Organization, 2008). Tourism receipts in Africa, growing at 10 per cent a year, account for US$21.5 billion, or 3.5 per cent, of Africa's GDP. (There are wide variations within Africa – tourism accounts for 20 per cent of GDP in Mauritius, 10 per cent in Namibia, Tanzania and The Gambia, 5 per cent in Botswana and Kenya, and 2.5 per cent in South Africa.) The World Tourism and Travel Council (WTTC) reports that tourism contributes 15 per cent of GDP and 16 per cent of employment in the Caribbean region (including indirect effects).

Tourism can benefit poor people if employment opportunities are opened to local people. Tourism can offer labour-intensive and small-scale opportunities, employing semi-skilled and casual workers, small and medium-sized enterprises and a high proportion of women, and providing an opportunity for self-employment. Tourism also provides opportunities in remote areas and in places which rate highly in respect of their natural resources and culture, all of which tends to favour the poor.

Tourism is a step towards diversification, but as countries become more developed they move increasingly into higher value-added sectors. Developing countries have already realised the importance of appropriate frameworks that provide for a transparent and non trade-distortionary rules-based system for investing in the tourism sector through commitments in international service negotiations. This relatively open stance has coincided with the large impact of tourism on development in terms of value added, incomes and employment in static terms, as well as dynamic effects on the rest of the economy. Rather than protecting the local tourism sector, especially the smaller players, from foreign involvement, it is more efficient to implement complementary policies to promote the (local) sector and its effect on development.

Governments can use various policy and regulatory tools to enhance tourism and its development impact.

A review of tourism policy and regulations based on experiences in developing countries, including several small states, has a number of important policy implications (Mitchell and te Velde, 2008):

1. A more liberal stance to air access will help to increase tourist arrivals. Evidence from Botswana, Mauritius and South Africa shows that this will help to increase tourist arrivals.

2. A more liberal regime in the tourism support services (e.g. transport handlers and other business indicators such as access to finance) has been an important factor behind the more rapid increase in tourist arrivals in Cape Verde.

3. Tourism is growing fast in Cambodia and Vietnam – notwithstanding their adverse regulatory environment – because they are cheap destinations located in a rapidly growing regional economy. Although tourism has a larger and more important share of the Cambodian economy, tourist activities have a greater developmental benefit per unit of activity in Vietnam because of better developed linkages with the rest of the economy.

4. There are contrasting experiences regarding the extent of linkages between tourism and the poor, and the role of Cambodia and The Gambia in promoting this. Some of the factors accounting for the lack of developmental impact in Cambodia also apply in The Gambia. Notably, poor human resources and economic infrastructure, and weak local food supply chains and governance characterise both locations. The difference, however, is that in The Gambia a local business association has spent the last six years providing an interface between established tourist facilities and resource-poor local people.

5. When the capacity to provide health services is available (as in India and Thailand) and there is a demand for these, regulatory co-ordination can help to facilitate trade in heath tourism.

6. There are various views on what caused the emergence of the tourism industry in St Lucia, but both public and private players suggest that government has facilitated the development of the sector by building infrastructure (especially in the north of the island) and using appropriate incentives which have helped the private sector.

7. Although Suriname is unlikely to attract mass tourism, its ability to build up tourism services has been hampered by the lack of domestic and foreign investment in the medium (and large) sized hotel sector. While there is weak infrastructure and high transport costs, probably the most important constraint is the weak regulatory framework, which hampers investment. A further major constraint is the limited passenger flight capacity due to restrictive regulation and failure to liberalise the air transport sector.

8. There has been an overall increase in tourism arrivals and spending in Tanzania. The govern-

ment has liberalised tourism services by transferring the non-core functions of the Tourism Department to the private sector by, for example privatising formerly state-owned tourist parastatals. The development of the tourism sector has been positive following reforms beginning in the mid-1990s.

9. While Uganda has liberalised the tourism sector by, for example, privatising hotels, with success, and has implemented several community-oriented tourism plans, challenges remain in developing the sector. Regulatory challenges relate to complementary issues such as business indicators. In particular, Uganda suffers from weak tax policies and costs to finance tax administration and from problems relating to the skills and education of workers, and to access to electricity and land.

The ICT sector

A well-functioning ICT sector is not only important for development because it improves the efficiency of households, firms, sectors and the country as a whole. It also provides significant new opportunities for exports of services from small and isolated states. Appropriate regulation, trade liberalisation and other complementary factors (e.g. good quality skills) play a key role in developing the ICT sector. This is explained below.

ICT and development: the role of regulation

Evidence (Calí *et al.*, 2008) suggests that a well-developed ICT sector contributes to faster growth, better economic performance at the level of the firm and improved household welfare, because it helps actors to engage in activities more efficiently. ICT enables firms to access knowledge and information, reduce transaction costs, more easily supply markets remotely, improve decision-making across the value chain through better and easier communication, and improve the flexibility of firms in responding to consumer demand. However, ICT is not available everywhere (internet penetration in 2007 was 1.8 per cent in Africa, 8.4 per cent in the Asia-Pacific region and 28.2 per cent in the Americas), and there is a digital divide between poor and rich countries (Campos, 2006; Torero and Braun, 2006; International Telecommunication Network, 2007). Development of the ICT sector depends on a good telecommunications system. Reform of telecommunications involves market liberalisation (e.g. ICT prices) and competition, allowing private sector participation, introducing effective regulation and trade liberalisation for foreign firms.

Market reforms can boost productivity and stimulate investment in ICT, enhancing the performance of the sector. Market-based strategies also allow governments to meet social and economic objectives such as increasing access to ICTs and raising government revenues from telecommunication services.

Competition has become more common in the ICT sector. Africa has the least competition (Campos, 2006; Torero and Brain, 2006; ITN, 2007), with 51 per cent of countries having some form of competition in basic voice services (compared with 61 per cent in the Americas and 55 per cent in Asia-Pacific), and 75 per cent in the mobile phone sector (76 per cent in the Americas and 78 per cent in Asia-Pacific) in 2006.

Private sector participation in telecommunications was lower in Africa in the 1990s (especially in terms of volume), but increased after 2003. Operators have been privatised in 78 developing countries, raising close to US$80 billion in 1990–2006.

Effective regulation of telecommunication is particularly important in countries with small markets which due to natural monopoly characteristics may allow only one or a few telecommunications firms to operate. When markets have been privatised, effective regulation is critical for benefits to be felt by households and firms, e.g. in the form of low-cost connection to broadband services. Empirical evidence suggests that effective regulators are independent of political influences and have the technical skills needed to monitor firms and the capacity to enforce regulation. Further, the spread of ICT benefits from a comprehensive ICT strategy that fosters innovation and adopts new technology.

Country case studies show that ***trade policy liberalisation*** and openness to foreign firms has also helped the development of the ICT sector (Calí *et al.*, 2008). Trade liberalisation is more beneficial in the presence of complementary regulation such as policies on competition.

ICT and offshore services

A competitive ICT sector opens up new export frontiers for developing countries, including those (landlocked) countries traditionally constrained by high transport costs. The adoption of ICT can enable specific services (and goods) to be traded or developed offshore without the need for using traditional transport systems. The rise in call centres, online programmers and software developers based in developing countries (e.g. India and Mauritius) provides examples of the trend for offshore services to move from developed to developing countries. Other opportunities for offshore development arise in a wide range of sectors, including legal, financial and health services. Offshoring has begun to bring large benefits to those developing countries that have a competitive ICT sector (e.g. those with low broadband costs, ICT associations and good quality skills, from experienced managers in call centres to engineering and computing skills). In India, IT-enabled services (worth US$9.5 billion in 2007) were responsible for a third of total services exports in 2007. The IT-enabled services sector in Mauritius grew by 25 per cent a year in 2005–2007.

Regulations in importing countries also affect offshoring opportunities. For instance, some US states have banned offshoring of services due to employee concerns about jobs. Protectionism has also been visible, but to a lesser extent, in Europe, where some groups feel threatened. (Unions were quite vocal when offshoring gained momentum in the UK and USA in 2004–205 because of direct job losses which would only be indirectly compensated for by economic gains.) There are also concerns about data protection issues which may constrain offshoring opportunities for developing countries. Such barriers to trade will be important interests (offensive interests in services negotiations) in trade negotiations for key developing country exporters of services.

Professional, education and cultural services: examples from small states

This section reviews a number of initiatives by countries to promote professional, education and cultural services.

Botswana is trying to develop its services sector. An important initiative in this regard was the establishment of the International Financial Services Centre (IFSC) in 2003. The government-sponsored IFSC aims to establish a cross-border financial services industry to make Botswana the regional (or African) base for business services such as management of companies' inbound telephone calls through call centres, administrative and shared service activities.

The IFCS operates as a special licensee for companies that carry out offshore financial services operations, allowing them to pay a lower taxation rate (15 per cent instead of the standard 25 per cent until 2020 and exemptions from withholding tax). It also helps new companies with the lengthy administrative procedures for starting their businesses. The IFSC approved five applications from companies in 2005, bringing the number of certified companies operating under the IFSC to 29.

While the IFSC has been successful in attracting these companies, conditions for establishing a significant back-office services sector remain weak. Two main types of complementary policies are required: developing skills and developing an appropriate IT infrastructure. Without these, even a favourable incentive framework supported by the IFSC cannot keep companies in Botswana. The relatively poor quality of IT infrastructure, including poor data exchange processes, is believed to have been the major cause of a well-known international bank's decision to relocate part of its back-office operations away from Botswana. The bank was not able to get the right calibre of staff on an ongoing basis and the IT infrastructure did not match the requirements of the company. Other banks also list the lack of skilled labour as one of their primary concerns – an issue made worse by the strict immigration regime.

Examples from Botswana show that the public sector can play an important role alongside the private sector in the development of services industries. A case in point is the Botswana Accountancy College, where the government assisted the private sector in promoting tertiary education in Botswana and plugged a significant skills gap in a ten-year timeframe (see Calí and te Velde, 2007). However, such examples are few and not sufficient to meet the requirements of the country. There need to be more efforts to improve the ICT infrastructure and the availability and quality of local skills to make Botswana the southern African regional hub of financial services and increase net services exports.

There are various examples of how Mauritius has promoted professional services, e.g. using the Scheme to Attract Professionals for Emerging Sectors (SAPES) and Ebène Cyber City, to become a centre for ICT services.

The emergence of Singapore as a regional and international hub of the services sector is due to close co-operation and partnership between the public and private sectors and their combined initiatives. The government actively plans the direction of the economy. It reviews economic performance, identifies niche markets with growth potential, sets targets for medium- and long-term growth, and devises and implements strategic plans to achieve its targets. The private sector builds on the services and facilities provided by government and makes full use of its potential. A classic example of this is the development of Singapore's education sector. The Economic Committee of Singapore stressed the need to develop a strong tertiary education sector in the mid-1980s and reaffirmed it in 2001. Since then, the government has undertaken numerous initiatives to promote tertiary education in the country. Besides establishing three world class public universities, the Economic Development Board has embarked on an ambitious plan to attract renowned foreign academic institutions and bring in more specialised programmes through tie-ups with local private educational institutions.

Strategic and practical implications

It is part of a normal development strategy for developing countries generally, but especially small states, to concentrate on the development of knowledge intensive services. Such services are less sensitive to high transport costs (compared to goods), help diversify the economic base, reduce vulnerability to macro shocks, are less sensitive to hurricanes (compare a call centre with a plantation) and reduce reliance on agriculture and manufacturing, which are subject to eroding trade preferences and problems of scale. With low-cost and high quality telecommunication systems and IT-enabled services, small and isolated states can obtain direct access to large developed markets.

Overall, the development of service sectors requires a set of actions at various levels, including government leadership to provide an appropriate framework and incentives for the economy to shift towards a more competitive sector in developing countries which over recent decades have relied on preferences and protection. For example, Mauritius implemented a set of initiatives (incentives and skills development) to move towards other pillars for development, such as financial services and ICT. The country had already been successful in diversifying into garments and tourism. Changes in policy may be required at all levels: trade negotiations, the development of an appropriate supply capacity and building an appropriate domestic regulatory framework. State-business relations need to be strengthened so that the private sector benefits further from government initiatives. Engagement in international trade and business is crucial so that important lessons can be learned from the experiences of other countries in general, and successful small states in particular. In addition, the international community can help by supporting such initiatives and assisting small states both technically and financially to build the domestic capacity that supports a strong services sector crucial for future growth prospects. Countries need to be proactive and consistent, yet flexible in their approach. Aid for trade can support this. Many small states are amongst the most disadvantaged countries in the world in terms of their economic and environmental vulnerability. Regional and international co-operation to devise appropriate plans to build domestic capacity to improve physical and human infrastructure is crucial for these states.

There are various supporting factors, e.g. domestic capabilities, regulatory frameworks and external conditions, in and across countries and sectors:

Sectors

- ***Tourism activity*** is often initially driven by the private sector, but the public sector can support tourism by building infrastructure (as it has done, for example, in St Lucia) and by co-ordinating the activities of different private sector agents, e.g.

the coalition of service industries in Barbados. The design of appropriate international trade-related policies can be instrumental in this regard. The success of the open skies policy of Dubai demonstrates how such liberalisation can work well, although recently there have been some problems related to the financial sector.

- Some small states, especially middle- and high-income states, are moving fast into knowledge-based service sectors beyond tourism services. For example, Mauritius has already experienced a rapid rise in the number of IT companies operating in the country. However, in other small states the government needs to consider following an proactive approach to support services, as even a small expansion requires an increase in domestic capabilities such as skills and improved IT networks. If a deliberate attempt is not supported on all fronts, IT companies may decide to move elsewhere (e.g. away from Botswana to South Africa).

- Offshore education and training could be promoted by small states by creating location advantages where investment in education (e.g. training local and foreign nurses) can improve exports of services and at the same time upgrade the skills of the local workforce so that they are appropriate for the development of the service sectors.

- Small states export other services, including professional services, but often there are no systematic data. The lack of available data suggests that such services may not receive priority policy support. A first step would be to compile data and assess the export capacity of these sectors. Considering the increase in global demand for business services, such sectors can play an important role in diversifying the economies of small states.

Supporting factors

- Building an appropriate and flexible supply capacity is key to the development of the services sector. Although this is part of normal development policies (skills enhancement, infrastructure, ICT, etc.), the situation is different for small states, which face stark choices because of their size and limited resources.

- The regulatory framework is very important for services. In some cases, bad frameworks can stifle development (e.g. lack of regulation of monopolies in the utilities sector in the Caribbean). In other cases, a change in the rules can enable new service activities, such as offshore schools or the provision of film sets.

- Small states need to embrace globalisation and use international trade negotiations to signal openness and their forward-looking approach. Creating a transparent framework for the non-discriminatory treatment of domestic and foreign investors is important for small states' efforts to attract significant foreign (and local) investment in services. Successful small states tend to be more active in regional service negotiations and they can try to gain access for their services providers in negotiations on temporary migration.

- Governments have also considered the institutional support structure of both the private and public sectors. Coalitions of service industries can play a useful role in small states through, for example, educating their members about international service conditions and policies; promoting the adoption of standards and codes of conduct of their members to prepare for competition; lobbying government on the importance of an appropriate environment for services; and assessing the capacity of the sector and identifying areas with market potential.

Notes

1 Director of Programmes, International Economic Development Group, ODI.

2 This article focuses on traded services such as tourism, cultural, educational and financial services. This may not cover all knowledge intensive service industries, and some parts of the above sectors are not very knowledge intensive.

3 http://web.worldbank.org/WEBSITE/EXTERNAL/DATASTATISTICS/0,,contentMDK:20398986~menuPK:64133163~pagePK:64133150~piPK:64133175~theSitePK:239419,00.html

4 Non-trade related external constraints also exist, such as the level of competition abroad.

References

Adlung, R (2007). 'The Contribution of Services Liberalization to Poverty Reduction: What Role for the GATS?' Staff working paper ERSD-2007-01. Geneva: WTO, Economic Research and Statistics Division.

Borchert, I and Mattoo, A (2009). 'The Crisis-Resilience of Services Trade', Policy Research Working Paper 4917. Washington, DC: World Bank.

Brandon, EP (2003). 'New External Providers of Tertiary Education in the Caribbean', Paper prepared for IESALC.

Briguglio, L, Persaud, B and Stern, R (2006). *Toward an Outward-Oriented Development Strategy for Small States: Issues, Opportunities and Resilience Building*. Washington, DC: World Bank.

Calí, M, Ellis, K and te Velde, DW (2008). 'Services and Development: The Role of Regulation and Trade Liberalisation', ODI working paper 298.

Calí, M and te Velde, DW, (2007). 'Assessment of Botswana's Services Sector: A Study for the BTPP/BIDPA'. London: Overseas Development Institute.

Campos, NF (2006). *The Impact of Information and Communication Technologies on Economic Growth in Latin America in an International Perspective*. Middlesex, UK: Centre for Economic Development, Brunel University.

Commonwealth Secretariat (2007). *Small States: Economic Review and Basic Statistics, Volume 11*. London: Commonwealth Secretariat.

Commonwealth Secretariat-World Bank (2000). 'Small States: Meeting Challenges in the Global Economy', Report of the Commonwealth Secretariat/World Bank Joint Task Force on Small States. Washington DC: World Bank. Also available online at http://www.worldbank.org/small states

Conrad, D (2007). 'Developing a Competitive Service Sector', Paper presented at the 8th Business Forum of the Greater Caribbean, Panama City, 7–10 March 2007.

Hoekman, B and Braga, CAP (1997). 'Protection and Trade in Services', World Bank Policy Research Working Paper 1747. Washington DC: World Bank.

International Telecommunication Network (2007). *World Telecommunication/ICT Indicators Database*. Geneva: ITU.

Lejarraga, I and Walkenhorst, P (2006). 'Of Linkages and Leakages: How Tourism Can Foster Economic Diversification', Draft paper. Washington DC: World Bank.

Matthijs, M and Subramanian, U (2007). 'Can Sub-Saharan Africa Leap into Global Network Trade?', Policy research working paper 4112. Washington DC: World Bank.

Mattoo, A and Subramanian, A (2004). 'The WTO and the Poorest Countries: The Stark Reality', IMF Working Paper No. WP/04/81. Washington, DC: International Monetary Fund.

Mitchell, J and te Velde, DW (2008). 'The Role of Regulation in Promoting Tourism and Development'. London, UK: Department for International Development.

ODI-PPT (2004). 'Tourism-Agricultural Linkages: Boosting Inputs from Local Farmers', Case Study Brief 3, http://www.odi.org.uk/tourism/resources/briefings/0501_pptpilots_casestudies_3.pdf

Qureshi, M and te Velde, DW (2008). *Growth Strategies for Small States in a Globalising World: The Role of Knowledge-based and Service Industries*. London: Commonwealth Secretariat.

Roy, D and Subramanian, A (2001). 'Who Can explain the Mauritian Miracle: Meade, Romer, Sachs, or Rodrik?', IMF Working Paper 01/116. Washington DC: International Monetary Fund.

te Velde, DW (2009). 'Temporary Migration of Natural Persons in EU Trade Agreements: Issues, Existing Provisions and Options for EPA Negotiations', in Razzaque, M (2009), *Trade, Migration and Labour Mobility*. Cameron and May, London.

te Velde, DW, (2006) 'Developing Trade in Services: Are the Constraints Economic, Regulatory or External?', in Page, S (ed.), *Trade and Aid: Partners or Rivals in Development Policy*. London: Cameron May.

te Velde, DW (2005). *Special and Differential Treatment in CARIFORUM-EC Services Negotiations – With Reference to Barbados, St Lucia and Suriname*, Report prepared for DFID Caribbean, Barbados.

te Velde, DW and Nair, S (2006). 'Foreign Direct Investment, Services Negotiations and Development. The Case of Tourism in the Caribbean', *Development Policy Review*, July.

te Velde, DW and Calí, M (2010). 'The Global Financial Crisis and Small States Supporting

Investment and Promoting Private Sector Development', Commonwealth Economic Paper, forthcoming.

Torero, M and von Braun, J (eds) (2006). *Information and Communication Technologies for Development and Poverty Reduction: The Potential of Telecommunications*. Baltimore: Johns Hopkins University Press.

UNCTAD (2004). *World Investment Report 2004: The Shift Towards Services Sector*. Geneva: United Nations Conference on Trade and Development

Winters, A and Martins PMG (2005). *Beautiful but Costly: Business Costs in Small Remote Economies*. London: Commonwealth Secretariat.

Yew, Lee Kuan (2000). *From Third World to First*. Time editions, Singapore Press holdings.

World Tourism Organization (2008). www.world-tourism.org

World Tourism and Travel Council (1996). Country Report on Caribbean, Regional and Country Reports. London: WTTC.

3. Exporting Health and Wellness: Prospects and Issues for Small States

Estella Aryada[1]

Introduction

This article examines the prospects and challenges faced by selected countries in the Caribbean region in exporting health and wellness services. It is based on the experience of the Commonwealth Secretariat's Trade Section in providing technical assistance to Commonwealth member states to help them enhance their export competitiveness. The vast majority of work in this area is in the Caribbean region, where technical assistance has been provided to Antigua and Barbuda, Barbados, Dominica, Guyana, Jamaica, St Lucia, and Trinidad and Tobago. The work has focused on identifying sub-sectors with export potential, assessing the demand and supply conditions, and developing frameworks to take advantage of opportunities. In this region, 'health and wellness' has featured highly among the sectors with export potential.

Trade is a vital part of many developing countries' development strategies, especially in small island states. Improving the composition, volume and value of exports, and strengthening the policy and institutional framework that governs export development is at the core of sustained growth. Research on the key determinants of growth has converged on three fundamentals: the ability to integrate with the global economy through trade and investment; capacity to maintain sustainable government finances and sound money; and the ability to put in place an institutional environment in which contracts can be enforced and property rights established (Summers, 2003). In addition, the importance of human capital has been highlighted by the growing recognition of the critical role that professional services play in adding value to both goods and other services. By definition, small states are generally more dependent on international trade: their small domestic markets require them to export more; their limited resource endowments necessitate them to import more. Their options for export diversification are fewer and their costs of production higher (due to the difficulty in achieving economies of scale and high infrastructure costs) (Briguglio, 2007). This dependence on international trade is reflected in the high trade openness of many small states[2] and has proved to be a double edged sword. On the one hand, it has increased their integration into the world economy, but on the other, it has made them more vulnerable to external shocks.

Experience has shown that a key ingredient in building resilience is improving competitiveness so as to quickly adapt to the changing global trade environment. Initially used in firm and industry-level analysis, competitiveness is now widely used to reflect the extent to which a country is able to address a wide array of domestic and exogenous shocks to provide rising prosperity to its citizens.[3] The quest for competitiveness is therefore continuous and the targets keep shifting in keeping with the dynamics of international trade.

Trade openness and the limitations in economies of scale have combined to raise the profile of trade in services such as tourism in many small states. Professional services are particularly suited to small states. This is because professional services are inherently unique to the provider: a spa experience in Antigua will vary with the different establishments; a holiday in St Vincent is distinct from one in St Lucia. Income derived from exporting such a service mainly arises out of the inelasticity of substitution and the preferences of consumers. For services that are more generic, such as call centres, small states are no less disadvantaged, since importers tend to favour key operations spread out in strategic locations around the world. It has also been argued that because of their small, cohesive populations, small states can adapt to change more easily and can realise the benefits of reform more quickly (Qureshi and te Velde, 2008).

A growing number of Commonwealth developing countries are exploring ways to improve their services exports. The main reasons for this are:

- Higher and more stable earnings through exporting a more diversified range of goods and services;
- Higher incomes and more employment opportunities for skilled professionals who are under- or unemployed at home
- The need to inject a new dynamism to counter economic stagnation and to move into higher value services;
- The need to adapt to the changing global trade environment, in particular, to new regional trade agreements (e.g. economic partnership agreements), commitments in the WTO and the expiry of preferential trade regimes.

Scope

The WTO General Agreement on Trade in Services (GATS) classifies health and wellness into two main categories:[4]

1. Business services

A. Professional Services

h. Medical and dental services

j. Services provided by midwives, nurses, physiotherapists and paramedical personnel

2. Health related and social services
(other than those listed under 1.A.h–j)

A. Hospital services

B. Other human health services

C. Social services

In the health profession, there has been a movement towards broadening the understanding of wellbeing. The Ottawa Charter for Health Promotion elaborates the diverse sectors of the economy that must work together to enable people to have greater control over and improve their health. By adopting this wider understanding, policy-makers, community-based organisations and professionals in different fields become important stakeholders in delivering health services. Further, it paves the way for business and export opportunities previously in the purview of public health, including lifestyle enhancement (sports and fitness, nutrition and overcoming substance abuse) and environmental health (detection, awareness and combating the effects of hazardous materials).

A functional understanding of what constitutes health and wellness has therefore developed over the years, to include four distinct but inter-related types of services:

1. ***Medical:*** general treatment and surgery for improved health or cosmetic purposes.
2. ***Wellness:*** therapeutic packages which may not necessarily be curative, but are designed to improve wellbeing through management of stress, weight or ageing.
3. ***Care:*** management of adverse health conditions, including recuperation, palliative care and care of the elderly.
4. ***Research and diagnostic services:*** development and trials for medical and cosmetic preparations

Exports

Health and wellness services can be exported in all the four modes summarised in the GATS. Mode 2 (consumption abroad) is by far the most common, with patients travelling from their home countries to seek health and medical services abroad. Foreign companies have taken advantage of the market opportunity and business-friendly environment to establish health facilities in the Caribbean region under Mode 3 (commercial presence), although on the whole the region tends to be a recipient rather than a source of FDI in this sector. Health professionals in the region are actively recruited to offer their services abroad on a temporary basis (Mode 4). Exports through Mode 1 (cross-border) are usually realised when health care professionals use the internet and postal services to care for patients abroad for consultation, follow-up and treatment.

Demand for health and wellness services is strong and growing, driven by a number of factors, including rising incomes, the ease of international travel, the dispersion of information through the internet and the widespread belief in physical self-improvement. Figures vary, but many analysts estimate that the world market for medical tourism alone will reach US$100 billion in 2010.[5] 750,000 Americans travelled abroad for medical care in 2007 (Deloitte and Touche). The main reasons for seeking health and wellness services abroad are comparable or better quality care at lower cost, shorter waiting periods, ease of access to procedures or treatment that may be subject to controls at home and the availability of advanced technology for treatment and surgery.

Countries in the Caribbean are well positioned to become competitive exporters of health and wellness services. This is due to a combination of two sets of factors. The first set are basic conditions that are necessary for international trade in any service to flourish and include the following:

- ***A stable macro and political environment:*** A stable environment is an important signal for investors and tourists alike.

- ***Availability of good quality infrastructure:*** Well-developed transport networks make it easier and less costly to move resources and connect markets. Access to reliable energy at reasonable cost is the key not only to improving productivity, but also to providing a modern lifestyle. Reliable and extensive telecommunications networks enable a rapid flow of information, which increases response and decision time and overall efficiency.

- ***A robust financial system:*** A robust financial sector and instruments for investment make various products available and facilitates the smooth flow of funds between consumers abroad and service providers at home.

- ***A well-educated, entrepreneurial and internationalised private sector:*** Education improves the efficiency of workers and increases their capacity to adapt to more advanced processes and techniques. A vibrant, internationalised private sector is ready to seize export market opportunities, and is able to interface with foreign partners and have effective dialogue with government.

On their own, none of these factors can deliver competitiveness, but the absence of one can undermine a country's efforts to achieve export-led growth.

The second set of factors are the drivers of competitiveness in the provision of health and wellness services. These are:

- ***Proximity and ease of travel from heavily populated areas:*** Patients travelling to consume health and wellness services aim to minimise the discomfort and time associated with travel. The Caribbean is within easy reach of clients based in the USA and Canada: flying time to Jamaica from Miami and Toronto is less than two and four hours, respectively. Islands like Barbados, Dominica and Jamaica share the same time zone as the east coast of the USA and Canada, minimising the effects of jet lag. Having a common language, being well attuned to the business culture, tastes and preferences of the American consumer, and familiarity with the American health insurance system also works in favour of the Caribbean.

- ***Reputation as a holiday destination:*** The region's strong brand image in tourism acts as a lever for the health and wellness sector. Tour and travel operators can provide information and arrange flights much more quickly than to less well-known destinations. As prospective clients are already aware of the region's tourism products, the decision to travel to the same 'exotic' location for a medical procedure or to combine it with tourism is relatively more easily made.

- ***Availability of world class facilities and skilled personnel:*** A recent McKinsey survey estimates that 40 per cent of all medical travellers do so in search of advanced technologies.[6] Some countries in the Caribbean have made significant investment in training health personnel and equipping medical facilities.

The region has developed areas of specialisation which attract clients from all over the world. For instance, in 2007 a fertility centre in Barbados achieved higher success rates across all age groups than similar facilities in both the USA and UK; an international centre of excellence for the treatment of alcohol and other drug addictions has been set up in Antigua. This demonstrates the region's potential for the development of world class facilities in other fields.

Major challenges

Outflow of health personnel: The permanent departure of skilled professionals is a worldwide phenomenon that cuts across all skill groups. In the healthcare sector, permanent migration of professionals exacerbates the shortages already prevalent in many developing countries, worsening access to and quality of healthcare. Many developing countries subsidise medical training, so a permanent outflow of personnel is a negative return on scarce public resources. Several proposals have been put forward to control the movement of professionals to ensure that migration is temporary, that they are treated fairly and that their home country reaps some benefit.[7] No permanent solution has been found so far.

In developing strategies for the export of health and wellness services, the Secretariat's Trade Section has concentrated on Modes 1 and 2 (cross-border supply and consumption abroad), where professionals need not leave their home country in order to export the service. For this to take place, it is essential that, first, the health sector is deepened so as to provide a wider range of services. Second, alternative funding arrangements must be made to supplement government resources. If managed well, increased private investment in the health and wellness sector can result in several positive outcomes arising out of the introduction of new techniques, equipment and facilities which would not have otherwise been available. A deeper health sector can go a long way towards discouraging professionals from migrating. Improvements in the health sector can also play an important role in reversing migration and encouraging professionals to return to take up new business and professional opportunities.

Achieving equity in healthcare provision: The export orientation of the health sector can have the unintended result of creating a system where foreign clients have access to high quality services that are not readily available to nationals. The result is a tiered system arising out of two major conditions. First, the profit motive of the private sector means that healthcare providers will seek to service clients who can pay. Where resources are directed to caring for foreign clients to the exclusion of local patients, the result may be the alienation of the poor and other marginalised groups in society. Second, private providers tend to offer more attractive conditions of work. The consequence of this could be under-resourced public facilities on which the majority of the population relies.

A range of policy options can be used to address this inequality, including:

- Charging a levy on foreign patients which is then used to subsidise local patients either directly through treatment, or indirectly by building or equipping public facilities.
- Introducing a system for foreign specialists to tutor local professionals in various fields.
- Bonding arrangements where health professionals can join the private sector only after serving in the public sector for a given period of time.
- Requirements for facilities that export their services to reserve a minimum percentage of beds, and person and equipment hours for local clients or disadvantaged groups.

Regulatory capacity: The greatest challenge is managing a globalised, dual healthcare system, often with limited market knowledge, insufficient funds, and inadequate technical and managerial expertise. A wide range of clinical issues need to be addressed, including control of unfamiliar and hospital-acquired infections, assurance of quality and ethical standards and the use of unauthorised or counterfeit drugs. Political questions also come into play: what role should the private sector play in health care? How far should government go in opening the sector to foreign providers and patients? Strategic choices must be made on what niches to develop and which markets to target, and how best to mobilise investment and ensure the availability of the required human resources. A host of managerial issues need to be addressed, including human resource planning, mobilising investment, ensuring value for money and dealing with foreign insurance providers, especially where malpractice claims arise.

The Secretariat's Trade Section promotes the creation of structures for regular dialogue between the different ministries, departments and agencies on the one hand, and private sector providers, experts and associations on the other. Such dialogue can be facilitated by an action plan endorsed by the stakeholders. A platform that brings together multiple stakeholders is essential to facilitate dissemination of the knowledge and expertise that exists, but its success depends on the representatives having the authority to take decisive action on a clear agenda. This has proved to be a valuable tool at the macro level. At corporate level, long-term advantage can be obtained through seeking international accreditation by agencies such as the Joint Commission International (JCI). About 100 health care facilities in 25 countries have so far been accredited, two of which are in the Caribbean.

Health and wellness strategy for St Lucia

In 2007, the Trade Section assisted St Lucia in identifying professional services with potential for export growth. Analysis revealed that St Lucia could increase exports in health and wellness, education; IT-enabled services and production for entertainment services. More significantly, there is room to maximise the synergies between medical and wellness tourism, medical education and medical research. All three subsectors depend on first class clinical facilities, high grade clinical staff and a robust quality assurance system. By strengthening these core services, therefore, the country can realise increased trade opportunities faster and more efficiently.

Conclusion

The Caribbean region has some potential for developing health and wellness into a valuable export sector. By leveraging its strength in tourism, good facilities and availability of expertise in some fields, the region can take advantage of the growing worldwide increase in travel for medical and wellness purposes. The strategic plans that have been formulated with the assistance of the Secretariat's Trade Section are important in articulating a framework

Figure 3.1. St Lucia's strategy for exporting health services

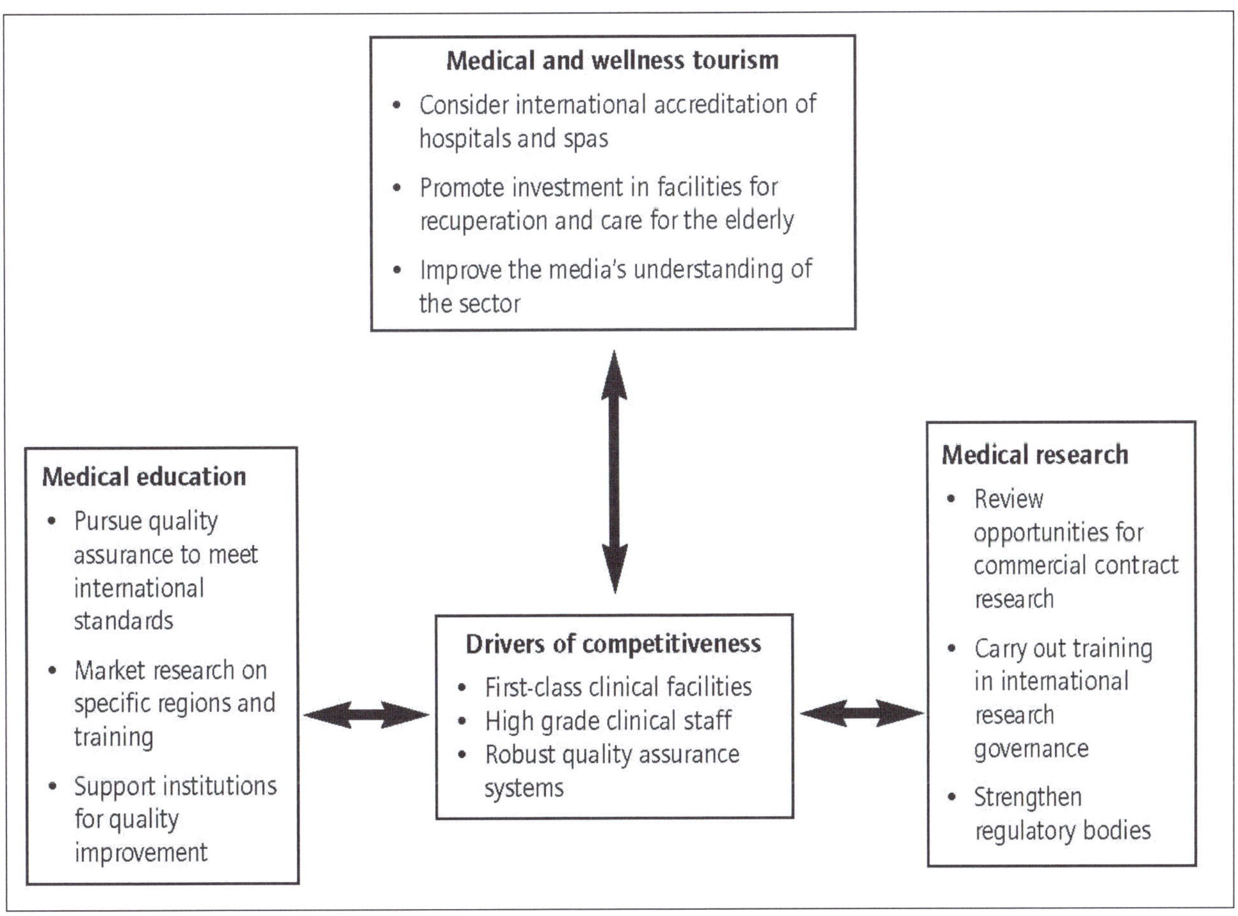

within which the sector can develop. Successful implementation of the strategies and sustaining market opportunity will depend largely on building strong partnerships within government (among the various agencies, departments and ministries); between different service providers in the private sector; and between governments and the private sector.

Notes

1 Adviser (Trade), Special Advisory Services Division, Commonwealth Secretariat.

2 Selected trade to GDP ratios: Antigua and Barbuda (142); Maldives (192); Seychelles (239.3). WTO statistics database (2005–2009).

3 Adapted from 'The Global Competitiveness Index: Prioritizing the Economic Policy Agenda' in *The Global Competitiveness Report*, 2008–2009, World Economic Forum.

4 Extracted from the WTO services sectoral classification list, MTN.GNS/W/120.

5 See 'Medical Tourism Consumers in Search of Value', Deloitte Center for Health Solutions.

6 *Mapping the Market for Medical Travel*, McKinsey Quarterly, 2008.

7 For instance, the Commonwealth Code of Practice for the International Recruitment of Health Workers, www.thecommonwealth.org/Internal/190698/172879/documents/

References

Briguglio, L (2007). 'Economic Vulnerability and Resilience: Concepts and Measurements' in *Commonwealth Small States, Issues and Prospects.*

Deloitte and Touche, 'Medical Tourism: Updates and Implications', available at www.deloitte.com

Ottawa Charter, www.who.int/hpr/NPH/docs/Ottawa_charter

Qureshi, M and te Velde, DW (2008). *Working Smart and Small: The Role of Knowledge-based and Service Industries in Growth Strategies for Small States.* London: Commonwealth Secretariat.

Summers, Lawrence H (2003). Godkin Lectures, John F Kennedy School of Government, Harvard University, April.

4. Pro-poor Tourism Interventions through the Creation of Agro-tourism Linkages

Chanda Chella[1]

Introduction

Tourism is an important sector in most Commonwealth small states, particularly the island states. It is often a major source of government revenue, employment and foreign exchange. In some countries, such as Antigua and Barbuda, Maldives, Seychelles, The Bahamas and Vanuatu, tourism contributes over 50 per cent to GDP. The tourism sector in small states has shown an upward trend, while other sectors have declined. In recent years, the annual growth in tourism in Caribbean and Pacific small states has been between 4 and 5 per cent. Growth in tourism can be expected to stimulate growth in other sectors, as tourism sources goods and services from other sectors. In developed economies most goods and services used in the tourism sector are supplied locally: this is not usually the case in small states, where most products are imported. In addition, services supplied locally tend to be basic and small scale.

While tourism in small states has grown over many years in terms of tourist arrivals, expenditure and investment, there has been minimum impact on other sectors. Government expectations of spin-offs from the growth in tourism have not been fully met. Furthermore, a large part of the earnings from tourism are not retained within the country, as a high proportion goes to pay foreign airlines and the international tour operators that arrange the holiday packages, and foreign investors repatriate their profits. The World Bank estimates that 55 per cent of tourism earnings leak from countries in the South. Other studies have estimates ranging from 75 per cent in the case of Caribbean countries and 60 per cent in the case of Fiji Islands.[2] Others estimate that leakages in the Caribbean amount to over 80 per cent of earnings from tourism, while African least developed countries (LDCs) have up to 85 per cent leakages.[3]

Thus many small states are faced with the challenge of making tourism relevant to the development needs of their own people, particularly in reducing poverty. One of the Commonwealth Secretariat's strategic goals is to support pro-poor policies for economic growth and sustainable development in member countries. One area through which the Secretariat works to realise this goal is by assisting member countries to develop competitive and sustainable tourism.

This article is based on examples of work that the Secretariat has undertaken in agro-tourism linkages in small states. The first example is a study of agro-tourism linkages in 19 Caribbean and Pacific countries. A second example is the development of a national strategy for agro-tourism linkages in Barbados. Lastly, the article presents an analysis of the tourist value chain and prospects for pro-poor tourism in The Gambia. The focus of the article is an examination of how local agricultural products can be supplied to the tourism sector.

Tourism, economic development and poverty reduction

Tourism is an important component of economic development in many countries. Recently, the United Nations and the World Economic Forum both noted that tourism is an important driver of economic growth and prosperity and can play a role in poverty reduction in developing countries.[4] Although the contribution of tourism to increases in GDP is recognised in most countries, economic growth has not necessarily led to poverty reduction. Tourism is often dismissed as a potential vehicle for poverty reduction because it is driven by foreign private sector interests. Such thinking partly explains why some countries have not made use of opportunities to develop tourism in order to address poverty.

The ways in which tourism can contribute to poverty reduction fall into three categories.

Traditional approaches

The traditional approaches through which tourism can contribute to the reduction of poverty are by creating employment and through the taxes that the government collects from the sector.

Taxes on tourism: The revenue which governments earn from tourism can support investment in education, health and infrastructure, all of which impact on people's lives. Some small states have utilised government revenue, most of which comes from tourism, towards such investment through prudent economic management. The result has been improvements in human development, so that some states, for example Antigua and Barbuda, The Bahamas, Barbados and Mauritius, are now ranked as countries with a high level of human development by the Human Development Index.[5] The importance of human capital in economic development is well known and documented. Not all countries manage their economies well and regardless of how much government revenue can be earned from tourism or other sources, in some small states little impact is made on human development.

Employment of poor people: Tourism creates jobs for local people. Jobs provide the income necessary to pay for people's basic needs and can mean that they have enough for personal savings and investment. In addition, jobs provide opportunities for the development of skills. Due to the labour intensity of tourism, it is estimated that one job in the core tourism industry creates one and half additional indirect jobs in tourism-related sectors.[6]

Dynamic effect

In order to develop a destination, increase its attractiveness, facilitate better movement of tourists and improve service provision, investment in infrastructure is required. A spin-off from investing in infrastructure aimed at boosting tourism is that poor people in the locality can also benefit from it and that it can enhance their income-earning activities. Other sectors that employ poor people can also benefit from use of the infrastructure.

Direct interventions

To maximise benefits to the poor, the traditional approaches need to be augmented by more direct interventions. The widely recognised approaches that constitute direct interventions have been well publicised by the United Nations World Tourism Organization (UNWTO) through the Sustainable Tourism-Eliminating Poverty (ST-EP) programme.[7]

One direct intervention is *voluntary giving or support from tourism enterprises and tourists*. This approach creates a culture of dependency. Voluntary giving and support should aim at building local capacity to manage and support activities that empower poor people and link them to markets.

Other direct interventions include:

- Direct sales of goods and services to visitors by poor people;
- Establishment and running of tourism enterprises by poor people;
- Supply of goods and services to tourism enterprises by the poor or by enterprises employing poor people.

In small states, these three approaches are largely undertaken by small, micro and medium enterprises (SMMEs). The approaches all require some level of business management skills in order to succeed. This is in addition to the need for a prevailing business enabling environment. On the supply side, there are requirements of quality, quantity, timeliness, and health and safety that have to be met consistently. Meeting these requirements is challenging.

Agri-tourism linkages: Supply of agricultural products to the tourism sector has been identified as one way through which the local economy and people can benefit from tourism. The following sections highlight some of the work that the Commonwealth Secretariat has undertaken in this area.

Commonwealth Secretariat initiatives

Agro-tourism linkages in the small states of the Caribbean and Pacific

In 2007, the Secretariat commissioned a study on agro-tourism linkages in Commonwealth small states of the Caribbean and Pacific that targeted 19 states.[8] The purpose of the study was to investigate the potential for increased linkages between agriculture and tourism.

Its findings showed that agricultural production has been in decline for many years due to erosion in preferential trading arrangements and loss of competitiveness. Meanwhile the tourism sector has been growing by an annual rate of 4 to 5 per cent in the Caribbean and Pacific regions. Traditionally, the many small states in the two regions, especially in the Caribbean, have mainly produced sugar and bananas for export. If the agriculture sector is looking at supplying the tourism market, diversification into agri-food is necessary. While sustaining the agriculture sector, agri-tourism linkages will also allow for greater retention of tourist earnings.

The study estimated that around US$680 million per annum is spent by tourists on food and drink in the 19 states, of which goods worth US$610 million are imported. Only about 10 per cent is supplied locally. There is scope to increase this and small states should take advantage of the current debate on global environmental issues and promote the purchase of local food, in addition to maximising the number of informed travellers who are concerned about issues of food miles and social responsibility.

Agricultural suppliers have yet to win the confidence of the tourism industry in their ability to meet high standards of food health and safety, high expectations of product quality and reliability of supply. While there is scope for increasing local supplies, not all imports can be replaced due to limited production capacity for some products. Existing food processing plants in some states can take advantage of regional free trade and replace the high volumes of imported processed foods, such as sauces, fruit juices and breakfast cereals.

The main supply chain bottlenecks identified by the the study are:

- The quality of local products is usually not of the standard required by hotels;
- The quantity and reliability are not good enough;
- Local producers are not aware of the requirements of the hotel industry;
- There is limited access to credit to upgrade production facilities and capacity;
- Agriculture skills and human resources are limited;
- Local producers have inadequate working capital and cannot wait 30 to 90 days for payment, as expected by most hotels;
- There is usually no formal market or any forum that puts farmers in touch with hotels so it does not feel like a formal supply chain as it might do in the retail sector. This makes it difficult to promote products, negotiate contracts and co-ordinate delivery;
- The seasonality of local produce does not necessarily coincide with tourist peak seasons and some parts of the tourism industry prefer products with an all year round supply;
- In some states there needs to be changes in government policy to allow agriculture to supply the tourism sector effectively.

In addition, there seems to be a lack of leadership and political will to change the status quo. There is also a culture of 'imported is better' that needs to be changed.

Barbados

In 2007, the Secretariat provided technical assistance to Barbados to develop a national strategy for the promotion of linkages between the agriculture and tourism sectors.

Tourism: Tourism contributes about 15 per cent to Barbados's GDP and employs 12,000 people (approximately 8 per cent of the total labour force). The island is the third leading destination among Caribbean Commonwealth small states after The Bahamas and Jamaica, as shown in Figure 4.1.

Figure 4.1. Tourist arrivals in Barbados and other Caribbean small states

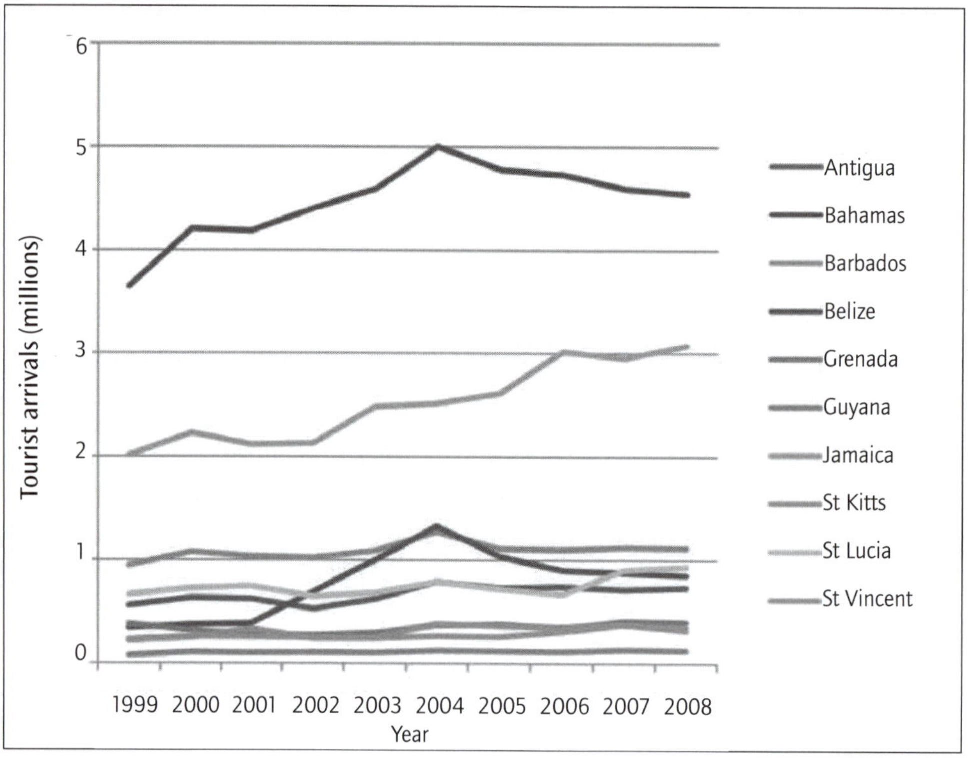

Source: World Travel and Tourism Council, 2009

Agriculture: Historically, agriculture played an important economic role, with the production and export of sugar. The food crop and livestock sub-sectors are important to the country and are critical for agri-tourism linkages. The agriculture sector employs 4,500 people (approximately 3 per cent of the total labour force).

Poverty: About 14 per cent of the population of Barbados are classified as poor, according to UN statistics. Poverty levels are among the lowest in the Caribbean. Barbados is ranked 37 out of the 179 countries listed in the Human Development Index and is classified as having high human development. It is the highest ranked small island country.

One of the challenges faced by Barbados is how to diversify its agriculture. Sugar production has declined, partly due to loss in competitiveness caused by rising production costs and falling world prices and partly due to the erosion of export preferences. Success in crop and market diversification depends on securing a market in the tourism sector.

Strategic issues

The national strategy outlines strategic approaches in four main areas: institutions; productive capacity; marketing and trade facilitation; and education and outreach. The strategy is based on the findings of a diagnostic study of the tourism and agriculture sectors carried out with the aim of finding ways to strengthen supply linkages between the two sectors. Some of the findings are briefly discussed in relation to each strategic approach.

Policies and institutions

A number of policies and plans have stated the need for stronger linkages between agriculture and tourism, starting with the overarching 2006–2025 National Strategic Plan. In agriculture and tourism each sector had its own set of policies which pointed to the need for stronger linkages (national sustainable tourism policy, destination marketing strategy and Ministry of Agriculture medium-term plan). However, there was no policy wholly dedicated to agri-tourism linkages.

To address this gap, the national strategy includes recommendations for actions aimed at rationalising existing policies and institutional roles and responsibilities. It also outlines a more specific agro-tourism policy.

Productive capacity

The agriculture sector has not maximised market opportunities in the tourism sector due to limited production capacity. Demand by the tourism sector for agriculture products is mostly met by imports. Production capacity has been affected by increased competition for limited land resources, natural factors such as weather (hurricanes, floods and droughts) and rising input costs. Agriculture is dominated by traditional methods and subsistence farming. Although there has been some modernisation of production methods through greenhouses and hydroponics technologies, this is not widespread. Support infrastructure such as packhouses and storage facilities is limited and inappropriate. The quality of products, particularly fruit, needs improving.

In order to increase productivity, the strategy recommends the setting up of a support organisation that will facilitate the acquisition and use of appropriate technology, particularly among subsistence farmers. Enhanced investment incentives in agriculture would lead to improved production. The strategy recommends clustering in order to address production constraints at both the input and output levels.

Market access and facilitation

Access to the tourism market by local farmers was highly competitive due to the ease of importation that resulted from trade liberalisation. This was compounded by individual farmers marketing their own products. The Barbados Agriculture Society sometimes marketed on behalf of its members. However, there were no governing contractual arrangements.

The strategy emphasises the need to create a buyer-seller network (BSN). The BSN would play a co-ordinating role in facilitating trading between the agriculture and tourism sectors. The strategy defines the players, key elements and supporting elements required to make it a successful operation. The players identified are from the public sector, the private sector, and regional and international agencies, pointing to the importance of partnerships in building linkages. Key elements of the BSN are the factors at the core of linkages, namely supply management, trading/brokering, a farmer certification scheme to ensure product standards are upheld and information networking. Elements required to support linkages identified in the strategy are the creation of a policy and institutional framework, finance and credit, and awareness building.

Education and awareness

Chefs in the tourism industry rarely make use of local products because they do not know what is available locally. In big hotels and chain restaurants this is attributed to lack of awareness on the part of those responsible for purchasing. On the agriculture side, farmers do not have full knowledge of the requirements of the tourism industry.

The strategy identifies actions required to increase awareness and education on issues related to practices, and behavioural changes required for sustainable linkages. Training is identified as a key means of achieving this and the setting up of a framework for ongoing training is recommended.

The Gambia

In 2008, the Secretariat commissioned the Overseas Development Institute (ODI) to undertake a study of the Gambian tourist value chain and identify prospects for pro-poor tourism.

Tourism: The Gambia is a small state in West Africa. It has a sea coast and is a winter sun destination, mainly for the European market. Most visitors are holidaymakers and there is a very small number of business travellers. The main means of access for tourists is by air and the country is mainly serviced by charter flights. In international terms, and relative to other African Commonwealth small states, The Gambia's tourism sector is small (Figure 4.2). However, it is a leading sector for the country and contributes about 16 per cent of GDP and over 30 per cent of export earnings (US$39 million in 2007). Directly and indirectly, it provides 10,000 jobs. Package holidays, which include flights, transfers, and bed and breakfast accommodation, are a major feature, making up 85 per cent of tourist arrivals.

Figure 4.2. Tourist arrivals in The Gambia and other African small states

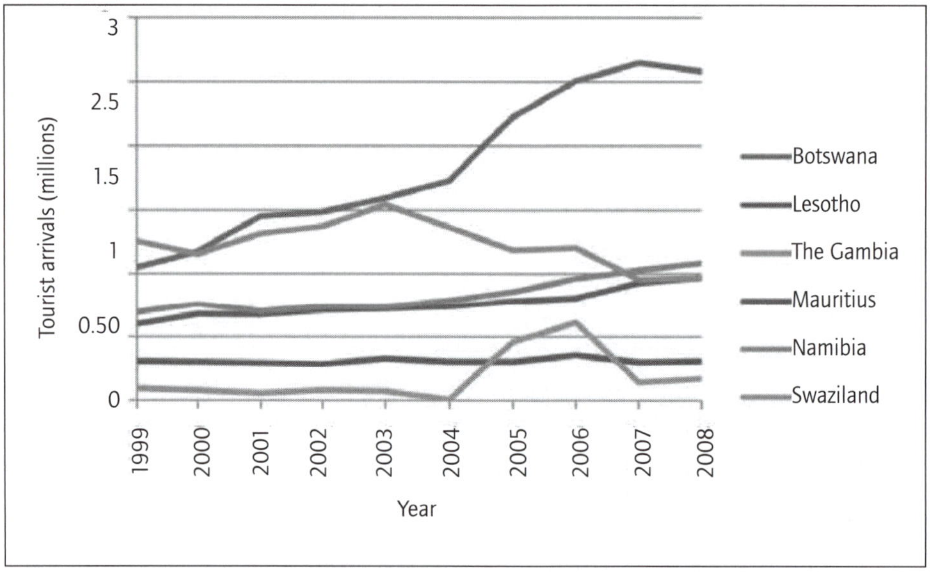

Source: World Travel and Tourism Council, 2009

Agriculture: Agriculture is the second biggest economic sector. It contributes 33 per cent to GDP and employs 75 per cent of the labour force. The sector is dominated by subsistence farming and productivity is low. The need to transform agricultural production remains a challenge. However, due to the supply linkages that have been created with the tourism sector, new and non-traditional crops have been introduced and this has contributed to growth in horticulture production.

Poverty: The Gambia is faced with high poverty levels: according to UN figures, about 61 per cent of the population lives in poverty. There is both urban and rural poverty, but it is more prevalent in the rural areas, where 68 per cent of the country's population live.

The Gambia will have to rely heavily on tourism and agriculture to address poverty. As pointed out above, 75 per cent of the workforce relies on agriculture. Securing lucrative markets for these people will impact positively on their livelihoods. The tourism sector is a huge potential market for fresh produce. It also offers opportunities for value addition through agro-processing.

The ODI study showed that in 2006 hotels bought 45 to 50 per cent of food and beverages locally. This was a marginal increase from estimates for 1986, which showed that 60 per cent was imported, implying that 40 per cent was locally purchased.

A major and well-known initiative that has helped poor small farmers access the tourism market has been through a company called Gambia is Good (GiG), formed in 2004. GiG is a fresh produce marketing company that also provides research and extension services for small farmers. It has set up a demonstration farm where farmers are trained. GiG acts as an intermediary between hotels and small farmers and provides transportation for produce from farmers and cold storage facilities. Transportation and communication are still a challenge because farmers are widely dispersed over the country, while GiG has its main premises in the capital city. Use of ICT to link farmers with GiG has not been fully exploited.

By 2008, between 800 and 1,000 rural farmers were trading through GiG, 90 per cent of whom were estimated to be women.[9] Some households claim that GiG has made a positive impact on their livelihoods through income generated from the sale of agriculture products to the tourism industry. This was heard in testimonials given by female farmers,[10] as well as estimates made in the study. The income of participating households was estimated to have increased fivefold from £81 to £458 per year. Benefits certainly extend beyond the participating households through multiplier effects.

Lessons

The study on agro-tourism linkages in the small states of the Caribbean and Pacific identifies the challenges to developing stronger linkages between tourism and agriculture. Although it is a general study, the issues identified apply to most Commonwealth small states, including Barbados and The Gambia, which are discussed in this paper. The study provides a good basis on which individual countries in the Caribbean and Pacific can initiate activities to improve the supply of local agricultural products to the tourism sector. The discussion in the paper is limited to the work conducted in Barbados to design a national strategy for the government. It does not include results achieved from implementing the recommended strategies. The following lessons can be drawn from The Gambia's experience.

Government policy: There is a need for governments to set out policies and strategies that promote linkages between tourism and agriculture. The objective of promoting linkages should not be an end in itself, but should be embedded in a country's overall development strategy. This ensures that requirements for multi-purpose infrastructure such as roads and bridges are addressed for the benefit of all sectors. Complementary policies from different sectors are required. In The Gambia, the government has indicated in its Poverty Reduction Strategy (PRS), actions to improve productivity in tourism and agriculture and subsequently boost linkages between the two sectors as a means of reducing poverty.

Intermediary organisation: There is a need to have in place an intermediary organisation to co-ordinate activities on the supply and demand sides. On the supply side, issues of quality and quantity should be addressed through research, training, extension services, and technology innovation and acquisition. On the demand side, individual small farmers can be overwhelmed and challenged by having to approach large hotels and restaurants. There is a need for an organisation with an understanding of the demands of the hotels and the business environment in which they operate, that can play a market facilitation role. The intermediary organisation's understanding of the demand side should be applied in formulating actions to improve supply, while its understanding of the supply side should enable it to structure and secure payment terms that are favourable to farmers. In The Gambia, GiG plays the role of intermediary.

Need to create awareness: This extends beyond agri-tourism. Other mechanisms aimed at linking the poor to the tourism market should ensure that systems are in place to inform the tourism industry about products that are available locally. Big hotels and chains tend to adhere to in-house practices of using imported international food brands. The task of creating awareness rests on local organisations, including relevant government ministries and producer associations. Although there is no evidence of this happening in The Gambia, the government could provide some non-financial incentives to hotels to encourage them to buy locally, particularly in the early stages of developing linkages.

Seasonality: Both tourism and agriculture are seasonal sectors. In The Gambia, horticultural demand is highest during the tourist high season, resulting in overproduction and oversupply. This pushes down prices and may not benefit poor farmers. Outside the tourist high season, most horticulture farmers shut down production, despite the fact that the tropical climate is suited to all year cultivation of horticultural products. In some small states, the tourist high season coincides with the low production season in the agriculture sector. To avoid the loss of income suffered by small farmers due to seasonality, other markets, including export markets, should be explored. Acquisition of technology for agro-processing would utilise the excess supply during the high season.

Notes

1 Adviser (Trade), Special Advisory Services Division, Commonwealth Secretariat.
2 Helen McBain, *Caribbean Tourism and Agriculture: Linking to Enhance Development and Competitiveness*, March 2007.
3 Pleumarom A, *Does Tourism Benefit the Third World?*, Third World Network.
4 World Economic Forum, *The Travel and Tourism Competitiveness Index 2009: Measuring Sectoral Drivers in a Downturn.*
5 HDI compiled by the UNDP measures a country's achievement in three basic areas of human development: standard of living (GNP per capita); life expectancy at birth; and adult literacy and school enrolment.
6 International Labour Organization (ILO), *Reducing Poverty through Tourism*, October 2008.
7 World Tourism Organization, *Tourism and Poverty Alleviation, Recommendations for Action*, March 2004.
8 Antigua and Barbuda, The Bahamas, Barbados, Belize, Dominica, Grenada, Jamaica, St Kitts and Nevis, St Lucia, St Vincent and the Grenadines, Trinidad and Tobago, Fiji Islands, Papua New Guinea Samoa, Solomon Islands, Tonga, Tuvalu and Vanuatu
9 Report of a Commonwealth Secretariat Tourism Technical Assistance Mission to The Gambia, October 2008.
10 Ibid.

References

Commonwealth Secretariat (March 2007). *Agro-Tourism Linkages in Small Commonwealth States of the Caribbean and Pacific.*

Commonwealth Secretariat (October 2008). *Report of a Tourism Technical Assistance Mission to The Gambia.*

International Labour Organization (October 2008). Reducing Poverty through Tourism.

McBain, H (March 2007). *Caribbean Tourism and Agriculture: Linking to Enhance Development and Competitiveness.*

Overseas Development Institute (March 2008). 'The Gambian Tourist Value Chain and Prospects for Pro-Poor Tourism', Working paper 289.

Pleumarom, A (2007/2008). *Does Tourism Benefit the Third World?* Third World Network.

UNDP (2007/2008). *Human Development Report.* New York: United Nations Development Programme.

World Economic Forum (2009). *The Travel and Tourism Competitiveness Report: Managing in a Time of Turbulence.* Geneva: World Economic Forum.

World Tourism Organization (March 2004). *Tourism and Poverty Alleviation, Recommendations for Action.* Madrid, World Tourist Organization.

World Travel and Tourism Council, http://www.wttc.org/eng/Tourism_Research/Tourism_Impact_Data_and_Forecast_Tool/index.php

PART II

Social and Economic Data on Small States

Basic Statistics

The set of statistical tables in this volume covers all small states (with populations of 1.5 million or less), as well as other countries with populations of up to 5 million. The 54 tables that follow set out basic data on country size, together with the latest information on selected economic, social development and environmental indicators, and characteristics of the major sectors of small economies. It is hoped that the statistical data presented will form a useful supplement to those available from other sources on larger countries. In order to indicate the scope of the data presented in the tables and to outline the concepts and methodology used in their computation, a series of technical notes are presented. The sources cited at the foot of the tables provide more comprehensive explanations of the concepts used. Apart from international sources, a large number of national sources have been used in the compilation wherever definitions are comparable.

Technical notes for tables

The criterion used in selecting the 60 countries covered in the tables is that their 2007 populations were under 5 million. Although more than 60 countries fall within this classification, some were excluded from the tabulation because of the absence of reliable statistical data.

The countries are grouped into three categories on the basis of their 2007 per capita GNI or by dominant characteristic. The three categories are: (a) low-income countries with per capita income of US$935 or less; (b) middle-income countries with per capita income of between US$935 and $11,456; (c) high-income countries with per capita income of US$11,456 or more.

Although the data are drawn from authoritative and reliable sources, they may not always be comparable because of the lack of standardised definitions used by different countries in collecting primary data. For comparative purposes, they should therefore be used with caution.

Economic indicators

Table 1. Gross national income at market prices

Gross national income is the market value of goods and services produced within a country and abroad in a given year. Total GNI at market prices was calculated using the World Bank Atlas method. GNI per capita is the quotient of GNI/mid-year population. All growth rates have been computed using the least squares method.

Table 2. Gross domestic product at current market prices

Table 3. Sectoral distribution of gross domestic product

Table 4. Growth of production

GDP measures the total final output of goods and services produced in the country by residents and non-residents, regardless of its allocation between local and foreign claimants.

The agricultural sector covers agriculture, forestry, hunting and fishing. The industrial sector comprises mining, manufacturing, construction, electricity, gas and water. All other economic activities are classified as services.

Growth of production in agriculture, industry, manufacturing and services is mainly derived from the sum of gross output minus the value of intermediate input used in production in each respective field.

Table 5. Structure of demand

Public consumption (or government consumption) includes all current expenditure for purchase of goods and services by all levels of government. Capital expenditure on national defence and security is regarded as consumption expenditure. Private consumption is the market value of all goods and services purchased or received as income in kind by households and non-profit institutions. It includes imputed rent for owner-occupied dwellings.

Gross domestic investment consists of the outlays for additions to the fixed assets of the economy, plus changes in the net value of inventories. Gross domestic savings shows the amount of gross domestic investment financed from domestic output; comprising public and private savings, it is gross domestic investment plus the net exports of goods and non-factor services.

Table 6. Percentage changes in the Consumer Price Index

The percentage change in the Consumer Price Index (CPI) has frequently been used to indicate the rate of inflation, which reflects the changes in the cost of a specified bundle of goods and services purchased by the average person.

Table 7. Merchandise exports and growth
Table 8. Merchandise imports and growth

Merchandise exports are the market value (fob) of movable goods, including non-monetary gold whose ownership changes from a resident to a foreigner. Merchandise imports are the market value (cif) of movable goods, including non-monetary gold whose ownership changes from a foreigner to a resident. The growth rates of merchandise exports and imports are in nominal terms.

Table 9. Trade balance

Trade balance is the difference between exports (fob) and imports (fob).

Table 10. Destination of merchandise exports
Table 11. Destination of merchant exports to selected regions

The destination of merchandise exports is the markets to which the goods of a country are exported.

Table 12. Source of merchandise imports
Table 13. Merchandise imports by selected regions

The source of merchandise imports is the countries from which goods are imported.

Table 14. Merchandise trade with Commonwealth countries

This table attempts to indicate the significance of the Commonwealth (53 countries) as a market for the external trade of small states.

Table 15. Export characteristics
Table 16. Selected indicators of openness and instability

Both concentration and diversification indices range between 0 and 1, with 1 representing the most extreme concentration. Export instability indices provide an indication of the relative magnitude of fluctuations in total merchandise export values and have been calculated in the same way as coefficients of variation. The indices range between 0 and 100, with 100 representing the most extreme volatility.

Table 17. Fish catches

The data relate to nominal catches of freshwater, brackish water and marine species of fish, crustaceans, molluscs and other aquatic animals and plants killed, caught, trapped, collected, bred or cultivated for all commercial, industrial, recreational and subsistence purposes. The concept 'nominal catches' refers to the landings, and in most cases, the quantity caught, converted to a live weight basis.

Table 18. Energy production, consumption and trade

Data on energy refer to commercial forms of primary energy: coal and lignite, crude petroleum, natural gas and natural gas liquids, and hydro and nuclear electricity, converted to the coal equivalent. Botswana, Lesotho and Swaziland have no separate data as they are incorporated in SACU.

Table 19. Tourist arrivals and earnings

Unless otherwise stated, the number of tourist arrivals refers to persons staying at least 24 hours or making at least one overnight stay. Tourist earnings are defined as a country's receipts from the payment of goods and services made by foreign tourists. Total export earnings are defined as the total value of goods and services, including tourism.

Table 20. International reserves

International reserves consist of a country's holdings of special drawing rights and foreign exchange, as well as its reserve position in the IMF. These data are also presented as months of imports which the reserves could finance at current import levels.

Table 21. External debt: selected categories

External debt refers to debt owed to non-residents, repayable in convertible currency, goods or services, which has an original or extended maturity of over one year. Debt outstanding (disbursed only) is total outstanding debt drawn by the borrower at the end of the year. Short-term debt is debt with an original maturity of less than one year. Concessional debt must contain a grant element of at least 25 per cent.

Table 22. Official net transfers

Official net transfers are net flows minus interest payments or disbursements minus total debt service payments.

Table 23. Principal indicators of debt
Table 24. Composition of debt

Exports of goods and services (XGS) are the total value of all goods and services (including workers' remittances) sold to the rest of the world.

Official debt comprises loans from international organisations (multilateral loans), governments (bilateral loans) and their agencies, and autonomous public bodies.

Commercial debt comprises loans from suppliers (manufacturers, exporters or other suppliers of goods), financial markets (private banks, other private financial institutions and publicly issued and privately placed bonds) and others (external liabilities on account of nationalised properties and unclassified debts).

Table 25. Foreign direct investment

Foreign direct investment is defined as a long-term investment by a foreign investor in an enterprise resident in an economy other than that in which the foreign direct investor is based. This table represents inward FDI flows.

Table 26. Total net financial flows from all sources
Table 27. Net financial flows by major categories
Table 28. ODA commitments, disbursements, per capita resource flows and IMF credit

All reported flows are in net terms. This refers to gross disbursements of grants and loans minus repayments of previous loans. Official development assistance is defined as those concessional flows to developing countries and multilateral institutions provided by official agencies, including state and local governments, or by their executive agencies. It must contain a grant element of at least 25 per cent. Bilateral flows are provided directly by a donor country to a developing country.

Use of IMF credit indicates any transactions in the Fund's general account that take place outside its gold tranche.

Table 29. Average exchange rates

Data refer to end of period of market exchange rates and official exchange rates for countries quoting rates in units of national currency per US dollar.

Table 30. Money supply and average national interest rates

Money supply equals the sum of currency outside banks and demand deposits other than those of the central government. In most cases the IMF's category *money* is used, but where this is not available other definitions such as *M1* and *M2* are used. The interest rates refer to the rate at which the monetary authorities lend for the short- and medium-term financing needs of the private sector. These rates are normally differentiated according to the creditworthiness of borrowers and financing objectives.

Social and demographic indicators

Table 31. Selected size indicators
Table 32. Population indicators

Surface area estimates include inland waters. Population values shown are mid-year estimates for 2007. GNI provides an estimate of total domestic and foreign output claimed by the residents of a country. The surface area used consists of both land and water bodies. Arable and permanently cropped land data was obtained from the Food and Agriculture Organisation (FAO) and includes FAO estimates, manual estimates and official data reported in FAO country questionnaires. Population density is defined as the number of individuals per given unit of land (usually per square kilometre) and is derived by dividing the total population by the surface area. Population estimates are based on national population censuses, which vary in frequency and quality.

Table 33. Distribution of labour force

Agricultural labour force refers to those engaged in farming, forestry, hunting and fishing as a percentage of the total labour force.

Table 34. Urban and rural population

Urban population refers to the percentage of the mid-year population classified as living in urban areas. These are usually defined as populated centres with certain characteristics, such as certain public and municipal services. They typically refer to centres of 2,000 people or more.

Table 35. Population distribution by age

Population data have been classified into four age groups: 0–4 for infants; 5–14 for youth; 15–59 for adults; and 60+ for elders. The projections are based on assumptions of the medium variant.

Table 36. Selected demographic indicators
Crude birth rate refers to annual live births per thousand of the mid-year population. Crude death rate refers to annual deaths per thousand of the mid-year population. Infant mortality rate gives annual deaths of infants under one year of age per 1000 live births.

Table 37. Life expectancy at birth
Life expectancy refers to the average number of years of life remaining at birth.

Table 38. Adult literacy rates
Adult literacy rate refers to literate adults, able to read and write, as a percentage of the total adult population aged 15 years and over.

Table 39. Primary education gross enrolment ratio
Table 40. Secondary education enrolment ratio
Table 41. Tertiary education gross enrolment ratio
Gross primary school enrolment refers to enrolment of all ages at the primary level as percentages of respective primary school age population. It includes children aged 6–11 years. For countries with universal education, enrolment may exceed 100 per cent, since some pupils are outside the above age limits. Secondary education requires at least four years of approved primary education and provides general vocational or teacher training instructions for pupils usually between 12 and 17 years of age. For the tertiary level, the population used is the five-year age group following on from the secondary school leaving age.

Table 42. Selected characteristics of female population
The female population is expressed as a percentage share of the total population. Women in total labour force is expressed as the number of females in the labour force as a percentage share of the total labour force. The total fertility rate represents the number of children who would be born per woman if the woman were to live to the end of her child-bearing years and bear children at each age in accordance with the prevailing age-specific fertility rates.

Table 43. Main components of government expenditure
Total government expenditure covers all agencies performing central government functions. It excludes government-owned and/or controlled agencies which sell goods and services to the public as well as government financial institutions. The table indicates the proportions of government expenditure with regard to the defence and social sectors.

Other development indicators

Table 44. Access to improved water sources
Access to an improved water source refers to the percentage of the population with reasonable access to an adequate amount of water from an improved source, such as a household connection, public standpipe, borehole, protected well or spring, or rainwater collection. Reasonable access is defined as the availability of at least 20 litres a person a day from a source within 1 kilometre of the dwelling.

Table 45. Access to improved sanitation
Access to improved sanitation facilities refers to the percentage of the population with at least adequate access to excreta disposal facilities that can effectively prevent human, animal and insect contact with excreta. Improved facilities range from simple but protected pit latrines to flush toilets with a sewerage connection.

Table 46. Human Development Index
The Human Development Index (HDI) is a composite index that measures the average achievement in a country in three basic dimensions of human development: a long and healthy life measured by life expectancy at birth; knowledge, measured by adult literacy rates and enrolment in primary, secondary and tertiary levels; and standard of living, measured by GDP per capita in PPP (purchasing power parity).

Table 47. Gender-related Development Index
While the HDI measures average achievement, the Gender-related Development Index (GDI) adjusts the average achievement to reflect the inequalities between men and women.

Table 48. Human Poverty Index
The Human Poverty Index (HPI-1) measures depriva-

tion in the three basic dimensions of human development captured in the HDI. These are vulnerability to death at an early age, as measured by the probability at birth of not surviving until age 40; knowledge – exclusion from the world of reading and communications as measured by the adult illiteracy rate; lack of access to economic provisioning as measured by the unweighted average of two indicators, the percentage of the population without sustainable access to an improved water source and the percentage of children underweight for their age.

Table 49. Births delivered by skilled health personnel and maternal mortality

Percentage of births attended by skilled health personnel – this includes births attended by appropriately trained doctors, nurses, midwives or auxiliary nurses. The year of the most recent survey is given alongside the percentage.

The maternal mortality ratio is the annual number of deaths of women from pregnancy-related causes per 100,000 live births. This 'reported' column shows country reported figures that are not adjusted for under-reporting or misclassification.

Table 50. Prevalence of underweight children

Prevalence of underweight children under five years old is the proportion of those falling below minus two standard deviations (moderate underweight) and minus three deviations (severe underweight) from the median weight for age of the reference population.

Table 51. Under fives mortality rate

Under fives mortality rate is the probability (expressed as a rate per 1000 live births) of a child born in a specified year dying before reaching the age of five if subject to current age specific mortality rates.

Table 52. Summary statistics of HIV/AIDS, malaria and tuberculosis

The estimated number of people living with HIV in 2005 and 2003. These estimates include all people with HIV infection, whether or not they have developed symptoms of AIDS, in 2005 and 2003. For some countries where sufficient data from the last six years were not available, no estimates have been made. Estimated prevalence refers to the percentage of the adult population carrying the virus. Death rates refers to the estimate of the total number of people who have died from AIDS or a related illness during the last year.

Deaths of children under five from malaria is a percentage of all deaths caused by malaria out of the total number of deaths for this age group.

Estimated deaths from tuberculosis is an estimate of the total number of deaths related to tuberculosis within a given country

Table 53. Environment

Carbon dioxide emissions are emissions from the burning of fossil fuels and the manufacture of cement. They account for the largest share of greenhouse gases, which are associated with global warming.

Forest change rate relates to the number of hectares of forest lost or gained and the percentage change.

The UN-HABITAT definition of a slum is a settlement in an urban area in which more than half the inhabitants live in inadequate houses and lack one or more of the following five conditions: durable housing; sufficient living area; access to improved water; access to sanitation; or secure tenure.

Table 54. Main indicators of communications

Internet users is based on nationally reported data. In some cases, surveys have been carried out that give a more precise figure for the number of internet users. The reported figure for internet users – which may refer only to users above a certain age – is divided by the total population to obtain *users per 1000 inhabitants*.

Mobile cellular telephone subscribers refers to users of portable telephones subscribing to an automatic public mobile telephone service using cellular technology that provides access to the public switched telephone network (PSTN). *Per 100 inhabitants* is obtained by dividing the number of cellular subscribers by the population and multiplying by 100

Table 1. Gross national income at market prices

Group/country	Total GNI at market prices 2004	2005	2006	2007	GNI growth rate 2000–2007	GNI per capita 2004	2005	2006	2007	GNI per capita real growth rates 1990–2000
	(US$ million)				(per cent/ year)	(US$)				(per cent)
Low-income										
Commonwealth countries										
Gambia, The	403	442	488	541	2.6	270	290	290	320	-0.3
Papua New Guinea	3,262	3,262	4,603	5,401	20.9	560	500	740	850	2.1
Solomon Islands	274	297	454	374	6.6	590	620	690	750	0.3
Other countries										
Central African Republic	1,218	1,400	1,566	1,608	5.7	310	350	350	370	-0.5
Comoros	326	389	411	425	9.1	550	650	660	680	-2.4
Guinea-Bissau	241	282	303	331	5.4	160	180	190	200	-1.1
Lao PDR	2,239	2,567	2,879	3,707	11.8	400	450	500	630	3.9
Mauritania	1,532	1,795	2,325	2,636	13.2	510	580	760	840	1.2
São Tomé & Principe	61	68	123	138	15.7	400	480	800	870	-0.8
Middle-income										
Commonwealth countries										
Belize	994	1,042	1,114	1,144	5.0	3,520	3,570	3,740	3,760	0.5
Botswana	7,755	9,864	10,358	11,515	9.1	4,380	5,590	5,570	6,120	0.9
Dominica	261	271	292	301	3.0	4,110	4,160	4,200	4,471	1.1
Fiji Islands	2,373	2,684	3,098	3,125	9.8	2,820	3,170	3,720	3,750	0.5
Grenada	408	496	507	414	1.4	3,810	4,660	4,680	3,920	1.8
Guyana	695	770	849	926	4.4	930	1,020	1,150	1,386	5.0
Jamaica	8,739	8,999	9,504	8,904	2.0	3,310	3,390	3,560	3,330	0.7
Kiribati	119	115	124	107	1.8	970	1,210	1,240	1,120	2.0
Lesotho	1,323	1,407	1,957	2,069	15.5	720	930	980	1,030	2.1
Maldives	768	762	903	974	6.6	2,390	2,320	3,010	3,190	4.1
Mauritius	5,759	6,526	6,812	7,029	5.9	4,670	5,250	5,430	5,580	3.8
Namibia	4,787	6,074	6,573	7,174	9.2	2,380	2,990	3,210	3,450	0.8
St Kitts & Nevis	369	401	434	488	6.9	7,840	8,350	8,960	9,990	4.9
St Lucia	744	820	888	928	4.7	4,580	4,970	5,350	5,520	1.3
St Vincent & the Grenadines	409	421	457	507	6.1	3,460	3,550	3,820	4,210	2.4
Samoa	329	373	421	489	9.0	1,790	2,020	2,270	2,700	1.1
Seychelles	675	691	751	762	3.6	8,080	8,180	8,870	8,960	1.4
Swaziland	1,900	2,579	2,737	2,934	34.3	1,700	2,080	2,400	2,560	-0.1
Tonga	178	207	225	254	19.6	1,750	1,970	2,250	2,480	1.2
Vanuatu	289	331	373	417	7.3	1,400	1,560	1,690	1,840	-2.9
Other countries										
Albania	7,487	8,345	9,257	10,979	10.0	2,389	2,646	2,918	3,442	–
Armenia	3,435	4,740	6,178	8,878	26.8	1,135	1,571	2,053	2,957	–
Bahrain	10,288	14,022	15,442	18,804	13.2	14,590	19,350	20,610	24,984	1.5
Bhutan	694	798	928	1,168	11.8	1,100	1,250	1,430	1,770	3.4
Bosnia-Herzegovina	10,513	11,200	12,766	15,375	10.0	2,692	2,861	3,251	3,907	–
Cape Verde	837	976	1,105	1,287	10.6	1,690	1,930	2,130	2,430	2.5
Congo Republic	2,924	3,793	5,073	5,797	16.3	830	1,050	1,370	1,540	-3.4
Costa Rica	18,754	20,333	21,894	24,648	6.8	4,410	4,700	4,980	5,520	2.0
Djibouti	754	803	864	908	5.4	970	1,010	1,060	1,090	2.0
Estonia	9,621	12,201	15,302	17,212	15.0	7,130	9,060	11,400	12,830	–

Table 1. Gross national income at market prices (continued)

Group/country	Total GNI at market prices 2004	2005	2006	2007	GNI growth rate 2000–2007	GNI per capita 2004	2005	2006	2007	GNI per capita real growth rates 1990–2000
	(US$ million)				(per cent/ year)	(US$)				(per cent)
Middle-income (contin.)										
Other countries										
Gabon	5,559	6,930	7,032	9,344	11.9	4,080	5,010	5,360	7,020	0.3
Georgia	5,220	6,505	7,921	10,400	18.8	1,156	1,454	1,787	2,366	–
Latvia	13,465	15,839	19,346	26,148	18.0	5,816	6,881	8,451	11,483	–
Lebanon	20,649	22,006	23,392	23,978	3.8	5,208	5,487	5,768	5,850	–
Lithuania	22,028	25,321	29,119	36,878	13.7	6,403	7.393	8,544	10,879	–
Macedonia FYR	4,949	5,719	6,316	6,945	8.8	2,440	2,810	3,100	3,410	–
Moldova	2,614	3,191	3,681	4,138	12.2	680	850	990	1,130	–
Mongolia	1,951	2,389	3,178	3,983	19.5	763	926	1,220	1,515	–
Montenegro	2,073	2,257	2,696	3,118	10.7	3,346	3,713	4,486	5,214	–
Panama	13,701	14,952	16,442	18,382	6.6	4,310	4,630	5,000	5,500	2.7
Suriname	1,011	1,141	1,918	2,166	11.6	2,270	2,540	4,210	4,730	0.1
Timor-Leste	506	588	865	1,604	28.3	550	750	950	1,510	–
Turkmenistan	6,924	7,855	9,109	11,092	12.5	1,450	1,630	1,860	2,230	–
High-income										
Commonwealth countries										
Antigua & Barbuda	855	867	929	1,070	6.9	9,900	10,440	11,140	12,610	2.8
Bahamas, The	5,196	5,767	6,002	6,337	4.3	17,210	17,838	18,338	19,130	–0.8
Barbados	2,709	2,962	3,285	3,579	4.8	9,312	10,146	11,213	12,178	1.7
Brunei Darussalam	7,872	9,531	11,561	12,388	6.0	21,527	25,497	30,269	31,759	–2.1
Cyprus	13,633	16,364	17,948	19,617	9.7	16,510	18,430	23,270	24,940	2.7
Malta	4,857	5,491	6,216	6,825	8.5	12,100	13,610	15,310	16,680	12.6
New Zealand	79,656	106,251	111,958	114,521	11.0	19,990	19,610	26,750	27,080	1.4
Singapore	106,265	119,757	128,816	148,400	5.1	25,060	27,580	28,730	32,340	6.7
Trinidad & Tobago	11,727	13,447	16,612	19,304	14.8	9,010	10,300	12.500	14,480	1.4
Other countries										
Croatia	35,824	42,666	47,329	53,240	10.4	7,675	8,273	9,159	11,169	–
Equatorial Guinea	1,577	2,724	4,216	6,27	43.5	3,200	5,410	6,099	12,860	18.9
Iceland	11,626	14,414	15,078	17,959	9.7	39,800	48,570	49,960	57,750	1.5
Ireland	142,419	171,122	191,315	207,880	11.3	35,010	41,140	44,830	47,610	6.1
Kuwait	65,568	92,692	115,476	122,780	16.3	24,540	31,640	40,114	43,063	17.5
Luxembourg	26,315	29,749	32,904	41,391	10.2	65,412	68,110	75,329	88,715	1.5
Norway	240,503	281,509	318,919	364,330	10.8	52,370	60,890	68,440	77,370	3.7
Oman	23,883	28,964	33,991	38,325	12.6	9,635	11,553	13,349	14,768	–
Qatar	29,492	41,055	54,409	61,194	17.0	38,588	51,564	66,246	72,795	–5.3
Slovenia	32,840	34,819	37,785	44,946	5.0	16,443	17,415	18,885	22,456	–
United Arab Emirates	99,810	125,397	154,762	179,733	14.1	25,287	30,553	36,428	41,031	–1.6

Table 1. Gross national income at market prices (continued)

Group/country	Total GNI at market prices 2004	2005	2006	2007	GNI growth rate 2000–2007	GNI per capita 2004	2005	2006	2007	GNI per capita real growth rates 1990–2000
	(US$ million)				(per cent/ year)	(US$)				(per cent)
Group averages										
Low-income	1,313	1,334	1,848	2,105	6	473	470	573	640	1
n	3	3	3	3	3	3	3	3	3	3
Middle-income	1,944	2,242	2,634	2,523	6	3,184	3,547	3,805	3,968	2
n	20	20	20	20	20	20	20	20	20	20
High-income	27,668	33,374	35,839	39,002	7	17,387	17,894	20,628	22,090	3
n	8	8	8	8	8	8	8	8	8	8
Under 0.5mn population	1,608	1,797	2,235	2,176	4	6,649	7,297	8,021	8,501	2
n	17	17	17	17	17	17	17	17	17	17
Over 0.5 mn population	4,818	5,593	6,307	6,839	10	3,681	4,197	4,885	5,273	2
n	13	13	13	13	13	13	13	13	13	13

Notes: – = not available; n = number of countries.

Source: World Bank website, www.devdata.worldbank.org; United Nations website, www.data.un.org

Table 2. Gross domestic product at current market prices

Group/country	GDP at current market price 2003	2004	2005	2006	2007	Growth rates[a] 1990–2000	Growth rates[a] 2000–2007
	(million US$)					(per cent/year)	(per cent/year)
Low-income							
Commonwealth countries							
Gambia, The	395	401	461	511	644	3.5	6.2
Papua New Guinea	3,182	3,926	4,945	5,579	6,259	1.7	7.3
Solomon Islands	257	265	298	336	388	4.7	4.8
Other countries							
Central African Republic	1,198	1,307	1,369	1,418	1,712	4.3	2.0
Comoros	323	362	387	403	449	–2.0	12.2
Guinea-Bissau	239	270	301	304	357	–0.8	7.5
Liberia	442	497	548	631	735	–8.5	4.4
Mauritania	1,093	1,548	1,850	2,663	2,644	–1.2	16.0
São Tomé & Principe	54	64	71	123	145	–1.4	17.5
Middle-income							
Commonwealth countries							
Belize	989	1,055	1,105	1214	1277	6.7	7.7
Botswana	7,388	9,731	10,317	10,598	12,311	5.1	12.5
Dominica	255	271	284	319	341	4.9	3.4
Fiji Islands	2,251	2,582	2,729	3,138	3,431	0.8	12.5
Grenada	439	437	474	525	605	7.4	5.7
Guyana	742	786	787	896	1080	5.5	6.9
Jamaica	8,147	8,865	9,574	10,023	11,430	5.7	6.4
Kiribati	58	73	66	71	78	0.8	10.0
Lesotho	1,139	1,367	1,450	1,494	1,600	3.5	8.6
Maldives	696	776	766	927	1,055	15.7	8.4
Mauritius	5,224	6,064	6,290	6,347	6,786	5.5	6.5
Namibia	4,271	5,712	6,126	6,566	7,015	4.2	10.5
Nauru	–	–	–	–	–	–	–
St Kitts & Nevis	370	403	453	477	527	10.1	6.9
St Lucia	693	765	823	899	980	7.6	5.1
St Vincent & the Grenadines	371	409	386	423	553	5.8	7.2
Samoa	323	358	404	424	525	10.4	11.8
Seychelles	720	703	694	775	728	5.0	2.8
Swaziland	1,845	2,517	2,731	2,648	2,894	5.0	10.1
Tonga	163	189	214	223	253	2.6	6.8
Tuvalu	7	7	7	7	7	1.6	0.0
Vanuatu	283	317	341	388	452	4.2	10.1
Other countries							
Albania	5,653	7,464	8,376	9098	10831	–	13.9
Armenia	2,807	3,577	4,900	6384	9204	–	26.8
Bahrain	9,100	11,102	12,914	16,069	18,443	7.4	12.7
Bhutan	645	729	844	942	1096	5.6	12.3
Bosnia-Herzegovina	8,370	10,023	10,764	12264	15144	–	12.6
Cape Verde	831	925	983	1144	1434	5.5	14.4
Congo Republic	3,564	4,343	5,091	7,385	7,646	1.2	13.2
Costa Rica	17,427	18,558	20,021	22,229	26267	10.7	7.5
Estonia	9,190	11,239	13,101	16,410	20,901	–	17.9
Gabon	6,057	7,229	8,055	9,546	11,568	–1.1	13.0

Table 2. Gross domestic product at current market prices (continued)

Group/country	GDP at current market price 2003	2004	2005	2006	2007	Growth rates[a] 1990–2000	Growth rates[a] 2000–2007
	(million US$)					(per cent/year)	(per cent/year)
Middle-income (contin.)							
Other countries							
Georgia	3,991	5,126	6,411	7,762	10,175	–	20.6
Latvia	11186	13762	16042	19935	28766	–	20.8
Lebanon	19802	21465	21558	22136	24731	–	4.5
Lithuania	18,609	22,552	25,962	30,089	38,894	–	15.9
Macedonia FYR	4,630	5,368	5,815	6,373	7,927	–	11.4
Moldova	1,981	2,598	2,988	3,408	4,402	–	17.3
Mongolia	1,448	1,816	2,306	3,132	3,930	–	22.1
Montenegro	1,708	2,073	2,257	2,696	3,846	–	17.6
Panama	12,887	14,204	15,467	17,097	19,485	7.0	10.2
Suriname	1,200	1,150	1,342	2,115	2,241	-6.7	14.7
Timor-Leste	336	339	349	356	395	–	3.3
Turkmenistan	5977	6837	8103	10280	12926	–	16.7
Uruguay	11,182	13,216	16,791	19,308	23,136	9.2	2.0
High-income							
Commonwealth countries							
Antigua & Barbuda	757	818	876	1155	7.0	8.3	
Bahamas, The	5,502	5,650	5,983	6,237	6,571	–	4
Barbados	2,628	2,797	3,091	3,430	3,409	4.3	3.9
Brunei Darussalam	4,738	5,485	9,531	11,562	12,252	1.9	16.1
Cyprus	11,385	15,418	16,996	18,371	21,277	4.6	13.6
Malta	4,900	5,320	5,570	6,375	7,449	4.5	10.9
New Zealand	79,572	98,467	109,291	104,519	135,667	1.4	15.4
Singapore	91,342	107,498	116,764	132,158	161,347	9.7	8.3
Trinidad & Tobago	10,511	12,207	14,358	18,136	20,886	3.7	16.2
Other countries							
Croatia	33,875	40,713	44432	49,038	58,558	–	11.6
Equatorial Guinea	2,894	3,235	3,231	8,565	9,923	15.6	27.9
Iceland	10,499	13,061	15,814	16,265	19,963	3.1	13.0
Ireland	153,719	184,451	201,817	220,137	259,018	7.7	15.6
Kuwait	41,748	59,267	80,781	101,647	112,116	7.6	21.8
Luxembourg	26,228	33,593	36,469	41,468	49,460	7.7	14.7
Norway	220,854	254,708	295,513	334,942	388,413	4.4	13.3
Oman	21,784	24,772	30,923	35,729	41,640	–	13.8
Qatar	19,500	31,734	42,463	52,722	71,041	8.6	22.9
Slovenia	29,058	33,724	35,695	38,899	47,182	–	10.2
United Arab Emirates	70,960	104,598	129,702	163,296	180,180	3.2	21.4

Notes: – = not available.
[a]The GDP growth rates shown are 1990–2000 and 2000-2007.

Source: World Bank, World Development Indicators, various issues, Washington, DC

Table 3. Sectoral distribution of gross domestic product

Group/country	Agriculture			Industry			Services		
	2005	2006	2007	2005	2006	2007	2005	2006	2007
	(per cent)			(per cent)			(per cent)		
Low-income									
Commonwealth countries									
Gambia, The	33	33	29	13	15	15	54	54	56
Papua New Guinea	42	42	35	39	39	45	19	19	20
Solomon Islands	35	36	33	8	7	7	57	57	60
Other countries									
Central African Republic	54	56	54	21	15	14	25	29	32
Comoros	51	45	47	11	12	12	38	43	41
Guinea-Bissau	60	62	64	12	11	12	28	27	24
Mauritania	24	13	13	29	48	47	47	39	41
São Tomé & Principe	16	15	14	21	15	15	63	70	71
Middle-income									
Commonwealth countries									
Belize	14	14	12	18	21	21	68	65	66
Botswana	2	2	2	53	53	49	44	45	49
Dominica	18	18	18	24	24	23	58	59	59
Fiji Islands	15	15	15	26	26	25	57	59	60
Grenada	8	7	7	23	29	29	69	64	64
Guyana	31	31	29	23	24	24	69	64	67
Jamaica	6	6	6	23	25	28	69	64	66
Kiribati	14	7	–	23	29	–	69	64	–
Lesotho	17	16	12	41	43	47	41	40	41
Mauritius	6	6	5	28	27	28	66	68	67
Namibia	10	11	11	32	31	30	58	58	59
St Kitts & Nevis	3	2	–	23	29	–	69	64	–
St Lucia	5	5	5	23	29	29	69	64	65
St Vincent & the Grenadines	9	9	8	23	29	27	69	64	64
Samoa	14	12	12	27	27	28	60	60	61
Seychelles	3	3	3	28	26	28	69	71	69
Swaziland	12	11	7	48	46	49	41	43	43
Tonga	29	29	28	15	15	13	56	56	60
Vanuatu	14	14	14	9	9	9	77	77	77
Other countries									
Albania	23	22	21	22	20	20	55	58	59
Armenia	21	20	20	45	45	44	34	35	36
Bahrain	1	1	1	23	29	29	69	64	65
Bhutan	25	22	21	37	38	43	38	40	36
Bosnia-Herzegovina	–	–	–	–	–	–	–	–	–
Cape Verde	7	9	9	20	17	17	73	74	75
Congo Republic	6	4	5	48	73	60	48	22	35
Costa Rica	9	9	9	30	29	29	61	62	63
Djibouti	4	4	4	14	16	17	82	80	79
Estonia	4	3	3	29	29	30	67	68	67
Gabon	8	5	5	58	31	60	35	64	35
Georgia	17	13	11	27	25	24	56	62	65
Latvia	4	4	3	22	22	22	74	74	75
Lithuania	5	4	4	33	33	33	62	63	63
Lebanon	6	7	6	23	24	24	71	69	70

Table 3. Sectoral distribution of gross domestic product (continued)

Group/country	Agriculture			Industry			Services		
	2005	2006	2007	2005	2006	2007	2005	2006	2007
	(per cent)			(per cent)			(per cent)		
Middle-income (contin.)									
Other countries									
Mongolia	25	22	23	34	42	41	41	36	36
Macedonia FYR	13	13	12	30	29	30	58	58	59
Moldova	20	17	12	16	16	15	64	67	73
Montenegro	10	10	9	21	20	18	69	69	73
Oman	2	2	2	23	29	29	69	64	65
Panama	8	8	7	16	19	17	76	73	77
Suriname	11	5	–	23	29	–	69	64	–
Timor-Leste	32	32	–	23	29	–	69	64	–
Turkmenistan	–	–	–	–	–	–	–	–	–
Uruguay	9	9	10	31	32	32	60	58	58
High-income									
Commonwealth countries									
Antigua & Barbuda	4	4	4	23	29	29	69	64	64
Bahamas, The	3	3	3	23	29	29	69	64	64
Barbados	6	6	6	23	29	29	69	64	64
Brunei Darussalam	1	1	1	72	73	71	28	26	28
Cyprus	4	4	4	23	29	29	69	64	64
Malta	3	3	3	23	29	29	69	64	64
New Zealand	5	5	5	23	29	30	69	64	64
Singapore	0	0	0	34	35	31	66	65	69
Trinidad & Tobago	1	1	0	60	62	59	40	38	41
Other countries									
Croatia	7	6	6	28	28	28	65	65	66
Equatorial Guinea	3	3	3	93	94	94	5	3	3
Iceland	11	11	11	23	29	29	69	64	64
Ireland	3	2	2	23	29	29	69	64	64
Kuwait	1	1	1	23	29	29	69	64	64
Luxembourg	0	0	0	16	15	14	83	85	85
Norway	2	2	1	43	45	43	55	54	46
Qatar	0	0	0	23	29	29	69	64	66
Slovenia	3	2	2	34	34	34	63	63	63
United Arab Emirates	2	2	2	23	29	29	69	64	66

Note: – = not available.

Source: World Bank, World Development Indicators 2009, Washington, DC, http://ddp-ext.worldbank.org/ext/DDPQQ/member.do?method=getMembers, accessed November 2009; CIA, *The World Factbook 2009*, Washington DC, http://www.cia.gov/library/publications/the-world-factbook/geos/xx.html, accessed November 2009

Table 4. Growth of production

Group/country	GDP 1990–00	GDP 2000–07	Agriculture 1990–00	Agriculture 2000–07	Industry 1990–00	Industry 2000–07	Manufacturing 1990–00	Manufacturing 2000–06	Services 1990–00	Services 2000–07
	(Average annual rates in real terms, percentage)									
Low-income										
Commonwealth countries										
Gambia, The	3.0	4.9	3.3	2.6	1.0	7.3	0.9	4.2	3.7	6.0
Papua New Guinea	3.8	2.3	4.5	1.4	5.4	3.2	4.6	3.2	-0.6	2.7
Solomon Islands	–	–	–	–	–	–	–	–	–	–
Other countries										
Central African Republic	2.0	0.0	3.8	0.7	0.7	0.8	-0.2	1.1	-0.3	-1.6
Comoros	–	–	–	–	–	–	–	–	–	–
Guinea-Bissau	1.2	0.4	3.9	4.8	-3.1	4.0	-2.0	4.0	-0.6	0.3
Liberia	4.1	-2.7	–	–	–	–	–	–	–	–
Mauritania	2.9	5.1	-0.2	0.6	3.4	4.2	5.8	-1.4	4.9	6.9
São Tomé & Principe	–	–	–	–	–	–	–	–	–	–
Timor-Leste	–	0.1	–	–	–	–	–	–	–	–
Middle-income										
Commonwealth countries										
Antigua & Barbuda	–	–	–	–	–	–	–	–	–	–
Barbados	–	–	–	–	–	–	–	–	–	–
Belize	–	–	–	–	–	–	–	–	–	–
Botswana	6.0	5.3	3.0	-1.5	-5.0	4.6	4.4	2.8	7.8	5.9
Dominica	–	–	–	–	–	–	–	–	–	–
Fiji Islands	–	–	–	–	–	–	–	–	–	–
Grenada	–	–	–	–	–	–	–	–	–	–
Guyana	–	–	–	–	–	–	–	–	–	–
Jamaica	1.8	1.0	-0.3	-1.4	-1.0	1.7	-2.2	-0.2	2.3	0.4
Lesotho	5.1	3.8	2.4	-5.5	5.3	5.8	6.6	6.7	7.1	3.7
Maldives	–	–	–	–	–	–	–	–	–	–
Mauritius	5.2	4.0	-0.5	0.6	5.5	1.4	5.3	0.2	6.4	6.0
Namibia	4	5	4	1	2	6	3	4	5	5
St Kitts & Nevis	–	–	–	–	–	–	–	–	–	–
St Lucia	–	–	–	–	–	–	–	–	–	–
St Vincent & the Grenadines	–	–	–	–	–	–	–	–	–	–
Seychelles	–	–	–	–	–	–	–	–	–	–
Swaziland	3.4	2.6	0.9	1.2	3.2	1.7	2.8	1.6	3.9	4.1
Tonga	–	–	–	–	–	–	–	–	–	–
Trinidad & Tobago	3.2	8.8	2.7	-10.8	3.2	12.3	4.9	8.7	3.2	5.2
Vanuatu	–	–	–	–	–	–	–	–	–	–
Other countries										
Albania	3.5	5.3	4.3	1.4	-0.5	3.6	–	-0.2	6.9	7.2
Armenia	-1.9	12.7	0.5	7.8	-7.8	15.9	-4.3	6.5	4.5	3.6
Bahrain	–	–	–	–	–	–	–	–	–	–
Bhutan	–	–	–	–	–	–	–	–	–	–
Bosnia-Herzegovina	–	5.3	–	5.0	–	7.1	–	8.1	–	3.9
Cape Verde	–	–	–	–	–	–	–	–	–	–
Congo Republic	1.0	4.1	0.7	–	1.7	–	-2.4	–	-0.7	–
Costa Rica	5.3	5.4	4.1	4.1	6.2	5.9	6.8	5.8	4.7	5.6
Djibouti	–	–	–	–	–	–	–	–	–	–
Equatorial Guinea	–	–	–	–	–	–	–	–	–	–
Estonia	0.4	8.1	-6.2	-3.0	-2.4	9.8	7.3	10.5	3.3	7.7
Gabon	2.3	2.0	2.0	1.4	1.6	1.2	3.0	3.4	3.1	2.7

Table 4. Growth of production (continued)

Group/country	GDP		Agriculture		Industry		Manufacturing		Services	
	1990–00	2000–07	1990–00	2000–07	1990–00	2000–07	1990–00	2000–06	1990–00	2000–07
	(Average annual rates in real terms, percentage)									
Middle-income (contin.)										
Other countries										
Georgia	-7.1	8.3	-11.0	1.6	-8.1	12.5	–	10.4	-0.3	9.5
Latvia	-1.5	9.0	-5.2	2.9	-8.3	8.4	-7.3	6.3	2.7	9.5
Lebanon	6.1	3.3	1.9	0.5	-1.8	4.0	-0.8	2.8	3.7	2.6
Lithuania	-2.7	8.0	-0.8	1.9	3.2	10.3	5.5	9.9	5.5	7.4
Macedonia FYR	-0.8	2.7	0.2	1.3	-2.3	2.0	-5.3	1.1	0.5	3.2
Moldova	-9.6	6.5	-11.2	-1.8	-13.6	0.8	-7.1	4.8	0.7	8.4
Mongolia	1.0	7.5	2.5	4.6	-2.5	7.9	-9.7	8.1	0.7	8.4
Montenegro	–	–	–	–	–	–	–	–	–	–
Oman	4.5	4.7	5.0	2.2	3.9	-0.5	6.0	9.3	5.0	7.5
Panama	4.7	6.0	3.1	4.1	6.0	4.0	2.7	0.6	4.5	6.5
Suriname	–	–	–	–	–	–	–	–	–	–
Turkmenistan	-4.8	–	-5.7	–	-3.4	–	–	–	-5.4	–
Uruguay	3.4	3.3	2.8	6.1	1.1	3.7	-0.1	5.3	3.7	2.3
High-income										
Commonwealth countries										
Brunei Darussalam	–	–	–	–	–	–	–	–	–	–
Cyprus	–	–	–	–	–	–	–	–	–	–
New Zealand	3.2	3.4	2.9	2.5	2.4	2.8	2.2	2.6	3.6	3.9
Singapore	7.6		-1.8	0.9	7.7	3.2	7.0	5.2	7.8	4.8
Other countries										
Croatia	0.6	4.8	-2.1	1.3	-1.1	5.9	-3.5	5.5	1.3	4.7
Iceland	–	–	–	–	–	–	–	–	–	–
Ireland	7.5	5.2	–	–	–	–	–	–	–	–
Kuwait	4.9	9.2	1.0	–	0.3	–	-0.1	–	3.5	–
Luxembourg	–	–	–	–	–	–	–	–	–	–
Norway	4.0	2.4	2.6	3.7	3.8	0.6	1.5	3.7	3.9	3.1
Oman	–	–	–	–	–	–	–	–	–	–
Qatar	–	–	–	–	–	–	–	–	–	–
Slovenia	2.7	6.0	0.4	1.4	3.8	7.0	9.3	10.7	5.3	5.4
United Arab Emirates	4.8	7.7	13.2	3.6	3.0	6.0	11.9	8.1	7.2	9.6

Notes: – = not available.

Source: World Bank, World Development Indicators 2009, Washington, DC

Table 5. Structure of demand

Group/country	Gross capital formation		Household consumption		Government consumption		Gross savings	
	1995	2007	1995	2007	1995	2007	1995	2007
	(as a percentage of GDP)							
Low-income								
Commonwealth countries								
Gambia, The	20	23	90	77	14	16	6	12
Papua New Guinea	22	20	44	47	17	11	36	35
Solomon Islands	8	19	70	–	28	–	–	–
Other countries								
Central African Republic	14	9	79	96	15	3	6	4
Comoros	19	9	80	101	26	13	0	14
Guinea-Bissau	22	17	95	70	6	16	5	23
Lao PDR	12	32	91	72	10	9	15	23
Liberia	–	20	56	116	14	15	–	40
Mauritania	20	26	77	61	11	20	17	29
Nicaragua	22	32	83	90	11	12	-1	14
São Tomé & Principe	–	38	105	–	30	–	–	–
Togo	16	18	77	81	12	19	11	7
Middle-income								
Commonwealth countries								
Belize	22	21	43	66	20	14	–	–
Botswana	25	41	34	29	29	20	36	55
Dominica	41	25	81	–	20	–	–	–
Fiji Islands	17	19	83	–	30	–	–	–
Grenada	38	50	62	–	22	–	–	–
Guyana	42	26	70	–	15	–	–	–
Jamaica	29	30	70	72	11	16	24	15
Lesotho	56	28	104	98	24	26	27	41
Mauritius	29	27	63	69	13	14	26	20
Namibia	22	30	54	50	30	25	32	40
St Kitts & Nevis	58	46	70	–	17	–	–	–
St Lucia	26	41	71	–	15	–	–	–
St Vincent & the Grenadines	20	25	64	–	18	–	–	–
Samoa	34	10	81	–	34	–	–	–
Seychelles	25	13	50	65	28	25	–	–
Swaziland	16	13	82	73	15	15	7	20
Vanuatu	43	20	63	–	28	–	–	–
Other countries								
Albania	21	30	87	88	14	9	21	20
Armenia	18	37	109	72	11	11	-7	31
Bahrain	24	20	48	–	24	–	–	–
Bhutan	33	60	60	–	20	–	–	–
Bosnia-Herzegovina	20	23	–	90	–	22	10	9
Cape Verde	33	39	83	–	20	–	–	–
Congo Republic	37	27	49	29	13	14	-3	36
Costa Rica	18	25	71	67	14	13	15	19
Djibouti	21	24	79	–	37	–	–	–
Estonia	28	38	54	56	26	17	24	20
Gabon	23	26	41	36	12	9	33	41
Georgia	4	35	102	70	11	22	-7	17
Latvia	14	37	63	65	24	18	14	15

Table 5. Structure of demand (continued)

Group/country	Gross capital formation		Household consumption		Government consumption		Gross savings	
	1995	2007	1995	2007	1995	2007	1995	2007
	(as a percentage of GDP)							
Middle-income (contin.)								
Other countries								
Lebanon	36	18	101	92	15	15	-3	0
Lithuania	22	30	67	66	22	17	13	16
Macedonia FYR	21	23	70	78	19	18	14	21
Moldova	25	38	57	95	27	19	19	22
Mongolia	32	40	56	48	13	13	35	42
Montenegro	–	–	–	–	–	–	–	–
Oman	15	19	51	39	25	18	–	–
Panama	30	23	52	60	15	11	30	23
Suriname	21	33	53	–	25	–	–	–
Timor-Leste	–	32	–	–	–	–	–	–
Turkmenistan	49	23	44	46	8	13	50	34
Uruguay	15	15	73	74	12	11	14	13
High-income								
Commonwealth countries								
Antigua & Barbuda	37	54	48	–	18	–	–	–
Barbados	19	21	63	–	19	–	–	–
Bahamas, The	18	30	74	–	14	–	–	–
Cyprus	27	20	74	–	14	–	–	–
Malta	33	23	63	–	18	–	–	–
New Zealand	23	23	58	60	17	19	18	15
Singapore	37	23	46	38	10	10	46	–
Trinidad & Tobago	21	13	53	55	12	12	26	30
Other countries								
Croatia	18	33	64	56	29	20	11	24
Equatorial Guinea	27	38	83	–	30	–	–	–
Iceland	18	29	61	–	19	–	–	–
Ireland	18	27	54	46	16	16	23	23
Kuwait	15	20	43	30	32	15	–	–
Luxembourg	28	21	55	–	16	–	–	–
Norway	22	23	50	42	22	20	26	38
Qatar	18	35	74	–	14	–	–	–
Slovenia	24	31	60	52	19	18	23	27
United Arab Emirates	30	21	48	45	16	10	–	–

Note: – = not available.

Source: World Bank, World Development Indicators 2008 and 2009, http://ddpext.worldbank.org/ext/DDPQQ/member.do?method=getMembers&userid=1&queryId=135, accessed November 2009

Table 6. Percentage changes in the Consumer Price Index

Group/country	Base year	2000	2003	2004	2005	2006	2007	2008
					(per cent)			
Low-income								
Commonwealth countries								
Gambia, The	2000	0.2	17.0	14.2	4.8	2.1	5.4	4.5
Papua New Guinea	2000	15.6	14.7	2.2	1.7	2.4	2.8	9.3
Solomon Islands	2000	6.0	10.0	6.7	7.2	11.2	7.7	17.3
Other countries								
Central African Republic	2000	3.2	3.1	–2.1	2.9	3.8	3.9	9.3
Comoros	2000	–1.9	3.5	2.5	7.2	1.7	4.5	9.6
Guinea-Bissau	2000	8.6	–3.5	0.9	3.3	2.0	4.6	10.5
Liberia	2000	–	15.0	–8.1	6.9	8.0	11.4	18.1
Mauritania	2000	3.3	5.2	8.0	12.1	6.1	7.3	7.3
Middle-income								
Commonwealth countries								
Belize	2000	0.6	2.6	3.1	3.6	4.2	2.3	6.4
Botswana	2000	8.6	9.2	7.0	8.6	11.6	7.1	12.7
Dominica	2000	0.8	1.6	2.0	2.2	2.4	3.1	5.1
Fiji Islands	2000	1.1	4.2	2.8	2.4	2.5	4.8	7.7
Grenada	2000	0.5	2.8	2.6	3.5	3.8	4.2	8.2
Guyana	2000	6.1	6.0	4.7	6.3	6.6	12.3	8.1
Jamaica	2000	8.2	7.0	10.6	15.3	8.6	9.3	22.0
Kiribati	2000	3.0	2.6	2.5	–	–	–	–
Lesotho	2000	6.1	6.7	5.9	3.4	6.0	8.0	10.7
Maldives	2000	–1.1	–2.9	6.4	3.3	0.3	7.4	12.3
Mauritius	2000	4.2	5.2	4.7	4.9	8.9	9.1	9.4
Namibia	2000	4.5	3.9	4.2	2.3	5.1	6.7	10.4
St Kitts & Nevis	2000	3.5	2.2	2.3	1.8	8.5	4.5	5.5
St Lucia	2000	1.5	0.9	1.5	3.9	2.3	2.5	7.2
St Vincent & the Grenadines	2000	0.8	0.3	2.9	3.7	3.0	7.0	10.1
Samoa	2000	1.0	0.1	16.3	1.9	3.7	5.6	11.5
Seychelles	2000	6.3	3.3	3.8	1.0	–0.3	5.3	37.0
Swaziland	2000	16.7	9.4	6.0	4.8	5.2	8.6	13.7
Tonga	2000	5.9	11.6	11.0	8.3	6.4	5.9	10.4
Tuvalu	2000	3.9	6.7	2.1	–	–	–	–
Vanuatu	2000	2.5	3.0	1.4	1.2	1.9	4.0	4.8
Other countries								
Albania	2000	0.1	0.5	2.3	2.4	2.4	2.9	3.4
Armenia	2000	–0.8	4.7	7.0	0.6	2.9	4.4	8.9
Bahrain	2000	–0.4	2.4	2.4	2.6	2.0	3.3	3.5
Bhutan	2000	4.0	2.1	4.6	5.3	5.0	5.2	8.4
Bosnia-Herzegovina	2000	–	–	–	–	–	–	–
Cape Verde	2000	–2.5	1.9	–1.9	0.4	5.4	4.4	6.8
Congo Republic	2000	–0.9	9.8	1.0	5.3	3.4	0.7	7.8
Costa Rica	2000	11.0	9.5	12.3	13.8	11.5	9.4	13.4
Estonia	2000	–	1.3	3.1	4.1	4.4	6.6	10.4
Gabon	2000	1.0	2.3	0.4	–0.1	–1.4	5.0	5.3
Georgia	2000	4.1	4.8	5.7	8.2	9.2	9.2	10.0
Latvia	2000	2.6	3.0	6.2	6.7	6.5	10.1	15.4
Lebanon	2000	–	–	–	–	–	–	–
Lithuania	2000	1.0	–1.1	1.1	2.7	3.7	5.7	10.9
Macedonia FYR	2000	6.6	1.1	0.9	0.2	3.3	3.6	7.2

Table 6. Percentage changes in the Consumer Price Index (continued)

Group/country	Base year	2000	2003	2004	2005	2006	2007	2008
					(per cent)			
Middle-income (contin.)								
Other countries								
Moldova	2000	31.3	11.7	12.5	12.0	12.8	12.4	12.8
Mongolia	2000	11.6	5.1	8.2	12.7	5.1	9.0	25.1
Montenegro	2000	–	–	–	–	–	–	–
Oman	2000	-1.1	-0.4	0.8	1.9	3.2	6.0	12.1
Panama	2000	1.4	1.4	0.4	3.3	2.1	4.2	8.8
Suriname	2000	64.3	23.0	10.0	10.0	11.3	6.7	13.2
Timor-Leste	2000	–	7.1	3.2	1.1	3.9	10.3	9.1
Turkmenistan	2000	–	–	–	–	–	–	–
Uruguay	2000	4.8	19.4	9.2	4.7	6.4	8.1	7.9
High-income								
Commonwealth countries								
Antigua & Barbuda	2000	2.0	0.4	1.5	–	–	–	–
Bahamas, The	2000	1.6	2.9	0.5	1.6	2.4	2.5	4.5
Barbados	2000	2.4	1.6	1.4	6.1	7.1	4.0	8.1
Brunei Darussalam	2000	1.5	-2.0	0.9	1.1	0.2	0.3	2.7
Cyprus	2000	4.1	4.1	2.3	2.6	2.5	2.4	4.7
Malta	2000	2.4	0.5	2.8	2.8	2.8	1.3	4.3
New Zealand	2000	2.6	1.8	2.3	3.0	3.4	2.4	4.0
Singapore	2000	1.4	0.5	1.7	0.5	1.0	2.1	6.5
Trinidad & Tobago	2000	3.6	3.8	3.7	6.9	8.3	7.9	12.0
Other countries								
Croatia	2000	4.6	1.8	2	3.3	3.2	2.9	6.1
Equatorial Guinea	2000	3.0	6.0	-8.3	–	–	–	–
Iceland	2000	5.2	2.1	2.8	4.2	6.7	5.1	12.7
Ireland	2000	5.6	3.5	2.2	2.4	3.9	4.9	4.1
Kuwait	2000	1.8	1.0	1.3	4.1	3.1	5.5	10.6
Luxembourg	2000	3.1	2.1	2.2	2.5	2.7	2.3	3.4
Norway	2000	3.1	2.5	0.5	1.5	2.3	0.7	3.8
Oman	2000	-0.5	0.2	0.8	1.9	3.2	6.0	12.1
Qatar	2000	1.7	2.3	6.8	8.8	11.8	13.8	15
Slovenia	2000	8.9	5.6	3.6	2.5	2.5	3.6	5.6
United Arab Emirates	2000	2.0	3.1	5.0	–	–	–	–

Note: – = not available.

Source: International Monetary Fund, *International Financial Statistics*, various issues, Washington, DC

Table 7. Merchandise exports and growth

Group/country	Exports (fob) 2000	2002	2003	2004	2005	2006	2007	Growth rate 1985–90	1990–2007
	(US$ million)							(per cent/year)	
Low-income									
Commonwealth countries									
Gambia, The	39	27	15	47	39	37	46	-0.7	-7.3
Papua New Guinea	2,797	2,655	3,667	4,265	5,236	6,268	7,419	2.1	10.3
Solomon Islands	87	91	117	179	210	237	326	2.6	8.5
Other countries									
Central African Republic	226	172	122	130	115	113	123	-17.8	0.7
Comoros	17	29	32	35	24	32	30	4.0	0.4
Guinea-Bissau	112	121	99	114	114	133	373	-1.8	15.8
Liberia	581	1,080	938	950	988	1563	1023	-24.1	4.5
Mauritania	533	549	578	803	933	1400	1692	2.2	7.1
São Tome & Principé	18	9	12	9	18	11	8	-6.3	-5.5
Middle-income									
Commonwealth countries									
Belize	184	193	248	298	309	420	359	-1.1	6.5
Botswana	3,752	2,700	3,500	4,400	4,400	4,800	5,158	0.7	6.2
Dominica	54	43	39	69	86	96	114	16.1	-0.1
Fiji Islands	674	609	723	881	866	927	1003	-2.0	4.8
Grenada	77	51	45	40	48	38	698	5.9	20.8
Guyana	596	545	570	648	640	684	808	4.7	6.2
Jamaica	1,307	1,114	1,175	1,405	1,531	1984	2219	0.6	3.9
Kiribati	2	8	5	6	7	6	9	18.5	1.5
Lesotho	211	357	475	640	673	699	805	2.5	15.6
Maldives	75	90	113	123	99	170	163	0.8	6.7
Mauritius	1,488	1,746	1,855	1,914	2,005	2,110	1,971	-0.1	3.0
Namibia	1,400	1,072	1,262	1,828	2,070	2,647	–	2.6	4.6
Nauru	3	3	3	2	3	3	3	-10.7	-13.3
St Kitts & Nevis	33	68	69	70	83	84	84	3.1	6.7
St Lucia	45	68	52	82	164	288	133	-4.3	0.8
St Vincent & the Grenadines	51	39	38	37	40	196	158	-4.2	5.2
Samoa	67	76	103	96	233	131	163	-7.8	19.4
Seychelles	124	175	214	368	426	350	334	5.0	5.5
Swaziland	967	1,079	1,667	1,806	1,637	1,663	2,000	1.6	7.4
Tonga	18	28	29	34	19	22	18	5.5	0.3
Trinidad & Tobago	3,041	3,851	6,615	8,456	11,124	13,420	14,769	0.0	12.5
Tuvalu	1	1	1	1	1	1	1	14.9	-4.0
Vanuatu	86	58	77	204	236	242	273	-1.7	15.7
Other countries									
Albania	–	339	447	604	632	759	1,012	–	–
Armenia	–	505	686	723	974	985	1,152	–	–
Bahrain	7,578	8,376	10,263	13,529	15,906	19,755	23,846	7.1	9.1
Bhutan	114	104	113	154	154	312	350	-2.2	10.2
Bosnia-Herzegovina	–	838	1,144	1,506	2,190	2763	3145	–	–
Cape Verde	11	22	29	21	26	37	30	-6.5	11.1
Congo Republic	2,775	1,934	2,592	839	5,421	8,164	7,049	-1.7	11.5
Costa Rica	5,850	5,264	6,102	6,302	7,021	13,362	14,887	1.8	14.1
Djibouti	136	154	191	253	275	340	422	10.0	9.2
Estonia	3,830	4,340	5,619	5,906	7,643	9,701	11,007	–	–
Gabon	3,765	2,993	3,664	4,492	5,105	4,666	6,272	0.3	5.5
Georgia	–	349	465	645	851	981	1529	–	–
Latvia	–	2,313	2,893	3,979	5,144	6145	8293	–	–

Table 7. Merchandise exports and growth (continued)

Group/country	Exports (fob) 2000	2002	2003	2004	2005	2006	2007	Growth rate 1985–90	1990–2007
	(US$ million)							(per cent/year)	
Middle-income (contin.)									
Other countries									
Lebanon	–	1,018	1,194	1,927	2,183	2544	3342	–	–
Lithuania	–	5,477	7,162	9,297	11,764	14154	17169	–	–
Macedonia FYR	–	1,115	1,367	1,675	2,041	2400	3603	–	–
Moldova	–	644	790	985	1,055	1,243	1,761	–	–
Mongolia	–	524	616	852	1,054	1,454	1,672	–	–
Montenegro	–	–	–	–	–	–	–	–	–
Oman	10,667	11,127	10,362	12,728	17,372	24,109	22,806	1.4	9.4
Panama	779	756	795	892	964	1,038	1,126	1.2	7.3
Suriname	502	491	576	880	944	1,234	1,399	–2.7	7.7
Timor-Leste	–	–	–	–	–	–	–	–	–
Turkmenistan	–	–	–	–	–	–	–	–	–
Uruguay	2,295	2,164	2,197	2,930	3,403	4,291	5,082	–1.7	7.1
High-income									
Commonwealth countries									
Antigua & Barbuda	83	63	48	64	91	113	184	–4.8	12.5
Bahamas, The	892	1,188	1,346	1,492	2,131	2,137	2,333	–2.7	6.0
Barbados	272	242	193	209	260	324	391	–0.3	3.8
Brunei Darussalam	3,161	3,435	4,422	4,510	5,633	6,907	6,944	2.2	6.3
Cyprus	949	847	925	1,171	1,452	1,330	1,391	0.6	2.1
Malta	2,442	2,494	2,461	2,624	2,273	2,668	2,992	2.8	5.1
New Zealand	12,716	14,148	16,271	20,340	21,766	22,441	26,997	0.3	6.3
Singapore	137,932	125,087	144,121	170,674	207,338	272,057	299,173	2.3	10.0
Trinidad & Tobago	3,041	3,851	6,615	8,456	11,124	13,420	14,769	0.0	12.5
Other countries									
Iceland	1,896	2,231	2,397	2,877	2,981	3,453	4,784	–0.5	6.9
Ireland	76,335	87,786	92,813	104,415	110,105	108,853	121,258	0.4	9.9
Croatia	–	4,834	6,054	7,859	8,733	10,304	12,130	–	–
Equatorial Guinea	1,033	1,737	2,605	3,935	6,196	7,467	8,204	1.1	37.4
Kuwait	18,826	15,980	19,519	25,530	35,250	42,235	46,789	-36.7	26.8
Luxembourg	8,245	10,191	13,342	16,258	18,318	22,853	22,459	0.0	7.8
Norway	57,600	60,458	68,143	82,369	103,260	122,122	136,376	–0.3	8.6
Oman	–	11,127	10,362	12,726	17,421	24,109	22,806	–	–
Qatar	11,593	10,977	13,380	18,546	26,081	25,090	38,624	–0.2	15.7
Slovenia	–	10,357	12,728	14,606	19,159	23,151	30,017	–	–
United Arab Emirates	40,626	38,971	49,889	67,310	93,966	112,758	125,238	1.4	10.3
Group averages (Commonwealth countries only)									
Low-income	974	924	1,266	1,497	1,828	2,181	2,597	1	4
	3	3	3	3	3	3	3	3	3
Middle-income	620	608	821	1,018	1,161	1,347	1,420	2	6
	23	23	23	23	23	23	23	23	23
High-income	17,943	16,817	19,600	23,282	28,008	35,711	39,464	0	7
	9	9	9	9	9	9	9	9	9
Under 0.5 mn population	404	438	500	544	639	747	808	2	6
	19	19	19	19	19	19	19	19	19
Over 0.5 mn population	1,405	1,424	2,033	2,515	3,010	3,521	3,975	1	6
	13	13	13	13	13	13	13	13	13

Note: – = not available.

Source: IMF, *Direction of Trade Statistics Yearbook 2007*, Washington, DC; Economist Intelligence Unit website, www.eiu.com, accessed November 2009

Table 8. Merchandise imports and growth

Group/country	Imports (cif)							Growth rate	
	2000	2002	2003	2004	2005	2006	2007	1985–1990	1990–2007
	(US$ million)							(per cent)	
Low-income									
Commonwealth countries									
Gambia, The	331	415	506	575	639	710	862	14.0	8.1
Papua New Guinea	1,167	1,086	1,229	1,458	1,835	2,360	2,697	7.7	4.3
Solomon Islands	112	90	117	144	189	256	304	3.6	6.8
Other countries									
Central African Republic	125	145	147	203	220	298	341	7.9	3.7
Comoros	30	97	126	127	132	143	156	15.4	3.6
Guinea-Bissau	105	102	159	136	213	200	240	16.4	4.0
Liberia	5,500	5,040	4,284	4,866	5,736	7,142	8,803	71.9	4.4
Mauritania	636	866	1,000	1,120	1,364	1,475	1,852	9.9	9.6
São Tomé & Principe	40	62	64	64	64	80	81	31.4	2.8
Timor-Leste	–	–	–	–	–	–	–	–	–
Middle-income									
Commonwealth countries									
Belize	443	459	531	554	770	735	826	10.5	8.4
Botswana	2100	1,760	2,170	3,696	4,444	4,521	4,463	23.5	5.0
Dominica	147	212	206	22	267	298	381	16.5	7.1
Fiji Islands	762	845	995	1,234	1,454	1,588	1,567	11.4	4.4
Grenada	246	209	246	272	339	344	393	9.6	7.8
Guyana	649	562	584	609	723	944	1,009	4.4	7.9
Jamaica	3,192	3,565	3,661	3,953	4,736	5,646	7,323	10.3	8.4
Kiribati	49	40	30	20	–	–	–	23.4	–
Lesotho	728	779	661	707	650	694	1604	15.3	5.0
Maldives	389	391	471	645	745	909	1,739	14.5	16.1
Mauritius	2,093	2,166	2,386	2,774	3,165	3,646	3,864	25.4	5.2
Namibia	1,550	1,450	1,726	1,828	2,070	2,647	3,300	14.9	6.3
Nauru	27	25	20	20	20			2.2	–
St Kitts & Nevis	196	187	241	405	296	383	468	34.0	9.0
St Lucia	350	568	352	402	614	708	1,789	36.0	13.8
St Vincent & the Grenadines	162	179	201	225	241	578	584	36.2	9.0
Samoa	271	179	254	288	641	319	346	10.2	8.8
Seychelles	338	415	414	554	764	830	1,008	14.6	10.5
Swaziland	1,066	1,133	1,902	1,741	1,825	1,908	–	15.0	–
Tonga	70	87	101	122	128	139	161	10.3	5.3
Trinidad & Tobago	2,353	3,660	3,711	5,479	5,809	5,886	6,933	-5.0	10.7
Tuvalu	13	15	22	20	–	–		5.9	-100.0
Vanuatu	124	139	212	230	268	272	318	36.7	0.6
Other countries									
Albania	–	1,500	1,842	2,287	2,606	3,029	4,091	–	–
Armenia	–	987	1,280	1,351	1,802	2,192	2,368	–	–
Bahrain	3,546	4,037	4,839	5,861	7,108	8,675	10,423	3.3	6.3
Bhutan	203	190	196	245	266	320	364	5.2	–
Bosnia-Herzegovina	–	3,370	3,998	4,876	5,758	6,001	7,522	–	–
Cape Verde	237	331	361	452	495	638	847	12.4	10.9
Congo Republic	493	630	858	326	1,519	2,007	3,673	1.0	11.3
Costa Rica	6,389	7,188	7,663	8,268	9,807	10,966	12,301	13.1	11.2
Djibouti	617	677	820	898	1,208	1,548	1,911	-7.0	13.7
Equatorial Guinea	312	443	1,220	738	1,119	1,614	1,326	32.7	16.2
Estonia	5,052	5,865	7,967	8,363	10,001	13,455	15,525	–	–

Table 8. Merchandise imports and growth (continued)

Group/country	Imports (cif)							Growth rate	
	2000	2002	2003	2004	2005	2006	2007	1985–1990	1990–2007
	(US$ million)							(per cent)	
Middle-income (contin.)									
Other countries									
Gabon	1,395	1,143	1,357	1,610	1,699	1,949	2,753	–	–
Georgia	–	796	1,141	1,846	2,490	3,678	5,217	–	–
Latvia	–	4,041	5,244	7,039	8,660	11,581	15,348	–	–
Lebanon	–	6,313	7,705	9,380	9,631	10,916	13,036	–	–
Lithuania	–	7,709	9,804	12,379	15,488	19,413	24,456	–	–
Macedonia FYR	–	1,995	2,306	2,931	3,225	3,762	4,546	–	–
Moldova	–	1,038	1,402	1,769	2,293	3,500	4,664	–	–
Mongolia	–	691	801	1,011	1,160	1,774	2,350	–	–
Montenegro	–	–	–	–	–	–	–	–	–
Oman	5,376	6,005	6,572	7,690	9,658	11,564	15,835	-2.9	10.9
Panama	3,406	3,036	3,086	3,592	4,155	5,392	6,459	1.7	8.9
Suriname	480	595	681	750	915	969	1,246	7.8	5.7
Turkmenistan	–	2,128	2,511	2,729	2,703	2,781	3,637	–	–
Uruguay	3,466	2,786	2,190	3,119	3,879	6,168	7,408	13.2	10.7
High-income									
Commonwealth countries									
Antigua & Barbuda	410	390	357	240	390	–	–	26.0	–
Bahamas, The	3,931	5,823	5,712	5,533	9,658	10,739	10,173	-6.3	9.1
Barbados	1,156	1,071	1,202	1,476	1,605	1,621	1,649	2.9	5.2
Brunei Darussalam	1,427	1,630	1,341	1,640	1,669	1,990	3,933	10.5	8.4
Cyprus	3,847	4,084	4,487	5,730	6,285	6,932	8,635	15.5	7.4
Malta	3,400	2,828	3,396	3,803	3,587	3,980	4,373	20.9	4.9
New Zealand	13,950	15,097	18,474	23,094	26,133	26,363	30,781	10.0	7.1
Singapore	134,630	116,482	127,996	162,967	189,745	238,797	263,325	18.4	9.0
Other countries									
Croatia	–	10,464	14,044	16,433	18,355	21,405	25,629	–	–
Iceland	2,591	2,275	2,829	3,707	4,848	6,140	6,630	13.1	8.4
Ireland	50,640	51,427	53,865	61,344	68,557	73,063	83,097	15.8	8.5
Kuwait	7,361	8,804	11,414	12,843	15,379	16,645	21,602	-8.0	10.3
Luxembourg	11,386	13,146	16,306	20,052	21,639	26,547	27,457	19.6	7.8
Norway	31,811	34,158	40,052	48,441	54,907	64,267	80,281	11.4	6.7
Oman	–	6,005	6,572	7,691	9,645	11,581	15,835	–	–
Qatar	3,252	4,051	4,897	6,052	10,475	12,688	22,800	8.3	16.5
Slovenia	10,148	13,853	17,571	19,626	23,014	29,481	–	–	–
United Arab Emirates	25,464	30,353	38,827	74,403	99,709	115,160	146,038	12.1	16.1
Group averages (Commonwealth countries only)									
Low-income	537	530	617	726	888	1,109	1,288	8	6
	3	3	3	3	3	3	3	3	3
Middle-income	753	827	917	1,122	1,427	1,650	2,004	16	2
	23	23	23	23	23	23	23	23	23
High-income	20,344	18,426	20,371	25,560	29,884	41,489	46,124	12	7
	8	8	8	8	8	8	8	8	8
Under 0.5 mn population	66,285	77,374	89,739	106,901	131,031	153,340	181,460	802	247
	19	19	19	19	19	19	19	19	19
Over 0.5 mn population	1,535	1,661	1,857	2,302	2,602	2,903	3,547	127	
	13	13	13	13	13	13	13	13	13

Note: – = not available.

Source: International Monetary Fund, *Direction of Trade Statistics Yearbook 2008*, Washington, DC

Table 9. Trade balance[a]

Group/country	2001	2002	2003	2004	2005	2006	2007
				(US$ million)			
Low-income							
Commonwealth countries							
Gambia, The	-369	-415	-79	-98	-114	-113	127
Papua New Guinea	881	563	1,014	1,096	1,753	4,263	4,722
Solomon Islands	-23	1	0	10	21	9	23
Other countries							
Central African Republic	35	27	9	-25	-44	-45	-35
Comoros	-43	-68	-94	-92	-108	-105	112
Guinea Bissau	1	-4	-0.3	-7	-43	-35	-40
Mauritania	-157	-317	-422	-317	-431	205	-150
Middle-income							
Commonwealth countries							
Belize	-209	-187	-207	-173	-234	-185	-216
Botswana	710	676	897	832	1,604	1,904	1,711
Dominica	-71	-59	-64	-85	-103	-103	-134
Fiji Islands	-502	-520	-305	-633	-764	-929	-1046
Grenada	-133	-140	-183	-185	-261	-232	268
Guyana	-56	-24	-17	-8	-171	-230	-308
Jamaica	-1,618	-1,871	-1,943	-1,945	-2,581	-2,944	-3,562
Lesotho	-400	-406	-519	-595	-656	668	-799
Maldives	-236	-212	-262	-386	-494	-590	-737
Mauritius	-218	-211	-303	-580	-797	-1,080	-1,357
Namibia	-202	-211	-464	-283	-256	102	-180
St Kitts & Nevis	-112	-115	-118	-118	-122	-161	-184
St Lucia	-218	-203	-283	-260	-329	-424	-441
St Vincent & the Grenadines	-106	-117	-137	-160	-170	-198	-226
Samoa	-340	-255	-357	-143	-175	-209	-213
Seychelles	-212	-143	-89	-155	-299	-290	-412
Swaziland	-82	52	127	91	-258	252	271
Tonga	-66	-75	-76	-90	-110	-119	-135
Vanuatu	-58	-58	-65	-75	-93	-110	-143
Other countries							
Albania	-1,027	-1,155	-1,336	-1,592	1,821	-2,123	-3,124
Armenia	-420	-369	-434	-458	-588	-903	-2,063
Bahrain	1,610	1,190	1,402	1,485	1,478	2,386	2,865
Bosnia-Herzegovina	-2,958	-3,340	-4,159	-4,570	-4,955	-4,298	-4,377
Cape Verde	-194	-236	-309	-378	-349	-442	-664
Congo Republic	1,374	1,598	1,805	2,464	3,440	4,062	2,950
Costa Rica	-821	-1,278	-1,089	-1,421	-2,159	-2,770	-3,024
Djibouti	-164	-161	-201	-223	-238	-281	-415
Estonia	-775	-1,118	-1,567	-2,019	-1,911	-3,022	-3,678
Gabon	1,766	1,621	2,136	2,856	4,105	3,507	3,750
Georgia	-550	-489	-638	-916	-1,214	-2,019	-3,976.5
Latvia	-1,336	-1,480	-2,003	-2,781	-3,018	-4,941	-7,287
Lebanon	-5,353	-4,700	-4,794	-6,452	-6,118	-5,755	-8,677
Lithuania	-1,108	-1,315	-1,704	-2,383	-2,916	-4,169	-7,283
Macedonia FYR	-536	-880	-939	-1,256	-1,187	-1,355	-1,875
Moldova	-315	-378	-623	-754	-1,192	-1,591	-2,348
Mongolia	-101	-156	-200	-29	-29	-189	-228
Montenegro	–	–	–	–	–	–	–
Oman	5,763	5,537	5,584	5,508	10,663	11,706	10,380

Table 9. Trade balance[a] (continued)

Group/country	2001	2002	2003	2004	2005	2006	2007
				(US$ million)			
Middle-income (contin.)							
Other countries							
Panama	–696	–1,035	–1,202	–1,538	–1,558	–1,712	–3,182
Suriname	140	47	30	42	22	161	174
Timor-Leste	–	–	–	–	–	–	–
Turkmenistan	345	688	938	1,333	2,996	3,449	3,646
Uruguay	–775	48	183	153	21	–460	–491
High-income							
Commonwealth countries							
Antigua & Barbuda	–280	–296	–308	–324	–358	–486	–570
Bahamas, The	–1,387	–1,327	–1,332	–1,429	–1,852	–2,206	–2,156
Barbados	–681	–702	–801	–971	–1,086	–1,201	–1,291
Cyprus	–2,577	–2,884	–3,183	–4,049	–4,231	–5,023	–6,345
Malta	–552	–339	–640	–879	–1,125	–1,206	–1,357
New Zealand	1,422	144	–511	–1,427	–2,578	–1,999	1,708
Singapore	17,249	18,818	29,567	31,239	36,687	44,747	49,099
Trinidad & Tobago	718	238	1,293	1,509	3,948	7,700	5,721
Other countries							
Croatia	–4,101	–5,648	–7,908	–8,350	–9,346	–10,511	–13,465
Equatorial Guinea	1,567	2,349	1,918	3,489	5,410	5,606	7,000
Iceland	–75	150	–210	–519	–1,482	–2,239	–1,388
Ireland	27,263	33,447	36,882	39,014	36,809	31,888	31,292
Kuwait	9,190	7,250	11,914	18,426	32,733	44,288	43,056
Norway	26,402	24,291	28,162	33,619	48,917	59,856	63,036
Slovenia	–620	–248	–622	–1,258	–1,258	–1,419	–2,928

Notes: – = not available.
[a]The difference between exports (fob) and imports (fob).

Source: International Monetary Fund, *International Financial Statistics*, various issues, 2008, Washington, DC

Table 10. Destination of merchandise exports

Group/country	Industrial countries						Developing countries					
	2002	2003	2004	2005	2006	2007	2002	2003	2004	2005	2006	2007
	(percentage of total exports)											
Low-income												
Commonwealth countries												
Gambia, The	74.0	57.4	43.8	21.4	37.9	31.1	26.0	42.6	56.2	78.6	62.1	68.9
Papua New Guinea	46.9	46.1	45.7	48.3	47.6	46.6	53.1	53.8	54.2	51.6	52.3	53.3
Solomon Islands	24.7	20.1	20.4	17.5	17.7	15.6	75.3	79.9	72.3	75.7	74.8	77.7
Other countries												
Central African Republic	89.6	79.8	75.5	71.0	67.0	55.2	10.4	20.2	24.5	28.6	33.0	44.8
Comoros	85.9	91.0	74.1	69.4	75.9	39.6	13.6	8.4	25.2	29.5	23.0	59.0
Guinea-Bissau	7.9	9.8	27.7	3.6	3.0	0.4	92.1	90.2	72.3	96.4	97.0	99.6
Lao PDR	32.4	30.5	31.5	22.9	14.7	14.9	42.9	42.0	37.9	50.2	64.5	63.4
Liberia	81.4	74.4	68.7	75.6	55.5	44.3	18.6	25.6	31.3	24.4	44.5	55.7
Mauritania	74.1	70.7	67.3	72.6	53.9	48.8	24.5	27.7	31.1	25.9	44.9	49.9
São Tomé & Principe	88.9	83.9	67.1	84.4	87.2	77.5	11.1	16.1	32.9	15.6	12.8	22.5
Middle-income												
Commonwealth countries												
Belize	75.5	80.9	68.8	72.3	80.7	66.7	24.5	19.1	31.2	27.7	19.3	33.3
Dominica	50.3	38.3	39.9	37.4	33.4	15.4	49.5	61.4	59.7	62.2	66.2	84.2
Fiji Islands	69.1	66.5	63.3	60.0	54.7	49.0	20.1	21.8	22.2	23.1	25.9	28.5
Grenada	52.4	56.0	44.3	44.7	25.9	2.1	47.3	43.5	54.9	54.6	73.0	97.8
Guyana	78.9	78.3	76.5	69.8	67.4	67.5	19.2	19.4	20.8	27.1	29.1	28.7
Jamaica	85.4	82.8	78.0	82.5	77.0	86.1	14.3	17.0	21.9	17.4	22.7	13.6
Kiribati	–	–	–	–	–	–	–	–	–	–	–	–
Maldives	70.2	58.4	57.7	48.2	42.5	46.4	29.8	41.6	42.3	51.8	57.5	53.6
Mauritius	87.8	86.3	85.2	77.3	72.9	78.6	12.2	13.7	14.4	22.3	27.1	21.4
Nauru	–	–	–	–	–	–	–	–	–	–	–	–
St Kitts & Nevis	90.1	90.6	87.0	86.7	82.4	77.1	9.7	9.0	12.6	12.9	17.0	22.3
St Lucia	77.8	74.7	60.2	65.0	88.9	68.0	22.2	25.3	39.8	35.0	11.1	32.0
St Vincent & the Grenadines	79.6	44.1	40.3	36.7	76.8	73.3	20.4	21.8	59.7	63.3	23.2	26.7
Samoa	79.5	74.1	77.7	84.9	50.3	54.2	20.5	25.9	20.1	14.9	49.3	45.4
Seychelles	80.1	97.0	87.3	85.7	82.0	75.6	19.9	2.8	12.6	14.2	17.9	24.2
Tonga	91.2	92.5	65.5	87.4	79.3	77.3	8.8	7.5	34.4	12.3	20.3	22.2
Tuvalu	–	–	–	–	–	–	–	–	–	–	–	–
Vanuatu	16.7	16.1	20.8	17.8	17.0	14.4	82.9	83.5	78.9	82.0	82.7	85.3
Other countries												
Albania	94.5	94.3	90.8	93.4	91.9	87.5	5.4	5.7	9.1	6.6	8.1	12.5
Armenia	50.9	51.9	56.3	62.2	62.0	55.6	49.0	48	43.3	37.6	37.6	44.3
Bahrain	10.9	9.2	8.7	9.1	9.8	9.0	21.3	21.1	20.8	22.4	22.5	20.9
Bosnia-Herzegovina	74.7	74.5	66.7	62.9	61.1	63.6	25.3	25.5	33.3	37.1	38.9	36.4
Cape Verde	97.4	97.9	94.4	91.7	89.2	83.2	2.4	2.0	5.3	8.1	10.6	16.5
Congo Republic	36.4	29.3	20.2	35.3	41.6	47.3	63.6	70.7	70.4	63.1	57.0	50.7
Costa Rica	26.4	24.7	65.2	60.5	57.9	55.8	16.8	15.7	34.6	39.3	42.0	44.0
Djibouti	4.2	4.0	3.5	3.4	3.4	2.5	95.8	96.0	96.5	96.6	96.6	97.5
Estonia	64.2	65.2	70.0	67.8	58.2	59.6	33.2	34.4	29.3	31.7	41.2	39.7
Gabon	70.7	70.9	67.8	68.3	44.4	50.4	8.0	20.8	23.3	22.8	43.6	39
Georgia	28.8	27.4	22.7	25.4	28.5	43.3	71.2	72.6	77.3	74.5	71.2	56.6
Latvia	67.8	69.3	61.3	56.5	49.6	44.8	31.9	30.4	35.5	43.2	50.3	55.1
Lebanon	33.4	38.0	26.2	23.8	20.1	23.4	65.5	60.8	72.9	75.2	78.9	75.7
Lithuania	58.1	60.8	58.5	53.2	47.9	44.2	41.8	39.1	41.4	46.7	52.0	55.7
Macedonia FYR	63.2	63.7	61.3	55.4	55.7	56.0	36.8	36.3	38.7	44.5	44.3	44

Table 10. Destination of merchandise exports (continued)

Group/country	Industrial countries 2002	2003	2004	2005	2006	2007	Developing countries 2002	2003	2004	2005	2006	2007
	(percentage of total exports)											
Middle-income (contin.)												
Other countries												
Moldova	30.1	28.8	31.8	27.0	34.9	29.8	69.9	71.2	68.1	72.8	64.9	70.0
Mongolia	42.8	37.6	45.3	40.6	24.0	22.6	57.2	62.3	54.7	59.4	76.0	77.4
Montenegro	–	–	–	–	–	–	–	–	–	–	–	–
Oman	32.5	22.2	18.9	20.7	16.8	59.6	67.5	77.8	81.1	79.3	83.2	39.7
Panama	71.7	77.6	75.6	73.5	74.2	70.0	28.1	22.3	23.3	25.1	24.1	29.7
Suriname	82.5	80.3	84.5	83.4	77.5	79.2	17.5	19.7	15.5	16.6	22.4	20.8
Timor-Leste	–	–	–	–	–	–	–	–	–	–	–	–
Turkmenistan	23.7	21.9	9.5	8.8	7.9	7.3	73.4	70.2	88.7	89.8	90.5	91.0
Uruguay	34.5	39.6	45.0	45.4	37.3	34.3	64.4	58.8	51.6	50.5	58.6	61.6
High-income												
Commonwealth countries												
Antigua & Barbuda	–	–	–	–	–	–	–	–	–	–	–	–
Bahamas, The	78.2	73.5	70.4	78.7	70.7	55.6	21.6	26.3	29.4	21.1	29.1	44.2
Barbados	33.1	40.4	42.0	38.0	45.2	23.8	49.9	59.6	58.0	62.0	54.8	76.2
Brunei Darussalam	61.7	59.8	63.6	57.9	55.8	54.9	38.3	40.2	36.4	42.1	44.2	45.1
Cyprus	52.3	59.8	61.1	62.9	55.2	56.8	40.2	30.4	30.6	20.3	24.9	26.4
Malta	52.8	47.8	64.7	66.5	66.4	64.2	40.9	45.5	30.2	32.5	32.9	34.7
New Zealand	64.7	65.1	63.3	63.3	60.9	58.4	34.4	34.1	35.2	35.3	37.8	40.0
Singapore	38.7	38.8	38.1	35.6	31.2	29.4	61.0	60.9	61.6	64.0	68.5	70.3
Trinidad & Tobago	66.8	72.8	75.3	75.6	74.4	70.6	31.5	25.8	23.6	23.5	24.6	28.3
Other countries												
Croatia	64.1	69.0	67.2	63.9	64.5	59.7	30.4	26.3	27.3	30.7	27.7	28.5
Equatorial Guinea	78.0	83.5	61.3	65.9	56.1	66.4	22.0	16.5	38.7	34.1	43.9	33.6
Iceland	91.9	92.1	90.7	89.1	88.2	90.1	8.1	7.8	9.3	10.9	11.8	9.9
Ireland	88.1	89.9	89.5	89.5	88.0	87.2	10.0	9.5	10.0	10.1	11.6	12.3
Kuwait	46.8	43.6	43.1	42.9	40.8	39.3	53.2	56.4	56.9	57.1	59.2	60.7
Norway	90.2	90.4	90.9	91.1	90.3	89.5	9.8	9.6	9.1	8.9	9.6	10.4
Qatar	50.3	50.6	47.4	45.8	50.3	48.4	37.9	42.9	45.0	46.9	42.5	51.6
Slovenia	64.6	64.4	63.2	61.5	60.3	57.3	35.4	35.6	36.8	38.4	39.7	42.7
United Arab Emirates	37.1	37.9	36.3	38.0	34.4	32.8	46.7	46.8	48.8	47.5	50.3	50.7
Group averages (Commonwealth countries only)												
Low-income	48.5	41.2	36.6	29.1	34.4	31.1	51.5	58.8	60.9	68.6	63.1	66.6
n	3	3	3	3	3	3	3	3	3	3	3	3
Middle-income	72.3	69.1	63.5	63.8	62.1	56.8	26.8	27.6	35.0	34.7	36.2	41.3
n	15	15	15	15	15	15	15	15	15	15	15	15
High-income	56.0	57.3	59.8	59.8	57.5	51.7	39.7	40.4	38.1	37.6	39.6	45.7
n	8	8	8	8	8	8	8	8	8	8	8	8
Under 0.5 mn population	65.9	62.9	59.3	60.5	59.8	51.3	32.4	34.2	40.0	39.2	39.9	48.5
n	15	15	15	15	15	15	15	15	15	15	15	15
Over 0.5 mn population	65.1	63.3	61.0	57.3	56.1	55.8	32.4	33.8	35.1	37.7	38.2	38.5
n	9	9	9	9	9	9	9	9	9	9	9	9

Notes: – = not available; n = number of countries. Percentages for the two groups do not add up to 100 because the distribution of some exports has not been specified.

Source: International Monetary Fund, *Direction of Trade Statistics Yearbook 2008*, Washington, DC

Table 11. Destination of merchandise exports to selected regions

Group/country	European Union 2003	2004	2005	2006	2007	NAFTA 2004	2005	2006	2007	Japan 2004	2005	2006	2007
	(percentage of total exports)												
Low-income													
Commonwealth countries													
Gambia, The	44.4	46.3	17.9	35.5	28.0	2.4	0.8	0.7	0.5	2.4	1.5	1.9	2.6
Papua New Guinea	10.1	10.0	8.7	7.3	7.7	1.2	1.1	1.3	1.5	5.8	8.6	8.2	9.5
Solomon Islands	2.5	0.0	8.5	5.6	7.4	1.8	1.0	1.3	0.9	7.6	6.4	9.0	5.8
Other countries													
Central African Republic	77.0	87.1	65.6	62.8	51.2	7.9	4.7	3.5	3.3	2.0	1.7	0.9	1.6
Comoros	71.9	29.4	48.8	71.9	43.3	4.4	6.0	6.3	3.3	2.9	14.6	0.3	0.0
Guinea-Bissau	8.1	5.2	3.4	2.3	0.5	22.4	0.2	0.3	0.0	0.0	0.1	0.0	0.0
Lao PDR	26.2	28.5	19.7	10.6	12.3	1.9	1.4	1.2	2.0	1.3	1.1	1.0	0.8
Liberia	67.5	75.6	70.8	56.0	102.2	9.7	10.5	12.4	28.0	0.0	0.0	0.8	0.0
Mauritania	57.5	54.1	58.9	44.3	42.7	0.9	0.1	3.5	0.1	13.1	12.3	5.5	5.5
Nicaragua	10.9	10.5	13.3	6.4	13.4	43.0	43.0	71.5	42.3	0.8	1.2	0.4	1.1
São Tomé & Principe	66.7	70.0	83.3	92.5	62.5	0.0	1.7	3.1	0.0	0.0	0.7	0.4	0.0
Timor-Leste	–	–	–	–	–	–	–	–	–	–	–	–	–
Togo	17.3	21.5	9.1	23.8	24.7	0.5	1.1	0.9	1.0	0.0	0.0	0.0	0.0
Middle-income													
Commonwealth countries													
Antigua & Barbuda	–	–	–	–	–	–	–	–		–	–	–	–
Barbados	18.7	14.0	16.5	14.2	12.8	17.3	21.2	30.2	11.8	0.0	0.0	0.1	0.3
Belize	37.1	33.2	39.2	452.2	32.9	41.5	35.9	37.8	33.7	3.2	2.4	1.2	1.7
Dominica	23.1	45.0	30.2	28.7	12.3	10.0	4.7	3.2	2.6	10.0	2.3	1.1	1.8
Fiji Islands	15.4	13.6	13.4	14.2	12.5	24.5	20.4	17.7	19.9	4.1	5.4	5.2	4.1
Grenada	36.2	25.0	31.3	10.5	0.9	15.0	12.5	13.2	1.4	0.0	0.0	0.3	0.0
Guyana	32.8	36.3	30.9	29.0	31.3	47.0	37.8	37.1	35.6	0.5	0.6	1.0	0.7
Jamaica	33.1	32.3	29.9	24.3	26.1	41.4	45.4	46.1	52.5	2.5	1.0	1.5	1.3
Kiribati	–	–	–	–	–	–	–	–	–	–	–	–	–
Maldives	15.2	19.7	24.2	30.3	36.8	27.0	1.0	1.8	3.1	11.5	23.2	10.2	6.7
Mauritius	66.2	65.8	65.4	63.0	69.3	14.6	9.8	8.6	8.1	0.8	0.8	0.8	0.5
St Kitts & Nevis	20.0	22.9	16.9	10.1	7.1	67.1	68.7	71.4	72.6	1.4	0.1	1.5	0.0
St Lucia	48.0	43.9	45.7	78.8	43.6	17.1	18.9	10.4	26.3	0.0	0.0	0.0	0.0
St Vincent & the Grenadines	5.9	35.1	27.5	74.6	74.7	5.4	10.0	1.1	1.3	0.0	0.0	0.0	0.3
Samoa	3.0	4.3	0.2	0.8	0.3	5.3	6.4	3.8	3.7	1.1	0.4	0.7	0.2
Seychelles	95.8	77.7	74.4	69.7	74.7	2.5	1.9	3.7	1.3	8.4	9.6	8.3	0.3
Tonga	3.6	8.8	5.3	1.4	5.6	38.2	36.8	40.9	38.9	50.0	42.1	27.3	22.2
Trinidad & Tobago	6.8	6.2	5.2	11.3	8.8	70.9	72.7	64.8	63.7	0.2	0.0	1.3	1.5
Vanuatu	3.0	0.0	14.5	3.4	1.7	0.0	2.6	1.0	0.4	0.0	6.8	11.4	11.4
Other countries													
Albania													
Armenia													
Bahrain	3.6	2.9	3.9	3.2	4.0	2.9	2.6	3.4	2.6	1.8	1.8	2.3	1.6
Bosnia-Herzegovina													
Cape Verde	79.3	76.2	80.8	86.5	76.7	19.0	7.7	2.7	6.7	0.0	0.0	0.0	0.0
Congo Republic	12.7	11.9	6.2	5.6	5.3	7.4	28.7	36.0	41.1	0.0	0.0	0.0	0.1
Costa Rica	15.4	17.1	16.3	25.3	25.1	50.3	46.0	35.8	33.0	0.7	0.7	1.9	1.8
Djibouti	3.7	3.2	2.9	2.4	1.4	0.4	0.4	0.9	0.9	0.0	0.1	0.1	0.0
Equatorial Guinea	38.1	23.4	30.2	26.5	35.5	35.9	31.9	25.0	23.4	0.0	3.3	3.9	6.5
Estonia	55.7	69.4	77.6	65.6	69.8	3.5	3.9	6.1	5.1	0.3	0.3	0.6	0.5
Gabon	5.3	4.9	12.7	14.8	15.1	53.3	52.7	27.6	32.6	0.2	0.2	1.5	2.2

Table 11. Destination of merchandise exports to selected regions
(continued)

Group/country	European Union 2003	2004	2005	2006	2007	NAFTA 2004	2005	2006	2007	2004	Japan 2005	2006	2007
	(percentage of total exports)												
Middle-income (contin.)													
Other countries													
Georgia													
Latvia													
Lebanon													
Lithuania													
Macedonia FYR													
Moldova													
Mongolia													
Montenegro													
Oman	2.1	3.1	2.8	2.0	1.8	3.2	3.1	3.7	4.4	11.5	14.2	10.9	14.3
Panama	9.6	25.4	28.2	33.6	33.7	52.3	46.9	41.2	36.7	0.2	0.4	0.4	0.4
Suriname	31.8	22.9	23.4	21.6	21.1	27.7	32.6	28.1	35.7	1.4	1.2	0.6	0.6
Turkmenistan													
Uruguay	23.4	23.2	17.6	20.4	19.7	24.6	25.7	19.7	17.7	1.7	0.9	2.6	1.7
High-income													
Commonwealth countries													
Bahamas, The	30.9	37.6	52.7	56.7	41.7	45.5	34.3	22.1	24.0	0.1	0.0	3.8	0.1
Brunei Darussalam	0.3	2.6	1.1	5.3	1.2	8.7	9.6	13.9	5.5	38.1	36.8	54.7	32.8
Cyprus	56.4	58.8	60.5	55.4	55.6	1.8	1.8	0.9	0.9	2.0	1.5	1.2	1.4
Malta	33.6	47.2	50.8	49.7	47.4	16.1	15.4	13.5	11.8	2.9	2.0	4.9	4.7
New Zealand	15.4	15.0	15.1	15.3	13.9	17.5	17.3	16.0	14.6	21.0	10.6	10.3	9.2
Singapore	14.2	14.5	13.3	11.3	10.7	13.8	12.2	10.8	9.9	6.4	6.0	5.5	4.8
Other countries													
Croatia													
Iceland	73.4	75.2	76.4	71.0	74.5	10.2	9.1	11.4	7.7	3.0	3.3	2.1	4.3
Ireland	62.3	62.5	63.4	63.5	6.3	20.6	19.6	19.6	18.9	2.8	2.7	2.3	2.0
Kuwait	9.9	7.7	11.4	10.9	10.2	12.4	13.2	9.1	8.4	20.5	21.5	20.4	19.9
Norway	75.8	78.2	80.7	82.2	81.0	12.5	10.7	8.9	9.1	1.2	1.0	1.0	1.0
Qatar	2.1	2.7	5.4	7.2	6.0	1.5	1.9	0.9	1.2	41.9	37.0	40.5	39.9
Slovenia													
United Arab Emirates	7.4	8.4	11.2	5.9	6.1	1.8	1.6	1.3	1.1	24.8	24.6	25.8	23.6
Group averages (Commonwealth countries only)													
Low-income	19.0	18.8	11.7	16.1	14.4	1.8	0.9	1.1	1.0	5.3	5.5	6.3	6.0
n	3	3	3	3	3	3	3	3	3	3	3	3	3
Middle-income	27.3	28.5	27.7	53.9	26.5	26.2	23.9	23.1	22.2	5.5	5.6	4.2	3.1
n	17	17	17	17	17	17	17	17	17	17	17	17	17
High-income	25.2	29.3	32.2	32.3	28.4	17.2	15.1	12.9	11.1	11.8	9.5	13.4	8.8
n	6	6	6	6	6	6	6	6	6	6	6	6	6
Under 0.5 mn population	25.0	27.8	28.7	59.1	26.2	21.1	18.7	17.9	15.9	8.4	8.4	8.4	5.5
n	15	15	15	15	15	15	15	15	15	15	15	15	15
Over 0.5 mn population	29.8	29.9	26.7	27.3	27.4	22.8	21.2	19.8	20.4	2.9	2.9	3.3	3.1
n	9	9	9	9	9	9	9	9	9	9	9	9	9

Notes: – = not available; n = number of countries.

Source: International Monetary Fund, *Direction of Trade Statistics Yearbook 2008*, Washington, DC

Table 12. Main sources of merchandise imports

Group/country	Industrial countries						Developing countries					
	2002	2003	2004	2005	2006	2007	2002	2003	2004	2005	2006	2007
	(percentage of total imports)											
Low-income												
Commonwealth countries												
Gambia, The	35.8	34.1	29.0	28.7	24.7	22.0	64.2	64.9	71.0	71.3	74.6	78
Papua New Guinea	64.2	61.3	61.1	68.5	59.0	66.2	34.2	37.0	36.9	29.7	30.2	31.9
Solomon Islands	43.3	41.8	41.1	39.5	41.0	39.0	56.7	58.2	57.5	59.3	48.8	59.9
Other countries												
Central African Republic	54.8	43.6	48.1	43.4	50.0	44.2	20.9	29.7	24.5	27.9	23.5	27.1
Comoros	52.9	56.3	38.7	35.7	39.9	28.2	46.2	42.9	60.2	63.1	58.7	70.2
Guinea-Bissau	42.1	40.1	42.0	55.1	49.0	45.0	46.1	48.8	41.8	33.1	35.5	39
Lao PDR	11.2	9.0	12.0	8.5	5.7	7.8	87.0	89.2	86.0	89.6	92.4	90.4
Liberia	49.4	38.5	32.6	31.4	23.4	25.7	50.6	61.5	67.4	68.6	76.7	74.3
Mauritania	57.3	59.6	58.2	59.5	51.1	50.3	34.7	32.0	31.7	31.0	48.5	38.9
São Tomé & Principe	92.3	90.3	86.4	82.1	86.7	86.2	7.7	9.7	13.6	17.9	13.3	13.8
Middle-income												
Commonwealth countries												
Belize	52.6	60.1	46.6	49.4	47.9	45.6	42.2	34.4	46.1	44.7	44.4	45.9
Dominica	41.8	41.4	39.2	42.8	39.7	45.7	58.0	58.3	60.4	56.8	60.3	53.9
Fiji Islands	64.7	62.8	57.9	53.5	50.0	47.9	34.2	36.1	40.9	45.3	48.7	50.4
Grenada	49.0	51.2	47.4	48.3	42.4	41.9	51.0	48.8	52.6	51.7	57.9	58.1
Guyana	49.1	54.5	42.9	44.4	40.1	38.1	45.4	39.0	48.7	47.4	50.8	52.9
Jamaica	65.8	64.2	57.9	57.4	55.5	47.8	32.0	33.4	39.7	41.0	43.0	50.6
Kiribati	–	–	–	–	–	–	–	–	–	–	–	
Maldives	18.5	20.7	19.2	21.7	17.1	46.9	81.5	79.2	80.6	78.2	80.6	53
Mauritius	40.2	39.8	38.4	39.0	40.4	37.0	59.8	60.1	61.4	60.9	59.6	62.9
Nauru	–	–	–	–	–	–	–	–	–	–	–	–
St Kitts & Nevis	75.3	76.6	38.2	71.6	71.3	69.9	24.6	23.2	61.6	28.1	27.4	29.9
St Lucia	31.3	57.1	56.2	65.1	73.2	21.4	68.5	42.7	43.6	34.7	38.8	78.4
St Vincent & the Grenadines	65.8	68.3	61.2	57.7	52.8	46.9	34.2	31.7	38.8	42.3	47.2	53.1
Samoa	61.0	55.2	47.7	76.0	47.8	43.8	38.4	44.3	51.5	23.9	51.5	55.3
Seychelles	50.5	44.0	45.9	41.5	36.1	42.8	49.5	45.0	43.2	49.5	53.6	46.8
Tonga	66.4	69.3	59.0	60.3	57.6	48.7	33.6	30.7	40.9	39.6	42.5	51.2
Tuvalu	–	–	–	–	–	–	–	–	–	–	–	–
Vanuatu	54.4	34.8	43.6	50.1	56.8	54.6	43.6	63.7	54.4	48.0	41.0	43
Other countries												
Albania	75.7	72.5	71.1	64.8	61.7	63.0	24.3	27.5	28.9	35.1	38.3	36.9
Armenia	33.3	38.2	36.6	37.6	35.1	36.8	66.6	61.0	63.2	62.2	64.9	63.1
Bahrain	48.1	47.3	45.1	37.8	38.8	37.5	51.4	52.2	54.4	61.7	60.7	61.9
Bosnia-Herzegovina	58.6	56.3	57.6	54.3	52.8	52.3	41.4	43.7	42.4	45.7	47.2	47.7
Cape Verde	82.1	80.3	82.6	77.5	74.9	76.4	16.4	18.1	15.6	20.6	23.0	21.9
Congo Republic	55.6	52.0	68.8	58.2	39.9	50.9	34.0	36.9	29.5	41.4	58.7	48.9
Costa Rica	49.4	39.8	64.1	61.6	61.0	59.5	22.8	27.3	35.3	37.8	38.8	39.7
Djibouti	36.9	29.8	27.2	20.6	21.0	20.5	60.5	67.5	69.5	76.6	76.4	76.8
Estonia	62.5	61.3	65.7	64.1	58.7	60.3	37.5	38.7	34.3	35.9	40.1	39.6
Gabon	83.3	81.2	79.7	74.9	72.2	73.6	16.1	18.2	19.6	24.3	27.0	25.6
Georgia	38.9	45.5	39.5	32.0	29.2	28.2	60.8	54.3	60.4	68.0	70.8	71.8
Latvia	58.5	56.8	49.6	47.8	49.7	48.7	40.8	42.7	47.9	52.1	50.3	51.3
Lebanon	61.3	63.7	57.1	52.4	51.9	48.6	36.6	34.2	40.6	45.0	45.4	48.5
Lithuania	53.6	53.1	49.4	45.1	45.5	49.1	44.8	45.6	50.6	54.9	54.4	50.9
Macedonia FYR	57.6	55.0	49.6	45.3	42.9	51.6	42.4	45.0	50.4	54.7	57.0	48.4
Moldova	33.4	32.9	29.7	29.7	25.7	25.9	66.0	67.1	70.3	70.1	74.2	74.0

Table 12. Main sources of merchandise imports (continued)

Group/country	Industrial countries						Developing countries					
	2002	2003	2004	2005	2006	2007	2002	2003	2004	2005	2006	2007
	(percentage of total imports)											
Middle-income (contin.)												
Other countries												
Mongolia	20.4	25.3	23.2	21.0	21.5	18.1	79.6	74.7	76.8	79.0	76.8	80.4
Montenegro	–	–	–	–	–	–	–	–	–	–	–	–
Oman	52.2	48.5	55.3	50.1	48.2	51.6	47.8	51.5	44.7	49.9	51.8	48.4
Panama	48.3	56.8	42.4	40.4	39.8	46.9	37.4	40.3	41.6	54.5	43.7	52.7
Suriname	61.9	68.9	65.1	64.7	63.2	62.9	37.6	30.5	34.1	34.6	36.1	36.3
Timor-Leste	–	–	–	–	–	–	–	–	–	–	–	–
Turkmenistan	17.4	15.1	34.4	26.7	24.3	22.0	68.3	78.8	65.3	73.0	75.4	77.7
Uruguay	31.4	24.4	21.6	19.6	28.8	26.8	68.6	75.6	78.2	80.3	71.2	73.1
High-income												
Commonwealth countries												
Antigua & Barbuda	–	–	–	–	–	–	–	–	–	–	–	–.
Bahamas, The	61.3	54.8	49.2	46.0	53.6	59.9	37.4	43.6	48.5	52.4	43.66	37.9
Barbados	67.3	64.7	62.6	61.5	61.1	56.0	32.7	35.3	37.4	38.4	38.8	43.8
Brunei Darussalam	37.7	36.9	28.6	21.9	29.1	57.9	62.1	62.9	71.2	77.9	70.8	42.0
Cyprus	51.3	67.2	72.4	70.6	69.8	71.4	44.8	28.0	26.0	27.8	28.7	28.3
Malta	67.3	69.7	81.2	83.7	77.2	80.2	32.7	30.3	18.7	16.3	22.7	19.7
New Zealand	70.2	68.3	67.1	63.6	60.1	58.6	29.3	31.7	32.8	36.3	39.8	41.4
Singapore	43.0	42.7	40.9	37.8	35.0	35.8	56.8	57.2	58.7	61.3	64.52	64.2
Trinidad & Tobago	58.7	59.3	61.2	50.2	50.1	48.7	41.2	40.5	38.7	49.7	48.5	51.2
Other countries												
Croatia	70.2	70.3	67.0	63.1	62.1	60.9	28.7	28.8	31.6	35.6	36.1	37.2
Equatorial Guinea	79.8	85.7	84.1	82.1	72.7	69.7	7.8	14.3	15.9	17.9	27.0	30.3
Iceland	79.6	78.5	81.4	79.6	80.9	80.9	20.4	21.5	18.6	20.4	19.06	19.1
Ireland	84.8	82.6	82.9	83.9	82.3	82.9	11.7	14.8	14.5	13.9	15.3	15.0
Kuwait	64.7	65.1	63.4	61.2	56.7	55.5	35.3	34.9	36.6	38.8	43.3	44.5
Norway	81.2	79.3	78.3	76.7	75.9	75.8	18.8	20.7	21.7	23.3	24.0	24.2
Qatar	71.1	61.6	63.4	64.8	83.8	66.2	28.9	38.4	36.0	34.7	15.3	33.7
Slovenia	74.3	73.5	78.7	72.9	71.1	66.9	25.6	26.5	21.2	27.1	28.8	32.8
United Arab Emirates	57.8	53.1	47.8	50.1	49.0	46.7	42.2	46.9	51.6	49.3	50.5	52.8
Group averages (Commonwealth countries only)												
Low-income	47.8	45.7	43.7	45.6	41.6	42.4	51.7	53.4	55.1	53.4	51.2	56.6
n	3	3	3	3	3	3	3	3	3	3	3	3
Middle-income	52.4	53.3	46.8	51.9	48.6	45.3	46.4	44.7	51.0	46.1	49.8	52.4
n	15	15	15	15	15	15	15	15	15	15	15	15
High-income	57.1	58.0	57.9	54.4	54.5	58.6	42.1	41.2	41.5	45.0	44.7	41.1
n	8	8	8	8	8	8	8	8	8	8	8	8
Under 0.5 mn population	53.3	53.7	48.4	53.2	50.9	50.8	46.0	44.9	50.0	45.5	48.1	47.5
n	15	15	15	15	15	15	15	15	15	15	15	15
Over 0.5 mn population	52.6	53.9	51.3	50.2	47.8	46.5	45.8	44.1	46.8	48.0	48.1	51.8
n	9	9	9	9	9	9	9	9	9	9	9	9

Notes: – = not available; n = number of countries.

Source: International Monetary Fund, *Direction of Trade Statistics Yearbook 2007*, Washington, DC

Table 13. Merchandise imports by selected regions

Group/country	European Union					NAFTA					Japan				
	2003	2004	2005	2006	2007	2003	2004	2005	2006	2007	2003	2004	2005	2006	2007
	(percentage share in imports)														
Low-income															
Commonwealth countries															
Gambia, The	22.7	23.8	22.1	20.7	18.7	3.4	4.5	5.3	3.4	2.7	0.7	0.7	0.6	0.7	0.6
Papua New Guinea	2.9	2.6	2.0	2.7	3.2	2.6	3.2	3.3	2.3	2.7	3.5	4.3	54.7	4.3	5.7
Solomon Islands	2.6	2.8	3.7	9.5	2.5	1.7	2.1	1.1	5.7	4.3	3.4	3.4	25.9	17.1	4.6
Other countries															
Central African Republic	36.8	30.0	36.0	40.3	37.2	5.3	16.7	7.6	9.4	6.5	1.3	1.0	0.4	0.3	0.6
Comoros	41.9	41.7	95.7	39.2	29.5	0.9	0.9	2.1	0.7	0.6	13.7	0.9	0.9	1.4	0.6
Guinea-Bissau	38.2	31.3	53.5	45.5	41.3	1.4	0.6	0.9	3.0	3.3	0.7	0.0	0.1	0.1	0.4
Liberia	18.3	10.8	29.1	51.5	39.0	1.0	1.5	4.9	4.9	4.2	16.2	21.2	67.4	54.8	58.1
Mauritania	50.4	46.2	48.2	42.4	42.3	4.1	8.0	7.2	7.1	6.6	4.3	2.8	2.3	1.2	1.1
São Tomé & Principe	85.5	77.3	64.1	92.8	74.1	3.2	6.1	17.2	5.8	11.7	0.5	3.0	1.6	0.2	0.0
Middle-income															
Commonwealth countries															
Belize	14.0	9.7	16.9	10.3	13.0	55.3	42.9	43.4	50.1	45.8	3.3	4.1	1.4	1.1	0.6
Dominica	13.2	16.2	9.4	10.5	9.2	21.5	19.1	27.2	27.4	26.0	6.3	4.3	4.5	2.0	11.0
Fiji Islands	2.8	4.0	4.5	4.3	3.4	2.7	2.5	2.7	2.4	2.4	4.9	3.9	3.5	3.3	2.8
Grenada	13.6	12.0	14.7	12.2	13.5	31.6	30.1	28.9	26.2	25.4	4.4	3.6	3.8	2.6	2.3
Guyana	26.0	12.6	10.6	12.6	10.9	23.8	26.8	26.9	23.8	23.9	2.8	3.0	3.1	3.3	2.7
Jamaica	16.4	12.8	7.4	8.5	6.2	44.6	44.9	45.9	43.0	5.1	4.2	4.7	4.6	3.8	3.1
Kiribati	–	–	–	–	–	–	–	–	–	–	–	–	–	–	–
Maldives	11.3	10.4	14.2	10.1	7.2	2.8	2.6	1.9	2.8	36.5	2.1	1.9	1.8	2.6	0.9
Mauritius	28.1	26.5	30.7	34.6	27.0	2.8	2.5	2.3	2.2	2.5	3.5	4.1	3.6	2.8	3.6
Nauru	–	–	–	–	–	–	–	–	–	–	–	–	–	–	–
St Kitts & Nevis	30.9	12.3	18.2	16.6	15.6	40.2	23.5	49.3	51.7	55.8	2.8	2.2	4.4	3.7	3.2
St Lucia	15.0	20.5	35.7	38.8	8.4	38.1	29.8	25.6	22.8	11.3	2.5	3.2	2.9	3.2	1.5
St Vincent & the Grenadines	54.7	16.4	14.9	37.6	27.6	11.2	40.4	37.8	12.8	15.1	1.6	3.6	4.1	2.4	3.9
Samoa	2.8	1.1	1.4	2.5	1.7	4.7	4.9	13.6	6.5	5.5	11.9	7.7	7.5	8.6	6.9
Seychelles	39.4	43.8	37.8	33.8	40.5	1.2	2.2	3.1	1.4	1.2	1.2	0.9	0.8	1.4	1.8
Tonga	6.1	4.1	5.5	12.2	2.5	7.1	6.6	8.6	8.6	9.9	2.0	2.5	10.2	1.4	1.9
Tuvalu	–	–	–	–	–	–	–	–	–	–	–	–	–	–	–
Vanuatu	2.3	4.3	12.3	3.7	3.9	0.9	4.3	4.1	4.1	8.5	10.6	11.2	16.8	19.9	1.9
Other countries															
Albania	71.7	68.4	64.1	61.4	58.8	1.2	1.7	1.7	1.3	1.4	0.4	0.5	0.4	0.4	0.5
Armenia	27.4	25.4	28.1	28.3	30.0	7.5	7.3	7.3	5.4	4.8	1.3	0.9	1.3	1.8	3.2
Bahrain	24.1	27.6	22.7	23.0	20.7	11.7	5.9	5.8	6.6	6.7	7.8	7.3	6.6	6.8	7.2
Bosnia-Herzegovina	68.4	67.5	64.4	60.9	61.2	0.6	0.7	0.4	1.0	0.4	0.0	0.0	0.1	0.0	0.1
Cape Verde	76.6	69.5	75.6	73.2	75.4	2.7	12.3	2.4	2.4	0.8	0.8	0.2	0.0	0.0	0.1
Congo Republic	42.8	53.1	49.3	42.5	42.6	7.1	10.4	8.2	7.8	5.3	0.7	3.4	0.5	0.5	0.3
Costa Rica	12.1	10.6	13.1	13.7	11.8	20.9	52.2	47.1	47.1	47.8	3.2	5.9	5.6	4.9	5.4
Djibouti	21.4	17.2	12.2	14.4	14.3	4.9	5.0	4.5	3.6	3.5	3.3	3.4	4.2	3.2	4.2
Equatorial Guinea	48.6	41.2	55.8	33.7	49.2	30.9	26.9	24.7	37.9	19.8	0.3	1.0	0.5	1.1	0.6
Estonia	62.0	77.7	75.9	74.2	78.4	3.3	0.1	1.6	1.3	1.4	4.1	1.4	2.0	1.1	0.8
Gabon	72.7	70.3	7.0	61.0	51.5	5.5	6.9	64.3	8.6	19.9	2.5	1.7	2.7	2.5	2.0
Georgia	37.7	33.4	24.8	25.8	23.7	8.1	6.2	6.2	3.9	5.3	0.2	0.3	0.3	1.1	1.8
Latvia	75.4	73.0	75.1	76.4	77.3	2.0	1.5	1.3	1.1	1.3	0.2	0.1	0.0	0.2	0.4
Lebanon	54.9	47.3	42.7	38.4	36.5	4.9	5.9	5.8	10.0	7.6	2.1	2.1	1.8	1.7	2.6
Lithuania	56.4	63.2	59.2	62.6	68.1	3.2	1.7	2.1	1.7	2.3	2.2	0.4	0.3	0.3	0.0

Table 13. Merchandise imports by selected regions (continued)

Group/country	European Union					NAFTA					Japan				
	2003	2004	2005	2006	2007	2003	2004	2005	2006	2007	2003	2004	2005	2006	2007
	(percentage share in imports)														
Middle-income (contin.)															
Other countries															
Macedonia FYR	53.2	49.8	45.5	43.9	57.9	2.6	2.0	2.1	2.1	1.2	0.8	0.8	0.7	0.7	0.1
Moldova	36.0	32.9	32.8	32.7	32.2	2.5	1.8	1.9	1.0	1.3	0.8	0.9	0.9	0.1	0.1
Mongolia	13.3	11.0	9.8	7.5	10.5	3.4	5.3	4.6	2.6	1.7	7.9	7.4	7.1	11.9	7.2
Montenegro	–	–	–	–	–	–	–	–	–	–	–	–	–	–	–
Panama	10.6	7.7	7.0	6.8	7.5	13.6	33.9	31.7	27.6	36.9	33.2	6.0	4.5	4.7	5.1
Suriname	29.8	30.5	29.1	27.4	29.3	32.2	27.7	31.5	30.5	28.5	6.4	6.5	5.1	5.1	5.1
Timor-Leste	–	–	–	–	–	–	–	–	–	–	–	–	–	–	–
Turkmenistan	12.1	20.6	16.5	17.6	14.5	1.9	12.4	10.8	5.1	5.8	0.1	2.1	0.6	2.1	2.8
Uruguay	13.4	15.1	11.0	17.7	14.3	9.0	10.1	8.8	9.7	11.2	1.3	1.6	1.1	1.2	1.2
High-income															
Commonwealth countries															
Antigua & Barbuda	–	–	–	–	–	–	–	–	–	–	–	–	–	–	–
Bahamas, The	26.7	14.8	22.4	14.9	18.6	21.4	23.1	20.7	25.2	27.9	5.6	7.9	2.5	13.0	13.5
Barbados	19.7	18.7	12.6	13.8	16.1	18.7	23.0	41.5	42.3	34.9	28.0	30.6	0.9	3.7	3.3
Brunei Darussalam	10.7	15.5	9.8	14.6	85.0	11.6	3.5	3.5	3.5	6.9	9.9	7.3	6.9	5.6	6.0
Cyprus	55.6	64.8	67.0	67.5	67.9	4.4	2.6	1.7	1.7	1.4	5.6	4.7	2.8	2.5	2.6
Malta	58.0	72.3	75.0	67.7	72.9	4.3	5.4	5.8	6.0	4.2	5.6	2.5	1.7	2.2	2.0
New Zealand	19.6	20.0	18.9	16.6	16.8	14.0	13.4	12.6	13.8	11.4	11.8	11.2	1.1	9.2	9.5
Singapore	12.5	13.5	12.2	11.4	12.3	14.7	13.4	82.6	13.3	13.1	12.5	11.7	10.1	8.3	8.2
Other countries															
Croatia	71.8	69.5	65.8	65.4	63.3	0.0	0.0	0.0	0.0	0.0	0.0	0.0	0.0	0.0	0.0
Iceland	56.9	61.2	61.9	57.8	60.5	8.4	11.3	10.7	15.6	15.5	3.8	3.9	4.7	4.1	3.7
Ireland	59.6	63.2	64.6	66.5	67.8	17.3	14.6	14.5	12.3	12.0	3.8	3.0	2.7	1.8	1.6
Kuwait	33.9	37.2	34.2	30.4	30.4	15.3	13.5	14.9	14.7	13.8	10.3	7.9	8.4	7.8	8.5
Norway	66.9	70.8	69.1	69.1	68.4	7.3	7.3	7.7	8.2	9.2	3.6	3.4	3.2	2.7	2.2
Oman	20.8	29.0	24.8	20.9	23.0	6.6	5.4	7.0	8.6	8.1	17.1	16.6	15.8	16.5	17.6
Qatar	35.1	45.5	40.7	44.8	41.6	13.1	10.0	11.1	9.9	14.0	10.5	5.2	1.0	10.2	8.9
Trinidad & Tobago	19.4	30.0	12.6	12.5	12.7	35.0	26.8	32.5	35.1	32.5	4.3	3.5	5.5	3.8	3.6
United Arab Emirates	34.4	33.1	33.8	29.8	28.7	7.3	6.5	9.9	12.2	9.7	7.2	6.8	5.4	5.8	6.1
Group averages (Commonwealth countries only)															
Low-income	9.4	9.7	9.3	11.0	8.1	2.6	3.2	3.2	3.8	3.2	2.6	2.8	27.1	7.4	3.6
n	3	3	3	3	3	3	3	3	3	3	3	3	3	3	3
Middle-income	18.4	13.8	15.6	16.6	12.7	19.2	18.9	21.4	19.0	18.3	4.3	4.0	4.9	4.1	3.2
n	15	15	15	15	15	15	15	15	15	15	15	15	15	15	15
High-income	28.9	31.4	31.1	29.5	41.4	12.7	12.0	24.1	15.1	14.3	11.3	10.9	3.7	6.4	6.4
n	7	7	7	7	7	7	7	7	7	7	7	7	7	7	7
Under 0.5 mn population	21.2	18.1	20.1	20.0	22.4	18.0	17.4	21.0	19.4	21.0	6.5	6.2	4.7	4.9	4.0
n	15	15	15	15	15	15	15	15	15	15	15	15	15	15	15
Over 0.5 mn population	19.6	18.8	18.5	20.1	17.5	10.8	11.1	11.2	10.6	5.6	3.6	3.6	12.4	4.7	3.2
n	8	8	8	8	8	8	8	8	8	8	8	8	8	8	8

Notes: – = not available; 0.0 = figure less than 0.1 per cent.

Source: International Monetary Fund, *Direction of Trade Statistics Yearbook 2008*, Washington, DC

Table 14. Merchandise trade with Commonwealth countries

Group/country	2001	2002	2003	2004	2005	2006	2007	2001	2002	2003	2004	2005	2006	2007
	(percentage of total exports)							(percentage of total imports)						
Low-income														
Commonwealth countries														
Gambia, The	56.0	37.9	40.0	41.5	71.8	59.5	51.5	14.0	16.4	14.8	15.0	15.0	15.9	14.5
Papua New Guinea	29.6	29.3	31.5	39.4	33.8	33.9	35.6	59.7	78.5	75.5	77.5	78.3	67.0	79.2
Solomon Islands	13.8	13.3	23.2	9.9	8.1	8.4	10.7	62.1	70.0	67.5	69.0	64.6	60.6	42.1
Other countries														
Central African Republic	10.8	1.2	1.6	2.3	1.7	1.8	5.9	10.0	6.5	12.5	13.8	13.0	12.8	36.1
Comoros	16.2	13.8	6.3	17.6	20.8	9.4	1.3	28.0	27.0	26.5	33.0	36.4	30.1	36.5
Guinea-Bissau	46.0	50.8	88.9	65.5	89.5	94.7	41.8	19.3	17.9	16.7	4.5	5.2	8.0	6.3
Lao PDR	3.5	4.3	4.4	6.5	5.0	3.07	6.4	8.6	7.3	5.7	5.2	6.5	5.2	4.5
Liberia	2.4	2.2	4.3	4.5	10.0	21.5	34.5	9.2	0.6	13.3	13.7	15.9	16.9	23.6
Mauritania	5.0	5.2	8.2	7.1	7.9	6.1	6.8	4.8	6.5	9.5	10.5	14.6	11.1	9.8
Nicaragua	4.4	4.4	4.1	7.5	4.4	4.2	14.9	1.7	1.4	1.3	1.7	1.2	2.8	1.2
São Tomé & Principe	9.1	12.5	25.0	10.0	11.1	11.1	8.8	11.3	8.5	11.3	7.6	12.5	6.3	3.7
Togo	32.3	30.9	26.4	29.2	35.4	29.6	28.4	29.0	11.8	13.9	5.9	14.2	17.1	7.1
Middle-income														
Commonwealth countries														
Belize	22.3	33.2	33.9	40.4	39.3	53.8	29.0	9.2	9.6	10.3	11.7	8.7	9.3	9.7
Dominica	79.5	75.4	76.9	73.0	70.1	72.3	69.8	44.3	28.6	31.7	10.2	31.3	32.9	36.2
Fiji Islands	48.0	49.0	49.6	49.1	49.7	50.4	48.0	58.0	63.0	77.5	76.4	76.2	76.2	204.7
Grenada	22.1	29.8	51.1	47.5	52.1	68.4	97.3	41.0	41.6	43.2	46.0	45.1	49.4	5.9
Guyana	50.5	48.9	51.8	50.5	50.3	47.4	48.9	24.3	56.0	35.7	38.8	38.2	36.7	38.4
Jamaica	34.4	33.1	28.0	36.0	33.8	28.9	27.6	19.7	18.5	18.1	23.4	22.2	21.4	29.7
Maldives	32.6	23.1	27.7	27.0	36.4	34.7	28.8	62.4	59.4	66.9	61.2	57.3	54.2	72.0
Mauritius	34.8	35.1	36.3	36.8	36.8	38.5	42.1	34.2	37.5	36.5	34.5	31.2	33.8	42.9
Samoa	72.5	64.9	94.3	70.2	85.0	48.1	52.8	34.3	63.3	59.8	65.3	66.1	60.8	65.9
St Vincent & the Grenadines	23.3	40.2	92.0	89.2	82.5	21.2	29.7	34.5	25.6	38.7	34.0	46.1	39.8	42.1
Seychelles	31.5	36.9	39.7	33.0	27.7	38.0	15.5	20.3	32.4	32.5	25.7	32.5	27.9	23.6
Tonga	8.3	7.7	7.1	2.9	15.8	18.2	27.8	81.1	60.9	82.8	73.0	77.3	74.1	43.5
Vanuatu	0.0	41.8	42.0	23.9	65.8	20.7	22.3	0.0	53.3	39.4	41.6	52.6	54.2	43.5
Other countries														
Albania	0.7	0.7	0.2	0.3	0.0	0.1	1.2	4.6	3.8	3.3	1.4	1.7	2.3	2.1
Armenia	7.1	11.2	7.2	3.0	2.0	2.3	1.3	13.4	8.8	4.9	4.1	3.6	3.7	3.7
Bahrain	3.7	9.7	9.8	6.8	8.1	8.4	11.9	14.5	14.9	12.9	12.6	14.1	19.1	11.1
Bosnia-Herzegovina	0.9	2.0	1.7	1.2	1.6	1.3	1.4	1.5	1.7	1.3	1.4	1.8	1.6	1.4
Cape Verde	0.0	20.6	17.2	14.3	3.0	2.7	5.0	4.0	4.0	1.9	3.7	4.6	2.5	2.2
Congo Republic	1.0	1.2	1.6	4.4	1.4	0.9	2.4	10.7	14.3	14.5	10.7	18.0	15.4	14.0
Costa Rica	2.4	7.1	3.1	7.4	5.7	14.3	27.5	0.5	1.9	2.6	3.0	2.9	2.6	3.1
Djibouti	1.0	6.5	4.7	2.8	2.5	2.7	2.1	13.2	13.3	16.8	19.8	24.8	24.6	25.9
Equatorial Guinea	7.3	13.3	12.3	7.5	7.8	3.2	3.0	17.9	18.1	11.8	8.0	9.0	10.2	8.7
Estonia	5.3	6.4	5.1	4.8	5.2	4.0	4.1	4.3	4.5	4.2	3.2	3.4	2.8	4.7
Gabon	3.9	7.7	6.0	6.1	10.3	15.1	5.1	10.3	9.7	12.3	13.8	12.7	14.1	11.7
Georgia	9.0	12.1	8.9	10.9	14.1	11.8	12.3	4.5	3.0	2.9	5.7	4.2	3.6	2.8
Latvia	16.0	9.5	10.2	18.6	12.9	7.3	7.3	3.1	3.6	2.9	2.7	2.9	3.5	3.0
Lebanon	8.6	7.1	6.3	6.9	8.7	10.2	5.0	7.7	8.6	7.5	6.9	7.1	8.0	6.7
Lithuania	14.2	7.9	10.2	11.7	6.9	9.8	5.1	3.9	4.3	3.8	2.9	3.9	4.1	3.2
Macedonia FYR	3.5	3.1	2.9	3.8	2.3	2.9	2.5	2.7	1.9	3.1	2.4	2.3	2.1	1.5
Moldova	1.9	2.1	2.1	3.0	1.7	1.9	2.7	2.2	1.9	2.4	1.0	1.3	1.2	0.8
Mongolia	4.6	3.9	5.4	6.5	8.9	10.9	11.5	3.0	2.9	2.7	2.3	3.6	3.7	3.9

Table 14. Merchandise trade with Commonwealth countries (continued)

Group/country	2001	2002	2003	2004	2005	2006	2007	2001	2002	2003	2004	2005	2006	2007
	(percentage of total exports)							(percentage of total imports)						
Middle-income (continued)														
Other countries														
Montenegro	–	–	–	–	–	–	–	–	–	–	–	–	–	–
Oman	12.5	11.7	8.3	6.4	7.2	14.1	5.4	17.9	16.0	17.1	19.8	17.5	14.0	14.2
Panama	1.7	4.8	12.9	4.4	4.7	6.0	7.3	2.2	2.8	9.1	2.9	3.1	3.1	2.9
Suriname	22.1	20.0	13.5	18.6	16.8	21.9	33.6	14.5	16.7	18.1	22.4	23.1	22.6	20.8
Timor-Leste	–	–	–	–	–	–	–	–	–	–	–	–	–	–
Turkmenistan	2.0	3.5	0.7	1.1	0.8	3.5	1.6	1.7	2.4	1.8	2.2	3.2	3.0	2.3
Uruguay	8.8	8.0	9.9	7.6	7.3	7.0	6.9	3.7	4.8	4.7	5.3	9.5	8.0	10.3
High-income														
Commonwealth countries														
Bahamas, The	6.7	6.7	7.1	6.0	7.9	11.0	22.3	8.0	5.0	9.9	6.2	4.8	5.9	7.7
Barbados	55.6	55.0	83.4	50.7	61.2	76.2	67.8	32.9	33.2	41.8	34.3	35.1	36.8	43.2
Brunei Darussalam	13.5	16.6	21.2	19.7	14.0	20.5	35.6	61.7	56.9	48.6	65.1	65.7	66.9	141.5
Cyprus	21.2	29.9	35.6	31.3	19.2	18.4	17.8	11.4	14.5	11.1	11.3	11.2	11.4	11.7
Malta	22.8	29.4	29.0	27.0	26.7	25.5	27.7	18.6	14.7	16.6	19.8	18.5	21.2	17.6
New Zealand	33.2	34.3	34.9	35.3	35.8	35.7	37.6	32.3	34.4	34.6	34.7	33.9	21.2	35.0
Singapore	28.4	27.9	27.8	25.3	28.4	25.7	26.4	23.8	24.7	23.2	21.4	21.4	19.6	19.7
Trinidad & Tobago	23.9	20.9	18.7	19.5	16.0	43.4	19.3	10.6	12.0	12.9	10.7	13.6	14.2	14.4
Other countries														
Croatia														
Iceland	21.2	20.7	20.4	22.3	21.2	47.4	15.1	12.6	13.2	11.6	8.7	8.6	36.7	9.5
Ireland	28.7	27.1	28.2	21.3	20.9	22.3	21.3	40.7	45.1	39.3	39.7	41.2	41.9	42.5
Kuwait	21.0	23.9	25.2	23.4	20.5	21.9	22.4	17.6	15.9	15.5	15.4	15.3	15.8	14.9
Norway	25.4	48.6	26.9	27.4	31.1	31.7	31.4	13.5	12.1	11.7	11.1	12.2	11.8	13.6
Oman	13.1	15.7	12.6	18.9	17.6	17.1	20.5	16.6	15.0	17.8	14.3	15.9	15.7	14.1
Qatar	9.5	12.5	12.5	17.8	15.6	13.8	30.8	14.6	15.8	20.1	12.4	14.6	16.9	12.7
United Arab Emirates	15.3	15.9	17.9	17.0	16.1	17.5	19.1	21.9	23.0	21.0	25.6	29.6	25.8	25.6

Note: – = not available.

Source: International Monetary Fund, *Direction of Trade Statistics Yearbook 2008*, Washington, DC

Table 15. Export characteristics

Group/country	Number of commodities exported				Diversification index				Concentration index			
	2005	2006	2007	2008	2005	2006	2007	2008	2005	2006	2007	2008
Low-income												
Commonwealth countries												
Gambia, The	9	9	14	21	0.577	0.606	0.611	0.594	0.438	0.506	0.302	0.259
Papua New Guinea	118	128	128	135	0.855	0.849	0.852	0.851	0.283	0.309	0.310	0.302
Solomon Islands	14	14	14	12	0.742	0.716	0.742	0.721	0.657	0.657	0.716	0.768
Other countries												
Central African Republic	68	18	18	20	0.665	0.715	0.713	0.702	0.451	0.467	0.465	0.463
Comoros	5	2	5	4	0.627	0.579	0.627	0.673	0.609	0.960	0.609	0.479
Guinea-Bissau	21	1	2	1	0.549	0.613	0.616	0.615	0.985	0.981	0.984	0.984
Liberia	8	170	16	28	0.852	0.806	0.841	0.730	0.841	0.697	0.717	0.474
Mauritania	3	4	3	5	0.497	0.496	0.497	0.497	0.763	0.716	0.763	0.740
São Tomé & Principe	2	3	4	4	0.606	0.579	0.613	0.606	0.882	0.869	0.597	0.642
Middle-income												
Commonwealth countries												
Antigua & Barbuda	36	58	42	69	0.698	0.651	0.641	0.605	0.690	0.484	0.560	0.445
Belize	34	134	133	20	0.800	0.710	0.727	0.577	0.385	0.356	0.386	0.460
Botswana	144	140	146	159	0.899	0.902	0.907	0.883	0.736	0.723	0.626	0.642
Dominica	20	17	20	14	0.722	0.762	0.722	0.749	0.376	0.406	0.376	0.398
Fiji Islands	232	231	230	160	0.739	0.763	0.748	0.735	0.289	0.292	0.280	0.247
Grenada	23	27	22	28	0.688	0.662	0.683	0.618	0.329	0.241	0.289	0.277
Guyana	221	217	82	71	0.816	0.830	0.814	0.822	0.325	0.291	0.297	0.342
Jamaica	111	114	115	123	0.788	0.785	0.792	0.767	0.660	0.576	0.585	0.559
Kiribati	6	16	6	9	0.540	0.610	0.540	0.637	0.383	0.565	0.383	0.478
Lesotho	21	36	21	18	0.675	0.845	0.675	0.648	0.399	0.442	0.399	0.369
Maldives	23	8	7	7	0.767	0.508	0.516	0.524	0.501	0.767	0.760	0.819
Mauritius	231	166	170	231	0.725	0.704	0.728	0.722	0.299	0.283	0.280	0.252
Namibia	257	257	255	256	0.809	0.843	0.828	0.814	0.298	0.298	0.250	0.271
Nauru	33	28	33	43	0.666	0.675	0.666	0.634	0.404	0.330	0.404	0.247
St Kitts	13	21	19	21	0.706	0.671	0.670	0.685	0.575	0.499	0.482	0.463
St Lucia	179	176	166	186	0.607	0.677	0.743	0.609	0.306	0.299	0.405	0.232
St Vincent & the Grenadines	27	28	33	36	0.731	0.706	0.707	0.672	0.347	0.337	0.302	0.258
Samoa	139	136	136	123	0.709	0.701	0.749	0.683	0.723	0.720	0.774	0.793
Seychelles	21	18	17	143	0.730	0.729	0.748	0.719	0.615	0.628	0.645	0.521
Swaziland	149	142	118	148	0.813	0.820	0.834	0.781	0.351	0.306	0.347	0.229
Tonga	10	12	10	12	0.659	0.658	0.659	0.628	0.483	0.554	0.483	0.453
Tuvalu	75	75	75	78	0.505	0.523	0.505	0.574	0.237	0.459	0.231	0.452
Vanuatu	15	15	15	13	0.705	0.695	0.705	0.737	0.607	0.484	0.607	0.718
Other countries												
Albania	117	119	128	136	0.734	0.737	0.707	0.720	0.283	0.267	0.230	0.197
Armenia	106	216	123	133	0.790	0.774	0.760	0.722	0.358	0.286	0.259	0.265
Bahrain	151	139	150	–	0.822	0.822	0.818	–	0.756	0.787	0.783	–
Bhutan	44	71	79	13	0.755	0.756	0.755	0.639	0.306	0.286	0.258	0.647
Bosnia-Herzegovina	198	209	208	243	0.640	0.683	0.629	0.583	0.142	0.142	0.133	0.122
Cape Verde	39	41	32	54	0.706	0.696	0.725	0.683	0.475	0.475	0.495	0.490
Congo Republic	90	102	100	88	0.803	0.792	0.793	0.772	0.759	0.767	0.770	0.762
Costa Rica	199	204	240	212	0.611	0.638	0.602	0.652	0.177	0.226	0.212	0.186
Djibouti	9	20	9	16	0.677	0.724	0.677	0.663	0.207	0.302	0.207	0.198
Gabon	61	60	96	99	0.823	0.797	0.814	0.800	0.818	0.837	0.822	0.837

Table 15. Export characteristics (continued)

Group/country	Number of commodities exported				Diversification index				Concentration index			
	2005	2006	2007	2008	2005	2006	2007	2008	2005	2006	2007	2008
Middle-income (contin.)												
Other countries												
Georgia	122	135	220	152	0.746	0.704	0.722	0.741	0.204	0.176	0.181	0.221
Latvia	247	250	249	251	0.523	0.479	0.431	0.462	0.125	0.107	0.001	0.001
Lebanon	244	216	190	246	0.640	0.636	0.543	0.638	0.105	0.115	0.371	0.117
Lithuania	252	253	254	254	0.533	0.507	0.473	0.493	0.214	0.189	0.111	0.203
Moldova	157	155	159	215	0.697	0.683	0.635	0.652	0.272	0.177	0.131	0.145
Mongolia	68	82	76	111	0.802	0.840	0.845	0.833	0.416	0.437	0.451	0.442
Oman	202	203	210	215	0.712	0.742	0.739	0.647	0.680	0.686	0.697	0.749
Panama	75	77	79	87	0.624	0.600	0.628	0.589	0.384	0.386	0.382	0.399
Suriname	167	184	162	161	0.770	0.729	0.742	0.731	0.874	0.880	0.887	0.820
Timor-Leste	29	59	29	38	0.511	0.581	0.642	0.593	0.250	0.251	0.353	0.593
Turkmenistan	60	70	71	75	0.775	0.783	0.778	0.770	0.792	0.806	0.798	0.808
Uruguay	171	179	181	185	0.714	0.698	0.678	0.671	0.192	0.207	0.212	0.228
High-income												
Commonwealth countries												
Bahamas, The	11	85	79	94	0.538	0.710	0.740	0.704	0.511	0.351	0.340	0.303
Barbados	220	221	223	223	0.661	0.618	0.676	0.652	0.270	0.251	0.237	0.219
Brunei Darussalam	82	87	115	111	0.802	0.845	0.810	0.811	0.644	0.716	0.677	0.671
Cyprus	219	160	163	168	0.551	0.529	0.543	0.589	0.249	0.208	0.191	0.215
Malta	217	213	212	212	0.633	0.616	0.689	0.623	0.397	0.443	0.420	0.397
New Zealand	254	253	253	251	0.629	0.633	0.627	0.609	0.133	0.134	0.146	0.154
Singapore	257	257	257	257	0.484	0.477	0.476	0.480	0.246	0.260	0.250	0.259
Trinidad & Tobago	172	167	176	174	0.783	0.785	0.769	0.748	0.383	0.415	0.357	0.376
Other countries												
Equatorial Guinea	34	27	119	38	0.793	0.774	0.740	0.726	0.925	0.913	0.852	0.771
Estonia	248	250	251	249	0.454	0.489	0.453	0.438	0.145	0.161	0.108	0.771
Iceland	200	207	209	212	0.781	0.779	0.779	0.762	0.391	0.391	0.376	0.426
Ireland	256	256	254	251	0.651	0.646	0.654	0.612	0.224	0.225	0.234	0.226
Kuwait	184	200	187	–	0.843	0.830	0.825	–	0.658	0.686	0.664	–
Luxembourg	252	254	256	255	0.567	0.563	0.565	0.587	0.136	0.151	0.160	0.188
Norway	254	252	254	253	0.651	0.644	0.628	0.611	0.454	0.431	0.406	0.417
Qatar	227	231	238	234	0.825	0.798	0.814	0.787	0.568	0.562	0.499	0.540
United Arab Emirates	245	251	246	252	0.664	0.607	0.607	0.580	0.497	0.425	0.483	0.452

Note: – = not available.

Source: United Nations Conference on Trade and Development, *Handbook of International Trade and Development Statistics 2009*, Geneva

Table 16. Selected indicators of openness and instability

Group/country	Merchandise exports as percentage of GDP				Merchandise imports as percentage of GDP				Export instability index	
	2004	2005	2006	2007	2004	2005	2006	2007	1990–2000	2000–2007
Low-income										
Commonwealth countries										
Gambia, The	11.7	8.5	7.2	7.1	143.4	138.6	138.9	133.9	53.5	28.5
Papua New Guinea	4.6	4.2	26.5	5.2	3.7	3.8	28.6	4.9	5.2	11.2
Solomon Islands	67.5	70.5	70.5	84.0	54.3	63.4	76.2	78.4	11.3	16.5
Other countries										
Central African Republic	9.9	1.8	2.1	7.2	15.5	16.1	19.9	19.9	17.4	13.6
Comoros	9.7	29.5	33.0	6.7	35.1	34.1	35.5	34.7	16.9	10.6
Guinea-Bissau	42.2	328.2	514.1	104.5	50.4	70.8	65.8	67.2	49.6	28.9
Liberia	38.7	170.3	221.9	139.2	198.5	1,046.7	1,131.9	1,197.7	25.2	17.3
Mauritania	161.6	3.3	1.7	64.0	225.4	248.9	233.8	70.0	7.0	15.5
São Tomé & Principe	0.6	1.0	0.4	5.5	4.1	3.5	3.0	55.9	41.0	24.0
Middle-income										
Commonwealth countries										
Belize	28.2	28.0	34.6	28.1	52.5	69.7	60.5	64.7	8.0	15.4
Botswana	45.2	42.6	45.3	0.0	38.0	43.1	42.7	36.3	3.1	9.0
Dominica	25.5	30.3	30.1	33.5	8.1	94.0	93.4	112.1	16.9	16.5
Fiji Islands	34.1	31.7	29.5	29.2	47.8	53.3	50.6	45.7	6.6	4.4
Grenada	9.2	10.1	7.2	115.4	62.2	71.5	65.5	65.0	14.1	64.2
Guyana	82.4	81.3	76.3	74.8	77.5	91.9	105.4	93.4	7.3	3.7
Jamaica	15.8	16.0	19.0	19.4	44.6	49.5	56.3	64.1	3.1	8.5
Kiribati	8.2	10.6	8.5	11.5	27.4	–	–	–	67.3	28.3
Lesotho	46.8	46.4	46.8	0.0	47.2	44.8	46.4	100.3	25.1	15.4
Maldives	15.9	12.9	18.3	15.5	91.1	97.3	98.1	164.8	18.6	13.8
Mauritius	31.6	31.9	33.2	29.0	45.7	50.3	57.4	56.9	4.3	5.7
Namibia	32.0	33.8	40.3	0.0	32.0	33.8	40.3	47.0	5.5	39.8
Nauru	–	–	–	–	–	–	–	–	–	14.1
St Kitts & Nevis	17.4	18.3	17.6	15.9	100.5	65.3	80.3	88.8	15.2	10.1
St Lucia	10.7	19.9	32.0	13.6	52.5	74.6	78.8	182.6	11.5	36.1
St Vincent & the Grenadines	9.0	10.4	46.3	28.6	55.0	62.4	136.6	105.6	26.3	43.0
Samoa	26.8	57.7	30.9	31.0	80.4	158.7	75.2	65.9	36.6	23.7
Seychelles	52.3	61.4	45.2	45.9	78.8	110.1	107.1	138.5	22.5	19.2
Swaziland	71.8	59.9	62.8	69.1	69.2	66.8	72.1	–	14.8	11.4
Tonga	18.0	8.9	9.9	7.1	64.6	59.8	62.3	63.6	10.6	17.5
Tuvalu	14.3	14.3	14.3	14.3	285.7	–	–	–	25.5	5.6
Vanuatu	64.4	69.2	62.4	60.4	72.6	78.6	70.1	70.4	22.6	30.3
Other countries										
Albania	8.1	7.5	8.3	9.3	30.6	31.1	33.3	37.8	–	–
Armenia	20.2	19.9	15.4	12.5	37.8	36.8	34.3	35.5	–	17.0
Bahrain	121.9	123.2	–	–	52.8	55.0	–	–	5.5	11.9
Bhutan	21.7	18.2	33.1	0.0	33.6	–	–	–	5.4	20.1
Bosnia-Herzegovina	15.0	20.3	22.5	20.8	48.6	53.5	48.9	49.7		18.6
Cape Verde	2.3	2.6	3.2	2.1	48.9	50.4	55.8	59.1	27.6	27.9
Congo Republic	145.1	106.5	110.5	92.2	190.4	29.8	27.2	48.0	25.5	44.4
Costa Rica	4.5	35.1	60.1	56.7	1.8	49.0	49.3	46.8	12.2	18.8
Djibouti	38.0	38.8	–	–	134.8	170.4	–	–	16.2	10.7
Gabon	62.1	63.4	48.9	54.2	22.3	21.1	20.4	23.8	6.9	8.5
Georgia	–	–	–	–	–	–	–	–	–	19.0

Table 16. Selected indicators of openness and instability (continued)

Group/country	Merchandise exports as percentage of GDP				Merchandise imports as percentage of GDP				Export instability index	
	2004	2005	2006	2007	2004	2005	2006	2007	1990–2000	2000–2005
Middle-income (contin.)										
Other countries										
Latvia	28.9	32.1	30.8	28.8	51.1	54.0	58.1	53.4	–	16.2
Lebanon	9.0	10.1	11.5	13.5	43.7	44.7	49.3	52.7	–	15.2
Lithuania	41.2	45.3	47.0	52.2	54.9	59.7	64.5	74.3	–	15.1
Macedonia FYR	31.2	35.1	37.7	45.5	54.6	55.5	59.0	57.3	–	13.5
Moldova	37.9	35.3	36.5	40.0	68.1	76.7	102.7	106.0	–	12.5
Panama	6.3	6.2	6.1	5.8	25.3	26.9	31.5	33.1	31.2	4.0
Suriname	76.5	70.3	58.3	62.4	65.2	68.2	45.8	55.6	6.5	13.1
Timor-Leste	–	–	–	–	–	–	–	0.0	–	–
Uruguay	22.2	20.3	22.2	22.0	23.6	23.1	31.9	32.0	5.5	10.3
High-income										
Commonwealth countries										
Antigua & Barbuda	7.8	10.4	11.3	–	29.3	44.5	–	–	–	20.3
Bahamas, The	–	–	–	–	–	–	–	–	17.1	12.3
Barbados	7.5	8.4	9.4	–	197.8	51.9	47.3	–	15.2	13.6
Brunei Darussalam	82.2	59.1	59.7	–	29.9	65.9	60.0	–	8.7	8.7
Cyprus	7.6	–	7.2	6.5	37.2	–	21.7	40.6	9.1	8.7
Malta	49.3	40.8	41.9	40.2	71.5	469.2	413.5	58.7	10.6	6.2
New Zealand	20.7	19.9	21.5	19.9	23.5	23.9	25.2	22.7	3.3	6.0
Singapore	158.8	177.6	205.9	185.4	151.6	162.5	180.7	163.2	4.6	10.3
Trinidad and Tobago	69.3	77.5	74.0	70.7	44.9	40.5	32.5	33.2	–	18.0
Other countries										
Equatorial Guinea	121.6	191.8	87.2	82.7	22.8	34.6	18.8	13.4	–	–
Estonia	52.5	58.3	59.1	52.7	74.4	76.3	82.0	74.3	9.4	11.5
Iceland	22.0	18.9	21.2	24.0	28.4	30.7	37.7	33.2	3.8	9.2
Ireland	56.6	54.6	49.4	46.8	33.3	34.0	33.2	32.1	3.5	3.1
Kuwait	43.1	43.6	–	41.7	21.7	19.0	–	19.3	22.1	13.9
Luxembourg	48.4	50.2	55.1	45.4	59.7	59.3	64.0	55.5	3.8	9.6
Norway	32.3	34.9	36.5	35.1	19.0	18.6	19.2	20.7	6.5	9.1
Qatar	58.4	61.4	47.6	73.3	19.1	24.7	–	43.2	12.9	15.9
Slovenia	43.3	53.7	59.5	63.6	52.1	55.0	59.2	62.5	–	–
United Arab Emirates	64.4	72.4	69.1	76.7	71.1	76.9	–	89.4	26.9	15.3

Note: – = not available.

Source: International Monetary Fund, *Direction of Trade Statistics Yearbook*, various issues; International Monetary Fund, *International Financial Statistics*, Washington, DC, various issues

Table 17. Fish catches

Group/country	2000	2001	2002	2003	2004	2005	2006	2007
	('000 MT)							
Low-income								
Commonwealth countries								
Gambia,The	29.0	34.5	45.7	37.4	32.4	34.6	36.9	43.6
Papua New Guinea	96.6	120.1	151.8	186.7	229.7	250.3	280.6	264.2
Solomon Islands	19.2	23.6	25.9	36.9	34.2	28.5	39.3	31.3
Other countries								
Central African Republic	15.0	15.0	15.0	15.0	15.0	15.0	15.0	15.0
Comoros	13.2	12.2	13.1	14.1	14.9	15.1	15.1	16.0
Guinea-Bissau	6.3	6.8	7.3	6.2	6.2	6.2	6.2	6.2
Liberia	11.7	11.3	11.0	10.7	10.4	13.3	10.5	16.2
Mauritania	114.5	140.1	156.1	199.7	270.7	304.9	165.3	201.6
São Tomé & Principe	4.0	3.7	3.8	4.0	4.1	4.2	4.2	4.2
Middle-income								
Commonwealth countries								
Belize	55.2	30.1	59.1	16.8	15.6	15.0	11.8	14.4
Botswana	0.2	0.1	0.1	0.1	0.1	0.1	0.1	0.0
Dominica	1.2	1.2	1.3	0.9	0.7	0.6	0.7	1.0
Fiji Islands	40.0	43.0	38.8	34.7	46.6	40.0	47.5	50.1
Grenada	1.7	2.3	2.2	2.5	2.0	2.1	2.2	2.4
Guyana	48.9	53.4	48.0	59.7	56.7	53.4	53.0	47.4
Jamaica	5.5	12.3	7.8	8.7	13.5	13.1	17.8	16.5
Kiribati	25.5	32.4	31.6	31.5	31.6	34.0	23.6	21.6
Lesotho	0.0	0.0	0.0	0.0	0.0	0.0	0.0	0.2
Maldives	119.0	127.1	163.4	155.4	158.6	185.9	184.2	143.6
Mauritius	9.7	11.0	10.7	11.0	10.3	10.3	9.1	8.5
Namibia	590.0	548.9	626.2	637.8	571.8	554.1	509.5	415.5
Nauru	0.2	0.1	0.0	0.0	0.0	0.0	0.0	0.1
St Kitts & Nevis	0.5	0.6	0.4	0.4	0.5	0.5	0.5	0.5
St Lucia	1.8	2.0	1.6	1.5	1.5	1.4	1.5	1.6
St Vincent & the Grenadines	27.7	52.5	44.5	4.8	8.6	1.7	4.7	5.3
Samoa	13.0	11.8	9.9	6.6	4.7	4.5	3.8	4.6
Seychelles	33.2	53.9	63.6	87.1	101.8	109.5	93.8	66.2
Swaziland	0.1	0.1	0.1	0.1	0.1	0.1	0.1	0.1
Tonga	3.8	4.7	4.8	4.4	1.6	1.9	2.9	2.7
Tuvalu	0.5	0.5	0.6	1.5	2.4	2.6	2.2	2.2
Vanuatu	70.5	36.0	44.3	57.7	121.2	151.0	88.1	85.4
Other countries								
Albania	3.6	3.6	4.5	4.3	6.1	6.5	7.7	7.5
Armenia	2.0	2.2	1.5	1.6	1.0	1.0	1.4	4.6
Bahrain	11.7	11.2	11.2	13.6	14.3	11.9	15.6	15.0
Bhutan	0.3	0.3	0.3	0.3	0.3	0.3	0.3	0.3
Bosnia-Herzegovina	2.0	2.0	6.7	8.6	8.4	9.1	9.6	9.6
Cape Verde	10.6	8.7	8.2	8.2	10.4	21.6	24.6	18.3
Congo Republic	46.0	48.9	51.9	54.7	54.3	58.4	59.5	59.9
Costa Rica	45.2	45.3	50.9	49.9	45.6	46.4	42.0	47.5
Croatia	27.9	29.0	30.2	28.3	40.5	45.8	51.4	53.1
Djibouti	0.3	0.3	0.3	0.3	0.3	0.3	0.3	0.3
Equatorial Guinea	3.6	3.6	3.5	3.5	3.5	3.5	3.5	3.6
Gabon	48.3	43.0	41.7	45.6	46.0	43.9	41.7	39.1
Georgia	1.9	1.7	1.9	3.4	12.1	10.0	9.8	18.4

Table 17. Fish catches (continued)

Group/country	2000	2001	2002	2003	2004	2005	2006	2007
				('000 MT)				
Middle-income (contin.)								
Other countries								
Latvia	136.7	128.6	114.1	115.2	125.9	151.2	140.9	156.0
Lebanon	4.1	4.0	4.8	4.7	4.6	3.8	3.8	3.8
Lithuania	81.0	152.8	151.9	159.6	164.7	141.8	156.7	190.9
Macedonia FYR	1.8	1.2	1.0	1.1	1.2	1.1	0.7	1.2
Moldova	1.3	1.6	2.3	2.9	5.0	5.0	5.6	5.9
Montenegro	–	–	–	–	–	–	0.9	0.9
Panama	215.5	265.5	229.7	215.4	203.2	220.3	226.8	206.7
Suriname	21.3	24.9	25.2	28.2	45.1	27.4	30.6	29.6
Timor-Leste	0.4	0.4	0.4	0.4	0.4	0.4	0.4	0.4
Turkmenistan	12.3	12.8	12.9	14.6	15.0	15.0	15.0	15.0
Uruguay	113.3	105.1	108.8	117.3	123.0	125.8	134.0	108.7
High-income								
Commonwealth countries								
Antigua & Barbuda	1.7	1.8	1.8	2.4	2.6	2.5	3.0	3.1
Bahamas, The	11.1	9.3	12.3	12.7	11.4	11.1	10.7	3.8
Barbados	3.2	2.7	2.5	2.8	2.1	2.2	2.0	1.8
Brunei Darussalam	2.5	1.6	2.1	2.2	2.4	2.4	2.0	2.2
Cyprus	67.5	81.0	1.7	2.0	1.6	1.9	2.2	2.4
Malta	1.1	0.9	1.1	1.1	1.1	1.4	–	–
New Zealand	553.3	569.8	588.7	550.9	545.9	535.4	–	–
Singapore	5.4	3.3	2.8	2.1	2.2	1.9	3.1	3.5
Trinidad & Tobago	10.0	11.9	14.1	9.9	10.0	13.4	8.4	8.4
Other countries								
Croatia	27.9	29.0	30.2	28.3	40.5	45.8	51.4	53.1
Estonia	113.6	106.0	102.6	80.6	88.9	100.1	87.6	100.2
Iceland	2,003.7	2,008.3	2,153.1	2,014.9	1,764.2	1,694.1	1,356.4	1,425.9
Ireland	363.6	453.7	381.3	363.7	356.6	352.1	293.7	313.7
Kuwait	7.3	6.0	5.4	4.4	5.2	5.2	6.2	4.7
Luxembourg	0.0	0.0	0.0	0.0	0.0	0.0	0.0	0.0
Norway	3,383.1	3,372.9	3,474.3	3,286.6	3,309.6	3,208.7	3,114.2	3,343.8
Oman	120.4	129.9	142.7	138.5	165.1	157.3	147.7	151.7
Qatar	7.1	8.8	7.2	11.3	11.1	13.9	16.4	15.2
Slovenia	3.0	3.1	3.0	2.6	2.6	2.6	2.5	2.5
United Arab Emirates	105.5	112.6	97.6	95.2	90.0	90.0	87.0	87.0
Total group								
Low-income	372 (0.4)	362.0 (0.3)	422.3 (0.5)	451.7 (0.6)	617.6(0.7)	672.1(0.7)	573.1(0.6)	598.3(0.6)
n	15	9	9	9	9	9	9	9
Middle-income	3,283 (3.5)	3,798.8 (4.1)	3,911.8 (4.2)	3,846.9 (4.3)	2,065.2 (2.2)	2,117.3 (2.3)	2,028.1(2.2)	1,871.8 (2.1)
n	45	36	36	36	44	44	45	45
High-income	5,661 (6.1)	5,836.2 (6.3)	5,889.6 (6.3)	5,491.1 (6.1)	6,413.1(6.8)	6,242.0(6.7)	5,194.5(5.4)	5,523.0(5.9)
n		16	15	15	20	20	18	18
Under 1.5 mn population	4,656 (5.0)	2,687.9 (2.9)	2,824.1 (3.0)	2,642.2 (2.9)	1,039.4 (1.1)	1,083.8(1.1)	998.2(1.1)	921.2(0.9)
n	39	31	30	30	37	37	37	37
Under 5 mn population	11,316 (12.1)	11,998.0 (12.9)	12,225.7 (13.1)	9,789.7 (10.8)	9,111.5(9.7)	90,464 .0 (9.7)	7,807.5(8.3)	8,007.0(8.4)
n	73	75	62	61	74	74	73	73
World total	95,609.0	93,045.0	93,198.0	90,354.0	94,363.0	93,253.0	93,565.0	95,650.0

Notes: Figures in brackets refer to percentage of world total; n = number of countries.

Source: Food and Agriculture Organisation, *Yearbook of Fishery Statistics*, Rome, various issues, http://faostat.fao.org

Table 18. Energy production, consumption and trade

Group/country	Primary energy production			Commercial consumption			Net energy imports as a proportion of total energy consumption		
	2004	2005	2006	2004	2005	2006	2004	2005	2006
	(000 tons of coal equivalent)						(per cent)		
Low-income									
Commonwealth countries									
Gambia, The	–	–	–	153	153	160	102	102	102
Papua New Guinea	3,311	3,971	4572	2,256	2,251	2,281	–45	–51	–64
Solomon Islands	–	–	–	83	85	85	106	104	105
Other countries									
Central African Republic	10	10	10	122	122	129	123	123	124
Comoros	0	0	0	46	46	47	100	100	100
Guinea-Bissau	–	–	–	128	128	132	112	115	111
Liberia	–	–	–	269	313	336	109	108	107
Mauritania	–	–	–	691	719	707	101	101	101
São Tomé & Principe	1	1	1	45	50	51	98	96	98
Timor-Leste	10,524	10,563	10,581	138	140	141	–7,464	–7,357	–7,326
Middle-income									
Commonwealth countries									
Belize	13	13	13	402	416	420	109	110	110
Botswana	–	–	–	–	–	–	–	–	–
Dominica	4	3	4	56	58	60	93	95	93
Fiji Islands	82	83	85	964	836	811	100	100	100
Grenada	–	–	–	106	112	116	111	110	109
Guyana	–	–	–	685	707	715	102	103	103
Jamaica	21	19	20	4,753	4,570	5,525	108	107	107
Lesotho	–	–	–	–	–	–	–	–	–
Maldives	–	–	–	357	322	412	100	100	100
Mauritius	15	14	9	1,456	1,538	1,708	124	125	118
Namibia	–	–	–	–	–	–	–	–	–
Nauru	–	–	–	66	66	66	115	115	115
St Kitts & Nevis	–	–	–	108	112	112	100	100	100
St Lucia	–	–	–	175	179	184	104	105	
St Vincent & the Grenadines	3	3	4	94	95	98	97	96	104
Samoa	5	5	5	79	80	80	94	94	94
Seychelles	–	–	–	365	326	348	153	156	155
Swaziland	–	–	–	–	–	–	–	–	–
Tonga	–	–	–	82	81	81	101	101	101
Vanuatu	–	–	–	42	42	44	33	33	30
Other countries									
Albania	1,332	1,355	1,392	2,451	2,287	2,239	58	60	59
Armenia	543	551	561	2,611	3,052	3,137	81	84	84
Bahrain	23,886	24,405	24,748	11,413	12,269	13,216	-82	-72	-62
Bosnia-Herzegovina	8,081	8,483	8,999	9,760	10,393	10,947	18	18	18
Bhutan	340	371	423	211	224	218	-62	-67	-92
Cape Verde	1	1	1	127	142	145	108	109	110
Congo Republic	16,684	18,167	20,545	547	573	649	-2,885	-3,042	-3,060
Costa Rica	977	993	994	3,790	3,930	4,249	78	76	78
Djibouti	–	–	–	190	199	204	231	228	232
Gabon	15,614	15,539	15,621	866	1,000	1,005	-1,693	-1,447	-1,446
Georgia	905	883	785	3,097	3,632	3,946	78	81	85

Table 18. Energy production, consumption and trade (continued)

Group/country	Primary energy production			Commercial consumption			Net energy imports as a proportion of total energy consumption		
	2004	2005	2006	2004	2005	2006	2004	2005	2006
	(000 tons of coal equivalent)						(per cent)		
Middle-income (contin.)									
Other countries									
Latvia	392	421	355	4,333	4,347	4,749	115	82	107
Lebanon	138	129	85	7,071	7,366	6,260	101	93	101
Lithuania	2,493	1,785	1,531	8,341	8,690	8,177	78	86	97
Macedonia FYR	2,971	2,832	2,759	4,518	4,589	4,504	35	37	40
Moldova	19	15	15	5,037	5,319	5,064	100	100	99
Mongolia	–	–	–	–	–	–	–	–	–
Montenegro	–	–	–	–	–	–	–	–	–
Panama	479	476	479	2,959	3,066	3,279	74	84	85
Suriname	969	1,012	1,044	949	994	1,020	20	21	19
Uruguay	587	821	442	3,333	3,365	3,664	103	91	105
High-income									
Commonwealth countries									
Antigua & Barbuda	–	–	–	193.0	196.0	204.0	139	139	136
Bahamas, The	–	–	–	949	995	1,009	145	145	144
Barbados	127	129	110	535	557	568	67	77	81
Brunei Darussalam	31,056	30,441	32,283	4,024	3,972	4,038	–688	–688	–727
Cyprus	–	–	–	2,944	3,056	3,191	116	131	132
Malta	–	–	–	1,190	1,187	1,168	115	114	112
New Zealand	14,021	13,165	13,620	19,951	19,202	19,181	38	37	36
Singapore	–	–	–	19,356	21,109	20,752	375	372	390
Trinidad & Tobago	45,496	48,477	56,977	17,595	18,795	21,389	–146	–148	–164
Other countries									
Croatia	5,537	5,475	5,938	12,875	13,057	12,966	61	61	58
Equatorial Guinea	25,871	26,315	25,131	708	708	714	–2,684	–3,559	–3,422
Estonia	4,600	4,830	4,714	7,342	7,193	7,047	39	36	41
Iceland	1,375	1,362	1,547	2,058	2,045	2,221	73	72	68
Ireland	2,685	2,241	2,158	20,818	20,486	21,357	96	97	96
Kuwait	193,248	214,378	221,508	44,124	46,720	45,760	–302	–322	–348
Luxembourg	113	118	124	6,167	6,281	6,823	108	108	100
Norway	346,850	341,745	328,623	38,480	39,468	40,520	–789	–737	–711
Oman	80,165	80,525	84,920	15,473	16,320	21,046	–427	–398	–297
Qatar	111,354	120,213	142,520	22,472	28,960	29,130	–383	–312	–383
Slovenia	2,674	2,563	2,540	7,750	7,832	7,913	81	85	86
United Arab Emirates	251,762	254,290	269,264	83,120	84,360	86,556	–172	–169	–178
Group (total or average)									
Low-income	13,846	14,545	15,164	3,931	4,007	4,069	–247	–243	–247
n	5	5	5	10	10	10	9	9	9
Middle-income	76,554	78,379	80,919	81,394	84,989	87,464	16	15	20
n	25	25	25	35	36	36	35	36	36
High-income	1,116,934	1,146,267	1,191,977	327,931	342,303	353,349	–205	–199	–204
n	16	16	16	20	20	20	20	20	20
Under 1.5 mn population	195,142	203,905	228,700	59,167	66,894	69,263			
n	18	18	18	31	32	32	31	32	31
Under 5 mn population	1,207,334	1,239,191	1,288,060	413,449	431,495	445,086	–162	–157	–160
n	46	46	46	66	67	67	66	67	67

Source: United Nations, *Energy Statistics Yearbook 2006*, New York, NY

Table 19. Tourist arrivals and earnings

Group/country	Number of tourist arrivals			Tourist receipts			Tourist receipts as a proportion of total export earnings		
	2005	2006	2007	2005	2006	2007	2005	2006	2007
	(thousand)			(US$ million)			(per cent)		
Low-income									
Commonwealth countries									
Gambia, The	460	613	–	57	69	77	47.9	53.5	48.1
Papua New Guinea	69	78	–	4	–	–	0.1	–	–
Solomon Islands	9	12	14	3	4	4	1.2	1.3	–
Other countries									
Central African Republic	12	14	–	–	–	–	–	–	–
Comoros	26	28	15	24	27	–	34.8	34.2	–
Guinea-Bissau	5	12	30	2	3	–	1.7	–	–
Liberia	–	–	–	–	–	–	–	–	–
Mauritania	–	–	–	–	–	–	–	–	–
São Tomé & Principe	16	12	–	7	7	3	19.4	77.8	–
Middle-income									
Commonwealth countries									
Belize	1,037	903	879	214	271	289	69.3	34.7	38.2
Botswana	1,885	–	–	561	537	549	10.7	9.6	9.0
Dominica	381	465	437	57	72	71	31.8	36.7	33.2
Fiji Islands	550	545	540	676	636	–	40.3	37.4	–
Grenada	380	342	406	71	93	110	43.0	55.4	13.0
Guyana	117	113	131	35	37	50	4.4	4.4	5.1
Jamaica	2,615	3,016	2,880	1,783	2,094	2,137	46.2	45.2	43.4
Kiribati	49	11	32	–	–	–	–	–	–
Lesotho	304	357	300	26	27	43	3.9	3.9	5.3
Maldives	395	602	676	287	512	586	68.0	70.9	74.2
Mauritius	782	802	933	1,189	1,302	1,663	32.8	34.4	39.8
Namibia	856	961	1,048	363	473	542	14.6	14.9	90.5
St Kitts & Nevis	365	350	376	121	122	106	52.4	48.4	43.3
St Lucia	720	670	905	356	285	296	62.0	45.8	61.7
St Vincent & the Grenadines	256	306	328	104	113	109	52.3	30.8	32.2
Samoa	102	116	122	80	91	107	23.1	34.5	35.4
Seychelles	135	151	171	269	323	366	33.8	41.4	45.4
Swaziland	1,182	1,200	1,230	78	74	32	4.1	3.8	1.3
Tonga	60	54	–	15	16	16	26.8	30.2	31.4
Tuvalu	1	1	1	–	–	–	–	–	–
Vanuatu	126	154	167	104	109	142	0.9	0.9	1.3
Other countries									
Albania	748	937	1,127	880	1,057	1,055	49.0	46.7	35.7
Armenia	319	381	–	240	307	343	17.3	20.9	19.8
Bahrain	6,313	7,289	7,833	1,603	1,786	1,854	8.5	7.7	6.8
Bhutan	14	17	21	19	24	30	8.6	6.3	8.6
Bosnia-Herzegovina	217	256	306	557	658	798	17.5	16.9	17.3
Cape Verde	198	242	267	177	286	426	60.0	68.3	81.8
Congo Republic	–	–	–	34	–	–	0.6	–	0.0
Costa Rica	1,959	2,071	2,302	1,810	1,890	2,224	18.8	11.6	12.0
Djibouti	30	40	40	7	9	–	1.3	1.5	–
Gabon	–	–	–	–	–	–	–	–	–
Georgia	560	983	1052	287	361	441	33.7	36.8	28.8

Table 19. Tourist arrivals and earnings (continued)

Group/country	Number of tourist arrivals			Tourist receipts			Tourist receipts as a proportion of total export earnings		
	2005	2006	2007	2005	2006	2007	2005	2006	2007
	(thousand)			(US$ million)			(per cent)		
Middle-income (contin.)									
Other countries									
Latvia	3791	4649	5209	446	622	880	8.7	10.1	10.6
Lebanon	1140	1063	1017	5969	5441	5573	273.4	213.9	166.8
Lithuania	2000	2180	1486	975	1077	1192	8.3	7.6	–
Macedonia FYR	3246	3369	3903	116	156	219	5.7	6.5	–
Moldova	25	14	15	138	145	221	13.1	11.7	12.5
Panama	1,070	1,215	1,428	1,108	1,450	1,796	34.4	36.8	–
Suriname	160	153	163	96	109	73	8.4	7.4	5.2
Turkmenistan	12	6	8	–	–	–	–	–	–
Uruguay	1,907	1,824	1,815	699	710	927	14.8	12.7	18.2
High-income									
Commonwealth countries									
Antigua & Barbuda	734	745	935	309.0	327.0	338.0	55.8	55.4	49.6
Bahamas, The	4,779	4,731	4,601	2,081	2,066	2,198	44.8	45.1	44.6
Barbados	1,111	1,102	1,191	905	974	–	52.7	55.1	–
Brunei Darussalam	815	836	877	191	224	–	3.1	2.9	–
Cyprus	2,657	2,626	2,671	2,644	2,691	3,109	33.2	31.7	30.5
Malta	1,491	1,532	1,732	924	966	1,143	21.6	18.1	17.9
New Zealand	2,366	2,409	2,455	5,161	4,777	5,406	17.0	15.6	14.9
Singapore	8,943	9,751	10,285	5,903	7,204	8,680	2.3	2.2	2.4
Trinidad & Tobago	530	543	526	539	514	621	4.5	3.6	4.0
Other countries									
Croatia	45,762	47,733	52,271	7,625	8296	9,576	40.9	39.3	38.9
Equatorial Guinea	–	–	–	–	–	–	–	–	–
Estonia	1,917	1940	1,900	1,229	1,362	1,415	11.3	10.3	9.2
Iceland	871	971	1,054	630	663	887	12.5	12.5	12.7
Ireland	7,333	8,001	8,332	6,780	7,661	8,863	4.0	4.5	6.8
Kuwait	3,474	3,899	4,482	410	469	512	0.9	0.9	0.8
Luxembourg	913	908	917	3,614	3,620	4,009	6.1	4.9	4.5
Norway	3,828	3,945	–	4,030	4,251	5,021	3.0	2.7	2.8
Oman	1,114	–	–	828	919	900	4.6	3.7	3.9
Qatar	913	946	964	760	874	–	2.6	3.0	–
Slovenia	21,125	19,820	–	18,152	16,853	–	78.5	61.3	–
United Arab Emirates	7,126	–	–	3,218	4,972	6,059	3.2	4.2	4.8
Group (total or average)									
Low-income	597	769	59	97	110	84	1.4	1.3	0.8
n	7	7	3	6	5	3	6	4	1
Middle-income	36,007	37,808	39,554	21,550	23,275	25,266	26.6	20.4	18.1
n	39	38	36	37	36	34	37	36	32
High-income	117,802	112,438	95,193	65,933	69,683	58,737	8.8	7.4	5.3
n	19	17	15	19	19	15	19	19	15
Under 1.5 mn population	29,960	27,411	28,740	16,694	17,597	16,535	12.4	9.7	7.3
n	36	35	31	34	34	28	34	34	26
Under 5 mn population	597	151,015	134,806	87,580	93,068	84,087	10.4	8.7	6.6
n	66	63	55	63	61	53	63	60	49

Notes: – = not available; n = number of countries.

Source: United Nations Conference on Trade and Development, *Handbook of International Trade and Development Statistics*, various issues, Geneva

Table 20. International reserves

Group/country	Total international reserves						Months of imports reserves could finance					
	2002	2003	2004	2005	2006	2007	2002	2003	2004	2005	2006	2007
	(US$ million)											
Low-income												
Commonwealth countries												
Gambia, The	107	59	84	98	121	143	3.1	1.4	1.8	1.8	2.0	2.0
Papua New Guinea	322	494	633	718	1,401	2,053	3.6	4.8	5.2	4.7	7.1	9.1
Solomon Islands	18	37	81	95	104	119	2.4	3.8	6.7	6.0	4.9	4.7
Other countries												
Central African Republic	123	132	148	139	125	83	10.2	10.8	8.8	7.6	5.0	2.9
Comoros	80	94	104	86	94	117	9.9	9.0	9.8	7.8	7.8	9.0
Guinea-Bissau	103	33	73	80	82	113	12.1	2.5	6.5	4.5	4.9	–
Liberia	3	7	19	25	72	119	0.0	0.0	0.0	0.1	0.1	0.2
Mauritania	396	415	34	65	187	198	5.5	5.0	0.4	0.6	1.5	1.3
São Tomé & Principe	17	25	20	27	34	39	3.4	4.7	3.8	5.1	5.1	5.8
Middle-income												
Commonwealth countries												
Belize	115	85	48	71	114	109	3.0	1.9	1.0	1.1	1.9	1.6
Botswana	5,474	5,340	5,654	6,309	7,992	9,789	37.3	29.5	18.4	17.0	21.2	26.3
Dominica	46	48	42	49	63	61	2.6	2.8	23.1	2.2	2.5	1.9
Fiji Islands	359	424	478	315	–	–	5.1	5.1	4.6	2.6	–	–
Grenada	88	83	122	94	100	111	5.0	4.1	5.4	3.3	3.5	–
Guyana	284	276	232	252	280	313	6.1	5.7	4.6	4.2	3.6	3.7
Jamaica	1,645	1,195	1,847	2,170	2,318	1,878	5.5	3.9	5.6	5.5	4.9	3.1
Kiribati	–	–	–	–	–	–	–	–	–	–	–	–
Lesotho	406	460	502	519	658	n.a	6.3	8.4	8.5	9.6	11.4	–
Maldives	133	159	204	186	232	308	4.1	4.1	3.8	3.0	3.1	2.1
Mauritius	1,227	1,577	17	1,366	1,301	–	6.8	7.9	0.1	5.2	4.3	–
Namibia	323	325	345	312	450	896	2.7	2.3	2.3	1.8	2.0	–
Nauru	–	–	–	–	–	–	–	–	–	–	–	–
St Kitts & Nevis	66	65	79	72	89	0.0	4.2	3.2	2.3	2.9	2.8	0.0
St Lucia	94	107	133	116	135	154	2.0	3.6	4.0	2.3	2.3	1.0
St Vincent & the Grenadines	53	51	75	70	87	84	3.6	3.1	4.0	3.5	1.8	1.7
Samoa	63	84	96	92	95	88	4.2	4.0	4.0	1.7	3.6	3.0
Seychelles	70	67	35	56	113	41	2.0	2.0	0.7	0.9	1.6	0.5
Swaziland	276	278	324	244	373	774	2.9	1.8	2.2	1.6	2.3	–
Tonga	25	40	55	47	48	65	3.4	4.8	5.4	4.4	4.1	4.9
Tuvalu	–	–	–	–	–	–	–	–	–	–	–	–
Vanuatu	37	44	62	67	105	120	3.2	2.5	3.2	3.0	4.6	4.5
Other countries												
Albania	839	1,009	1,357	1,404	1,769	2,104	6.7	6.6	7.1	6.5	7.0	6.2
Armenia	417	502	548	669	1,072	1,659	5.1	4.7	4.9	4.5	5.9	6.1
Bahrain	1,726	1,778	1,941	–	–	–	5.1	4.4	4.0	–	–	–
Bhutan	355	367	399	467	545	699	22.4	22.5	19.5	–	–	–
Bosnia-Herzegovina	1,321	1,796	2,408	2,531	3,372	4,525	4.7	5.4	5.9	5.3	6.7	7.2
Cape Verde	80	94	140	174	255	281	2.9	3.1	3.7	4.2	4.8	4.0
Congo Republic	32	35	120	732	1,841	2,174	0.6	0.5	4.4	5.8	11.0	7.1
Costa Rica	1,502	1,839	1,922	2,313	3,115	4,113	2.5	2.9	2.8	2.8	3.4	4.0
Djibouti	74	100	94	89	120	132	1.3	1.5	1.3	0.9	0.9	0.8
Gabon	140	197	443	669	1,113	1,227	1.5	1.7	3.3	4.7	6.9	–
Latvia	1,241	1,432	1,911	2,232	4,353	5,553	3.7	3.3	3.3	3.1	4.5	10.3

Table 20. International reserves (continued)

Group/country	Total international reserves 2002	2003	2004	2005	2006	2007	Months of imports reserves could finance 2002	2003	2004	2005	2006	2007
	(US$ million)											
Middle-income (contin.)												
Other countries												
Lebanon	7,244	12,519	11,734	11,887	13,376	12,910	13.8	19.5	15.0	14.8	14.7	11.9
Lithuania	2,350	3,372	3,512	3,720	5,654	7,565	3.7	4.1	3.4	2.9	3.5	25.0
Macedonia FYR	722	898	905	1,229	1,751	2,082	4.3	4.7	3.7	4.6	5.6	5.5
Panama	1,183	1,011	631	1,211	1,335	1,935	4.7	3.9	2.1	3.5	3.0	18.6
Suriname	106	106	129	125	215	401	2.1	1.9	2.1	1.6	2.7	0.6
Turkmenistan	–	–	–	–	–	–	–	–	–	–	–	–
Uruguay	769	2,083	2,508	3,074	3,085	4,114	3.3	11.4	9.6	9.5	6.0	6.7
High-income												
Commonwealth countries												
Antigua & Barbuda	87.6	113.8	120.1	127	142.6	143.9	3.0	3.5	3.9	3.6	3.3	3.1
Bahamas, The	381	491	674	586	461	465	0.8	1.1	1.5	0.8	0.5	0.5
Barbados	669	738	580	603	636	839	7.5	7.4	4.9	4.5	4.7	6.1
Brunei Darussalam	438	482	505	492	514	667	3.2	4.3	3.7	3.5	3.1	2.0
Cyprus	3,022	3,257	3,910	4,429	5,647	6,119	8.9	8.7	8.2	8.5	9.8	8.5
Malta	2,209	2,729	2,732	2,576	2,977	3,785	9.4	9.6	8.6	8.6	9.0	10.4
New Zealand	4,963	6,085	6,947	8,893	14,069	17,247	3.9	4.0	3.6	4.1	6.4	6.7
Singapore	82,221	96,245	112,579	116,172	136,260	162,957	8.5	8.5	7.8	7.0	6.8	7.4
Trinidad & Tobago	2,028	2,451	3,168	4,856	6,586	6,694	6.6	8.1	7.5	11.0	13.5	11.6
Other countries												
Croatia	5,885	8,191	8,758	8,800	11,487	13,674	6.7	7.0	6.4	5.8	6.4	6.4
Equatorial Guinea	89	238	945	2,102	3,067	3,845	2.4	2.3	15.4	22.5	22.8	34.8
Estonia	1,000	1,373	1,788	1,943	2,781	3,262	2.0	2.1	2.6	2.3	2.5	2.5
Iceland	440	792	1,046	1,036	2,301	2,578	2.3	3.4	3.4	2.6	4.5	4.7
Ireland	5,415	4,079	2,831	779	720	779	1.3	0.9	0.6	0.1	0.1	0.1
Kuwait	9,208	7,577	8,242	8,863	12,566	166,666	12.6	8.0	7.7	6.9	9.1	92.6
Luxembourg	152	280	298	241	218	144	0.1	0.2	0.2	0.1	0.1	0.1
Norway	32,000	37,220	44,307	46,986	56,842	60,840	11.2	11.2	11.0	10.3	10.6	9.1
Oman	3,174	3,594	3,597	4,358	5,014	9,523	6.3	6.6	5.6	5.4	5.2	5.0
Qatar	1,567	2,944	3,396	4,542	5,383	9,416	4.6	7.2	6.7	5.2	5.1	5.0
Slovenia	6,980	8,497	8,793	8,076	7,036	980	7.7	7.4	5.7	4.8	3.5	0.4
United Arab Emirates	15,219	15,088	18,530	21,010	27,617	77,238	6.0	4.7	3.0	2.5	2.9	6.3
Group (total or average)												
Low-income	1,213	1,359	1,377	1,486	2,304	3,214	1.8	2.1	1.9	1.7	2.2	2.5
n	10	10	10	10	10	10	9	9	9	9	9	8
Middle-income	30,881	39,844	41,048	44,933	59,529	66,263	5.8	6.5	5.6	5.1	5.7	5.3
n	36	36	36	35	35	32	36	36	36	34	34	27
High-income	177,146	202,464	233,747	247,470	302,325	547,862	6.5	6.3	5.6	5.0	5.3	8.1
n	21	21	21	21	21	21	21	21	21	21	21	21
Under 1.5 mn population	18,970	23,651	25,224	30,619	38,275	48,878	3.6	3.9	3.5	3.6	3.7	4.0
n	35	35	35	35	34	33	35	35	35	34	33	29
Under 5 mn population	209,240	243,668	276,172	293,890	366,164	617,340	6.3	6.2	5.6	5.0	5.4	7.6
n	67	67	67	66	67	63	66	66	66	64	65	56

Note: n = number of countries.

Source: International Monetary Fund, *International Financial Statistics Yearbook 2009* and monthly September 2009, Washington, DC

Table 21. External debt: selected categories

Group/country	Total external debt outstanding (disbursed only)				Short-term debt as a proportion of total debt (disbursed)				Concessional debt as a proportion of total debt outstanding (disbursed)			
	2004	2005	2006	2007	2004	2005	2006	2007	2004	2005	2006	2007
	(US$ million)				(per cent)				(per cent)			
Low-income												
Commonwealth countries												
Gambia, The	672	668	725	733	4.0	3.4	2.5	3.1	90.3	91.9	93.9	94.9
Papua New Guinea	2,286	2,276	2,372	2,245	4.8	10.2	7.0	4.1	39.3	34.3	32.9	35.6
Solomon Islands	177	166	173	178	6.1	9.2	9.0	3.0	84.6	85.7	85.7	81.1
Other countries												
Central African Republic	1,065	1,002	992	973	9.3	10.1	9.5	9.1	79.4	79.2	78.6	80.7
Comoros	307	291	296	291	11.0	11.5	12.3	4.1	85.8	85.5	84.7	95.9
Guinea-Bissau	765	693	711	744	1.5	1.4	1.1	1.1	92.6	94.4	95.3	95.8
Liberia	2,715	2,576	2,697	2,475	43.9	44.3	46.2	49.0	23.2	23.3	22.9	24.2
Mauritania	2,333	2,316	1,624	1,704	6.9	7.2	14.0	14.9	82.7	82.0	70.4	72.6
São Tomé & Principe	366	340	355	169	4.6	4.1	4.2	11.2	90.3	90.7	88.7	78.2
Middle-income												
Commonwealth countries												
Belize	957	1,003	1,018	1,057	0.0	0.6	0.6	0.6	12.3	14.2	14.9	15.1
Botswana	510	473	408	402	4.3	7.4	5.9	5.5	63.0	61.9	63.5	69.5
Dominica	304	274	254	290	23.0	14.8	8.7	21.7	46.5	49.9	49.4	43.4
Fiji Islands	202	229	234	387	37.4	48.7	47.4	28.4	17.9	11.4	12.2	7.4
Grenada	432	406	492	525	17.7	1.6	7.1	9.4	26.5	35.6	36.7	38.0
Guyana	1,363	1,216	1,141	735	9.6	6.7	14.2	12.7	78.3	81.3	76.7	73.1
Jamaica	6,482	6,557	7,999	10,085	16.9	9.4	14.7	15.1	15.4	13.6	10.7	8.5
Lesotho	767	662	652	680	0.9	1.2	0.0	0.0	76.4	82.5	85.3	87.6
Maldives	372	369	477	562	10.9	14.3	19.5	23.1	57.7	54.2	47.6	43.7
Mauritius	2,289	3,125	2,624	4,253	59.1	74.7	75.8	85.1	14.1	9.8	11.2	6.7
St Kitts & Nevis	316	295	292	275	0.9	0.6	0.8	0.6	36.6	38.7	38.9	39.7
St Lucia	366	425	373	441	29.8	41.4	31.3	39.3	27.4	23.6	31.3	29.4
St Vincent & the Grenadines	257	281	299	254	13.0	12.2	19.3	21.4	38.1	33.4	31.1	38.1
Samoa	571	656	858	1,140	67.5	73.0	76.0	80.2	32.2	26.8	23.9	19.8
Seychelles	445	670	1,088	1,308	22.5	40.7	54.5	59.8	30.2	18.4	11.6	9.5
Swaziland	412	431	403	393	14.1	18.6	12.2	9.3	32.3	30.7	32.9	34.6
Tonga	86	82	85	91	1.2	0.9	1.1	1.0	92.8	94.6	94.3	94.2
Vanuatu	121	82	86	94	30.8	12.4	16.4	21.4	64.0	80.9	70.7	?
Other countries												
Albania	1,547	1,837	2,327	2,776	0.1	15.7	24.7	29.8	78.3	64.4	57.5	53.4
Armenia	1,970	1,842	2,004	2,888	20.8	16.2	15.3	15.9	47.0	48.8	51.1	43.8
Bosnia-Herzegovina	5,245	5,295	5,669	6,479	6.9	15.8	20.2	26.1	31.3	29.8	32.5	30.1
Bhutan	593	649	713	775	0.0	1.9	2.2	0.0	40.5	37.8	38.8	40.0
Cape Verde	501	520	573	599	8.5	9.4	9.6	4.3	82.0	81.8	83.3	89.4
Congo Republic	6,619	5,831	6,011	5,156	16.2	12.3	12.2	6.0	39.3	41.7	44.1	53.4
Costa Rica	5,514	5,996	6,591	7,846	30.5	35.1	35.3	37.8	7.9	6.4	6.3	6.2
Djibouti	417	412	463	472	3.2	4.0	4.1	3.5	88.8	88.9	88.1	89.6
Gabon	4,150	3,846	4,287	5,746	6.0	5.1	8.7	9.5	20.1	18.0	18.7	16.0
Georgia	2,064	1,911	1,973	2,292	5.1	2.7	5.6	11.2	61.2	65.3	66.6	61.8
Latvia	–	–	–	–	–	–	–	–	–	–	–	–
Lebanon	22,173	22,363	23,986	24,634	17.9	15.4	17.5	17.2	5.5	4.9	4.7	4.4

Table 21. External debt: selected categories (continued)

Group/country	Total external debt outstanding (disbursed only)				Short-term debt as a proportion of total debt (disbursed)				Concessional debt as a proportion of total debt outstanding (disbursed)			
	2004	2005	2006	2007	2004	2005	2006	2007	2004	2005	2006	2007
	(US$ million)				(per cent)				(per cent)			
Middle-income (contin.)												
Other countries												
Lithuania	–	–	–	–	–	–	–	–	–	–	–	–
Macedonia FYR	2,551	2,853	3,177	3,760	21.6	23.3	23.3	31.8	23.8	19.8	19.5	17.8
Moldova	1,946	2,053	2,417	3,203	30.4	35.0	34.0		18.0	17.1	16.1	14.1
Mongolia	1,351	1,302	1,394	1,596	0.0	0.0	0.0	0.0	95.7	96.3	96.7	92.4
Montenegro	–	–	1,240	1,174	–	–	–	–	–	–	65.5	63.6
Panama	9,397	9,743	9,989	9,862	4.1	5.0	5.1	–	3.2	2.7	2.4	2.2
Uruguay	15,160	14,465	11,190	12,363	27.7	27.2	19.7	19.3	0.9	0.9	1.0	0.9
Group (total or average)												
Low-income	10,686	10,328	9,945	9,512	15.5	16.8	18.4	18.0	59.6	58.5	54.3	56.6
n	9	9	9	9	9	9	9	9	9	9	9	9
Middle-income	97,450	98,153	102,787	116,600	16.2	18.6	19.7	25.2	19.2	18.2	20.3	23.1
n	34	34	35	36	34	34	34	33	34	34	35	35
Under 1.5 mn population	17,087	17,925	20,173	26,258	26.8	25.1	24.2	31.8	27.0	24.7	27.8	29.0
n	21	21	22	23	21	21	21	21	21	21	22	22
Under 5 mn population	108,136	108,481	112,732	126,112	16.1	18.4	19.5	24.3	23.2	22.0	23.3	25.8
n	43	43	44	45	43	43	43	42	43	43	44	44

Source: World Bank, *Global Development Finance 2009*, Washington, DC

Table 22. Official net transfers

Group/country	2001	2002	2003	2004	2005	2006
			(million US$)			
Low-income						
Commonwealth countries						
Gambia, The	16.5	52.2	12.5	8.1	31.2	22.3
Papua New Guinea	5.0	-8.0	3.0	39.0	66.0	179.0
Solomon Islands	-30.2	-10.7	-35.7	-8.4	-58.3	-26.8
Other countries						
Central African Republic	-8.9	0.0	2.0	-9.0	-6.0	-60.0
Comoros	3.2	10.1	1.7	1.9	-1.3	0.4
Guinea-Bissau	20.3	9.1	2.3	15.2	15.4	23.2
Liberia	-6.0	-1.0	3.0	12.0	-6.0	8.0
Mauritania	24.0	63.0	67.0	118.0	–	–
São Tomé & Principe	2.3	5.8	-13.4	3.3	0.4	-4.4
Middle-income						
Commonwealth countries						
Belize	71.8	50.2	143.0	-192.0	-23.0	-51.0
Botswana	38.7	63.9	24.0	33.5	0.9	63.3
Dominica	20.4	24.0	55.2	10.1	-45.3	-30.5
Fiji Islands	-18.2	11.8	47.5	-13.8	32.9	-4.6
Grenada	38.6	103.7	-7.2	26.5	-32.9	39.4
Guyana	5.0	-8.0	3.0	39.0	66.0	179.0
Jamaica	426.0	-398.0	-368.0	373.0	-103.0	780.0
Lesotho	-30.2	-10.7	-35.7	-8.4	-58.3	-26.8
Maldives	31.3	14.7	-5.9	36.5	36.0	67.1
Mauritius	-26.0	-54.0	536.0	-381.0	-133.0	-270.0
St Kitts & Nevis	49.8	20.9	22.0	-34.6	-40.4	-22.7
St Lucia	22.3	18.0	20.9	4.7	45.9	-72.1
St Vincent & the Grenadines	-7.0	4.8	11.3	19.2	17.6	6.3
Samoa	6.8	11.6	109.8	173.4	81.9	170.4
Seychelles	9.1	36.0	-0.8	-21.2	162.7	158.7
Swaziland	9.4	-6.9	-17.4	52.0	82.4	-17.9
Tonga	0.5	2.5	8.2	-2.5	0.5	-0.4
Vanuatu	1.2	11.2	-1.2	18.5	-29.6	0.3
Other countries						
Bhutan	71.7	92.4	88.5	76.2	83.1	43.1
Cape Verde	44.6	22.1	30.3	11.2	51.5	27.1
Congo Republic	-378.0	151.0	-277.0	128.0	-356.0	-80.0
Costa Rica	-48.0	-158.0	229.0	-21.0	229.0	99.0
Djibouti	6.3	24.1	12.2	12.4	19.0	31.6
Estonia	-14.0	1,589.0	1,458.0	2,643.0	1,015.0	
Gabon	-450.0	-415.0	-496.0	-30.0	-77.0	4.0
Oman	-996.0	-1,536.0	-930.0	-301.0	-35.0	618.0
Panama	739.0	-443.0	-189.0	100.0	-241.0	570.0
Uruguay	1,015.0	227.0	-60.0	2212.0	-617.0	-5,277.0

Table 22. Official net transfers (continued)

Group/country	2001	2002	2003	2004	2005	2006
	(million US$)					
Group total						
Low-income	–14.4	102.3	42.4	149.7	10.6	95.3
n	9	9	9	9	8	8
Middle-income	562.7	–678.5	362.7	4,896.7	131.1	–4,262.3
n	28	28	28	28	28	27
Under 1.5 mn population	–151.1	1558.3	1970.0	2444.4	1254.1	227.0
n	23	23	23	23	23	22
Under 5 mn population	548.3	–576.2	405.1	5,046.4	141.7	4,167.0
n	37	37	37	37	36	35

Source: World Bank, *Global Development Finance 2008*, Washington, DC

Table 23. Principal indicators of debt

Group/country	External debt (EDT) as a percentage of GNI				External debt as a percentage of exports of goods and services (XGS)				Total debt service (TDS) as a percentage of exports of goods and services (XGS)			
	2004	2005	2006	2007	2004	2005	2006	2007	2004	2005	2006	2007
Low-income												
Commonwealth countries												
Gambia, The	183.6	160.0	157.6	122.8	273.7	278.0	270.3	256.3	15.2	11.8	12.4	12.4
Papua New Guinea	64.2	50.0	48.0	40.0	82.1	63.0	–	–	17.1	11.2	4.5	–
Solomon Islands	66.6	56.4	51.3	46.4	137.1	105.6	82.8	–	12.9	8.9	2.0	–
Other countries												
Central African Republic	84.0	74.3	67.3	57.2	829.2	883.5	902.7	–	10.8	5.2	61.9	–
Comoros	85.2	75.6	73.4	64.7	431.0	418.8	357.0	–	4.2	5.8	4.6	–
Guinea-Bissau	295.9	239.6	238.7	213.6	684.9	545.7	534.8	–	40.2	25.7	25.4	–
Liberia	727.9	617.4	607.7	442.1	847.4	730.1	529.5	440.3	0.2	0.3	0.2	111.6
Mauritania	144.6	121.8	58.9	62.0	596.6	229.0	116.4	–	14.8	–	6.9	–
São Tomé & Principe	598.1	307.5	297.0	117.1	2,109.4	1,753.0	1,488.4	852.7	37.4	29.5	39.1	39.2
Middle-income												
Commonwealth countries												
Belize	101.6	100.3	93.1	91.8	165.2	147.8	117.2	117.3	57.6	34.5	15.5	69.3
Botswana	5.8	4.9	4.0	3.4	10.8	8.1	6.9	6.0	1.0	0.9	0.9	0.9
Dominica	120.1	99.8	89.9	–	199.3	175.9	148.0	173.1	10.8	10.4	10.5	11.6
Fiji Islands	7.4	7.6	7.7	11.4	13.1	13.5	13.9	–	0.9	1.0	1.0	–
Grenada	113.7	89.8	109.7	116.4	173.9	217.2	243.4	221.3	11.9	5.6	7.7	7.8
Guyana	201.7	163.1	132.4	73.3	151.1	135.4	120.4	65.0	5.3	3.8	3.4	2.4
Jamaica	76.9	72.2	85.6	101.2	115.0	110.3	115.1	136.0	15.1	16.3	11.9	17.3
Lesotho	47.1	38.4	34.8	33.7	65.4	61.3	55.8	48.2	4.6	7.4	3.9	7.0
Maldives	51.7	53.2	54.4	56.4	53.3	78.0	60.2	64.1	4.7	7.0	4.4	5.1
Mauritius	38.0	49.7	41.2	62.1	65.4	80.1	60.0	81.0	7.4	7.8	7.1	4.9
St Kitts & Nevis	88.8	75.9	63.2	55.2	137.7	110.1	105.2	103.5	20.4	17.9	16.8	17.3
St Lucia	50.6	52.9	44.7	47.6	73.7	79.5	79.6	91.4	5.0	6.1	7.4	7.6
St Vincent & the Grenadines	66.4	68.7	65.3	49.2	122.1	121.8	120.7	94.2	9.8	10.8	14.4	10.7
Samoa	154.0	163.2	194.7	223.0	513.6	499.8	573.0	714.5	19.1	17.1	19.7	26.9
Seychelles	66.7	98.2	148.7	190.8	69.0	90.4	124.5	147.9	6.2	7.5	20.6	11.2
Swaziland	18.0	16.0	15.0	13.3	18.9	19.7	18.4	15.8	2.0	1.5	1.6	1.9
Tonga	43.0	38.8	35.0	34.6	74.9	64.9	70.4	60.8	3.1	3.2	2.7	2.8
Vanuatu	38.7	23.9	21.9	22.4	64.3	40.1	40.0	36.6	1.8	1.3	1.7	1.5
Other countries												
Albania	20.2	21.5	24.9	24.9	54.5	57.2	61.2	80.9	2.6	2.5	3.7	4.1
Armenia	53.5	36.6	30.4	30.5	130.4	95.4	90.7	107.7	11.2	7.2	6.8	7.0
Bhutan	85.2	79.5	76.5	68.6	7.6	2.2	–	–	7.6	2.2	–	–
Bosnia-Herzegovina	49.9	47.2	44.6	41.4	102.9	93.0	82.6	77.0	4.8	4.5	8.6	8.0
Cape Verde	55.2	53.5	50.4	43.2	117.2	99.8	85.1	76.0	5.8	7.0	4.8	3.8
Congo Republic	203.8	129.3	100.5	86.1	181.4	117.0	94.6	83.8	6.0	2.1	1.4	1.2
Costa Rica	30.9	31.3	30.3	30.8	60.9	54.9	52.0	55.2	7.8	5.5	4.7	4.4
Croatia	94.7	81.3	92.5	97.7	170.7	148.6	164.9	176.6	27.3	26.3	33.8	33.0
Djibouti	57.0	53.1	54.3	51.8	145.2	127.7	131.9	–	6.2	4.7	6.4	–
Gabon	69.3	49.9	50.8	56.2	97.8	60.1	82.2	–	5.3	1.9	1.6	?
Georgia	39.5	29.4	24.9	22.0	105.2	75.1	64.8	58.6	11.9	7.4	8.8	4.6
Latvia	94.6	92.2	118.2	150.3	195.5	174.8	231.1	293.9	22.1	39.1	33.3	73.3
Lebanon	107.4	104.6	106.1	101.8	123.2	114.7	109.9	101.4	24.2	18.2	20.3	18.7
Macedonia FYR	47.9	50.0	50.1	49.2	109.7	102.7	95.4	–	10.5	9.1	16.8	–
Moldova	66.3	61.3	63.4	66.5	95.5	84.2	87.7	89.7	15.0	10.3	12.1	9.5

Table 23. Principal indicators of debt (continued)

Group/country	External debt (EDT) as a percentage of GNI				External debt as a percentage of exports of goods and services (XGS)				Total debt service (TDS) as a percentage of exports of goods and services (XGS)			
	2004	2005	2006	2007	2004	2005	2006	2007	2004	2005	2006	2007
Middle-income (contin.)												
Other countries												
Mongolia	74.9	57.7	45.8	41.5	95.0	77.9	62.6	–	2.4	2.3	2.1	–
Montenegro	–	–	45.4	33.5	–	–	–	–	–	–	–	–
Oman	16.3	13.5	15.5	–	26.3	20.0	20.3	–	6.8	7.5	1.3	–
Panama	71.4	67.9	63.1	54.3	96.0	82.7	71.5	60.5	14.3	17.6	24.8	5.3
Turkmenistan	22.6	14.0	9.0	5.9	–	–	–	–	–	–	–	–
Uruguay	120.2	89.8	59.4	54.4	322.6	252.7	169.0	158.5	32.9	38.4	88.1	19.1

Source: World Bank, *Global Development Finance 2009*, Washington, DC

Table 24. Composition of debt

Group/Country	Official debt as a percentage of total debt outstanding (disbursed)				Commercial debt as a percentage of total debt outstanding (disbursed)			
	2004	2005	2006	2007	2004	2005	2006	2007
Low-income								
Commonwealth countries								
Gambia, The	99.8	99.8	99.9	99.9	0.2	0.2	0.1	0.1
Papua New Guinea	64.7	59.4	53.5	51.8	35.3	40.6	46.5	48.2
Solomon Islands	90.9	95.1	94.9	84.7	9.1	4.9	5.1	15.3
Other countries								
Central African Republic	96.7	96.5	96.5	96.3	3.3	3.5	3.5	3.7
Comoros	100.0	100.0	100.0	100.0	0.0	0.0	0.0	0.0
Guinea-Bissau	100.0	100.0	100.0	100.0	0.0	0.0	0.0	0.0
Liberia	82.4	82.2	82.2	77.7	17.6	17.8	17.8	22.3
Mauritania	99.5	98.9	98.5	98.6	0.5	1.1	1.5	1.4
São Tomé & Principe	100.0	100.0	100.0	100.0	0.0	0.0	0.0	0.0
Middle-income								
Commonwealth countries								
Belize	30.5	31.2	36.9	32.4	69.5	68.8	63.1	67.6
Botswana	97.1	97.3	97.6	98.2	2.9	2.7	2.4	1.8
Dominica	73.5	72.9	72.5	72.1	26.5	27.1	27.5	27.9
Fiji Islands	94.5	95.9	97.1	44.8	5.5	4.1	2.9	55.2
Grenada	40.8	44.1	46.1	48.6	59.2	55.9	53.9	51.4
Guyana	98.3	99.0	99.1	98.6	1.7	1.0	0.9	1.4
Jamaica	44.6	36.2	29.7	23.0	55.4	63.8	70.3	77.0
Lesotho	90.3	95.4	96.5	97.2	9.7	4.6	3.5	2.8
Maldives	71.6	70.8	73.3	–	28.4	29.2	26.7	–
Mauritius	61.5	63.3	68.8	71.8	38.5	36.7	31.2	28.2
St Kitts & Nevis	52.4	53.7	53.7	54.2	47.6	46.3	46.3	45.8
St Lucia	63.8	64.6	68.0	71.6	36.2	35.4	32.0	28.4
St Vincent & the Grenadines	50.2	46.0	50.9	67.3	49.8	54.0	49.1	32.7
Samoa	99.8	100.2	100.0	100.0	0.2	-0.2	0.0	0.0
Seychelles	70.8	56.9	40.6	38.6	29.2	43.1	59.4	61.4
Swaziland	86.5	87.4	87.8	88.5	13.5	12.6	12.2	11.5
Tonga	100.0	100.0	100.0	100.0	0.0	0.0	0.0	0.0
Vanuatu	100.0	100.0	100.0	100.0	0.0	0.0	0.0	0.0
Other countries								
Albania	95.2	92.7	93.6	94.9	4.8	7.3	6.4	5.1
Armenia	71.5	67.3	67.6	56.0	28.5	32.7	32.4	44.0
Bhutan	100.0	100.0	100.0	100.0	0.0	0.0	0.0	0.0
Bosnia-Herzegovina	52.4	54.6	59.0	58.9	47.6	45.4	41.0	41.1
Cape Verde	95.6	95.4	96.6	97.3	4.4	4.6	3.4	2.7
Congo Republic	60.0	58.6	59.3	68.1	40.0	41.4	40.7	31.9
Costa Rica	44.4	48.7	34.9	30.3	55.6	51.3	65.1	69.7
Djibouti	98.6	98.4	98.7	99.0	1.4	1.6	1.3	1.0
Gabon	93.6	93.7	93.4	74.3	6.4	6.3	6.6	25.7
Georgia	94.0	91.8	90.0	86.4	6.0	8.2	10.0	13.6
Lebanon	9.9	8.5	8.2	8.3	90.1	91.5	91.8	91.7
Macedonia FYR	67.2	57.4	55.3	48.3	32.8	42.6	44.7	51.7
Moldova	58.0	53.7	48.9	39.1	42.0	46.3	51.1	60.9

Table 24. Composition of debt (continued)

Group/Country	Official debt as a percentage of total debt outstanding (disbursed)				Commercial debt as a percentage of total debt outstanding (disbursed)			
	2004	2005	2006	2007	2004	2005	2006	2007
Middle-income (contin.)								
Other countries								
Mongolia	99.9	99.9	98.9	93.9	0.1	0.1	1.1	6.1
Montenegro	–	–	97.5	100.0	–	–	2.5	0.0
Oman	41.7	35.7	28.5	–	58.3	64.3	71.5	–
Panama	15.6	14.2	14.3	15.1	84.4	85.8	85.7	84.9
Turkmenistan	67.5	75.3	78.3	80.5	32.5	24.7	21.7	19.5
Uruguay	38.7	39.1	29.3	26.2	61.3	60.9	70.7	73.8

Source: World Bank, *Global Development Finance 2009*, Washington, DC

Table 25. Foreign direct investment

Group/country	Foreign direct investment inward flows								
	2000	2001	2002	2003	2004	2005	2006	2007	2008
	(US$ million)								
Low-income									
Commonwealth countries									
Gambia, The	44	35	43	15	49	45	71	76	63
Papua New Guinea	96	63	18	101	26	34	–7	96	–30
Solomon Islands	1	–12	–4	–2	6	19	34	67	76
Other countries									
Central African Republic	1	5	6	13	15	17	35	57	121
Comoros	0	1	0	1	0	1	1	8	8
Guinea-Bissau	1	0	4	4	2	9	18	19	15
Liberia	21	8	3	372	237	–1,384	108	132	143
Mauritania	40	92	67	102	392	814	155	153	103
São Tomé & Principe	4	3	3	3	4	16	38	35	33
Middle-income									
Commonwealth countries									
Belize	23	60	24	–11	112	127	109	140	179
Botswana	57	31	405	420	392	281	486	495	–4
Dominica	20	18	20	31	26	19	29	61	60
Fiji Islands	–18	43	37	45	255	160	374	289	274
Grenada	39	61	54	89	65	70	96	190	168
Guyana	67	56	44	26	30	77	102	152	178
Jamaica	469	614	481	721	602	682	882	867	789
Kiribati	18	15	15	16	19	1	13	–8	2
Lesotho	31	28	27	42	53	57	92	106	199
Maldives	13	12	12	14	15	9	14	15	15
Mauritius	266	–28	32	62	11	42	105	339	383
Namibia	188	365	182	149	226	349	387	733	746
Nauru	0	0	1	2	1	1	0	1	1
St Kitts & Nevis	99	90	81	76	46	93	115	164	94
St Lucia	58	63	57	106	77	78	238	259	110
St Vincent & the Grenadines	38	21	34	55	66	40	109	117	96
Samoa	–2	1	0	1	2	–4	12	3	6
Seychelles	24	65	48	58	37	86	146	238	364
Swaziland	91	51	90	–61	71	–50	36	37	10
Tonga	5	1	1	3	5	17	10	28	6
Tuvalu	–1	1	25	0	0	0	5	0	0
Vanuatu	13	9	13	15	18	13	43	34	34
Other countries									
Albania	144	206	133	177	346	264	324	190	209
Armenia	104	70	111	121	248	239	453	1,816	2,622
Bahrain	364	80	217	517	865	1,049	2,915	1,896	2,021
Bhutan	0	0	2	3	3	9	6	195	234
Bosnia-Herzegovina	146	119	265	381	704	613	718	1,726	1,290
Cape Verde	32	9	39	34	68	82	131	269	20
Congo Republic	166	77	137	323	–13	402	1919	1,750	1,564
Costa Rica	409	460	659	575	794	861	1,469	2,247	1,426
Djibouti	3	3	4	14	39	59	164	2,731	3,606
Equatorial Guinea	108	945	323	1,431	1,651	1,873	1,656	2,017	1,815
Gabon	–43	–89	30	206	194	60	268	493	713

Table 25. Foreign direct investment (continued)

Group/country	Foreign direct investment inward flows								
	2000	2001	2002	2003	2004	2005	2006	2007	2008
	(US$ million)								
Middle-income (contin.)									
Other countries									
Georgia	131	110	160	334	492	453	1,170	360	683
Latvia	413	132	254	304	637	713	1,664	1,907	2,402
Lebanon	964	1,451	1,336	2,860	1,899	2,624	2,675	316	–234
Lithuania	379	446	732	179	773	1,032	1,840	2,017	1,815
Moldova	128	55	84	74	88	191	251	1,288	2,205
Mongolia	–	–	78	132	93	185	191	360	683
Panama	624	467	99	771	1,004	962	2,498	1,907	2,402
Suriname	–97	–27	–74	201	286	399	323	316	–234
Turkmenistan	–	–	276	226	354	418	731	801	820
Uruguay	273	297	194	416	332	847	1,493	1,288	2,505
High-income									
Commonwealth countries									
Antigua & Barbuda	67	112	66	166	80	214	316	952	879
Bahamas, The	250	102	312	642	443	563	706	746	700
Barbados	19	19	17	58	–12	62	105	233	133
Brunei Darussalam	549	526	1,035	3,375	334	289	434	260	239
Cyprus	855	944	1,057	893	1,090	1,186	1,864	2,181	2,164
Malta	618	247	–448	968	396	675	1,871	952	879
New Zealand	3,863	820	1,755	2,426	2,827	1,666	7,758	4,982	4,383
Singapore	16,484	15,649	7,200	11,664	19,830	13,930	27,680	31,550	22,724
Trinidad & Tobago	680	835	791	808	998	940	883	830	3,047
Other countries									
Croatia	1,109	1,582	1,099	2,049	1,079	1,788	3,457	4,982	4,382
Estonia	387	542	284	919	966	2,493	1,788	2,736	1,986
Iceland	171	174	87	332	737	3,081	4,029	3,473	–2,592
Ireland	25,779	9,651	29,324	22,781	–10,608	–31,689	–5,542	24,706	–20,030
Kuwait	16	–111	3	–67	24	234	122	123	56
Luxembourg	–	–	4,058	2,914	5,192	5,828	28,482	–31,692	3,012
Norway	5,967	2,127	637	3,484	2,473	3,413	6415	4,433	–95
Oman	83	5	122	494	229	1,688	1688	3,124	2,928
Qatar	252	296	624	625	1,199	1,298	3,500	4,700	6,700
United Arab Emirates	–515	1,184	1,307	4,256	10,004	10,900	12,806	14,186	13,700

Note: – = data not available.

Source: UNCTAD, *Handbook of Statistics*, 2009, Geneva

Table 26. Total net financial flows from all sources

Group/country	2001	2002	2003	2004	2005	2006	2007
				(US$ million)			
Low-income							
Commonwealth countries							
Gambia, The	45.8	47.2	68.1	59.8	67.9	73.0	87.2
Papua New Guinea	235.4	252.7	237.5	205.2	495.4	423.3	296.2
Solomon Islands	54.4	25.1	61.5	125.0	170.0	216.3	255.7
Other countries							
Central African Republic	75.4	54.3	51.6	111.1	93.2	137.2	187.5
Comoros	5.6	-105.4	25.5	24.7	43.1	30.6	-41.5
Guinea-Bissau	58.6	60.3	92.7	75.2	76.9	75.3	103.0
Liberia	1,032.1	-287.1	4,521.6	1,255.9	-2317.2	298.1	1,152.9
Mauritania	259.5	304.7	238.6	224.9	207.2	175.9	316.8
São Tomé & Principe	40.5	27.8	45.3	31.9	31.9	25.2	12.6
Timor-Leste	248.0	396.4	366.5	536.8	185.9	146.3	279.4
Middle-income							
Commonwealth countries							
Belize	92.8	38.3	6.1	51.0	23.5	-92.5	189.6
Botswana	45.4	57.8	-20.9	41.9	81.6	92.7	34.1
Dominica	-42.4	55.7	6.2	54.6	6.5	16.7	38.4
Fiji Islands	4.3	40.9	47.4	97.0	118.1	0.6	36.3
Grenada	20.2	11.3	30.4	24.2	95.5	34.9	23.8
Guyana	96.0	72.6	94.8	289.3	483.2	-23.7	114.6
Jamaica	201.9	0.8	85.4	280.0	-1637.2	332.3	262.4
Kiribati	12.7	20.9	18.4	17.3	28.8	24.5	19.2
Lesotho	-40.8	-43.9	-48.4	89.2	51.4	61.4	111.3
Maldives	37.3	51.6	55.0	76.3	127.3	142.3	121.2
Mauritius	321.6	-100.7	340.9	2,878.9	147.0	740.6	4,615.7
Namibia	130.4	62.0	170.9	62.9	158.3	491.2	248.0
Nauru	7.5	13.0	22.4	237.1	11.7	17.8	26.0
St Kitts & Nevis	6.4	5.4	2.6	-14.4	-18.0	0.4	-420.4
St Lucia	15.3	37.9	20.5	1.8	34.3	32.5	47.3
St Vincent & the Grenadines	-2.5	-11.1	-12.5	27.9	-12.4	16.4	499.8
Samoa	43.1	38.2	40.1	20.8	73.1	49.9	66.2
Seychelles	14.9	102.6	0.9	8.6	21.7	-43.9	127.9
Swaziland	35.3	26.8	41.9	55.2	50.9	37.8	54.6
Tonga	20.3	23.2	39.1	29.4	33.9	23.5	23.2
Tuvalu	10.1	36.7	6.3	8.0	8.3	19.0	11.0
Vanuatu	373.8	24.0	32.1	21.1	51.3	78.8	46.8
Other countries							
Albania	343.8	321.0	379.6	524.5	481.9	499.6	642.2
Armenia	209.8	301.4	250.6	250.0	236.2	362.2	563.2
Bahrain	2,601.7	168.2	250.8	828.5	–	–	–
Bhutan	59.6	96.0	57.2	77.8	95.4	93.0	87.9
Bosnia-Herzegovina	712.7	717.1	643.2	953.6	744.8	1,152.8	1,127.5
Cape Verde	129.9	160.3	185.9	209.4	260.4	191.5	110.8
Congo Republic	-220.6	-125.2	515.8	230.9	1,320.5	609.7	802.0
Costa Rica	51.5	70.7	149.0	179.9	654.2	1,317.9	737.8
Djibouti	70.7	94.3	99.2	73.9	98.0	184.5	133.3
Gabon	45.8	-166.0	158.6	398.7	-76.0	171.7	581.1
Georgia	–	–	843.7	358.7	363.6	576.6	580.7

Table 26. Total net financial flows from all sources (continued)

Group/country	2001	2002	2003	2004	2005	2006	2007
				(million US$)			
Middle-income (contin.)							
Other countries							
Lebanon	524.9	486.1	1,377.3	282.5	386.4	561.0	778.5
Macedonia FYR	247.3	237.9	93.2	326.7	383.0	546.6	232
Moldova	95.0	148.7	114.4	116.5	180.4	369.7	397.3
Montenegro	–	–	–	–	–	142.2	172.1
Panama	794.3	2,403.4	–5,867.6	1,959.5	5,942.1	6,021.9	4,904.3
Suriname	12.1	61.5	–4.6	21.2	19.0	37.4	71.1
Turkmenistan	42.7	–241.8	176.0	118.7	36.2	–167.1	129.7
Uruguay	474.7	734.5	–115.4	–199.8	516.5	1,270.0	1889.4
Group total							
Low-income	2,392.7	1,128.9	5,997.6	2,650.5	-945.7	1,601.2	2,649.8
n	11	11	11	10	10	10	10
Middle-income	5,802.1	6,032.1	286.5	11,069.3	11,581.4	15,994.4	20,237.9
n	39	39	40	40	39	40	40
Under 1.5 mn population	1,076.5	1,187.8	1,824.0	5,464.1	2,279.0	2,683.7	7,647.2
n	29	29	29	29	29	30	30
Under 5 mn population	8,194.8	7,161.0	6,284.1	13,719.8	10,635.7	17,595.6	22,887.7
n	50	50	51	50	49	50	50

Source: Organisation for Economic Co-operation and Development, *Geographical Distribution of Financial Flows to Developing Countries*, Paris, various issues

Table 27. Net financial flows by major categories

Group/country	Bilateral flows from DAC countries			Multilateral flows			Private flows			Net bilateral flows from EU member countries		
	2005	2006	2007	2005	2006	2007	2005	2006	2007	2005	2006	2007
	(US$ million)			(US$ million)			(US$ million)			(US$ million)		
Low-income												
Commonwealth countries												
Gambia, The	21.7	23.9	48.0	46.0	43.4	36.3	6.6	–1.2	13.9	14.5	8.3	47.5
Papua New Guinea	477.5	430.4	354.8	22.1	–7.7	–58.0	232.4	187.4	69.2	–34.3	47.2	68.7
Solomon Islands	144.2	189.7	242.5	25.9	25.5	14.0	–16.5	9.5	3.7	–2.5	20.3	5.7
Other countries												
Central African Republic	63.6	69.0	132.5	29.6	68.2	54.7	1.1	3.0	15.0	77.6	54.4	132.6
Comoros	35.4	20.2	–56.5	7.7	9.9	15.1	18.3	0.2	–76.1	18.2	37.5	–44.1
Guinea-Bissau	37.7	32.6	23.4	39.2	42.7	79.2	–1.6	–2.5	–19.8	50.3	58.7	59.4
Liberia	–2,404.1	217.5	904.4	86.8	80.1	247.5	–2,459.1	30.1	676.2	–1,010.1	438.2	768.7
Mauritania	125.5	88.2	100.6	81.1	87.1	215.0	2.4	–9.2	–39.5	105.6	80.5	170.6
São Tomé & Principe	17.8	21.9	7.7	14.0	3.3	4.9	–0.6	3.6	–17.2	20.0	19.7	4.5
Middle-income												
Commonwealth countries												
Belize	20.2	–99.1	155.7	4.2	7.2	31.6	12.8	–113.3	149.4	12.6	–98.2	204.6
Botswana	49.7	64.1	10.3	33.8	30.2	25.2	17.7	27.8	–53.2	40.2	65.4	–1.0
Dominica	–12.9	–0.3	23.4	13.6	16.9	14.7	–17.4	–2.2	20.3	–4.2	22.4	47.3
Fiji Islands	82.8	–17.9	6.5	34.8	16.0	28.4	41.9	–59.1	–27.1	37.1	26.9	–1.2
Guyana	371.0	–152.6	29.0	112.1	128.8	84.9	331.0	–199.2	–11.0	350.8	–197.2	14.1
Jamaica	–1,574.9	294.9	279.6	–65.7	37.9	–15.8	–1,580.6	311.8	294.5	15.8	163.0	164.0
Kiribati	22.3	18.8	14.5	6.5	5.6	4.4	0.8	–1.3	–8.3	4.3	5.0	–4.5
Lesotho	30.4	35.5	52.9	22.0	26.7	59.0	–9.0	–3.0	–9.4	18.7	25.3	39.5
Maldives	47.1	99.8	81.8	66.6	40.3	40.4	8.5	79.9	67.7	13.4	114.3	115.2
Mauritius	148.8	762.9	4,548.3	–3.8	–20.4	69.5	128.9	750.3	4,505.5	–261.0	220.6	2,678.6
Namibia	112.4	429.9	170.8	41.8	59.6	76.1	27.5	325.4	–14.3	85.0	379.4	94.3
Nauru	11.4	17.7	25.4	0.1	0.1	0.4	2.3	–0.3	0.0	1.4	–1.2	0.4
St Kitts & Nevis	–20.0	–3.7	–427.3	2.9	5.7	7.9	–19.7	–5.5	–429.0	–23.0	–4.1	–48.1
St Lucia	29.3	8.1	25.4	5.5	22.6	19.0	22.8	5.5	17.9	25.9	3.1	29.0
St Vincent & the Grenadines	–13.9	0.6	471.0	1.9	16.4	29.3	–19.6	–1.7	446.1	–15.2	3.8	480.6
Samoa	59.6	40.2	45.4	13.4	8.7	15.6	29.2	1.4	15.9	30.1	1.6	23.9
Seychelles	15.8	–25.6	128.4	5.6	–17.7	0.0	7.9	–32.7	127.5	9.9	–23.5	127.8
Swaziland	34.8	6.4	7.1	16.7	32.0	47.8	13.9	–5.9	–5.1	–9.6	14.4	16.2
Tonga	26.0	20.5	19.2	7.0	2.8	3.8	0.9	2.3	0.2	2.5	2.5	–1.6
Tuvalu	5.2	16.4	8.3	3.1	2.6	2.7	0.0	3.7	–0.7	2.3	4.2	1.5
Vanuatu	45.2	71.4	42.2	6.1	7.4	4.5	11.1	28.6	–11.3	4.1	45.9	5.7
Other countries												
Albania	249.1	227.7	436.4	201.7	148.0	144.5	55.4	49.1	222.6	258.1	253.8	471.9
Armenia	201.4	266.2	397.4	33.9	94.1	163.8	53.6	132.7	155.4	157.8	208.3	245.4
Bhutan	62.3	49.9	43.0	33.2	42.9	44.4	1.0	–1.2	–0.1	38.5	23.2	19.3
Bosnia-Herzegovina	451.9	845.5	784.6	266.9	234.5	309.8	161.6	525.5	481.0	544.6	870.7	897.4
Cape Verde	195.8	152.9	62.6	62.1	36.8	47.7	91.6	54.1	–51.6	195.5	152.2	65.6
Congo Republic	1,263.9	537.3	735.8	56.5	71.5	64.6	–554.3	469.2	779.8	1,304.8	446.5	829.4
Costa Rica	785.3	1,386.8	833.5	–131.6	–70.2	–99.9	753.1	1,362.4	791.0	90.0	79.2	65.5
Djibouti	75.5	148.8	96.3	23.5	34.0	36.9	21.7	53.2	20.8	63.1	120.2	95.8
Gabon	–54.3	185.1	601.3	–21.7	–13.9	–21.7	–112.2	226.7	637.7	103.9	299.8	326.7
Georgia	165.9	351.2	309.3	126.4	181.9	248.1	–32.3	144.7	149.1	71.6	266.8	229.2

Table 27. Net financial flows by major categories (continued)

Group/country	Bilateral flows from DAC countries 2005	2006	2007	Multilateral flows 2005	2006	2007	Private flows 2005	2006	2007	Net bilateral flows from EU member countries 2005	2006	2007
	(US$ million)			(US$ million)			(US$ million)			(US$ million)		
Middle-income (contin.)												
Other countries												
Lebanon	317.9	266.4	163.4	72.5	259.6	289.4	190.8	-75.2	-226.5	235.6	365.2	264.3
Macedonia FYR	251.7	423.8	187.9	124.1	116.2	30.4	103.6	304.5	58.9	241.0	435.8	237.9
Moldova	125.3	231.3	230.2	36.7	104.7	150.8	19.6	123.5	143.3	122.1	215.6	266.3
Mongolia	109.9	205.1	268.9	54.0	48.4	55.3	-22.6	86.1	128.6	44.6	82.3	104.7
Montenegro	–	108.3	206.7	–	31.6	-57.0	–	44.0	162.1	–	102.6	213.0
Oman	2,289.3	1,879.7	1,437.2	54.4	101.4	5.3	2,094.7	1,728.0	1,396.4	792.8	1,718.5	1,487.8
Panama	5,976.6	5,990.0	4,648.5	-56.2	-26.0	-51.2	5,961.8	6,002.0	4,749.8	-212.9	358.5	1,390.1
Suriname	9.4	24.4	30.5	9.5	12.9	40.2	-23.6	-25.2	-91.7	10.6	24.7	57.6
Timor-Leste	161.3	110.1	226.6	24.4	35.0	50.7	0.1	-64.3	-0.6	63.7	24.9	123.6
Turkmenistan	-85.8	-126.3	-473.9	-6.5	-34.4	-1.9	-69.1	-60.4	-408.7	-27.6	-112.1	-355.5
Uruguay	460.8	1,830.4	1,809.5	55.1	-560.7	79.4	453.8	1,818.2	1,790.0	317.6	612.7	781.0
Group (total or average)												
Low-income	-1,480.7	1,093.4	1,757.4	352.4	352.5	608.7	-2,217.0	220.9	625.4	-764.6	752.2	1,213.6
n	9	9	9	9	9	9	9	9	9	9	9	9
Middle-income	12,563.2	16,693.4	18,757.3	1,380.9	1,302.0	2,100.0	8,192.9	14,010.6	15,960.7	4,814.3	7,336.7	11,806.2
n	42	43	43	42	43	43	42	43	43	42	43	43
Under 1.5 mn population	1,754.5	3,000.5	6,848.7	756.8	698.7	986.3	560.1	1,855.4	5,520.9	1,110.1	2,323.1	4,908.6
n	27	27	27	27	27	27	27	27	27	27	27	27
Under 5 mn population	11,082.5	17,786.8	20,514.7	1,733.3	1,654.5	2,708.7	5,975.9	14,231.5	16,586.1	4,049.7	8,088.9	13,019.8
n	51	52	52	51	52	52	51	52	52	51	52	52

Note: – = not available.

Source: Organisation for Economic Co-operation and Development, *Geographical Distribution of Financial Flows to Developing Countries 2003–2007*, Paris

Table 28. ODA commitments, disbursements,[a] per capita resource flows and IMF credit

Group/country	Commitments			Disbursement as a proportion of commitment			Per capita net resource flows from all sources			Use of IMF credit		
	2005	2006	2007	2005	2006	2007	2005	2006	2007	2005	2006	2007
	(US$ million)			(per cent)			(US$)			(US$ million)		
Low-income												
Commonwealth countries												
Gambia, The	84.0	60.0	52.9	73.0	123.5	136.9	42.0	43.9	51.1	20.8	17.8	6.3
Papua New Guinea	233.6	381.0	333.4	113.9	73.3	95.1	81.6	68.3	46.8	0.0	0.0	0.0
Solomon Islands	156.8	239.0	275.3	126.4	85.6	90.1	360.2	446.9	516.6	0.0	0.0	0.0
Other countries												
Central African Republic	89.9	166.9	196.3	102.4	80.0	89.9	22.2	32.2	43.2	36.0	42.0	49.4
Comoros	56.8	28.8	40.9	43.8	105.6	108.8	71.8	49.8	–66.3	0.0	0.0	0.0
Guinea-Bissau	55.2	60.4	113.1	142.6	135.9	108.9	48.2	45.7	60.8	11.5	8.2	5.2
Liberia	218.4	285.0	428.2	106.5	94.0	162.6	–673.2	83.3	307.2	320.0	336.0	352.0
Mauritania	148.0	269.6	164.5	135.5	70.5	221.2	69.9	57.8	101.5	69.0	0.0	13.0
São Tomé & Principe	17.1	24.9	44.5	190.1	86.3	80.9	208.5	162.6	79.7	3.2	4.1	2.6
Middle-income												
Commonwealth countries												
Belize	23.0	29.2	24.8	52.2	26.0	94.4	80.5	–310.4	623.7	0.0	0.0	0.0
Botswana	111.3	76.0	290.0	43.2	86.3	36.0	44.4	49.9	18.1	0.0	0.0	0.0
Dominica	36.6	9.2	33.6	57.1	212.0	57.7	90.3	231.9	526.0	11.6	14.0	12.1
Fiji Islands	43.4	43.4	43.8	151.8	134.6	131.3	142.6	0.7	43.3	0.0	0.0	0.0
Grenada	62.2	18.3	22.1	84.7	146.4	102.7	892.5	323.1	220.4	8.4	9.5	7.7
Guyana	61.4	169.2	161.2	243.8	102.2	76.9	653.9	–32.1	155.1	90.9	55.8	58.6
Jamaica	86.5	87.5	167.3	45.9	42.3	15.5	–616.8	124.6	98.0	1.0	0.0	0.0
Kiribati	27.7	15.7	30.5	100.4	160.5	88.9	290.9	245.0	188.2	–	–	–
Lesotho	76.2	104.4	179.5	90.7	69.1	72.1	25.9	30.8	55.5	35.0	36.3	35.4
Maldives	66.2	46.1	31.6	114.5	81.3	118.4	431.5	474.3	397.4	5.9	6.2	6.5
Mauritius	46.5	72.8	172.7	73.5	25.5	43.2	118.3	591.1	3654.6	0.0	0.0	0.0
Namibia	118.2	224.7	212.1	96.4	64.7	96.7	78.4	240.0	119.6	–	–	–
Nauru	16.4	25.2	23.8	55.5	69.0	107.6	900.0	1271.4	1857.1	–	–	–
St Kitts & Nevis	12.0	11.8	24.2	20.8	44.1	12.0	–375.0	8.3	–8,579.6	0.0	0.0	0.0
St Lucia	35.7	11.5	15.0	29.4	160.8	157.3	207.9	195.8	281.5	0.0	0.0	0.0
St Vincent & the Grenadines	7.4	12.0	72.9	59.5	39.2	90.0	–104.2	136.7	4165.0	0.0	0.0	0.0
Samoa	78.5	63.5	96.1	55.5	74.2	38.4	397.4	269.7	354.0	0.0	0.0	0.0
Seychelles	14.7	32.3	4.1	102.0	43.3	68.3	261.4	–516.5	1504.7	0.0	0.0	0.0
Swaziland	53.1	46.6	78.2	87.9	74.7	80.3	45.0	33.2	47.7	0.0	0.0	0.0
Tonga	16.4	24.2	40.3	193.9	88.8	75.7	342.4	235.0	229.7	0.0	0.0	0.0
Tuvalu	16.6	7.2	19.2	54.2	212.5	60.9	53,091.7	147,133.3	164,550.0	–	–	–
Vanuatu	73.8	103.8	66.4	53.5	47.0	85.4	38.6	86.0	48.7	–	–	–
Other countries												
Albania	279.9	408.1	282.9	114.0	78.6	107.9	152.8	157.5	201.9	92.0	93.0	90.0
Armenia	311.4	429.5	274.8	62.0	49.7	127.9	78.3	120.3	187.7	176.0	164.0	158.0
Bahrain	–	–	–	–	–	–	–	–	–	–	–	–
Bhutan	99.8	56.3	80.6	89.8	167.3	110.7	149.8	143.3	133.8	0.0	0.0	0.0
Bosnia-Herzegovina	388.9	416.2	419.4	142.3	118.8	105.7	197.0	305.2	298.8	62.0	20.0	2.0
Cape Verde	260.1	134.1	165.2	62.3	103.2	98.9	513.6	369.0	209.1	12.3	13.0	13.5
Congo Republic	1,563.1	396.0	116.2	92.4	65.4	109.2	365.8	165.3	212.9	26.0	35.0	37.0

Table 28. ODA commitments, disbursements,[a] per capita resource flows and IMF credit (continued)

Group/country	Commitments			Disbursement as a proportion of commitment			Per capita net resource flows from all sources			Use of IMF credit		
	2005	2006	2007	2005	2006	2007	2005	2006	2007	2005	2006	2007
	(US$ million)			(per cent)			(US$)			(US$ million)		
Middle-income (contin.)												
Other countries												
Costa Rica	102.7	191.8	64.1	28.5	12.3	82.2	151.2	299.6	165.3	0.0	0.0	0.0
Djibouti	99.9	107.8	127.9	76.4	108.7	88.0	121.9	225.3	160.0	18.7	18.0	16.1
Estonia	–	–	–	–	–	–	–	–	–	–	–	–
Gabon	65.0	138.2	157.9	81.1	22.6	30.7	-58.9	131.0	436.9	68.0	57.0	25.0
Georgia	256.1	625.3	275.3	120.7	57.6	138.8	81.3	130.1	132.1	232.0	236.0	252.0
Latvia	–	–	–	–	–	–	–	–	–	–	–	–
Lebanon	247.7	1,003.6	1,115.2	98.2	70.4	84.2	96.3	138.3	190.0	0.0	0.0	0.0
Lithuania	–	–	–	–	–	–	–	–	–	–	–	–
Macedonia FYR	183.6	209.2	190.1	124.6	95.5	112.3	188.3	268.5	63.0	62.0	56.0	0.0
Moldova	172.6	143.0	231.8	110.9	156.6	116.1	46.5	96.5	104.8	95.0	141.0	160.0
Mongolia	133.1	293.3	193.8	165.8	69.0	117.6	79.9	116.8	157.2	35.0	31.0	26.0
Montenegro	–	102.0	89.0	–	94.1	119.0	–	236.6	286.8	–	0.0	0.0
Oman	9.3	6.4	2.7	-58.1	539.1	-1,159.3	938.1	847.2	639.0	0.0	0.0	–
Panama	42.8	74.7	216.9	46.5	41.6	-62.1	1838.5	1831.5	1,467.9	24.0	15.0	5.0
Suriname	51.0	57.0	149.2	86.3	111.9	101.1	41.8	82.2	155.2	–	–	–
Turkmenistan	25.4	31.9	79.2	115.4	82.1	36.0	-9.0	19.8	-93.9	0.0	0.0	0.0
Timor-Leste	181.6	234.6	295.3	101.8	89.2	94.2	190.5	142.2	262.1	–	–	–
Uruguay	73.2	21.5	63.2	20.1	96.7	53.5	1.8	383.2	569.3	2,304.0	0.0	0.0
High-income												
Commonwealth countries												
Antigua & Barbuda	3.2	0.5	7.2	243.8	660.0	58.3	-1,468.7	-438.1	-2.4	–	–	–
Bahamas, The	–	–	–	–	–	–	–	–	–	–	–	–.
Barbados	6.2	8.0	28.6	7,191.9	2,7931.3	3,813.3	1,527.1	7,626.3	3,709.5	–	–	–
Brunei Darussalam	–	–	–	–	–	–	–	–	–	–	–	
Cyprus	–	–	–	–	–	–	–	–	–	–	–	
Malta	–	–	–	–	–	–	–	–	–	–	–	
Singapore	–	–	–	–	–	–	–	–	–	–	–	
Trinidad & Tobago	38.2	39.6	28.3	1,668.1	4,458.6	6,977.4	4,81.3	1,329.5	1,481.3	–	–	–
Other countries												
Croatia	205.7	233.7	260.1	413.7	1,160.2	3,737.6	191.5	610.5	2,190.5	0.0	0.0	0.0
Equatorial Guinea	56.5	37.0	32.2	832.4	3,057.3	-643.5	971.7	2,280.6	-407.9	–	–	–
Kuwait	–	–	–	–	–	–	–	–	–	–	–	–
Qatar	–	–	–	–	–	–	–	–	–	–	–	–
Slovenia	–	–	–	–	–	–	–	–	–	–	–	–
United Arab Emirates	–	–	–	–	–	–	–	–	–	–	–	–
Group total (average)												
Low-income	117.8	168.4	183.2	114.9	95.0	121.6	25.7	110.1	126.7	51.2	45.3	47.6
n	9	9	9	9	9	9	9	9	9	9	9	9
Middle-income	134.1	146.9	148.8	84.5	98.5	121.6	1481.0	3651.9	4105.8	93.3	27.0	25.1
n	42	43	43	42	43	43	42	43	43	36	37	36
High-income	62.0	63.8	71.3	2,070.0	7,453.5	2,788.6	340.6	2,281.8	1,394.2	–	–	–
n	5	5	5	5	5	5	5	5	5	–	–	–

Table 28. ODA commitments, disbursements,[a] per capita resource flows and IMF credit (continued)

Group/country	Commitments			Disbursement as a proportion of commitment			Per capita net resource flows from all sources			Use of IMF credit		
	2005	2006	2007	2005	2006	2007	2005	2006	2007	2005	2006	2007
	(US$ million)			(per cent)			(US$)			(US$ million)		
Under 1.5 mn population	57.5	60.9	77.6	399.5	1213.2	394.3	1955.4	5098.9	5538.2	10.4	8.1	6.5
n	30	31	31	31	32	32	31	32	32	21	22	22
Under 5 mn population	125.0	143.0	147.5	266.6	743.1	304.6	1145.3	2972.5	3239.7	83.0	30.0	29.0
n	56	57	57	56	57	57	56	57	57	46	47	46

Notes: [a]Disbursements as a percentage of all commitments; – = not available; n = number of countries.

Sources: Organisation for Economic Co-operation and Development, *Geographical Distribution of Financial Flows to Developing Countries, 2003–2007*, 2009 edition, Paris; World Bank, *Global Development Finance 2008*, Washington, DC

Table 29. Average exchange rates

Group/country		2003	2004	2005	2006	2007	2008
				(National currency per US$)			
Low-income							
Commonwealth countries							
Gambia, The	Dalasis	27.31	30.03	28.58	28.07	24.88	–
Papua New Guinea	Kina	3.56	3.22	3.10	3.06	2.97	2.70
Solomon Islands	Island Dollars	7.51	7.48	7.53	7.61	7.65	7.73
Other countries							
Central African Republic	Francs	581.20	528.28	527.47	522.89	479.27	447.81
Comoros	Francs	435.90	396.21	395.60	392.17	359.45	335.85
Guinea-Bissau	Francs	581.20	528.28	527.47	522.89	479.27	447.81
Liberia	Liberian Dollars	59.38	54.91	57.10	58.01	61.27	–
Mauritania	Ouguiyas	263.03	–	265.53	268.60	258.59	–
São Tomé & Principe	Dobras	9,347.60	9,902.30	10,558.00	12,448.60	13,536.80	–
Middle-income							
Commonwealth countries							
Belize	Belize Dollars	2.00	2.00	2.00	2.00	2.00	2.00
Botswana	Pula	4.95	4.69	5.11	5.84	6.14	6.83
Dominica	E Caribbean Dollars	2.70	2.70	2.70	2.70	2.70	2.70
Fiji Islands	Fiji Dollars	1.90	1.73	1.69	1.73	1.61	1.59
Grenada	E Caribbean Dollars	2.70	2.70	2.70	2.70	2.70	2.70
Guyana	Guyanese Dollars	193.90	198.30	199.90	200.20	202.30	203.60
Jamaica	Jamaica Dollars	57.74	61.20	62.28	65.74	68.95	72.80
Kiribati	Australian Dollars	–	–	–	–	–	–
Lesotho	Loti	7.56	6.46	6.36	6.77	7.05	8.26
Maldives	Rufiyaa	12.80	12.80	12.80	12.80	12.80	12.80
Mauritius	Rupees	27.90	27.50	29.50	31.71	31.31	28.45
Namibia	Namibian Dollars	7.56	6.46	6.36	6.77	7.05	8.26
St Kitts & Nevis	E Caribbean Dollars	2.70	2.70	2.70	2.70	2.70	2.70
St Lucia	E Caribbean Dollars	2.70	2.70	2.70	2.70	2.70	2.70
St Vincent & the Grenadines	E Caribbean Dollars	2.70	2.70	2.70	2.70	2.70	2.70
Samoa	Tala	2.97	2.78	2.71	2.78	2.62	2.64
Seychelles	Rupes	5.40	5.50	5.50	5.52	6.70	9.46
Swaziland	Lilangeni	7.56	6.46	6.36	6.77	7.05	8.26
Tonga	Pa'anga	2.15	1.97	1.94	2.03	1.97	1.94
Tuvalu	Australian Dollars	1.53	–	–	–	–	–
Vanuatu	Vatu	122.19	111.79	109.25	110.64	102.44	101.33
Other countries							
Albania	Leks	121.86	102.78	99.87	98.10	90.43	83.89
Armenia	Dram	578.76	533.45	457.69	416.04	342.08	305.97
Bahrain	Dinar	0.38	0.38	0.38	0.38	0.38	0.38
Bhutan	Ngultrum	46.58	45.32	44.10	45.31	41.35	43.51
Bosnia-Herzegovina	Convertible Marka	1.73	1.58	1.57	1.56	1.43	1.34
Cape Verde	Escudos	97.70	88.81	88.67	87.90	80.57	75.28
Congo Republic	Francs	581.20	528.28	527.47	522.89	479.27	447.81
Costa Rica	Colones	398.66	437.94	477.79	511.30	516.62	526.24
Djibouti	Francs	177.72	177.72	177.72	177.72	177.72	177.89
Estonia	Krooni	13.86	12.60	12.58	12.47	11.43	10.69
Gabon	Francs	581.20	528.28	527.47	522.89	479.27	447.81
Georgia	Lari	2.15	1.92	1.81	1.78	1.67	1.49
Latvia	Lats	0.57	0.54	0.57	0.56	0.51	0.48

Table 29. Average exchange rates (continued)

Group/country		2003	2004	2005	2006	2007	2008
		(National currency per US$)					
Middle-income (contin.)							
Other countries							
Lebanon	Pounds	1,507.50	1,507.50	1,507.50	1,507.50	1,507.50	1,507.50
Lithuania	Litai	3.06	2.78	2.77	2.75	2.52	2.36
Macedonia FYR	Denar	54.32	49.41	49.28	48.80	44.73	41.87
Moldova	Lei	13.94	12.33	12.60	13.13	12.14	10.39
Mongolia	Togrogs	1,146.54	1,185.28	1,205.22	1,165.37	1,170.97	1,165.74
Montenegro	Euros	0.89	0.81	0.80	0.80	0.73	0.68
Oman	Rials	0.38	0.38	0.38	0.38	0.38	0.38
Turkmenistan	Manat	–	–	–	–	–	–
Other countries							
Panama	Balbaos	1.00	1.00	1.00	1.00	1.00	1.00
Suriname	Surinamese Dollars	2.60	2.73	2.73	2.74	2.75	2.75
Timor-Leste	US Dollars	–	–	–	–	–	–
Uruguay	Pesos	28.21	28.70	24.48	24.07	23.47	20.95
High-income							
Commonwealth countries							
Antigua & Barbuda	E Caribbean Dollars	2.70	2.70	2.70	2.70	2.70	2.70
Bahamas, The	Bahamian Dollars	1.00	1.00	1.00	1.00	1.00	1.00
Barbados	Barbados Dollars	2.00	2.00	2.00	2.00	2.00	2.00
Brunei Darussalam	Brunei Dollars	1.74	1.69	1.66	1.59	1.51	1.41
Cyprus	Pound/Euro	1.93	2.13	2.15	2.18	2.35	1.46
Malta	Lira/Euro	2.65	2.90	2.89	2.93	3.21	0.68
New Zealand	NZ Dollars	1.72	1.51	1.42	1.54	1.36	1.40
Singapore	Singapore Dollars	1.74	1.69	1.66	1.59	1.51	1.41
Trinidad & Tobago	T T Dollars	6.30	6.30	6.30	6.31	6.33	6.29
Other countries							
Croatia	Kuna	6.71	6.03	5.95	5.84	5.37	4.94
Equatorial Guinea	Francs	581.20	528.28	527.47	522.89	479.27	447.81
Iceland	Kronar	76.71	70.19	62.98	70.18	64.06	88.47
Ireland	Euro	0.89	0.81	0.84	0.80	0.73	0.68
Kuwait	Dinar	0.30	0.29	2.92	2.90	0.28	0.27
Luxembourg	Euro	0.89	0.81	0.80	0.80	0.73	0.68
Norway	Kroner	7.08	6.74	6.44	6.41	5.86	5.64
Qatar	Riyals	3.64	3.64	3.64	3.64	3.64	3.64
Slovenia	Tolars/Euros	207.11	192.38	192.71	191.03	0.73	0.68
United Arab Emirates	Dirhams	3.67	3.67	3.67	3.67	3.67	3.67

Note: – = not available.

Source: International Monetary Fund, *International Financial Statistics*, September 2009, Washington, DC

Table 30. Money supply and average national interest rates

Group/country		Money supply					Interest rates				
		2004	2005	2006	2007	2008	2004	2005	2006	2007	2008
		(national currency million)					(per cent per annum)				
Low-income											
Commonwealth countries											
Gambia, The	Dalasis	3,108	3,321	4,185	4,209	–	36.5	34.9	29.8	27.9	–
Papua New Guinea	Kina	2,232	3,017	3,790	4,923	5511	13.3	11.5	10.6	9.8	9.2
Solomon Islands	S I Dollars	295	399	521	724	701	14.3	14.1	13.9	14.1	–
Other countries											
Central African Republic	Francs	98	114	105	97	114	18.0	17.7	15.3	15.0	–
Comoros	Francs	2,3368	25,380	24,652	25,626	25,850	11.0	11.0	10.5	10.5	7.0
Guinea-Bissau	Francs	4,2964	51,679	53,260	63,509	–	4.0	4.0	4.3	4.3	4.8
Liberia	Liberian Dollars	3728	4872	4,872	6,635	9,100	18.1	17.0	15.5	15.1	–
Mauritania	Ouguiyas	–	–	–	–	–	21.0	21.0	23.1	24.0	23.5
Middle-income											
Commonwealth countries											
Belize	Belize Dollars	407	423	618	704	706	13.9	14.3	14.2	14.3	14.1
Botswana	Pula	4,224	3,968	5,087	6,167	7,580	15.8	15.7	16.5	16.2	16.6
Dominica	E Caribbean Dollars	111	143	138	159	183	8.9	9.9	9.5	9.2	9.1
Fiji Islands	Fiji Dollars	995	1, 172	1,124	1,615	–	7.2	6.8	7.4	9.0	–
Grenada	E Caribbean Dollars	340	315	309	356	356	10.2	10.2	9.9	9.8	9.5
Guyana	Guyanese Dollars	34,606	37,839	48,070	54,241	61,035	14.5	14.5	14.5	14.6	14.6
Jamaica	Jamaican Dollars	55,308	62,573	77,619	89,073	91,018	18.1	17.4	17.6	17.2	–
Lesotho	Maloti	1,592	1, 832	2,689	3,066	3,877	12.4	11.7	12.2	14.3	16.2
Maldives	Rufiyaa	2,477	3, 033	3,707	4,405	6,082	13.0	13.0	13.0	13.0	13.0
Mauritius	Rupees	23,617	25,958	28,164	35,051	–	21.0	21.0	21.1	21.9	21.5
Namibia	Namibian Dollars	9,570	9,409	13,701	14,636	18,571	11.4	10.6	11.2	12.9	13.7
St Kitts & Nevis	E Caribbean Dollars	166	164	184	205	252	10.3	10.0	9.3	9.3	8.7
St Lucia	E Caribbean Dollars	481	547	561	639	661	11.1	10.6	10.8	10.1	10.1
St Vincent & the Grenadines	E Caribbean Dollars	287	328	344	372	375	9.7	9.6	9.7	9.6	9.5
Samoa	Tala	125	161	170	179	174	11.2	11.4	11.7	12.7	12.7
Seychelles	Rupees	1,204	1,374	1,392	1,602	1,695	10.0	9.8	10.1	10.9	–
Swaziland	Emalangeni	1,079	1,288	1,357	1,666	1,971	11.3	10.6	11.2	13.2	14.8
Tonga	Pa'anga	71,694	73,442	69,862	87,654	77,025	11.6	11.4	12.0	12.2	12.5
Vanuatu	Vatu	12,730	14,036	15,764	18,496	20,012	7.6	7.5	8.3	8.2	5.2
Other countries											
Albania	Leks	142	170	224	242	243	11.8	13.1	12.9	14.1	13.0
Armenia	Dram	132,414	202,056	295,328	458,558	416,786	18.6	18.0	16.5	17.5	17.1
Bahrain	Dinars	861	1, 063	1,286	1,584	–	8.0	7.9	8.1	8.4	–
Bhutan	Ngultrum	8,546	9,600	10,646	8,683	–	15.0	14.0	14.0	14.0	–
Bosnia-Herzegovina	Convertible Marka	3,788	4,422	5,553	6,823	6,331	10.3	9.6	8.0	7.2	7.0
Cape Verde	Escudos	24,405	28,716	35,854	40,340	42,170	12.7	12.3	9.9	10.6	10.0
Congo Republic	Francs	279	396	585	624	853	18.0	17.7	15.3	15.0	–
Costa Rica	Colones	697	864	1,192	1,459	1,482	23.4	24.6	22.2	12.8	15.8
Djibouti	Francs	47,443	47,728	57,271	67,541	82,236	11.3	11.2	–	11.2	–
Estonia	Krooni	42,041	57,364	72,118	75,370	67,203	5.7	4.9	5.0	6.5	8.6
Gabon	Francs	387	529	618	689	774	18.0	17.7	15.3	15.0	–
Georgia	Lari	846	1,070	1,393	2,149	1,863	31.2	21.6	18.8	20.4	21.2
Latvia	Lats	2,000	2,870	4,066	3,935	3,345	7.5	6.1	7.3	10.9	11.9
Lebanon	Pounds	3,031	2,952	3,322	3,578	4,269	10.8	10.6	10.3	10.3	10.0

Table 30. Money supply and average national interest rates (continued)

Group/country		Money supply					Interest rates				
		2004	2005	2006	2007	2008	2004	2005	2006	2007	2008
		(national currency million)					(per cent per annum)				
Middle-income (contin.)											
Other countries											
Lithuania	Litai	15,126	20,903	24,834	27,938	23,322	5.7	5.3	5.1	6.9	8.4
Macedonia FYR	Denar	28,842	30,675	36,153	47,257	54,119	12.4	12.1	11.3	10.2	9.7
Moldova	Lei	5,564	7,333	8,268	10,924	11,609	20.9	19.3	18.1	18.8	21.1
Mongolia	Togrogs	221,328	269,124	331,903	590,472	660,616	25.4	23.6	21.4	17.5	18
Montenegro	Euros	98,267	192,445	402,502	983,480	1,023,334	–	–	11.2	9.2	9.2
Oman	Rials	907	1,128	1,230	1,917	1,993	7.6	7.1	7.4	7.29	7.1
Turkmenistan	Manat	–	–	–	–	–	–	–	–	–	–
Panama	Balbaos	–	–	–	–	–	8.8	8.7	8.4	8.3	8.2
Suriname	Suriname Dollars	699,500	772,600	941,200	1,177,700	1,363,000	20.4	17.4	15.6	13.8	12.2
Timor-Leste	US Dollars	33	39	54	75	104	15.5	16.7	16.5	15.0	13.1
Uruguay	Pesos	122,281	29,731	35,711	47,051	55,267	23.7	13.6	9.3	8.9	12.5
High-income											
Commonwealth countries											
Antigua & Barbuda	E Caribbean Dollars	445	525	642	672	720	12.0	11.4	10.9	10.4	10.4
Bahamas, The	Bahamian Dollars	1,134	1,248	1,251	1,300	1,275	6.0	5.5	5.5	5.5	5.5
Barbados	Barbados Dollars	2,796	3,127	3,147	3,792	3,945	8.3	9.2	10.3	10.8	10.0
Cyprus	Pounds	1,524	1,805	2,264	2,593	–	7.6	7.1	6.7	6.7	–
Malta	Lira	1,581	1,670	1,657	1,586	–	5.3	5.5	5.7	6.2	5.9
New Zealand	NZ Dollars	22,227	21,903	22,672	23,025	23,707	9.2	10.3	10.9	11.6	12.1
Singapore	Singapore Dollars	44,162	46, 086	52,243	63,939	75,703	5.3	5.3	5.3	5.3	5.4
Trinidad & Tobago	TT Dollars	8,375	13, 293	14,995	16,777	19,197	9.3	9.1	10.9	11.8	12.4
Other countries											
Croatia	Kuna	34,562	38,817	48,521	57,878	55,222	11.8	11.2	9.9	9.3	10.1
Equatorial Guinea	Francs	171	234	261	372	523	18.0	17.7	15.3	15.0	–
Iceland	Kronur	141,669	174, 017	202,583	410,780	–	12.0	14.8	17.9	19.3	–
Ireland	Euro	–	–	–	–	–	2.6	2.7	–	–	–
Kuwait	Dinars	3,174	3,727	3,550	4,147	4,370	5.6	7.5	8.6	8.5	7.6
Luxembourg	Euro	–	–	–	–	–	–	–	–	–	–
Norway	Kroner	–	–	–	–	–	4.0	4.0	–	6.7	7.3
Qatar	Riyals	14,598	22,362	27,883	40,737	50,870	7.0	6.7	7.2	7.4	6.8
Slovenia	Tolars	1,370	1,682	1,834	–	–	8.7	7.8	7.4	5.9	6.7
United Arab Emirates	Dirhams	80,818	104,449	120,020	181,664	208,138	–	–	–	–	–

Note: – = not available.

Source: International Monetary Fund, *International Financial Statistics*, September 2009, Washington, DC

Table 31. Selected size indicators

Group/country	Surface area 2007	Arable and permanent cropped land 2007	Population 2007	Population density 2007	Total GNI at current prices 2007
	(sq. km)	(sq. km)	('000)	(per sq. km)	(US$ million)
Low-income					
Commonwealth countries					
Gambia, The	11,300	1,750	1,615	152.0	541
Papua New Guinea	462,840	4,600	6,324	14.0	5,402
Solomon Islands	28,900	600	495	18.0	518
Other countries					
Central African Republic	622,980	20,200	4,343	7.0	1,608
Comoros	2,230	1,000	628	338.0	435
Guinea-Bissau	36,120	3,400	1,541	55.0	340
Liberia	111,370	3,700	3,627	38.0	531
Mauritania	1,025,520	2,080	3,121	3.0	2,636
São Tomé & Principe	960	410	158	165.0	145
Middle-income					
Commonwealth countries					
Belize	22,960	1,020	304	13.0	1,144
Botswana	581,730	2,520	1,881	3.0	11,484
Dominica	750	210	73	97.0	328
Fiji Islands	18,270	2,530	834	46.0	3,078
Grenada	340	120	106	311.0	565
Guyana	214,970	4,500	764	4.0	894
Jamaica	10,990	2,840	2,676	247.0	11,824
Kiribati	730	370	95	117.0	171
Lesotho	30,350	3,040	2,006	66.0	2,077
Maldives	300	120	305	1018.0	984
Mauritius	2,040	940	1,261	621.0	7,067
Namibia	824,290	8,050	2,080	3.0	8,536
Nauru	21	0	14	2	–
St Kitts & Nevis	260	40	49	188.0	481
St Lucia	620	100	168	275.0	893
St Vincent & the Grenadines	390	120	109	280.0	532
Samoa	2,840	830	181	64.0	499
Seychelles	460	60	85	73.0	940
Swaziland	17,360	1,920	1,151	67.0	2,934
Tonga	750	270	103	143.0	254
Tuvalu	30	20	12	400.0	–
Vanuatu	12,190	1,050	226	19.0	445
Other countries					
Albania	28,750	6,980	3,132	114.0	10,513
Armenia	29,800	4,600	3,072	109.0	7,912
Bahrain	710	60	753	1,060.0	18,804
Bhutan	47,000	1,550	676	14.0	999
Bosnia-Herzegovina	51,210	11,170	3,778	74.0	14,297
Cape Verde	4,030	530	492	122.0	1,320
Costa Rica	51,100	5,000	4,462	87.0	24,650
Djibouti	23,200	13	833	36.0	895
Estonia	45,230	6,070	1,342	32.0	17,233
Gabon	267,670	4,950	1,422	6.0	9,175

Table 31. Selected size indicators (continued)

Group/country	Surface area 2007	Arable and permanent cropped land 2007	Population 2007	Population density 2007	Total GNI at current prices 2007
	(sq. km)	(sq. km)	('000)	(per sq. km)	(US$ million)
Middle-income (contin.)					
Other countries					
Georgia	69,700	5,770	4,399	63.0	9,178
Latvia	64,590	11,980	2,276	37.0	22,971
Lebanon	10,400	2,871	4,097	400.0	25,365
Lithuania	65,300	18,650	3,376	54.0	33,437
Macedonia FYR	25,710	5,913	2,037	80.0	6,945
Moldova	33,840	21,230	3,667	112.0	4,138
Mongolia	1,566,500	8,530	2,608	2.0	3,361
Montenegro	14,026	1,900	621	45.0	3,246
Oman	309,500	990	2,726	9.0	38,325
Panama	75,520	6,950	3,341	45.0	18,384
Suriname	163,270	650	510	3.0	2,271
Timor-Leste	14,870	2,380	1,064	72.0	1,621
Turkmenistan	488,100	19,130	4,963	11.0	11,092
Uruguay	176,220	13,830	3,324	19.0	22,017
High-income					
Commonwealth countries					
Antigua & Barbuda	440	90	85	193.0	1,070
Bahamas, The	13,880	120	331	33.0	6,337
Barbados	430	170	255	592.0	3,579
Brunei Darussalam	5,770	80	389	74.0	12,388
Cyprus	9,250	1,560	855	92.0	19,617
Malta	320	93	409	1,279.0	6,825
New Zealand	267,710	9,320	4,228	16.0	114,544
Singapore	699	8	4,589	6,660.0	146,339
Trinidad & Tobago	5,130	470	1,333	260.0	19,302
Other countries					
Croatia	56,540	9,320	4,436	79.0	53,240
Equatorial Guinea	28,050	2,200	642	23.0	6,235
Iceland	103,000	70	311	3.0	17,961
Ireland	70,270	10,630	4,366	63.0	207,895
Kuwait	17,820	180	2,663	149.0	122,780
Luxembourg	2,590	630	480	185.0	37,948
Norway	323,800	8,590	4,709	15.0	364,350
Qatar	11,000	210	1,138	103.0	61,194
Slovenia	20,270	2,030	2,018	100.0	43,412
United Arab Emirates	83,600	2,900	4,365	52.0	179,733

Table 31. Selected size indicators (continued)

Group/country	Surface area 2007	Arable and permanent cropped land 2007	Population 2007	Population density 2007	Total GNI at current prices 2007
	(sq. km)	(sq. km)	('000)	(per sq. km)	(US$ million)
Group averages (Commonwealth countries only)		Total	Total	Total	Wtd average
Low-income	143,695	3,088	2,811	46	2,154
n	3	3	3	3	3
Middle-income	79,211	1,394	658	184	2,757
n	22	22	22	22	22
High-income	33,737	1,323	1,386	1,022	36,667
n	9	9	9	9	9
Under 0.5 mn population	3,341	257	174	272	2,202
n	19	19	19	19	19
Over 0.5 mn population	170,571	2,717	1,790	123	7,175
n	13	13	13	13	13

Notes: – = not available; n = number of countries.

Source: Food and Agriculture Organisation, *Production Yearbook*, various issues, Rome; World Bank, World Bank website, www.worldbank.org, accessed November 2009; CIA, *World Factbook*, various issues, Washington, DC

Table 32. Population indicators

Group/country	Total population							Population growth rate
	2001	2002	2003	2004	2005	2006	2007	1990–2006
				('000)				(per cent/year)
Low-income								
Commonwealth countries								
Gambia, The	1,341	1,375	1,341	1,478	1,617	1,663	1,707	4.0
Papua New Guinea	5,252	5,373	5,656	5,772	6,070	6,202	6,324	2.9
Solomon Islands	431	443	454	466	472	484	495	2.5
Other countries								
Central African Republic	3,771	3,828	3,937	3,986	4,191	4,265	4,343	2.1
Comoros	572	590	576	588	600	614	628	1.7
Guinea-Bissau	1,252	1,253	1,494	1,540	1,597	1,646	1,695	3.3
Liberia	3,214	3,295	3,222	3,241	3,442	3,579	3,714	2.2
Mauritania	2,642	2,721	2,801	2,882	2,963	3,044	3,121	2.7
São Tomé & Principe	143	145	148	150	153	155	158	1.5
Middle-income								
Commonwealth countries								
Belize	257	265	274	283	292	298	304	2.8
Botswana	1,695	1,711	1,722	1,769	1,836	1,858	1,881	2.4
Dominica	72	72	71	71	72	72	73	–0.7
Fiji Islands	807	813	818	823	828	833	834	0.6
Grenada	103	104	105	106	106	108	106	0.7
Guyana	735	736	738	739	739	739	739	–0.5
Jamaica	2,590	2,613	2,630	2,642	2,654	2,667	2,676	0.7
Kiribati	93	95	96	98	99	100	95	1.8
Lesotho	1,796	1,800	1,950	1,966	1,981	1,995	2,006	0.7
Maldives	277	282	286	291	295	300	305	2.0
Mauritius	1,200	1,212	1,222	1,233	1,234	1,253	1,261	0.9
Namibia	1,792	1,823	1,986	2,009	2,020	2,047	2,080	0.9
Nauru	10	13	12	10	10	10	10	0.6
St Kitts & Nevis	45	46	47	47	48	48	49	1.2
St Lucia	157	158	161	162	165	166	168	0.7
St Vincent & the Grenadines	116	117	118	118	119	120	120	0.3
Samoa	179	180	181	183	184	185	181	0.5
Seychelles	82	84	83	84	83	85	85	1.3
Swaziland	1,068	1,088	1,106	1,120	1,131	1,138	1,148	2.2
Tonga	98	98	99	99	99	100	102	0.2
Tuvalu	10	10	11	10	10	10	10	0.6
Vanuatu	194	199	204	210	215	221	226	2.2
Other countries								
Albania	3,069	3,076	3,087	3,099	3,111	3,122	3,132	–
Armenia	3,065	3,061	3,060	3,062	3,065	3,068	3,072	–
Bahrain	651	672	706	716	725	739	753	2.4
Bhutan	574	591	607	623	637	649	657	–
Bosnia-Herzegovina	3,748	3,776	3,783	3,782	3,781	3,781	3,778	–
Cape Verde	446	458	484	495	507	519	530	2.1
Congo Republic	3,285	3,367	3,449	3,530	3,610	3,689	3,767	3.0
Costa Rica	3,873	3,942	4,176	4,253	4,327	4,399	4,462	2.8
Djibouti	644	657	765	779	793	819	833	4.0
Estonia	1,364	1,359	1,354	1,349	1,346	1,344	1,061	–

Table 32. Population indicators (continued)

Group/country	Total population 2001	2002	2003	2004	2005	2006	2007	Population growth rate 1990–2006
				('000)				(per cent/year)
Middle-income (contin.)								
Other countries								
Gabon	1,205	1,228	1,249	1,270	1,291	1,311	1,342	1.0
Georgia	4,666	4,614	4,564	4,517	4,473	4,433	4,399	–
Latvia	2,359	2,338	2,325	2,313	2,301	2,288	2,276	–
Lebanon	3,821	3,869	3,918	3,965	4,011	4,055	4,139	–
Lithuania	3,481	3,469	3,454	3,436	3,414	3,394	3,376	–
Macedonia FYR	2,016	2,022	2,026	2,030	2,034	2,036	2,037	–
Moldova	4,033	3,961	3,888	3,820	3,759	3,709	3,667	–
Mongolia	2,421	2,449	2,480	2,515	2,554	2,585	2,608	–
Montenegro	657	650	640	631	625	621	621	–
Panama	2,897	2,940	3,119	3,175	3,232	3,288	3,341	1.9
Suriname	420	423	444	446	452	455	458	0.1
Timor-Leste	787	831	876	925	976	1,029	1,061	–
Turkmenistan	4,564	4,630	4,698	4,766	4,833	4,899	4,963	–
Uruguay	3,308	3,309	3,304	3,302	3,306	3,314	3,324	0.4
High-income								
Commonwealth countries								
Antigua & Barbuda	78	80	81	82	83	84	85	0.4
Bahamas, The	310	314	314	319	323	327	331	1.5
Barbados	288	289	290	291	292	293	294	0.8
Brunei Darussalam	344	351	358	366	374	382	389	2.5
Malta	395	397	399	401	404	406	409	0.9
Cyprus	797	807	816	740	758	771	855	0.6
New Zealand	3,849	3,900	4,009	4,061	4,099	4,185	4,228	1.3
Singapore	4,131	4,164	4,185	4,240	4,342	4,484	4,589	3.2
Trinidad & Tobago	1,310	1,318	1,297	1,301	1,324	1,328	1,333	0.2
Other countries								
Croatia	4,440	4,440	4,440	4,439	4,442	4,440	4,436	–
Equatorial Guinea	441	451	462	473	484	496	508	1.0
Iceland	282	284	290	292	297	302	311	0.9
Ireland	3,839	3,877	3,996	4,068	4,159	4,268	4,366	1.2
Kuwait	2,044	2,104	2,396	2,460	2,535	2,599	2,663	1.1
Luxembourg	441	444	450	453	457	462	480	1.2
Norway	4,513	4,538	4,577	4,592	4,623	4,660	4,709	0.6
Oman	2,427	2,444	2,459	2,479	2,507	2,546	2,600	3.1
Qatar	598	610	733	777	796	821	836	3.8
Slovenia	1,992	1,994	1,996	1,997	2,001	2,007	2,018	–
United Arab Emirates	3,424	3,603	3,779	3,947	4,104	4,248	4,365	5.9

Table 32. Population indicators (continued)

Group/country	Total population 2001	2002	2003	2004	2005	2006	2007	Population growth rate 1990–2006
	('000)							(per cent/year)
Group averages (Commonwealth countries only)			**Total**					
Low-income	3,039	3,107	3,143	3,263	2,720	2,783	2,842	-23
n	3	3	3	3	3	3	3	3
Middle-income	608	615	633	640	646	652	657	1
n	22	22	22	22	22	22	22	22
High-income	1,278	1,291	1,305	1,311	1,333	1,362	1,390	1
n	9	9	9	9	9	9	9	9
Under 0.5 mn population	164	166	168	170	172	174	176	1
n	19	19	19	19	19	19	19	19
Over 0.5 mn population	1,601	1,624	1,672	1,697	1,743	1,768	1,795	1
n	13	13	13	13	13	13	13	13

Notes: – = not available; n = number of countries.

Source: World Bank data website, www.devdata.worldbank.org, accessed October 2009

Table 33. Distribution of labour force

Group/country	Agriculture			Industry			Services		
	2004	2005	2006	2004	2005	2006	2004	2005	2006
	(per cent)			(per cent)			(per cent)		
Low-income									
Commonwealth countries									
Gambia, The	33.1	33.0	32.4	13.3	13.0	13.5	53.6	53.9	54.2
Papua New Guinea	40.1	38.2	39.5	37.6	36.9	37.1	22.3	24.9	23.4
Solomon Islands	44.5	44.5	44.5	10.1	10.1	10.1	45.4	45.4	45.4
Other countries									
Central African Republic	52.0	52.0	51.8	20.0	19.0	19.2	28.0	29.0	29.0
Comoros	40.0	40.0	49.1	12.0	12.0	11.6	48.0	48.0	39.4
Guinea-Bissau	57.0	57.0	60.8	13.0	13.0	12.2	30.0	30.0	27.0
Liberia	64.0	69.0	65.2	13.0	10.0	13.3	24.0	21.0	21.5
Mauritania	24.0	21.0	25.6	21.0	21.0	27.0	29.0	29.0	47.4
Middle-income									
Commonwealth countries									
Belize	14.9	15.0	15.3	17.7	18.1	17.8	67.5	66.8	66.9
Botswana	2.0	3.0	2.5	49.0	49.0	49.6	49.0	48.0	47.9
Dominica	17.2	17.1	17.1	22.0	21.9	21.7	60.8	60.9	61.2
Fiji Islands	14.0	13.7	14.1	22.5	21.0	21.6	63.5	65.4	64.3
Grenada	7.9	4.8	4.9	21.7	30.9	31.0	70.4	64.3	64.1
Guyana	37.8	34.7	34.9	20.5	19.9	19.4	41.7	45.4	45.7
Jamaica	5.0	6.0	5.6	31.0	30.0	30.6	64.0	64.0	63.8
Lesotho	17.0	17.0	16.2	40.0	40.0	39.5	43.0	43.0	44.2
Maldives	8.2	9.7	8.4	16.0	17.3	16.8	75.8	73.0	74.8
Mauritius	6.0	5.0	5.1	28.0	26.0	25.8	67.0	69.0	69.1
Namibia	10.0	11.0	10.6	31.0	30.0	30.2	59.0	60.0	59.2
St. Kitts & Nevis	2.9	2.7	2.2	25.2	24.8	26.1	71.9	72.5	71.8
St. Lucia	4.8	3.4	4.3	16.2	17.4	16.6	79.0	79.2	79.1
St. Vincent & the Grenadines	7.6	7.6	7.8	23.3	23.1	23.1	69.0	69.3	69.0
Samoa	13.4	12.9	13.0	27.2	27.1	27.1	59.4	59.9	59.9
Seychelles	2.6	2.6	2.6	26.5	29.0	27.7	70.9	68.4	69.6
Swaziland	13.0	14.0	11.6	47.0	45.0	47.8	40.0	41.0	40.6
Tonga	27.3	27.9	28.1	14.6	15.2	14.9	58.1	56.9	57.0
Vanuatu	14.4	14.5	14.4	8.6	8.5	8.5	77.0	77.0	77.1
Other countries									
Bahrain	0.4	0.3	0.4	35.3	39.1	37.4	64.3	60.5	62.1
Bhutan	25.7	23.5	22.2	37.6	37.7	39.2	36.7	38.7	38.5
Cape Verde	12.0	12.0	11.5	16.0	16.0	15.6	73.0	73.0	72.9
Congo Republic	6.0	6.0	6.1	63.0	67.0	62.0	31.0	27.0	31.9
Costa Rica	8.3	8.3	8.3	28.3	28.0	28.7	63.5	63.8	63.1
Estonia	3.8	3.7	4.0	28.1	28.5	28.4	68.1	67.8	67.6
Gabon	9.0	8.0	7.8	68.0	56.0	55.5	22.0	36.0	36.7
Oman	1.7	1.4	1.7	54.2	60.1	55.1	44.1	38.5	43.2
Panama	7.2	7.1	6.7	16.6	16.2	16.3	76.2	76.7	77.0
Suriname	6.8	6.4	6.1	41.4	44.5	42.5	51.8	49.0	51.7
Timor-Leste	31.6	31.8	32.2	14.9	15.2	12.8	53.5	53.0	55.0
Uruguay	11.6	9.1	9.1	28.8	31.1	32.0	59.6	59.8	58.9

Table 33. Distribution of labour force (continued)

Group/country	Agriculture			Industry			Services		
	2004	2005	2006	2004	2005	2006	2004	2005	2006
	(per cent)			(per cent)			(per cent)		
High-income									
Commonwealth countries									
Antigua & Barbuda	3.4	3.4	3.4	18.9	21.4	20.0	77.6	75.2	76.6
Bahamas, The	2.0	2.0	2.2	16.0	16.0	16.2	82.0	82.0	81.5
Barbados	4.0	4.0	4.0	16.0	16.0	16.2	80.0	80.0	79.8
Cyprus	3.0	2.9	2.8	19.7	19.8	19.6	77.3	77.3	77.6
Malta	2.5	2.5	2.5	23.7	23.0	24.1	73.8	74.5	73.4
New Zealand	7.6	7.0	7.0	24.0	24.0	24.0	68.5	69.0	69.0
Singapore	0.1	0.1	0.1	32.7	32.2	33.0	67.2	67.7	66.9
Trinidad & Tobago	0.7	1.0	1.0	51.3	45.8	46.0	48.0	53.2	53.1
Other countries									
Equatorial Guinea	3.0	5.0	4.4	94.0	91.0	91.8	3.0	4.0	3.8
Iceland	6.6	7.7	7.3	24.5	24.5	24.6	68.9	67.8	68.2
Ireland	2.5	2.1	2.4	36.9	36.1	37.2	60.6	61.8	60.5
Kuwait	0.4	0.3	0.4	55.5	63.4	56.8	44.1	36.3	42.8
Luxembourg	0.5	0.4	0.4	17.2	16.2	14.6	82.2	83.4	85.0
Norway	1.6	1.6	1.6	39.9	43.0	44.9	58.5	55.4	53.6
Qatar	0.3	0.2	0.2	70.0	73.2	74.1	29.7	26.6	25.8
United Arab Emirates	2.6	2.2	2.6	54.2	56.4	53.9	46.8	49.3	46.4

Source: UNCTAD, *Handbook of Statistics 2007*, website database, http://www.unctad.org/Templates/Page.asp?intItemID=1890&lang=1, accessed August 2008

Table 34. Urban and rural population

Group/country	Urban				Rural				Average annual urban growth rate
	2004	2005	2006	2007	2004	2005	2006	2007	1990–2007
	(per cent)				(per cent)				(per cent)
Low-income									
Commonwealth countries									
Gambia, The	26.1	26.0	55.0	56.0	74.0	74.0	45.0	44.0	5.9
Papua New Guinea	13.0	13.0	13.0	14.0	87.0	87.0	87.0	86.0	2.9
Solomon Islands	17.0	17.0	17.0	18.0	83.0	83.0	83.0	82.0	4.4
Other countries									
Central African Republic	43.0	44.0	38.0	38.0	57.0	57.0	62.0	62.0	2.5
Comoros	36.0	36.0	38.0	38.0	64.0	64.0	62.0	62.0	4.8
Guinea-Bissau	35.0	36.0	30.0	30.0	65.0	64.0	70.0	70.0	3.5
Liberia	47.0	48.0	59.0	60.0	53.0	52.0	41.0	40.0	5.2
Mauritania	63.0	64.0	41.0	41.0	37.0	36.0	59.0	59.0	3.1
São Tomé & Principe	38.0	38.0	59.0	60.0	62.0	62.0	41.0	40.0	3.9
Middle-income									
Commonwealth countries									
Belize	48.0	49.0	48.0	49.0	52.0	51.0	52.0	51.0	2.9
Botswana	52.0	53.0	58.0	59.0	48.0	47.0	42.0	41.0	4.1
Dominica	72.0	73.0	73.0	73.0	28.0	28.0	27.0	27.0	0.3
Fiji Islands	52.0	53.0	51.0	52.0	48.0	47.0	49.0	48.0	2.3
Grenada	41.0	42.0	31.0	31.0	59.0	58.0	69.0	69.0	0.3
Guyana	38.0	38.0	28.0	28.0	62.0	62.0	72.0	72.0	-0.2
Jamaica	52.0	52.0	53.0	54.0	48.0	48.0	47.0	46.0	1.4
Kiribati	49.0	50.0	50.0	50.0	51.0	50.0	50.0	50.0	4.1
Lesotho	18.0	18.0	19.0	19.0	82.0	82.0	81.0	81.0	2.1
Maldives	29.0	30.0	30.0	31.0	71.0	70.0	70.0	69.0	3.2
Mauritius	44.0	44.0	42.0	42.0	56.0	56.0	58.0	58.0	0.9
Namibia	33.0	33.0	36.0	36.0	67.0	67.0	64.0	64.0	4.1
Nauru	100.0	100.0	100.0	100.0	0.0	0.0	0.0	0.0	0.6
St Kitts & Nevis	32.0	32.0	32.0	32.0	68.0	68.0	68.0	68.0	0.8
St Lucia	31.0	31.0	28.0	28.0	69.0	69.0	72.0	72.0	0.8
St Vincent & the Grenadines	59.0	60.0	46.0	47.0	41.0	40.0	54.0	53.0	1.5
Samoa	22.0	22.0	23.0	23.0	78.0	78.0	77.0	77.0	1.4
Seychelles	50.0	50.0	50.0	50.0	50.0	50.0	50.0	50.0	1.2
Swaziland	24.0	24.0	24.0	25.0	76.0	76.0	76.0	75.0	2.2
Tonga	34.0	34.0	24.0	24.0	66.0	66.0	76.0	76.0	0.8
Tuvalu	56.0	57.0	57.0	57.0	44.0	43.0	43.0	43.0	2.8
Vanuatu	23.0	24.0	24.0	24.0	77.0	76.0	76.0	76.0	4.2
Other countries									
Albania	44.0	45.0	46.0	47.0	56.0	55.0	54.0	53	1.4
Armenia	64.0	64.0	64.0	64.0	36.0	36.0	36.0	36	–1.4
Bahrain	90.0	90.0	97.0	97.0	10.0	10.0	3.0	3	3.2
Bhutan	9.0	9.0	11.0	12.0	91.0	91.0	89.0	88	4.2
Bosnia-Herzegovina	45.0	45.0	46.0	47.0	55.0	55.0	54.0	53	0.5
Cape Verde	57.0	58.0	58.0	59.0	43.0	42.0	42.0	41	4.3
Congo Republic	54.0	54.0	61.0	61.0	46.0	46.0	39.0	39	3.5
Costa Rica	61.0	62.0	62.0	63.0	39.0	38.0	38.0	37	3.7

Table 34. Urban and rural population (continued)

Group/country	Urban 2004	Urban 2005	Urban 2006	Urban 2007	Rural 2004	Rural 2005	Rural 2006	Rural 2007	Average annual urban growth rate 1990–2007
	(per cent)				(per cent)				(per cent)
Middle-income (contin.)									
Other countries									
Djibouti	84.0	85.0	87.0	87.0	16.0	15.0	13.0	13	3.3
Estonia	70.0	70.0	69.0	69.0	30.0	30.0	31.0	31	-1.2
Gabon	85.0	85.0	84.0	85.0	15.0	15.0	16.0	15	3.6
Georgia	52.0	51.0	52.0	52.0	48.0	49.0	48.0	48.0	-1.7
Latvia	66.0	66.0	68.0	68.0	34.0	34.0	32.0	32.0	-1.1
Lebanon	88.0	88.0	87.0	87.0	12.0	12.0	13.0	13.0	2.3
Lithuania	67.0	67.0	66.0	66.0	33.0	33.0	34.0	34.0	-0.7
Macedonia FYR	–	–	–	–	–	–	–	–	–
Moldova	46.0	46.0	47.0	47.0	54.0	54.0	53.0	53.0	-0.9
Mongolia	57.0	57.0	57.0	57.0	43.0	43.0	43.0	43.0	1.1
Montenegro	–	–	–	–	–	–	–	–	–
Oman	78.0	79.0	71.0	72.0	22.0	21.0	29.0	28.0	2.7
Panama	57.0	58.0	72.0	73.0	43.0	42.0	28.0	27.0	3.9
Suriname	77.0	77.0	74.0	75.0	23.0	23.0	26.0	25.0	1.4
Timor-Leste	8.0	8.0	27.0	27.0	92.0	92.0	73.0	73.0	4.5
Turkmenistan	46.0	46.0	47.0	47.0	54.0	54.0	53.0	53.0	2.1
Uruguay	93.0	93.0	92.0	92.0	7.0	7.0	8.0	8.0	0.7
High-income									
Commonwealth countries									
Antigua & Barbuda	38.4	38.0	38.0	38.0	62.0	62.0	62.0	62.0	2.5
Bahamas, The	90.0	90.0	91.0	91.0	10.0	10.0	9.0	9.0	2.2
Barbados	52.0	53.0	53.0	54.0	48.0	47.0	47.0	46.0	1.7
Brunei Darussalam	77.0	78.0	74.0	74.0	23.0	22.0	26.0	26.0	3.4
Cyprus	69.0	69.0	69.0	70.0	31.0	31.0	31.0	30.0	1.7
Malta	92.0	92.0	96.0	96.0	8.0	8.0	4.0	4.0	1.1
New Zealand	86.0	86.0	86.0	86.0	14.0	14.0	14.0	14.0	1.4
Singapore	100.0	100.0	100.0	100.0	0.0	0.0	0.0	0.0	2.4
Trinidad & Tobago	76.0	76.0	76.0	13.0	24.0	24.0	24.0	87.0	3.1
Other countries									
Croatia	59.0	60.0	57.0	57.0	41.0	40.0	43.0	43.0	0.4
Equatorial Guinea	49.0	50.0	39.0	39.0	51.0	50.0	61.0	61.0	3.3
Iceland	93.0	93.0	93.0	93.0	7.0	7.0	7.0	7.0	1.2
Ireland	60.0	60.0	61.0	61.0	40.0	40.0	39.0	39.0	1.7
Kuwait	96.0	96.0	98.0	98.0	4.0	4.0	2.0	2.0	1.8
Luxembourg	92.0	92.0	83.0	83.0	8.0	8.0	17.0	17.0	1.4
Norway	80.0	80.0	77.0	78.0	20.0	20.0	23.0	22.0	1.1
Qatar	92.0	92.0	96.0	96.0	8.0	8.0	4.0	4.0	3.9
Slovenia	51.0	51.0	51.0	51.0	49.0	49.0	49.0	49.0	0.4
United Arab Emirates	85.0	85.0	77.0	77.0	15.0	15.0	23.0	23.0	5.1

Note: – = not available.

Source: UNICEF, *The State of the World's Children*, 2006, 2007, 2008, and 2009, New York

Table 35. Population distribution by age

Group/country	Age 0–4			Age 5–14			Age 15–64			Age 65+		
	2005	2010	2015	2005	2010	2015	2005	2010	2015	2005	2010	2015
	(per cent)			(per cent)			(per cent)			(per cent)		
Low-income												
Commonwealth countries												
Gambia, The	16.5	15.7	14.9	26.3	26.4	25.7	54.4	55.1	56.4	2.8	2.9	3.0
Papua New Guinea	15.0	14.1	13.1	25.7	25.4	24.2	56.9	58.1	56.5	2.4	2.5	2.8
Solomon Islands	14.8	13.8	12.6	25.8	24.8	23.8	56.5	58.2	60.3	3.0	3.1	3.3
Other countries												
Central African Republic												
Comoros	14.6	14.5	13.3	23.8	23.5	24.0	58.5	58.8	59.6	3.1	3.1	3.1
Guinea-Bissau	16.9	16.7	16.1	26.3	26.4	25.7	54.4	55.1	56.4	2.8	2.9	3.0
Liberia	16.8	16.0	15.2	26.7	26.5	25.9	53.5	54.4	55.7	3.0	3.1	3.2
Mauritania	15.2	14.5	13.6	25.4	24.8	24.2	56.7	58.1	59.4	2.7	2.7	2.8
Middle-income												
Commonwealth countries												
Botswana	11.6	11.4	11.1	23.5	21.5	20.6	61.4	63.2	64.0	3.5	3.9	4.3
Fiji Islands	10.9	10.0	9.4	21.9	20.9	19.3	62.9	64.1	65.3	4.2	5.0	6.0
Guyana	10.2	8.4	7.8	20.8	20.7	17.9	63.3	64.7	67.0	5.7	6.2	7.3
Jamaica	9.8	9.3	8.9	21.7	19.7	17.9	60.9	63.3	65.0	7.7	7.7	8.2
Lesotho	13.7	13.0	12.5	26.4	25.5	24.3	55.1	56.7	58.3	4.8	4.8	4.9
Maldives	9.0	8.9	9.0	23.8	18.3	16.0	63.2	68.5	70.8	4.0	4.4	4.3
Mauritius	7.7	6.8	6.9	17.0	15.3	13.8	68.8	70.3	70.4	6.5	7.5	9.0
Namibia	13.4	12.7	12.0	25.5	23.6	22.5	57.5	59.9	61.5	3.5	3.7	4.0
St Lucia	8.6	8.7	8.1	19.9	17.1	16.0	64.5	67.4	68.9	7.0	6.8	7.0
St Vincent & the Grenadines	8.9	8.5	8.1	19.7	18.0	16.7	64.3	66.8	68.3	7.2	6.7	6.9
Samoa	13.8	11.3	10.3	27.3	27.4	23.8	54.3	56.4	60.8	4.7	4.9	5.0
Swaziland	14.1	13.4	13.1	27.8	25.4	24.0	54.9	57.8	59.3	3.2	3.4	3.7
Tonga	13.6	13.2	11.6	24.0	24.2	25.1	56.6	56.7	57.3	5.8	5.9	6.0
Other countries												
Albania	7.1	7.0	7.3	19.3	15.9	13.5	64.8	67.4	68.5	8.7	9.7	10.7
Armenia	6.8	7.3	7.4	15.1	12.9	13.7	66.1	68.7	68.0	12.0	11.0	10.9
Bahrain	9.3	8.6	7.9	18.2	17.3	15.9	69.9	71.8	73.5	2.6	2.3	2.8
Bhutan	11.2	9.8	9.5	22.9	20.1	18.2	61.3	65.3	67.1	4.6	4.9	5.1
Bosnia-Herzegovina	4.8	4.5	4.5	11.8	10.7	9.4	69.9	70.9	71.1	13.4	13.9	15.0
Cape Verde	12.9	11.4	10.8	26.4	24.1	21.7	56.1	60.4	63.8	4.5	4.1	3.7
Congo Republic	15.5	14.9	13.6	25.7	25.3	24.6	55.0	56.0	58.0	3.8	3.8	3.8
Costa Rica	9.1	8.0	7.8	19.3	17.4	15.6	65.8	68.2	69.1	5.8	6.5	7.5
Djibouti	13.3	12.4	11.6	25.1	23.2	21.9	58.6	61.1	62.8	3.0	3.3	3.7
Estonia	4.9	5.8	6.3	10.3	9.5	10.7	68.2	67.6	65.3	16.7	17.1	17.7
Gabon	13.2	12.3	11.7	25.4	23.3	21.7	57.0	60.1	62.1	4.4	4.3	4.5
Georgia	5.2	5.9	5.8	13.2	10.8	11.3	67.1	69.0	68.2	14.4	14.3	14.7
Latvia	4.4	5.1	5.4	10.1	8.8	9.7	68.9	68.7	67.4	16.6	17.4	17.5
Lebanon	8.2	7.6	7.5	19.3	17.2	14.8	65.3	67.9	70.1	7.1	7.4	7.7
Lithuania	4.5	4.7	4.9	12.3	9.9	9.3	12.3	9.9	9.3	15.2	16.4	17.1
Macedonia FYR	5.8	5.3	5.4	14.1	12.3	11.0	69.0	70.5	70.6	11.1	11.9	13.0
Moldova	5.0	6.0	6.2	14.0	10.7	10.9	69.9	72.2	71.1	11.1	11.1	11.8
Mongolia	8.5	8.8	8.6	20.3	16.8	15.8	67.5	70.4	71.3	3.7	4.1	4.3
Montenegro	6.5	6.0	6.0	13.7	13.3	12.3	67.3	68.0	68.0	12.6	12.8	13.7
Oman	11.1	10.3	10.2	22.8	20.5	18.5	63.6	66.0	67.7	2.6	3.1	3.6
Panama	10.6	9.8	9.1	19.7	19.2	18.2	63.6	64.4	65.2	6.0	6.7	7.5

Table 35. Population distribution by age (continued)

Group/country	Age 0–4			Age 5–14			Age 15–64			Age 65+		
	2005	2010	2015	2005	2010	2015	2005	2010	2015	2005	2010	2015
	(per cent)			(per cent)			(per cent)			(per cent)		
Middle-income (contin.)												
Other countries												
Turkmenistan	10.6	10.0	9.5	21.7	19.0	18.3	63.1	66.8	67.9	4.6	4.1	4.3
Suriname	10.5	9.1	8.6	19.3	19.5	17.8	64.1	65.0	66.7	6.1	6.5	6.9
Timor-Leste	16.7	17.2	17.2	29.5	27.5	26.0	51.0	52.3	53.7	2.8	3.0	3.1
Uruguay	7.7	7.3	7.0	16.1	15.2	14.4	62.7	63.6	64.3	13.5	13.9	14.4
High-income												
Commonwealth countries												
Bahamas, The	8.6	8.1	7.7	18.9	16.9	15.3	66.6	68.0	69.0	6.0	7.0	8.0
Barbados	5.7	5.5	5.4	13.0	11.5	10.9	71.2	72.5	71.5	10.1	10.4	12.2
Brunei Darussalam	9.8	9.2	8.4	19.1	17.1	15.7	67.9	70.2	71.5	3.2	3.5	4.4
Cyprus	5.8	5.7	5.8	14.0	11.8	10.9	68.0	69.3	68.8	12.2	13.2	14.5
Malta	4.9	4.5	4.6	12.4	10.7	9.3	69.4	70.0	68.1	13.2	14.8	17.9
New Zealand	6.9	6.8	6.6	14.6	13.5	13.0	66.4	66.8	65.9	12.1	13.0	14.5
Singapore	5.0	4.1	3.9	14.5	11.5	9.0	71.9	74.2	73.6	8.5	10.2	13.6
Trinidad & Tobago	6.9	7.1	7.1	15.0	13.5	13.4	71.8	72.5	71.6	6.3	6.9	8.0
Other countries												
Croatia	4.7	4.8	4.9	11.2	10.2	9.6	67.1	67.7	67.0	17.0	17.3	18.6
Equatorial Guinea	15.9	15.6	15.6	26.4	25.1	24.6	54.6	56.4	57.0	3.2	2.8	2.7
Iceland	7.1	7.1	6.9	15.0	13.2	12.8	66.2	67.9	67.4	11.7	11.8	12.9
Ireland	7.3	7.6	7.2	13.1	13.2	13.9	68.6	67.9	66.4	11.0	11.4	12.5
Kuwait	8.5	8.5	7.7	15.2	14.8	14.7	74.5	74.4	74.4	1.8	2.3	3.1
Luxembourg	5.9	5.6	5.6	12.6	12.0	11.2	67.4	68.4	68.8	14.1	14.0	14.5
Norway	6.2	6.1	5.8	13.5	12.7	12.1	65.8	66.2	65.4	14.5	15.0	16.6
Qatar	6.7	5.8	5.4	11.2	10.2	10.6	80.8	83.0	82.5	1.3	1.1	1.5
Slovenia	4.4	4.8	4.9	9.8	9.0	9.2	70.3	69.8	67.9	15.5	16.4	17.9
United Arab Emirates	7.3	6.6	6.2	12.3	12.6	12.3	79.3	79.9	80.1	1.1	1.0	1.4

Source: Population Division of the Department of Economic and Social Affairs of the United Nations Secretariat, *World Population Prospects: The 2008 Revision*, http://esa.un.org/unpp, accessed October 2009

Table 36. Selected demographic indicators

Group/country	Crude birth rate				Crude death rate				Infant mortality rate			
	2004	2005	2006	2007	2004	2005	2006	2007	2004	2005	2006	2007
	(per 1,000 mid-year population)				(per 1,000 mid-year population)				(per 1,000 live births)			
Low-income												
Commonwealth countries												
Gambia, The	35.0	34.0	36.0	35.0	12.0	11.0	11.0	10.0	89.0	97.0	84.0	82.0
Papua New Guinea	30.0	30.0	31.0	30.0	10.0	10.0	10.0	10.0	68.0	55.0	54.0	50.0
Solomon Islands	33.0	32.0	31.0	31.0	7.0	7.0	7.0	7.0	34.0	24.0	55.0	53.0
Other countries												
Central African Republic	37.0	37.0	37.0	36.0	22.0	22.0	19.0	18.0	115.0	115.0	115.0	113.0
Comoros	36.0	35.0	34.0	34.0	7.0	7.0	7.0	7.0	52.0	53.0	51.0	49.0
Guinea-Bissau	50.0	50.0	50.0	50.0	20.0	20.0	19.0	19.0	126.0	124.0	119.0	118.0
Liberia	50.0	50.0	50.0	50.0	21.0	21.0	19.0	18.0	157.0	157.0	157.0	93.0
Mauritania	41.0	41.0	33.0	33.0	14.0	14.0	8.0	8.0	78.0	78.0	78.0	75.0
São Tomé & Principe	34.0	33.0	33.0	33.0	9.0	8.0	8.0	8.0	75.0	75.0	63.0	64.0
Middle-income												
Commonwealth countries												
Belize	27.0	26.0	26.0	25.0	5.0	5.0	4.0	4.0	32.0	15.0	14.0	22.0
Botswana	26.0	26.0	25.0	25.0	27.0	28.0	15.0	15.0	84.0	87.0	90.0	33.0
Dominica	–	–	–		–	–	–		13.0	13.0	13.0	9.0
Fiji Islands	23.0	23.0	22.0	21.0	6.0	6.0	7.0	7.0	16.0	16.0	16.0	16.0
Grenada	–	–	18.0	15.0	–	–	8.0	8.0	18.0	17.0	16.0	15.0
Guyana	21.0	21.0	18.0	17.0	9.0	9.0	9.0	8.0	48.0	47.0	46.0	45.0
Jamaica	20.0	20.0	20.0	20.0	8.0	8.0	7.0	7.0	17.0	17.0	26.0	26.0
Kiribati	–	–	–	–	–	–	–	–	49.0	48.0	47.0	46.0
Lesotho	28.0	28.0	30.0	29.0	25.0	26.0	19.0	19.0	61.0	102.0	102.0	68.0
Maldives	31.0	30.0	23.0	23.0	6.0	6.0	6.0	6.0	35.0	33.0	26.0	26.0
Mauritius	16.0	16.0	15.0	15.0	7.0	7.0	7.0	7.0	14.0	13.0	13.0	13.0
Namibia	28.0	27.0	26.0	26.0	15.0	16.0	13.0	13.0	47.0	46.0	45.0	47.0
St Kitts & Nevis	–	–	–	–	–	–	–	–	18.0	18.0	17.0	16.0
St Lucia	19.0	19.0	19.0	19.0	7.0	7.0	7.0	7.0	13.0	12.0	12.0	14.0
St Vincent & the Grenadines	20.0	20.0	20.0	20.0	7.0	7.0	7.0	7.0	18.0	17.0	17.0	17.0
Samoa	28.0	27.0	26.0	25.0	6.0	6.0	5.0	5.0	25.0	24.0	23.0	22.0
Seychelles	–	–	–	–	–	–	–	–	12.0	12.0	12.0	12.0
Swaziland	29.0	29.0	29.0	29.0	29.0	30.0	20.0	21.0	108.0	110.0	112.0	66.0
Tonga	24.0	23.0	25.0	25.0	6.0	6.0	6.0	6.0	20.0	20.0	20.0	19.0
Tuvalu	–	–	–	–	–	–	–	–	36.0	31.0	31.0	30.0
Vanuatu	31.0	30.0	29.0	29.0	6.0	5.0	5.0	5.0	32.0	31.0	30.0	28.0
Other countries												
Albania	17.0	17.0	16.0	16.0	7.0	7.0	6.0	6.0	17.0	16.0	15.0	13.0
Armenia	11.0	11.0	12.0	12.0	9.0	9.0	9.0	10.0	29.0	26.0	21.0	22.0
Bahrain	18.0	18.0	18.0	17.0	3.0	3.0	3.0	3.0	9.0	9.0	9.0	9.0
Bhutan	30.0	30.0	19.0	19.0	8.0	8.0	7.0	7.0	67.0	65.0	63.0	56.0
Bosnia-Herzegovina	9.0	9.0	9.0	9.0	9.0	9.0	9.0	9.0	13.0	13.0	13.0	13.0
Cape Verde	30.0	30.0	30.0	29.0	5.0	5.0	5.0	5.0	27.0	26.0	25.0	24.0
Congo Republic	44.0	44.0	36.0	35.0	13.0	13.0	12.0	12.0	81.0	81.0	129.0	79.0
Costa Rica	19.0	18.0	18.0	18.0	4.0	4.0	4.0	4.0	11.0	11.0	11.0	10.0
Djibouti	35.0	34.0	29.0	29.0	13.0	12.0	12.0	11.0	101.0	88.0	86.0	84.0
Estonia	10.0	10.0	11.0	11.0	14.0	14.0	14.0	14.0	6.0	6.0	5.0	4.0
Gabon	31.0	30.0	26.0	26.0	13.0	13.0	12.0	12.0	60.0	60.0	60.0	60.0

Table 36. Selected demographic indicators (continued)

Group/country	Crude birth rate				Crude death rate				Infant mortality rate			
	2004	2005	2006	2007	2004	2005	2006	2007	2004	2005	2006	2007
	(per 1,000 mid-year population)				(per 1,000 mid-year population)				(per 1,000 live births)			
Middle-income (contin.)												
Other countries												
Georgia	11.0	11.0	11.0	11.0	11.0	11.0	12.0	12.0	41.0	41.0	28.0	27.0
Latvia	9.0	9.0	9.0	9.0	13.0	13.0	11.0	14.0	10.0	9.0	8.0	7.0
Lebanon	19.0	18.0	18.0	18.0	7.0	7.0	7.0	7.0	27.0	27.0	26.0	26.0
Lithuania	9.0	9.0	9.0	9.0	12.0	12.0	12.0	12.0	8.0	7.0	7.0	7.0
Macedonia FYR	–	–	–	–	–	–	–	–	–	–	–	–
Moldova	10.0	10.0	11.0	11.0	11.0	11.0	12.0	12.0	23.0	14.0	16.0	16.0
Mongolia	22.0	22.0	19.0	19.0	7.0	7.0	7.0	7.0	41.0	39.0	34.0	35.0
Montenegro	–	–	13.0	14.0	–	–	9.0	10.0	–	–	9.0	9.0
Oman	25.0	25.0	22.0	22.0	3.0	3.0	3.0	3.0	10.0	10.0	10.0	11.0
Panama	22.0	22.0	21.0	21.0	5.0	5.0	5.0	5.0	19.0	19.0	18.0	18.0
Turkmenistan	22.0	22.0	22.0	22.0	8.0	8.0	8.0	8.0	80.0	81.0	45.0	45.0
Suriname	21.0	20.0	20.0	20.0	7.0	7.0	7.0	7.0	30.0	30.0	29.0	27.0
Timor-Leste	50.0	51.0	42.0	42.0	12.0	12.0	9.0	9.0	64.0	52.0	47.0	77.0
Uruguay	17.0	16.0	15.0	15.0	9.0	9.0	9.0	9.0	15.0	14.0	11.0	12.0
High-income												
Commonwealth countries												
Antigua & Barbuda	–	–	–	–	–	–	–	–	11.0	11.0	10.0	10.0
Bahamas, The	19.0	19.0	17.0	17.0	7.0	7.0	6.0	6.0	10.0	13.0	13.0	12.0
Barbados	12.0	12.0	11.0	11.0	9.0	8.0	7.0	7.0	10.0	11.0	11.0	11.0
Brunei Darussalam	23.0	23.0	22.0	22.0	3.0	3.0	3.0	3.0	8.0	8.0	8.0	8.0
Cyprus	12.0	12.0	12.0	12.0	7.0	7.0	7.0	7.0	5.0	4.0	3.0	3.0
Malta	10.0	10.0	10.0	10.0	8.0	8.0	8.0	8.0	5.0	5.0	5.0	4.0
New Zealand	14.0	14.0	14.0	14.0	7.0	7.0	7.0	7.0	5.0	5.0	5.0	5.0
Singapore	9.0	9.0	9.0	8.0	5.0	5.0	5.0	5.0	3.0	3.0	2.0	2.0
Trinidad & Tobago	14.0	14.0	15.0	15.0	8.0	8.0	8.0	8.0	18.0	17.0	33.0	31.0
Other countries												
Croatia	9.0	9.0	9.0	9.0	12.0	12.0	12.0	12.0	6.0	5.0	5.0	5.0
Equatorial Guinea	43.0	43.0	39.0	39.0	20.0	21.0	15.0	15.0	122.0	123.0	124.0	124.0
Iceland	14.0	14.0	16.0	14.0	6.0	6.0	7.0	6.0	2.0	2.0	2.0	2.0
Ireland	16.0	16.0	16.0	16.0	8.0	7.0	7.0	7.0	5.0	5.0	4.0	4.0
Kuwait	19.0	19.0	18.0	18.0	2.0	2.0	2.0	2.0	10.0	9.0	9.0	9.0
Luxembourg	13.0	12.0	12.0	11.0	8.0	8.0	9.0	9.0	5.0	4.0	4.0	2.0
Norway	12.0	12.0	12.0	12.0	10.0	9.0	9.0	9.0	4.0	3.0	3.0	3.0
Qatar	19.0	18.0	17.0	16.0	3.0	3.0	2.0	2.0	18.0	18.0	18.0	12.0
Slovenia	9.0	9.0	9.0	9.0	10.0	10.0	10.0	10.0	4.0	3.0	3.0	3.0
United Arab Emirates	16.0	16.0	16.0	16.0	1.0	1.0	1.0	1.0	7.0	8.0	8.0	7.0

Note: – = not available.

Source: UNICEF, *The State of the World's Children*, 2006, 2007, 2008 and 2009, New York

Table 37. Life expectancy at birth

Group/country	Total 2004	Male 2004	Female 2004	Total 2005	Male 2005	Female 2005	Total 2006	Male 2006	Female 2006	Total 2007	Male 2007	Female 2007
	(years)			(years)			(years)			(years)		
Low-income												
Commonwealth countries												
Gambia, The	56.0	55.0	58.0	57.0	55.0	58.0	59.0	58.0	60.0	59.0	59.0	60.0
Papua New Guinea	56.0	55.0	57.0	56.0	56.0	57.0	57.0	55.0	60.0	57.0	55.0	60.0
Solomon Islands	63.0	62.0	63.5	63.0	68.0	72.0	67.0	65.0	68.0	64.0	66.0	68.0
Other countries												
Central African Republic	39.0	39.0	40.0	39.0	39.0	40.0	44.0	43.0	46.0	44.0	43.0	46.0
Comoros	63.0	61.2	64.6	64.0	62.0	67.0	65.0	62.0	67.0	65.0	63.0	67.0
Guinea-Bissau	45.0	44.0	46.0	45.0	44.0	47.0	46.0	45.0	48.0	46.0	45.0	48.0
Liberia	42.0	42.0	43.0	42.0	42.0	43.0	45.0	44.0	46.0	45.0	45.0	47.0
Mauritania	53.0	52.0	55.0	53.0	52.0	55.0	64.0	62.0	66.0	64.0	62.0	66.0
São Tomé & Principe	63.0	62.3	64.3	63.0	57.0	60.0	65.0	60.0	63.0	65.0	59.0	63.0
Middle-income												
Commonwealth countries												
Belize	72.0	69.0	74.0	72.0	67.0	74.0	69.0	65.0	74.0	76.0	64.0	72.0
Botswana	35.0	36.0	35.0	34.0	35.0	34.0	50.0	50.0	50.0	50.0	50.0	51.0
Dominica	77.0	–	–	–	72.0	76.0	74.0	72.0	76.0	–	56.0	56.0
Fiji Islands	68.0	66.0	70.4	68.0	66.0	72.0	69.0	66.0	72.0	69.0	67.0	72.0
Guyana	64.0	60.8	66.9	64.0	63.0	64.0	64.0	63.0	66.0	66.0	57.0	63.0
Jamaica	71.0	69.0	73.0	71.0	69.0	73.0	71.0	70.0	73.0	72.0	70.0	75.0
Kiribati	63.0	–	–	–	62.0	68.0	65.0	68.0	63.0	–	63.0	68.0
Lesotho	35.0	35.0	37.0	34.0	34.0	36.0	43.0	43.0	43.0	42.0	43.0	42.0
Maldives	67.0	67.6	66.8	67.0	67.0	69.0	72.0	73.0	72.0	68.0	72.0	75.0
Mauritius	72.0	69.0	76.0	73.0	70.0	77.0	73.0	70.0	77.0	59.0	69.0	76.0
Namibia	47.0	47.0	48.0	46.0	47.0	47.0	52.0	52.0	53.0	57.0	52.0	53.0
St Kitts & Nevis	71.0	–	–	–	69.0	72.0	71.0	73.0	70.0	64.0	69.0	76.0
St Lucia	73.0	71.8	75.1	73.0	72.0	78.0	75.0	72.0	78.0	74.0	72.0	78.0
St Vincent & the Grenadines	71.0	68.6	74.2	71.0	66.0	74.0	70.0	74.0	66.0	71.0	66.0	75.0
Samoa	70.0	67.3	73.4	71.0	66.0	70.0	68.0	66.0	70.0	71.0	66.0	70.0
Seychelles	73.0	–	–	–	68.0	77.0	72.0	77.0	68.0	–	68.0	75.0
Swaziland	31.0	43.0	42.0	30.0	42.0	41.0	41.0	42.0	40.0	40.0	40.0	39.0
Tonga	72.0	71.2	73.8	73.0	72.0	70.0	71.0	73.0	69.0	73.0	71.0	69.0
Vanuatu	69.0	67.4	71.1	69.0	67.0	70.0	69.0	67.0	70.0	70.0	67.0	70.0
Other countries												
Albania	74.0	71.0	77.0	74.0	73.0	79.0	76.0	73.0	80.0	76.0	73.0	80.0
Armenia	72.0	68.0	75.0	72.0	70.0	76.0	72.0	68.0	75.0	72.0	68.0	75.0
Bahrain	75.0	73.3	76.1	75.0	73.0	76.0	75.0	74.0	76.0	76.0	75.0	76.0
Bhutan	64.0	62.3	64.8	64.0	62.0	65.0	64.0	62.0	67.0	66.0	61.0	65.0
Bosnia-Herzegovina	74.0	72.0	77.0	74.0	72.0	77.0	75.0	72.0	77.0	75.0	72.0	77.0
Cape Verde	70.0	67.4	73.6	71.0	67.0	72.0	70.0	66.0	72.0	72.0	73.0	78.0
Congo Republic	52.0	51.0	54.0	53.0	52.0	54.0	55.0	54.0	56.0	55.0	54.0	57.0
Costa Rica	78.0	76.0	81.0	78.0	77.0	81.0	79.0	76.0	81.0	79.0	76.0	81.0
Djibouti	53.0	52.0	54.3	53.0	53.0	56.0	56.0	53.0	58.0	55.0	53.0	58.0
Estonia	72.0	66.0	77.0	72.0	67.0	78.0	73.0	67.0	78.0	71.0	67.0	79.0
Gabon	54.0	54.0	55.0	54.0	53.0	54.0	57.0	56.0	57.0	57.0	56.0	57.0
Georgia	71.0	67.0	74.0	71.0	68.0	75.0	71.0	67.0	75.0	71.0	67.0	75.0
Latvia	72.0	66.0	78.0	72.0	66.0	77.0	72.0	65.0	77.0	73.0	66.0	77.0
Lebanon	72.0	70.0	75.0	72.0	70.0	75.0	72.0	70.0	74.0	72.0	70.0	74.0

Table 37. Life expectancy at birth (continued)

Group/country	Total	Male 2004	Female	Total	Male 2005	Female	Total	Male 2006	Female	Total	Male 2007	Female
		(years)			(years)			(years)			(years)	
Middle-income (contin.)												
Other countries												
Lithuania	73.0	66.0	78.0	73.0	65.0	77.0	73.0	65.0	77.0	73.0	65.0	77.0
Macedonia FYR	–	71.0	76.0	–	71.0	76.0	–	72.0	76.0	–	72.0	77.0
Moldova	68.0	65.0	72.0	69.0	65.0	72.0	69.0	65.0	72.0	69.0	65.0	72.0
Mongolia	65.0	62.0	68.0	65.0	65.0	68.0	66.0	66.0	69.0	67.0	64.0	70.0
Montenegro	–	–	–	–	–	–	74.0	–	–	74.0	72.0	76.0
Oman	74.0	73.0	76.0	75.0	73.0	76.0	76.0	74.0	77.0	76.0	74.0	77.0
Panama	75.0	73.0	78.0	75.0	73.0	78.0	75.0	73.0	78.0	75.0	73.0	78.0
Suriname	69.0	66.3	72.8	70.0	66.0	71.0	70.0	65.0	71.0	70.0	66.0	73.0
Timor-Leste	56.0	–	–	56.0	63.0	68.0	57.0	56.0	58.0	61.0	60.0	62.0
Turkmenistan	63.0	59.0	67.0	63.0	59.0	67.0	63.0	59.0	67.0	63.0	59.0	68.0
Uruguay	76.0	72.0	79.0	76.0	72.0	79.0	76.0	72.0	80.0	76.0	72.0	80.0
High-income												
Commonwealth countries												
Bahamas, The	70.0	67.3	73.8	71.0	70.0	76.0	74.0	71.0	77.0	59.0	71.0	77.0
Barbados	75.0	72.8	78.2	76.0	71.0	78.0	76.0	72.0	79.0	57.0	72.0	78.0
Brunei Darussalam	77.0	74.5	79.2	77.0	76.0	79.0	77.0	76.0	79.0	64.0	74.0	77.0
Cyprus	79.0	76.9	81.5	79.0	77.0	82.0	80.0	79.0	82.0	79.0	78.0	82.0
Malta	79.0	76.7	80.9	79.0	77.0	81.0	79.0	77.0	81.0	79.0	78.0	82.0
New Zealand	79.0	77.0	81.0	79.0	78.0	82.0	80.0	78.0	82.0	80.0	78.0	82.0
Singapore	79.0	77.0	81.0	79.0	78.0	82.0	80.0	78.0	82.0	80.0	78.0	83.0
Trinidad & Tobago	70.0	67.0	73.0	70.0	67.0	73.0	70.0	68.0	72.0	70.0	68.0	72.0
Other countries												
Croatia	75.0	72.0	79.0	75.0	72.0	79.0	76.0	–	–	76.0	72.0	79.0
Equatorial Guinea	43.0	42.2	43.1	42.0	45.0	47.0	46.0	46.0	47.0	51.0	52.0	54.0
Iceland	80.0	–	–	81.0	79.0	83.0	81.0	79.0	83.0	82.0	80.0	83.0
Ireland	78.0	76.0	81.0	78.0	77.0	82.0	79.0	79.0			77.0	82.0
Kuwait	77.0	75.0	79.0	77.0	75.0	80.0	78.0	76.0	80.0	78.0	76.0	80.0
Luxembourg	78.0	75.2	81.3	79.0	76.0	82.0	80.0	77.0	83.0	79.0	77.0	83.0
Norway	80.0	78.0	82.0	80.0	78.0	83.0	80.0	78.0	83.0	80.0	78.0	83.0
Qatar	74.0	71.5	76.3	73.0	77.0	78.0	77.0	77.0	77.0	76.0	76.0	76.0
Slovenia	77.0	73.0	80.0	77.0	74.0	81.0	78.0	–	–	78.0	74.0	82.0
United Arab Emirates	78.0	77.0	81.0	79.0	77.0	82.0	79.0	77.0	82.0	79.0	77.0	81.0

Note: – = not available.

Source: World Bank, World Development Indicators 2006, 2007, 2008 and 2009; UNICEF, *The State of the World's Children*, 2007, 2008 and 2009, New York; WHO, *World Health Statistics*, 2006, 2007, 2008 and 2009

Table 38. Adult literacy rates

Group/country	Total	Male 2005	Female	Total	Male 2006	Female	Total	Male 2007	Female
		(per cent)			(per cent)			(per cent)	
Low-income									
Commonwealth countries									
Gambia, The	–	–	–	–	–	–	–	–	–
Papua New Guinea	56.9[a]	61.9[a]	51.9[a]	57.3[a]	62.0[a]	52.6[a]	57.8	62.1	53.4
Solomon Islands	–	–	–	–	–	–	–	–	–
Other countries									
Central African Republic	–	–	–	–	–	–	–	–	–
Comoros	73.3[a]	78.9[a]	67.8[a]	74.2[a]	79.6[a]	68.8[a]	75.1	80.3	69.8
Guinea-Bissau	61.0[a]	72.4[a]	50.2[a]	62.8[a]	73.8[a]	52.4[a]	–	–	–
Liberia	53.2[a]	59.0[a]	47.5[a]	54.4[a]	59.6[a]	49.2[a]	55.5[a]	60.2[a]	50.9[a]
Mauritania	54.6[a]	62.5[a]	46.7[a]	55.2[a]	62.9[a]	47.5[a]	55.8	63.3	48.3
São Tomé & Principe	87.0[a]	93.1[a]	81.1[a]	87.5[a]	93.3[a]	81.9[a]	87.9[a]	93.4[a]	82.7[a]
Middle-income									
Commonwealth countries									
Belize	–	–	–	–	–	–	–	–	–
Botswana	81.4[a]	81.4[a]	81.4[a]	82.2[a]	82.1[a]	82.2[a]	82.9	82.8	82.9
Dominica	–	–	–	–	–	–	–	–	–
Fiji Islands	–	–	–	–	–	–	–	–	–
Grenada	–	–	–	–	–	–	–	–	–
Guyana	–	–	–	–	–	–	–	–	–
Jamaica	85.0[a]	79.4[a]	90.3[a]	85.5[a]	80.0[a]	90.7[a]	86.0	80.5	91.1
Kiribati	–	–	–	–	–	–	–	–	–
Lesotho	–	–	–	–	–	–	–	–	–
Maldives	96.9[a]	96.8[a]	96.9[a]	97.0	96.9[a]	97.0[a]	97.0	97.0	97.1
Mauritius	86.6[a]	89.7[a]	83.6[a]	87.0[a]	89.9[a]	84.1[a]	87.4	90.2	84.7
Namibia	887.2[a]	88.1[a]	86.4[a]	87.6[a]	88.4[a]	86.9[a]	88[a]	88.6[a]	87.4[a]
St Kitts & Nevis	–	–	–	–	–	–	–	–	–
St Lucia	–	–	–	–	–	–	–	–	–
St Vincent & the Grenadines	–	–	–	–	–	–	–	–	–
Samoa	98.6[a]	98.9[a]	99.4[a]	98.7[a]	98.9[a]	99.4[a]	98.7	98.9	98.4
Seychelles	–	–	–	–	–	–	–	–	–
Swaziland	–	–	–	–	–	–	83.8	84.0	83.7
Vanuatu	76.4[a]	78.4[a]	74.2[a]	77.3[a]	79.3[a]	75.2[a]	–	–	–
Other countries									
Albania	–	–	–	–	–	–	99.0	99.3	98.8
Armenia	–	–	–	–	–	–	99.5	99.7	99.3
Bahrain	87.9[a]	89.7[a]	85.2[b]	88.3[a]	90.0[a]	85.8[a]	88.8	90.4	86.4
Bhutan	52.8	65.0	38.7	54.3[a]	66.2[a]	40.5[a]	–	–	–
Bosnia-Herzegovina	–	–	–	–	–	–	–	–	–
Cape Verde	82.1[a]	88.3[a]	97.2[a]	83.0[a]	88.9[a]	97.6[a]	83.8	89.4	78.8
Congo Republic	85.2[a]	91.0[a]	79.6[a]	86.0[a]	91.6[a]	80.7[a]	–	–	–
Costa Rica	95.7[a]	95.5[a]	95.9[a]	95.8[a]	95.6[a]	96.0[a]	95.9	95.7	96.2
Djibouti	–	–	–	–	–	–	–	–	–
Estonia	99.8[a]	99.8[a]	99.8[a]	99.8[a]	99.8[a]	99.8[a]	99.8	99.8	99.8
Gabon	84.6[a]	89.0[a]	80.3[a]	85.4[a]	89.6[a]	81.3[a]	86.2[a]	90.2[a]	82.2[a]
Georgia	–	–	–	–	–	–	–	–	–
Latvia	–	–	–	–	–	–	99.8	99.8	99.8
Lebanon	–	–	–	–	–	–	89.6	93.4	86.0
Lithuania	–	–	–	–	–	–	99.7	99.7	99.7

Table 38. Adult literacy rates (continued)

Group/country	Total	Male	Female	Total	Male	Female	Total	Male	Female
		2005			2006			2007	
		(per cent)			(per cent)			(per cent)	
Middle-income (contin.)									
Other countries									
Macedonia FYR	–	–	–	–	–	–	97.0	98.6	95.4
Moldova	–	–	–	–	–	–	99.2	99.6	98.9
Mongolia	–	–	–	–	–	–	97.3	96.8	97.7
Montenegro	–	–	–	–	–	–	–	–	–
Oman	83.0[a]	88.4[a]	75.4[a]	83.7[a]	88.9[a]	76.5[a]	84.4	89.4	77.5
Panama	93.1[a]	93.7[a]	96.0[a]	93.2[a]	93.9[a]	96.1[a]	93.4	94.0	92.8
Suriname	89.9[a]	92.3[a]	94.3[a]	90.1[a]	92.5[a]	94.5[a]	90.4	92.7	88.1
Timor-Leste	–	–	–	–	–	–	–	–	–
Turkmenistan	–	–	–	–	–	–	99.5	99.7	99.3
Uruguay	–	–	–	97.8	97.4	98.1	97.9	97.4	98.2
High-income									
Commonwealth countries									
Antigua & Barbuda	–	–	–	–	–	–	–	–	–
Bahamas, The	–	–	–	–	–	–	–	–	–
Barbados	–	–	–	–	–	–	–	–	–
Brunei Darussalam	94.2[a]	96.1[a]	92.3[a]	94.6[a]	96.3[a]	92.7[a]	94.9	96.5	93.1
Cyprus	97.4[a]	98.8[a]	96.1[a]	97.6[a]	98.9[a]	96.3[a]	97.7	99.0	96.6
Malta	92.4	91.2	93.5	91.4[a]	89.7[a]	93.0[a]	–	–	–
New Zealand	–	–	–	–	–	–	–	–	–
Singapore	93.9[a]	97.1[a]	90.8[a]	94.2[a]	97.2[a]	91.2[a]	94.4	97.3	91.6
Trinidad & Tobago	98.5[a]	99.0[a]	98.1[a]	98.6[a]	99.1[a]	98.2[a]	98.7	99.1	98.3
Other countries									
Croatia	–	–	–	–	–	–	98.7	99.5	98.0
Equatorial Guinea	–	–	–	–	–	–	–	–	–
Iceland	–	–	–	–	–	–	–	–	–
Ireland	–	–	–	–	–	–	–	–	–
Luxembourg	–	–	–	–	–	–	–	–	–
Norway	–	–	–	–	–	–	–	–	–
Slovenia							99.7	99.7	99.6

Notes: – = not available.
[a]UIS estimate.
[b]National estimate.

Source: UNESCO Institute for Statistics database, http://stats.uis.unesco.org/unesco/TableViewer/document.aspx?ReportId=136&IF_Language=eng&BR_Topic=0, accessed October 2009

Table 39. Primary education gross enrolment ratio

Group/country	Total 2004	Male 2004	Female 2004	Total 2005	Male 2005	Female 2005	Total 2006	Male 2006	Female 2006	Total 2007	Male 2007	Female 2007
Low-income												
Commonwealth countries												
Gambia, The	78	77	80	76	74	78	85	82	87	86	84	89
Papua New Guinea	56	60	51	57	61	52	55	60	50	–	–	–
Solomon Islands	97b	98b	95b	101	102	98	–	–	–	–	–	–
Other countries												
Central African Republic	54	65	43	61	72	49	61	72	49	71	83	58
Comoros	85	91	80	85b	91b	80b	–	–	–	–	–	–
Guinea-Bissau	–	–	–	–	–	–	–	–	–	–	–	–
Mauritania	99	98	101	99	96	102	102	99	104	103	100	106
Middle-income												
Commonwealth countries												
Belize	120	121	118	122	124	119	123	125	121	123	124	122
Botswana	107	108	106	107	107	106	–	–	–	–	–	–
Fiji Islands	103	104	102	103b	104b	102b	100	100	99	94	96	93
Guyana	125[b]	127[b]	124[b]	124	125	124	115	116	115	112	113	111
Jamaica	96	96	96	95	95	95	–	–	–	91	91	92
Lesotho	116	116	116	114	114	114	114	115	114	–	–	–
Maldives	126	128	124	119	120	117	116	118	114	111	112	109
Mauritius	103	102	103	102	102	102	102	102	102	103	100	106
Namibia	105	105	105	105	105	105	106	106	106	109	110	109
Samoa	100	100	100	100b	100b	100b	–	–	–	95	96	95
Swaziland	103	107	100	106	110	102	111	115	107	113	118	109
Timor-Leste	106	110	102	99	103	95	–	–	–	91	93	88
Vanuatu	117	118	116	114	115	112	108	110	107	108	110	106
Other countries												
Albania	105	106	105	–	–	–	–	–	–	–	–	–
Armenia	94	92	96	94	92	96	98	96	100	110	108	111
Bahrain	110	110	110	111	111	111	120	120	119	103	103	103
Bhutan	–	–	–	97	98	95	102	103	101	–	–	–
Bosnia-Herzegovina	–	–	–	–	–	–	–	–	–	98	101	94
Cape Verde	111	113	108	108	111	105	106	108	103	101	105	98
Costa Rica	112	112	111	110	110	109	111	112	111	110	111	110
Djibouti	40	45	35	42	46	37	44	49	39	47	50	43
Estonia	100	101	98	100	101	98	99	100	98	99	100	98
Georgia	95	96	95	94	94	94	96	94	97	99	100	98
Latvia	95	97	94	95	96	93	95	96	93	95	97	94
Lebanon	96	98	94	95	97	94	94	96	93	95	97	94
Lithuania	96	97	96	94	95	94	95	95	94	95	96	95
Macedonia FYR	98	98	98	98	98	98	–	–	–	95	95	95
Moldova	101[a]	102[a]	101[a]	98[a]	99[a]	97[a]	97[a]	97[a]	96[a]	94[a]	95[a]	94[a]
Mongolia	106	105	106	97	96	98	101	99	102	100	99	101
Montenegro	–	–	–	–	–	–	–	–	–	–	–	–
Oman	88	88	87	85	85	85	82	82	83	80	80	81
Panama	112	114	111	111	113	109	112	113	110	113	114	111
Suriname	–	–	–	120	120	120	121	121	121	119	120	118
Turkmenistan	–	–	–	–	–	–	–	–	–	–	–	–
Uruguay	113	115	112	114	115	112	115	117	113	114	116	113

Table 39. Primary education gross enrolment ratio (continued)

Group/country	Total 2004	Male 2004	Female 2004	Total 2005	Male 2005	Female 2005	Total 2006	Male 2006	Female 2006	Total 2007	Male 2007	Female 2007
High-income												
Commonwealth countries												
Bahamas, The	97[b]	97[b]	97[b]	100	101	100	98	98	98	103	103	103
Barbados	98	99	97	100	100	100	103	104	102	105	105	105
Brunei Darussalam	109	109	109	107	108	107	107	107	106	106	106	105
Cyprus	98[a]	98[a]	97[a]	101[a]	101[a]	101[a]	102[a]	103[a]	102[a]	102[a]	103[a]	102[a]
Malta	103	104	103	100	101	99	–	–	–	–	–	–
New Zealand	101	101	101	102	102	102	102	102	102	102	101	102
Singapore	–	–	–	–	–	–	–	–	–	–	–	–
Trinidad & Tobago	97[a]	98[a]	95[a]	95[a]	96[a]	94[a]	–	–	–	100	101	99
Other countries												
Croatia										99	99	99
Iceland	99	100	97	98	100	97	98	98	97	97	97	98
Ireland	104	104	104	104	104	103	104	104	103	104	105	104
Kuwait	96	96	97	98	99	97	96	97	96	98	100	97
Luxembourg	101	101	101	101	101	102	102	101	102	102	102	103
Norway	99	99	99	98	98	98	98	98	98	99	99	99
Qatar	100	101	99	105	106	104	105	105	104	109	110	109
Slovenia	97	97	96	98	99	98	100	100	100	104	104	103
United Arab Emirates	98	99	97	101	102	101	104	104	103	107	107	106

Notes: – = not available.
[a]national estimate.
[b]UNESCO Institute for Statistics (UIS) estimate.

Source: UNESCO Institute for Statistics database, http://stats.uis.unesco.org/unesco/TableViewer/document.aspx?ReportId=136&IF_Language=eng&BR_Topic=0, accessed October 2009

Table 40. Secondary education gross enrolment ratio

Group/country	Total	Male 2004	Female	Total	Male 2005	Female	Total	Male 2006	Female	Total	Male 2007	Female
Low-income												
Commonwealth countries												
Gambia, The	43	47	39	49	53	44	63	67	58	49	51	46
Papua New Guinea	–	–	–	–	–	–	–	–	–	–	–	–
Solomon Islands	30[b]	33[b]	28[b]	30	32	27	–	–	–	–	–	–
Other countries												
Central African Republic	–	–	–	–	–	–	–	–	–	–	–	–
Comoros	35	40	30	35[b]	40[b]	30[b]	–	–	–	–	–	–
Guinea-Bissau	–	–	–	–	–	–	–	–	–	–	–	–
Mauritania	24	25	22	24	25	23	25[a]	27[a]	23[a]	25[a]	27[a]	24[a]
Middle-income												
Commonwealth countries												
Belize	85	84	87	84b	83b	85b	79	77	81	79	76	81
Botswana	77[b]	75[b]	79[b]	76	75	78	–	–	–	–	–	–
Fiji Islands	86	83	89	86[b]	83v	89[b]	84	80	88	82	78	87
Guyana	100[b]	99[b]	102[b]	104	105	103	105[b]	105[b]	104[b]	107	111	103
Jamaica	88	87	89	87	86	88	–	–	–	90	87	92
Lesotho	36	31	40	37	33	42	37	33	41	–	–	–
Maldives	73[b]	69[b]	78[b]	–	–	–	83[b]	80[b]	86[b]	–	–	–
Mauritius	86	87	85	88[b]	89[b]	88[b]	–	–	–	–	–	–
Namibia	58	55	62	58	54	62	58	54	62	59	54	64
Samoa	81	76	86	81[b]	76[b]	86[b]	–	–	–	–	–	–
Swaziland	45	46	44	47	47	47	51	50	51	54	58	51
Timor-Leste	55	55	54	53	53	53	–	–	–	–	–	–
Vanuatu	40	43	37	–	–	–	–	–	–	–	–	–
Other countries												
Albania	77	78	75	–	–	–	–	–	–	–	–	–
Armenia	86	85	87	88	86	89	89	88	91	89	87	91
Bahrain	101	98	103	101	99	104	102	100	104	–	–	–
Bhutan	–	–	–	46	49	43	49	51	46	–	–	–
Bosnia-Herzegovina	–	–	–	–	–	–	–	–	–	85	84	87
Cape Verde	66	63	69	68	65	70	80	75	86	79	73	86
Costa Rica	77	75	80	79	77	82	86	83	89	87	85	90
Djibouti	20	24	17	23	27	18	22	27	18	25	30	21
Estonia	98	97	99	100	99	101	100	99	101	100	99	101
Georgia	80	80	81	83	83	83	85	83	86	90	90	90
Latvia	97	97	96	99	99	99	99	98	99	98	98	98
Lebanon	81	78	85	81	78	85	81	78	85	81	77	86
Lithuania	100	100	100	100	100	100	99	99	99	98	98	98
Macedonia FYR	84	85	83	84	85	83	–	–	–	84	85	83
Moldova	87[a]	85[a]	89[a]	88[a]	86[a]	90[a]	89[a]	87[a]	91[a]	89[a]	87[a]	90[a]
Mongolia	89	83	94	91	85	96	89	84	95	92	87	97
Montenegro	–	–	–	–	–	–	–	–	–	–	–	–
Oman	87	88	85	88	90	86	89	90	87	90	91	88
Panama	70	68	73	70	68	73	70	67	73	70	68	73
Suriname	–	–	–	74	64	85	77	66	90	80	67	93
Turkmenistan	–	–	–	–	–	–	–	–	–	–	–	–
Uruguay	107	99	115	101	94	109	101	94	109	92	93	91

Table 40. Secondary education gross enrolment ratio (continued)

Group/country	Total	Male 2004	Female	Total	Male 2005	Female	Total	Male 2006	Female	Total	Male 2007	Female
High-income												
Commonwealth countries												
Bahamas, The	88[b]	88[b]	88[b]	90	90	91	91	90	91	94	92	96
Barbados	101	100	102	103	103	103	102	100	104	103	102	105
Brunei Darussalam	94	91	96	96	94	98	98	96	100	97	96	99
Cyprus	98[a]	96[a]	99[a]	97[a]	96[a]	97[a]	97[a]	96[a]	97[a]	98[a]	97[a]	99[a]
Malta	107	110	103	99	99	100	–	–	–	–	–	–
New Zealand	117	113	121	121	117	125	120	117	123	121	119	123
Singapore	–	–	–	–	–	–	–	–	–	–	–	–
Trinidad & Tobago	79[b]	76[b]	81[b]	76[b]	75[b]	78[b]	–	–	–	86[b]	83[b]	89[b]
Other countries												
Croatia	–	–	–	91	89	92	91	90	93	92	90	93
Iceland	108	106	109	109	108	110	110	108	111	111	108	114
Ireland	111	107	115	112	107	117	112	108	116	113	110	117
Kuwait	90	88	93	95	93	98	89	87	91	91	90	92
Luxembourg	96	94	98	96	93	98	96	94	98	97	96	99
Norway	115	113	116	113	112	113	113	113	112	113	114	112
Qatar	93	93	93	97	97	96	101	103	100	103	105	102
Slovenia	96	97	96	96	96	96	95	95	95	94	94	93
United Arab Emirates	83	82	83	86	85	86	90	89	91	92[b]	91[b]	94[b]

Notes: – = not available.
[a]National estimate.
[b]UNESCO Institute for Statistics (UIS) estimate.

Source: UNESCO Institute for Statistics database, http://stats.uis.unesco.org/unesco/TableViewer/document.aspx?ReportId=136&IF_Language=eng&BR_Topic=0, accessed October 2009

Table 41. Tertiary education gross enrolment ratio

Group/country	Total	Male 2004	Female	Total	Male 2005	Female	Total	Male 2006	Female	Total	Male 2007	Female
Low-income												
Commonwealth countries												
Gambia, The	1	2	–	–	–	–	–	–	–	–	–	–
Papua New Guinea	–	–	–	–	–	–	–	–	–	–	–	–
Other countries												
Central African Republic	2	–	–	2[b]	–	–	1	2	–	–	–	–
Comoros	2[b]	3[b]	2[b]	–	–	–	–	–	–	–	–	–
Guinea-Bissau	–	–	–	–	–	–	–	–	–	–	–	–
Liberia	–	–	–	–	–	–	–	–	–	–	–	–
Mauritania	3	5	2	3	5	2	4	5	2	4	–	–
Middle-income												
Commonwealth countries												
Botswana	5	5	5	5	5	5	–	–	–	–	–	–
Fiji Islands	15	14	17	15[b]	14[b]	17[b]	–	–	–	–	–	–
Guyana	10	7	13	11	7	15	12	7	16	12	8	17
Jamaica	–	–	–	–	–	–	–	–	–	–	–	–
Lesotho	–	–	–	3	3	4	4	3	4	–	–	–
Mauritius	17	14	20	17	15	19	17	16	18	–	–	–
Namibia	6	6	7	7	7	6	6	7	6	–	–	–
Swaziland	5	5	5	4	4	5	4	4	4	–	–	–
Other countries												
Albania	19	15	23	–	–	–	–	–	–	–	–	–
Armenia	26	24	29	28	25	31	32	29	34	34	31	37
Bahrain	33[b]	23[b]	44[b]	33	20	48	32	19	47	–	–	–
Bosnia-Herzegovina	–	–	–	–	–	–	–	–	–	37	–	–
Congo Republic	–	–	–	–	–	–	–	–	–	–	–	–
Costa Rica	25	23	28	25[b]	23[b]	28[b]	–	–	–	–	–	–
Djibouti	1	2	1	2	2	2	2	3	2	3	3	2
Estonia	65	49	82	66	50	83	65	49	82	65	50	81
Gabon	–	–	–	–	–	–	–	–	–	–	–	–
Georgia	41	41	42	46	45	47	38	36	41	37	35	39
Latvia	75	55	95	75	54	97	74	53	95	71	50	93
Lebanon	44	42	46	46	44	49	48	45	51	52	47	56
Lithuania	73	58	89	76	60	94	76	60	93	76	59	93
Macedonia FYR	28	24	33	30	25	35	–	–	–	36	31	40
Moldova	34[a]	29[a]	40[a]	36[a]	29[a]	43[a]	39[a]	33[a]	46[a]	41[a]	35[a]	48[a]
Mongolia	39	30	49	43	33	54	47	37	58	48	37	58
Montenegro	–	–	–	–	–	–	–	–	–	–	–	–
Oman	16	15	17	18	18	19	25	25	26	25	23	28
Panama	45	34	57	44	34	55	45	35	56	–	–	–
Suriname	–	–	–	–	–	–	–	–	–	–	–	–
Timor-Leste	–	–	–	–	–	–	–	–	–	–	–	–
Turkmenistan	–	–	–	–	–	–	–	–	–	–	–	–
Uruguay	–	–	–	–	–	–	64	47	82	–	–	–

Table 41. Tertiary education gross enrolment ratio (continued)

Group/country	Total	Male	Female	Total	Male	Female	Total	Male	Female	Total	Male	Female
		2004			2005			2006			2007	
High-income												
Commonwealth countries												
Bahamas, The	–	–	–	–	–	–	–	–	–	–	–	–
Barbados	–	–	–	–	–	–	–	–	–	53	34	73
Brunei Darussalam	15	10	20	15	10	20	15	10	20	15	11	20
Cyprus	36[a]	36[a]	35[a]	33[a]	31[a]	35[a]	33[a]	33[a]	34[a]	36[a]	36[a]	36[a]
Malta	26	23	30	32	27	36	–	–	–	–	–	–
New Zealand	86	70	102	82	66	99	80	64	96	80	64	96
Singapore	–	–	–	–	–	–	–	–	–	–	–	–
Trinidad & Tobago	11	10	13	11[b]	10[b]	13[b]	–	–	–	–	–	–
Other countries												
Croatia	–	–	–	43	39	47	44	40	49	46	41	51
Equatorial Guinea	–	–	–	–	–	–	–	–	–	–	–	–
Iceland	68	48	90	70	49	93	73	51	96	73	52	96
Ireland	58	51	65	58	52	65	59	52	66	61	54	68
Kuwait	19[b]	12[b]	27[b]	19	10	29	18	11	26	–	–	–
Luxembourg	12[b]	11[b]	13[b]	–	–	–	10	10	11	–	–	–
Norway	79	63	96	78	62	95	78	61	94	76	60	94
Qatar	19	9	34	19[b]	10[b]	33[b]	19[b]	10[b]	33[b]	16	9	27
Slovenia	72	61	84	79	66	94	83	68	99	86	70	102
United Arab Emirates	–	–	–	–	–	–	–	–	–	–	–	–

Notes: – = not available.
[a]National estimate.
[b]UIS estimate.

Source: UNESCO Institute for Statistics database, http://stats.uis.unesco.org/unesco/TableViewer/document.aspx?ReportId=136&IF_Language=eng&BR_Topic=0, accessed October 2009

Table 42. Selected characteristics of female population

Group/country	Percentage of females in total labour force					Total fertility rate (number of children who would be born per female)				
	2003	2004	2005	2006	2007	2003	2004	2005	2006	2007
	(per cent)					(per female)				
Low-income										
Commonwealth countries										
Gambia, The	41.6	41.7	41.6	41.5	41.5	4.7	4.6	4.5	4.8	4.8
Papua New Guinea	47.8	47.6	47.5	47.5	47.5	4.0	3.9	3.8	4.0	3.8
Solomon Islands	38.6	38.6	38.6	38.6	38.5	4.4	4.2	4.1	4.0	3.9
Other countries										
Central African Republic	46.2	46.2	46.1	46.0	45.8	4.9	4.9	4.8	4.7	4.6
Comoros	40.2	40.2	40.1	40.0	39.9	4.8	4.7	4.6	4.5	4.4
Guinea-Bissau	41.0	40.9	40.9	40.9	40.9	7.1	7.1	7.1	7.1	7.1
Liberia	39.8	39.8	39.9	39.9	40.0	6.8	6.8	6.8	6.8	6.8
Mauritania	40.5	40.4	40.4	40.3	40.3	5.8	5.7	5.6	4.5	4.4
Middle-income										
Commonwealth countries										
Belize	33.3	33.7	34.1	34.4	34.8	3.1	3.1	3.0	3.0	3.0
Botswana	43.7	42.0	41.7	41.5	41.1	3.7	3.1	3.0	3.0	2.9
Dominica	–	–	–	–	–	–	–	–	–	–
Fiji Islands	37.7	38.3	38.5	38.7	38.8	2.9	2.9	2.8	2.8	2.8
Grenada	–	–	–	–	–	–	–	–	2.3	2.3
Guyana	36.4	36.7	36.9	37.0	37.1	2.3	2.2	2.2	2.4	2.3
Jamaica	44.4	43.7	43.5	43.4	43.3	2.3	2.4	2.4	2.3	2.5
Kiribati	–	–	–	–	–	–	–	–	–	–
Lesotho	45.0	44.7	44.5	44.2	44.0	3.8	3.5	3.4	3.5	3.4
Maldives	35.2	37.9	38.9	39.7	40.5	5.3	4.1	4.0	2.6	2.6
Mauritius	34.3	35.3	35.6	35.9	36.1	1.9	2.0	2.0	2.0	1.9
Namibia	43.6	43.7	43.6	43.5	43.4	4.5	3.8	3.7	3.3	3.2
Nauru	–	–	–	–	–	–	–	–	–	–
St Kitts & Nevis	–	–	–	–	–	–	–	–	–	–
St Lucia	41.0	41.3	41.5	41.6	41.7	2.3	2.2	2.2	2.2	2.2
St Vincent & the Grenadines	39.8	40.5	40.9	41.3	41.7	2.2	2.2	2.2	2.2	2.2
Samoa	31.9	31.9	31.9	32.0	32.0	4.1	4.3	4.2	4.1	4.0
Seychelles	–	–	–	–	–	–	–	–	–	–
Swaziland	33.1	33.1	32.8	32.6	32.3	4.5	3.8	3.7	3.6	3.5
Tonga	37.7	37.8	37.8	37.8	37.8	3.7	3.4	3.3	3.8	3.8
Trinidad & Tobago	40.4	38.9	38.9	38.9	38.9	1.6	1.6	1.6	1.6	1.6
Vanuatu	46.6	46.7	46.7	46.7	46.8	4.1	4.0	3.9	3.9	3.8
Other countries										
Albania	42.0	42.1	42.2	42.3	42.3	2.3	2.2	2.2	2.1	2.1
Armenia	49.1	49.0	49.1	49.2	49.2	1.1	1.3	1.3	1.3	1.4
Bahrain	18.1	18.6	18.7	18.8	18.9	2.6	2.4	2.4	2.4	2.3
Bhutan	32.2	35.1	36.5	37.9	39.1	5.0	4.2	2.4	3.5	2.2
Bosnia-Herzegovina	45.8	47.8	48.2	48.5	48.7	1.3	1.3	1.3	1.2	1.2
Cape Verde	33.5	33.8	33.8	33.8	33.8	3.3	3.6	3.6	3.5	3.4
Congo Republic	40.7	40.3	40.3	40.2	40.2	6.3	6.3	6.3	4.6	4.5
Costa Rica	33.5	34.5	35.1	35.8	36.5	2.3	2.2	2.2	2.1	2.1
Djibouti	39.4	39.4	39.3	39.2	39.2	5.6	4.9	4.8	4.1	4.0
Equatorial Guinea	41.0	40.9	40.9	40.9	40.9	5.9	5.9	5.9	5.4	5.4
Estonia	49.4	49.3	49.4	49.4	49.4	1.2	1.4	1.4	1.5	1.5

Table 42. Selected characteristics of female population (continued)

Group/country	Percentage of females in total labour force					Total fertility rate (number of children who would be born per female)				
	2003	2004	2005	2006	2007	2003	2004	2005	2006	2007
	(per cent)					(per female)				
Middle-income (contin.)										
Other countries										
Gabon	42.9	43.4	43.4	43.3	43.2	3.9	3.9	3.8	3.1	3.1
Georgia	47.0	43.9	43.4	43.0	42.6	1.4	1.4	1.4	1.4	1.4
Latvia	49.0	48.6	48.6	48.6	48.6	1.1	1.3	1.3	1.3	1.3
Lebanon	29.1	30.0	30.4	30.8	31.2	2.2	2.3	2.2	2.2	2.2
Lithuania	49.4	49.2	49.2	49.3	49.3	1.3	1.3	1.3	1.3	1.3
Macedonia FYR	–	–	–	–	–	–	–	–	–	–
Moldova	48.0	47.8	47.7	47.5	47.4	1.4	1.2	1.2	1.4	1.4
Mongolia	40.2	40.2	40.2	40.1	40.1	2.4	2.4	2.3	1.9	1.9
Montenegro	–	–	–	–	–	–	–	–	1.8	1.8
Oman	14.2	15.6	16.4	17.2	18.0	4.9	3.6	3.4	3.1	3.0
Panama	36.6	38.3	38.8	39.4	39.9	2.7	2.7	2.6	2.6	2.6
Suriname	36.8	34.8	34.9	35.0	35.0	2.4	2.6	2.5	2.5	2.4
Timor-Leste	36.8	37.1	37.6	38.0	38.3	3.8	7.8	7.8	7.3	6.6
Turkmenistan	46.8	46.6	46.7	46.7	46.6	2.7	2.7	2.6	2.6	2.5
Uruguay	43.6	43.9	44.2	44.4	44.7	2.3	2.3	2.3	2.1	2.1
High-income										
Commonwealth countries										
Antigua & Barbuda	–	–	–	–	–	–	–	–	–	–
Bahamas, The	49.1	49.7	49.8	49.9	49.9	2.3	2.3	2.2	2.0	2.0
Barbados	47.9	47.4	47.4	47.3	47.2	1.5	1.5	1.5	1.5	1.5
Brunei Darussalam	33.6	34.1	34.1	34.1	34.1	2.5	2.4	2.4	2.4	2.3
Cyprus	44.0	44.5	45.1	45.7	46.1	1.9	1.6	1.6	1.6	1.6
Malta	31.2	32.6	33.6	34.7	35.7	1.8	1.5	1.5	1.4	1.4
New Zealand	46.1	46.4	46.5	46.7	46.9	2.0	2.0	2.0	2.0	2.0
Singapore	39.2	39.8	39.9	40.1	40.2	1.3	1.3	1.3	1.3	1.3
Other countries										
Croatia	44.6	44.8	45.0	45.2	45.4	1.7	1.3	1.3	1.3	1.3
Iceland	47.0	46.7	46.7	46.7	46.7	1.9	2.0	1.9	2.0	2.0
Ireland	41.7	42.5	43.0	43.5	43.9	1.9	1.9	2.0	1.9	2.0
Kuwait	23.4	24.7	25.4	26.0	26.6	2.6	2.3	2.3	2.3	2.2
Luxembourg	41.7	41.6	42.0	42.4	42.7	1.7	1.7	1.7	1.7	1.7
Norway	47.1	47.2	47.3	47.4	47.5	1.8	1.8	1.8	1.9	1.8
Qatar	14.0	13.7	13.7	13.9	14.3	3.2	2.9	2.9	2.7	2.7
Slovenia	45.8	46.1	46.1	46.2	46.2	1.1	1.2	1.2	1.3	1.3
United Arab Emirates	12.6	13.1	13.4	13.8	14.2	2.8	2.5	2.4	2.3	2.3

Note: – = not available.

Source: World Bank, World Development Indicators 2006, 2007, and 2009, Washington, DC; UNICEF, *The State of the World's Children*, 2005, 2006, 2007, 2008 and 2009, New York; UNCTAD, *Handbook of Statistics 2008*, website database http://stats.unctad.org/Handbook/TableViewer/tableView.aspx?ReportId=2063, accessed October 2009

Table 43. Main components of government expenditure

Group/country	Defence			Education			Health			Social security and welfare		
	2005	2006	2007	2005	2006	2007	2005	2006	2007	2005	2006	2007
Low-income												
Commonwealth countries												
Gambia, The	–	–	–	–	–	–	–	–	–	–	–	–
Papua New Guinea	–	–	–	–	–	–	–	–	–	–	–	–
Other countries												
Central African Republic	–	–	–	–	–	–	–	–	–	–	–	–
Comoros	–	–	–	–	–	–	–	–	–	–	–	–
Guinea-Bissau	–	–	–	–	–	–	–	–	–	–	–	–
Liberia	–	–	–	–	–	–	–	–	–	–	–	–
Mauritania	–	–	–	–	–	–	–	–	–	–	–	–
São Tomé & Principe	–	–	–	–	–	–	–	–	–	–	–	–
Middle-income												
Commonwealth countries												
Belize	–	–	–	–	–	–	–	–	–	–	–	–
Botswana	–	–	–	–	–	–	–	–	–	–	–	–
Fiji Islands	6.0	5.4	–	21.4	22.4	–	9.7	9.4	–	4.5	4.0	–
Grenada	–	–	–	–	–	–	–	–	–	–	–	–
Jamaica	1.8	2.3	2.0	17.7	19.4	17.7	6.9	8.3	7.9	1.3	0.8	1.3
Lesotho	–	–	–	–	–	–	–	–	–	–	–	–
Maldives	–	5.9	5.0	–	14.9	14.2	–	9.7	8.1	–	4.3	5.0
Mauritius	0.7	0.7	0.7	16.3	15.4	15.0	8.4	9.2	8.7	23.2	24.2	24.9
Namibia	–	–	–	–	–	–	–	–	–	–	–	–
St.Vincent & the Grenadines	–	–	–	–	–	–	–	–	–	–	–	–
Seychelles	–	4.0	4.4	–	9.1	11.2	–	8.2	7.9	–	15.4	11.3
Swaziland	–	–	–	–	–	–	–	–	–	–	–	–
Tonga	–	–	–	–	–	–	–	–	–	–	–	–
Other countries												
Albania	–	–	–	–	–	–	–	–	–	–	–	–
Armenia	–	–	–	–	–	–	–	–	–	–	–	–
Bahrain	14.2	–	–	15.0	–	–	8.0	–	–	1.9	–	–
Bhutan	–	–	–	–	–	–	–	–	–	–	–	–
Bosnia-Herzegovina	–	–	–	–	–	–	–	–	–	–	–	–
Costa Rica	0.0	–	–	29.9	30.5	31.8	2.6	2.6	2.5	16.1	16.0	16.0
Georgia	19.1	23.4	35.9	3.8	11.3	9.2	8.1	6.7	5.9	26.0	20.2	18.8
Latvia	5.2	6.5	6.5	7.7	7.9	15.9	13.8	15.2	14.6	6.7	6.3	6.2
Lebanon	9.7	8.8	9.2	9.4	7.8	6.9	2.9	3.1	2.2	1.6	3.3	7.5
Lithuania	6.6	7.5	8.8	10.4	10.1	10.1	8.0	11.0	11.1	7.0	7.3	9.9
Macedonia FYR	–	–	–	–	–	–	–	–	–	–	–	–
Moldova	1.8	1.8	1.9	7.6	7.5	10.3	3.9	14.7	4.5	5.3	12.4	7.0
Mongolia	–	–	–	–	–	–	–	–	–	–	–	–
Montenegro	–	–	–	–	–	–	–	–	–	–	–	–
Oman	–	–	–	–	–	–	–	–	–	–	–	–
Panama	–	–	–	–	–	–	–	–	–	–	–	–
Turkmenistan	–	–	–	–	–	–	–	–	–	–	–	–
Uruguay	5.2	5.2	–	14.0	14.3	–	7.9	8.6	–	22.9	32.1	–

Table 43. Main components of government expenditure (continued)

Group/country	Defence			Education			Health			Social security and welfare		
	2005	2006	2007	2005	2006	2007	2005	2006	2007	2005	2006	2007
High-income												
Commonwealth countries												
Bahamas, The	3.0	–	–	18.6	–	–	16.7	–	–	6.0	–	–
Cyprus	5.9	6.3	–	19.3	19.4	–	8.2	8.5	–	10.3	10.1	–
Malta	2.2	1.9	–	12.3	12.3	–	14.8	15.2	–	30.9	32.5	–
New Zealand	3.0	–	–	17.9	–	–	20.0	–	–	35.0	–	–
Singapore	33.0	28.6	27.4	14.3	19.7	20.0	5.8	5.6	6.0	2.0	7.9	4.0
Other countries												
Croatia	4.0	4.1	4.1	8.5	8.4	8.4	14.4	14.4	15.2	40.9	38.9	37.1
Iceland	0.1	0.2	0.2	10.9	11.1	10.6	25.9	25.8	25.2	23.7	23.4	23.6
Ireland	1.8	1.8	–	15.3	14.9	–	28.4	28.3	–	19.5	19.3	–
Kuwait	–	15.2	9.5	–	9.5	6.9	–	6.7	4.8	–	16.1	26.5
Luxembourg	0.8	0.8	0.9	13.2	13.4	13.9	2.1	1.5	1.3	42.2	42.3	42.5
Norway	3.6	3.6	3.6	4.4	3.9	3.8	12.7	10.7	11.1	30.9	28.4	28.7
Slovenia	5.3	5.8	–	19.6	19.6	–	1.0	1.1	–	28.8	27.7	–
United Arab Emirates	–	–	–	–	–	–	–	–	–	–	–	–

Note: – = not available.

Source: International Monetary Fund, *Government Finance Statistics Yearbook 2008*, Washington, DC

Table 44. Access to improved water sources

Group/country	Urban 2002	Urban 2004	Urban 2006	Rural 2002	Rural 2004	Rural 2006
		(per cent)			(per cent)	
Low-income						
Commonwealth countries						
Gambia, The	95	95	91	77	77	81
Papua New Guinea	88	88	88	32	32	32
Solomon Islands	94	94	94	65	65	65
Other countries						
Central African Republic	93	93	90	61	61	51
Comoros	90	92	91	96	82	81
Guinea-Bissau	45	79	82	42	49	47
Liberia	66	72	72	38	52	52
Mauritania	72	59	70	52	44	54
São Tomé & Principe	93	89	88	65	73	83
Middle-income						
Commonwealth countries						
Belize	100	100	100	82	82	–
Botswana	100	100	100	90	90	90
Dominica	100	100	100	90	90	–
Fiji Islands	–	43	43	–	51	51
Grenada	97	97	97	93	93	–
Guyana	83	83	98	83	83	91
Jamaica	98	98	97	87	88	88
Kiribati	77	77	77	53	53	53
Lesotho	88	92	93	74	76	74
Maldives	99	98	98	78	76	76
Mauritius	100	100	100	100	100	100
Namibia	98	98	99	72	81	90
Nauru	–	–	–	–	–	–
St Kitts & Nevis	99	99	99	99	99	99
St Lucia	98	98	98	98	98	98
St Vincent & the Grenadines	–	–		93	93	–
Samoa	91	90	90	88	87	87
Seychelles	100	100	100	75	75	–
Swaziland	87	87	87	42	54	51
Tonga	100	100	100	100	100	100
Tuvalu	94	94	94	92	92	92
Vanuatu	85	86	–	52	52	–
Other countries						
Albania			97			97
Armenia			99			96
Bahrain	100	100	100	100	100	–
Bhutan	86	86	98	60	60	79
Bosnia-Herzegovina			100			98
Cape Verde	86	86	–	73	73	–
Congo Republic	72	84	95	17	27	35
Costa Rica	100	100	99	92	92	96
Djibouti	82	76	98	67	59	54
Estonia	–	100	100	–	99	99
Gabon	95	95	95	47	47	47

Table 44. Access to improved water sources (continued)

Group/country	Urban 2002	Urban 2004	Urban 2006	Rural 2002	Rural 2004	Rural 2006
		(per cent)			(per cent)	
Middle-income (contin.)						
Other countries						
Georgia			100			97
Latvia			100			96
Lebanon			100			100
Lithuania			–			–
Macedonia FYR			–			–
Moldova			–			
Mongolia			90			48
Montenegro			100			96
Panama	99	99	96	79	79	81
Suriname	98	98	97	73	73	79
Timor-Leste	89	77	77	73	56	56
Turkmenistan			–			–
Uruguay	98	100	100	93	100	100
High-income						
Commonwealth countries						
Antigua & Barbuda	95	95	95	89	89	–
Bahamas, The	98	98	98	86	86	–
Barbados	100	100	100	100	100	100
Brunei Darussalam	–	–	–	–	–	–
Cyprus	100	100	100	100	100	100
Malta	100	100	100	100	100	100
New Zealand	100	100	100	–	–	–
Singapore	100	100	100	–	–	–
Trinidad & Tobago	92	92	97	88	88	93
Other countries						
Croatia			100			98
Equatorial Guinea	73	45	45	51	42	42
Iceland	100	100	100	100	100	100
Ireland	100	100	100	–	–	–
Kuwait	–	–	–	–	–	–
Luxembourg	–	100	100	–	100	100
Norway	100	100	100	100	100	100
Oman	81	–	–	72	–	–
Qatar	100	100	100	100	100	100
Slovenia			–			–
United Arab Emirates	–	100	100	–	100	100

Source: World Health Organisation, *World Health Statistics*, various editions, available at http://www.who.int/whosis/whostat2006/en/index.html

Table 45. Access to improved sanitation

Group/country	Urban 2002	Urban 2004	Urban 2006	Rural 2002	Rural 2004	Rural 2006
		(per cent)			(per cent)	
Low-income						
Commonwealth countries						
Gambia, The	72	72	50	46	46	55
Papua New Guinea	67	67	67	41	41	41
Solomon Islands	98	98	98	18	18	18
Other countries						
Central African Republic	47	47	40	12	12	25
Comoros	38	41	49	15	29	26
Guinea-Bissau	60	57	48	46	23	26
Liberia	61	49	49	14	7	7
Mauritania	49	49	44	7	8	10
São Tomé & Principe	78	32	29	51	20	18
Middle-income						
Commonwealth countries						
Belize	71	71	–	25	25	–
Botswana	57	57	60	25	25	30
Dominica	86	86	–	75	75	–
Fiji Islands	99	87	87	98	55	55
Grenada	96	96	96	97	97	97
Guyana	86	86	85	60	60	80
Jamaica	90	91	82	68	69	84
Kiribati	59	59	46	22	22	20
Lesotho	61	61	43	32	32	34
Maldives	100	100	100	42	42	42
Mauritius	100	95	95	99	94	94
Namibia	66	50	66	14	13	18
Nauru	–	–	–	–	–	–
St Kitts & Nevis	96	96	96	96	96	96
St Lucia	89	89	–	89	89	–
St Vincent & the Grenadines	–	–	–	96	96	96
Samoa	100	100	100	100	100	100
Seychelles	–	–	–	100	100	100
Swaziland	78	59	64	44	44	46
Tonga	98	98	98	96	96	96
Tuvalu	92	93	93	83	84	84
Vanuatu	78	78	–	42	42	–
Other countries						
Albania			98			97
Armenia			96			81
Bahrain	100	–	100	–	100	–
Bhutan	65	65	71	70	70	50
Bosnia-Herzergovina			99			92
Cape Verde	61	61	–	19	19	–
Congo Republic	14	28	19	2	25	21
Costa Rica	89	89	96	97	97	95
Djibouti	55	88	76	27	50	11
Estonia	93	97	96	–	96	94
Gabon	37	37	37	30	30	30

Table 45. Access to improved sanitation (continued)

Group/country	Urban 2002	Urban 2004	Urban 2006	Rural 2002	Rural 2004	Rural 2006
		(per cent)			(per cent)	
Middle-income (contin.)						
Other countries						
Georgia			94			92
Latvia			82			71
Lebanon			100			–
Lithuania			–			–
Macedonia FYR			–			–
Moldova			–			–
Mongolia			64			31
Montenegro			96			86
Panama	89	89	78	51	51	63
Suriname	99	99	89	76	76	60
Timor-Leste	32	66	64	20	33	32
Turkmenistan			–			–
Uruguay	95	100	100	85	99	99
High-income						
Commonwealth countries						
Antigua & Barbuda	98	98	98	94	94	–
Bahamas, The	100	100	100	100	100	100
Barbados	99	99	99	100	100	100
Brunei Darussalam	–	–	–	–	–	–
Cyprus	100	100	100	100	100	100
Malta	100	100	100	–	–	–
New Zealand	–	–	–	–	–	–
Singapore	100	100	100	–	–	–
Trinidad & Tobago	100	100	92	100	100	92
Other countries						
Croatia			99			98
Equatorial Guinea	65	60	60	30	46	46
Iceland	–	100	100	–	100	100
Ireland	–	–	–	–	–	–
Kuwait	–	–	–	–	–	–
Luxembourg	–	100	100	–	100	100
Norway	–	100	–	–	100	–
Oman	97	97	97	61	–	–
Qatar	100	100	100	100	100	100
Slovenia			–			–
United Arab Emirates	100	98	98	100	95	95

Source: World Health Organisation, *World Health Statistics*, various editions, available at http://www.who.int/whosis/whostat2006/en/index.html

Table 46. Human Development Index

Group/country	Human Development Index value 2003		Human Development Index value 2004		Human Development Index value 2005		Human Development Index value 2006	
	Rank	0–1 Value	Rank	0–1 Value	Rank	0–1 Value	Rank	0–1 Value
Low-income								
Commonwealth countries								
Gambia, The	155	0.470	155	0.479	155	0.502	160	0.471
Papua New Guinea	137	0.523	139	0.523	145	0.530	149	0.516
Solomon Islands	128	0.594	128	0.592	129	0.602	134	0.591
Other countries								
Central African Republic	171	0.355	172	0.353	171	0.384	178	0.352
Comoros	132	0.547	132	0.556	134	0.561	137	0.572
Guinea-Bissau	172	0.348	173	0.349	175	0.374	171	0.383
Liberia							176	0.364
Mauritania	152	0.477	153	0.486	137	0.55	140	0.557
São Tomé & Principe	126	0.604	127	0.607	123	0.645	128	0.643
Middle-income								
Commonwealth countries								
Belize	91	0.753	95	0.751	80	0.778	88	0.771
Botswana	131	0.565	131	0.570	124	0.654	126	0.664
Dominica	70	0.783	68	0.793	71	0.798	77	0.797
Fiji Islands	92	0.752	90	0.758	92	0.762	103	0.743
Grenada	66	0.787	85	0.762	82	0.777	86	0.774
Guyana	107	0.72	103	0.725	97	0.75	110	0.725
Jamaica	98	0.738	104	0.724	101	0.736	87	0.771
Kiribati	–	–	–	–	–	–		
Lesotho	149	0.497	149	0.494	138	0.549	155	0.496
Maldives	96	0.745	98	0.739	100	0.741	99	0.749
Mauritius	65	0.791	63	0.800	65	0.804	74	0.802
Namibia	125	0.627	125	0.626	125	0.65	129	0.634
Nauru	–	–	–	–	–	–		
St Kitts & Nevis	49	0.834	51	0.825	54	0.821	60	0.830
St Lucia	76	0.772	71	0.790	72	0.795	66	0.821
St Vincent & the Grenadines	87	0.755	88	0.759	93	0.761	92	0.766
Samoa (Western)	74	0.776	75	0.778	77	0.785	96	0.760
Seychelles	51	0.821	47	0.842	50	0.843	54	0.836
Swaziland	147	0.498	146	0.500	141	0.547	141	0.542
Tonga	54	0.810	55	0.815	55	0.819	85	0.774
Tuvalu	–	–	–	–	–	–		
Vanuatu	118	0.659	119	0.670	120	0.674	123	0.686
Other countries								
Albania		0.793		0.800		0.804	69	0.807
Armenia		0.752		0.759		0.767	83	0.777
Bahrain	43	0.846	39	0.859	41	0.866	32	0.902
Bhutan	134	0.536	135	0.538	133	0.579	131	0.613
Bosnia-Herzegovina						0.797	75	0.802
Cape Verde	105	0.721	106	0.722	102	0.736	118	0.705
Congo Republic	142	0.512	140	0.520	139	0.548	130	0.619
Costa Rica	47	0.838	48	0.841	48	0.846	50	0.847

Table 46. Human Development Index (continued)

Group/country	Human Development Index value 2003		Human Development Index value 2004		Human Development Index value 2005		Human Development Index value 2006	
	Rank	0–1 Value	Rank	0–1 Value	Rank	0–1 Value	Rank	0–1 Value
Middle-income (contin.)								
Other countries								
Djibouti	150	0.495	148	0.494	149	0.516	151	0.513
Estonia	38	0.853	40	0.858	44	0.86	42	0.871
Gabon	123	0.635	124	0.633	119	0.677	107	0.729
Georgia		0.747		0.751		0.759	93	0.763
Latvia		0.84		0.848		0.856	44	0.863
Lebanon						0.795	78	0.796
Lithuania		0.854		0.858		0.864	43	0.869
Macedonia FYR		0.798		0.800		0.804	68	0.808
Moldova		0.702		0.708		0.714	113	0.719
Mongolia		0.698		0.709		0.714	112	0.72
Montenegro		0.81		0.813		0.816	64	0.822
Panama	56	0.804	58	0.809	62	0.812	58	0.832
Suriname	86	0.755	89	0.759	85	0.774	89	0.77
Timor-Leste	140	0.513	142	0.512	150	0.514	158	0.483
Turkmenistan						0.727	108	0.728
Uruguay	46	0.840	43	0.851	46	0.852	47	0.859
High-income								
Commonwealth countries								
Antigua & Barbuda	60	0.797	59	0.808	57	0.815	59	0.830
Bahamas, The	50	0.832	52	0.825	49	0.845	49	0.845
Barbados	30	0.878	31	0.879	31	0.892	37	0.889
Brunei Darussalam	33	0.866	34	0.871	30	0.894	27	0.919
Cyprus	29	0.891	29	0.903	28	0.903	30	0.912
Malta	32	0.867	32	0.875	34	0.878	36	0.894
New Zealand	19	0.933	20	0.936	19	0.943	20	0.944
Singapore	25	0.907	25	0.916	25	0.922	28	0.918
Trinidad & Tobago	57	0.801	57	0.809	59	0.814	57	0.833
Other countries								
Croatia		0.846		0.850		0.857	45	0.862
Equatorial Guinea	121	0.655	120	0.653	127	0.642	115	0.717
Iceland	2	0.956	2	0.960	1	0.968	1	0.968
Ireland	8	0.946	4	0.956	5	0.949	5	0.960
Kuwait	44	0.844	33	0.871	33	0.891	29	0.912
Luxembourg	4	0.949	12	0.945	18	0.944	9	0.956
Norway	1	0.963	1	0.965	2	0.968	2	0.968
Oman	71	0.781	56	0.810	58	0.814	53	0.839
Qatar	40	0.849	46	0.844	35	0.875	34	0.899
Slovenia		0.914		0.911		0.917	26	0.923
United Arab Emirates	41	0.849	49	0.839	39	0.868	31	0.903

Table 46. Human Development Index (continued)

Group/country	Human Development Index value 2003		Human Development Index value 2004		Human Development Index value 2005		Human Development Index value 2006	
	Rank	0–1 Value	Rank	0–1 Value	Rank	0–1 Value	Rank	0–1 Value
Group average								
Low-income		0.490		0.493		0.519		0.494
n		8		8		8		9
Middle-income		0.713		0.716		0.732		0.955
n		32		32		32		32
High-income		0.870		0.874		0.883		1.052
n		17		17		17		17
Under 1.5 mn population		0.746		0.749		0.784		0.790
n		35		35		35		35
Under 5 mn population		0.732		0.736		0.751		0.750
n		56		56		56		57

Source: UNDP, *Human Development Report*, various editions, available at http://hdr.undp.org/reports/global/

Table 47. Gender-related Development Index

Group/country	Gender-related Development Index 2003		Gender-related Development Index 2004		Gender-related Development Index 2005		Gender-related Development Index 2006	
	Rank	0–1 Value	Rank	0–1 Value	Rank	0–1 Value	Rank	0–1 Value
Low-income								
Commonwealth countries								
Gambia, The	119	0.464	–	–	155	0.496	137	0.465
Papua New Guinea	103	0.518	103	0.521	145	0.529	–	–
Solomon Islands	–	–	–	–	129	–	–	–
Other countries								
Central African Republic	–	–	132	0.336	171	0.368	156	0.336
Comoros	101	0.541	99	0.550	134	0.554	119	0.565
Guinea-Bissau	135	0.326	–	–	175	0.355	150	0.37
Liberia	–	–	–	–	–	–	153	0.351
Mauritania	118	0.471	115	0.478	137	0.543	120	0.55
São Tomé & Principe	–	–	–	–	123	0.637	111	0.626
Middle-income								
Commonwealth countries								
Belize	76	0.734	–	–	80	–	–	–
Botswana	100	0.559	98	0.555	124	0.639	109	0.66
Dominica	–	–	–	–	71	–	–	–
Fiji Islands	71	0.742	–	–	92	0.757	88	0.737
Grenada	–	–	–	–	82	–	–	–
Guyana	79	0.716	–	–	97	0.742	94	0.719
Jamaica	75	0.736	77	0.721	101	0.732	76	0.767
Kiribati								
Lesotho	114	0.487	112	0.486	138	0.541	135	0.487
Maldives	–	–	–	–	100	0.744	85	0.745
Mauritius	54	0.781	53	0.792	65	0.796	66	0.795
Namibia	96	0.621	94	0.622	125	0.645	110	0.629
Nauru								
St Kitts & Nevis	–	–	–	–	54	–	–	–
St Lucia	–	–	–	–	72	–	–	–
St Vincent & the Grenadines	–	–	–	–	93	–	–	–
Samoa (Western)	–	–	63	0.77	77	0.776	82	0.752
Seychelles	–	–	–	–	50	–	–	–
Swaziland	115	0.485	114	0.479	141	0.529	126	0.527
Tonga	–	–	46	0.809	55	0.814	75	0.767
Tuvalu	–	–	–	–	–	–	–	–
Vanuatu	–	–	–	–	120	–	103	0.685
Other countries								
Albania							64	0.804
Armenia							73	0.773
Bahrain	41	0.837	38	0.849	41	0.857	32	0.889
Bhutan	–	–	–	–	133	–	114	0.604
Bosnia-Herzegovina							–	–
Cape Verde	81	0.714	78	0.714	102	0.723	101	0.692
Congo Republic	108	0.507	104	0.519	139	0.54	113	0.612
Costa Rica	44	0.829	42	0.831	48	0.842	49	0.844

Table 47. Gender-related Development Index (continued)

Group/country	Gender-related Development Index 2003		Gender-related Development Index 2004		Gender-related Development Index 2005		Gender-related Development Index 2006	
	Rank	0–1 Value	Rank	0–1 Value	Rank	0–1 Value	Rank	0–1 Value
Middle-income (contin.)								
Other countries								
Djibouti	–	–	–	–	149	0.507	130	0.504
Estonia	35	0.852	34	0.856	44	0.858	40	0.869
Gabon	–	–	–	–	119	0.67	–	–
Georgia							–	–
Latvia							43	0.862
Lebanon							71	0.783
Lithuania							41	0.868
Macedonia FYR							65	0.803
Moldova							97	0.715
Mongolia							95	0.718
Montenegro							55	0.819
Panama	47	0.800	47	0.806	62	0.081	52	0.83
Suriname	–	–	–	–	85	0.767	77	0.763
Timor-Leste	–	–	–	–	150	–	–	–
Turkmenistan							–	–
Uruguay	42	0.836	39	0.847	46	0.849	46	0.856
High-income								
Commonwealth countries								
Antigua & Barbuda	–	–	–	–	57	–	–	–
Bahamas, The	–	–	–	–	49	0.841	47	0.835
Barbados	29	0.876	–	–	31	0.887	34	0.882
Brunei Darussalam	–	–	–	–	30	0.886	29	0.895
Cyprus	28	0.884	27	0.9	28	0.899	26	0.91
Malta	32	0.858	29	0.869	34	0.873	33	0.889
New Zealand	17	0.929	20	0.932	19	0.935	20	0.937
Singapore	–	–	–	–	25	–	27	0.899
Trinidad and Tobago	48	0.796	48	0.805	59	0.808	53	0.827
Other countries								
Croatia							44	0.859
Equatorial Guinea	95	0.641	93	0.639	127	0.631	98	0.708
Iceland	3	0.953	2	0.958	1	0.962	1	0.963
Ireland	11	0.939	4	0.951	5	0.94	13	0.944
Kuwait	39	0.843	31	0.864	33	0.884	31	0.891
Luxembourg	7	0.944	6	0.949	18	0.924	18	0.938
Norway	1	0.960	1	0.962	2	0.957	3	0.958
Oman	60	0.759	57	0.785	58	0.788	59	0.816
Qatar	–	–	–	–	35	0.863	38	0.87
Slovenia							24	0.92
United Arab Emirates	–	–	43	0.829	39	0.855	35	0.876

Table 47. Gender-related Development Index (continued)

Group/country	Gender-related Development Index 2003		Gender-related Development Index 2004		Gender-related Development Index 2005		Gender-related Development Index 2006	
	Rank	0–1 Value	Rank	0–1 Value	Rank	0–1 Value	Rank	0–1 Value
Group average								
Low-income		0.464		0.471		0.497		0.466
n		5		4		7		7
Middle-income		0.706		0.715		0.691		0.752
n		17		16		22		22
High-income		0.875		0.878		0.876		0.889
n		11		11		15		16
Under 1.5 mn population		0.772		0.779		0.735		0.746
n		16		13		24		24
Under 5 mn population		0.732		0.749		0.706		0.748
n		32		30		43		43

Source: UNDP, *Human Development Report*, various editions, available at http://hdr.undp.org/reports/global/

Table 48. Human Poverty Index

Group/country	Human Poverty Index (HPI-1) 2004		Human Poverty Index (HPI-1) 2005		Human Poverty Index (HPI-1) 2006		Human Poverty Index (HPI-1) 2007	
	Rank	100–0 Value	Rank	100–0 Value	Rank	100–0 Value	Rank	100–0 Value
Low-income								
Commonwealth countries								
Gambia, The	88	44.7	86	44.7	94	40.9	121	40.9
Papua New Guinea	78	40.5	75	40.5	90	40.3	116	40.1
Solomon Islands	–	–	–	–	53	22.4	79	22.4
Other countries								
Central African Republic	92	47.8	91	47.8	98	43.6	126	44.6
Comoros	57	31.2	56	31.6	61	31.3	77	21.2
Guinea-Bissau	93	48.2	92	48.2	99	44.8	109	36.7
Liberia	–	–	–	–	–	–	118	40.5
Mauritania	79	40.5	81	41.0	87	39.2	106	35.9
São Tomé & Principe	–	–	–	–	39	15.8	59	13.3
Middle-income								
Commonwealth countries								
Belize	38	16.7	–	–	43	17.5	70	17.5
Botswana	94	48.4	93	48.3	63	31.4	90	31.2
Dominica	–	–	–	–	–	–	–	–
Fiji Islands	49	21.3	45	21.3	50	21.2	78	21.2
Grenada	–	–	–	–	–	–	–	–
Guyana	31	14.8	–	–	33	14.0	52	12.4
Jamaica	21	10.5	30	14.8	34	14.3	47	10.8
Kiribati	–	–	–	–	–	–	–	–
Lesotho	91	47.6	89	47.5	71	34.5	103	34.6
Maldives	37	16.6	36	16.9	42	17.0	68	17.1
Mauritius	24	11.4	24	11.3	27	11.4	45	9.7
Namibia	60	33.0	57	32.5	58	26.5	84	25.9
Nauru	–	–	–	–	–	–	–	–
St Kitts & Nevis	–	–	–	–	–	–	–	–
St Lucia	12	8.3	–	–	8	6.5	24	6.5
St Vincent & the Grenadines	–	–	–	–	–	–	–	–
Samoa (Western)	–	–	–	–	–	–	–	–
Seychelles	–	–	–	–	–	–	–	–
Swaziland	97	52.9	97	52.5	73	35.4	104	35.5
Tonga	–	–	–	–	–	–	–	–
Tuvalu	–	–	–	–	–	–	–	–
Vanuatu	52	24.7	49	24.7	56	24.6	83	23.9
Other countries								
Albania							15	4.6
Armenia							14	4.5
Bahrain	–	–	–	–	–	–	–	–
Bhutan	–	–	71	39.0	86	38.9	97	32.9
Bosnia-Herzegovina							5	3.1
Cape Verde	45	18.7	43	18.7	38	15.8	63	15.0
Congo Republic	54	30.1	51	27.9	57	26.2	82	23.7

Table 48. Human Poverty Index (continued)

Group/country	Human Poverty Index (HPI-1) 2004		Human Poverty Index (HPI-1) 2005		Human Poverty Index (HPI-1) 2006		Human Poverty Index (HPI-1) 2007	
	Rank	100–0 Value	Rank	100–0 Value	Rank	100–0 Value	Rank	100–0 Value
Middle-income (contin.)								
Other countries								
Costa Rica	3	4.0	4	4.4	5	4.4	10	3.8
Djibouti	53	29.5	52	30.0	59	28.5	85	26.5
Estonia	–	–	–	–	–	–	–	–
Gabon	–	–	50	27.3	49	20.4	74	20.2
Georgia							18	5.5
Latvia							–	–
Lebanon							38	8.5
Lithuania							–	–
Macedonia FYR							9	3.3
Moldova							21	6.0
Mongolia							58	13.0
Montenegro							12	4.1
Panama	9	7.7	12	7.9	15	8.0	28	6.9
Suriname	23	10.9	23	10.3	25	10.2	46	10.1
Timor-Leste	–	–	–	–	95	41.8	122	41.0
Turkmenistan							–	–
Uruguay	1	3.6	1	3.3	2	3.5	7	3.3
High-income								
Commonwealth countries								
Antigua & Barbuda	–	–	–	–	–	–		
Bahamas, The	–	–	–	–	–	–		
Barbados	4	4.5	5	4.5	1	3.0	4	3.0
Brunei Darussalam	–	–	–	–	–	–		
Cyprus	–	–	–	–	–	–		
Malta	–	–	–	–	–	–		
New Zealand	–	–	–	–	–	–		
Singapore	6	6.3	7	6.3	7	5.2	13	4.1
Trinidad & Tobago	15	8.8	17	8.8	12	7.3	27	6.9
Other countries								
Croatia							2	2.1
Equatorial Guinea	71	38.1	69	38.1	66	32.4	95	32.3
Iceland	–	–	–	–	–	–		
Ireland	–	–	–	–	–	–		
Kuwait	–	–	–	–	–	–		
Luxembourg	–	–	–	–	–	–		
Norway	–	–	–	–	–	–		
Oman	46	21.1	–	–	–	–	–	–
Qatar	10	7.8	13	7.9	13	7.8	29	7.2
Slovenia							–	–
United Arab Emirates	34	15.9	34	15.9	17	8.4	33	7.8

Table 48. Human Poverty Index (continued)

Group/country	Human Poverty Index (HPI-1) 2004		Human Poverty Index (HPI-1) 2005		Human Poverty Index (HPI-1) 2006		Human Poverty Index (HPI-1) 2007	
	Rank	100–0 Value	Rank	100–0 Value	Rank	100–0 Value	Rank	100–0 Value
Group average								
Low-income		42.150		42.300		34.788		32.844
n		6		6		6		8
Middle-income		22.707		21.590		24.367		23.459
n		15		20		18		22
High-income		12.300		13.567		13.583		10.683
n		4		6		6		6
Under 1.5 mn population		18.355		19.763		22.860		20.152
n		11		16		15		21
Under 5 mn population		25.458		23.406		25.290		21.546
n		24		31		29		35

Source: UNDP, *Human Development Report*, various editions, available at http://hdr.undp.org/reports/global/2005/

Table 49. Births delivered by skilled health personnel and maternal mortality

Group/country	Percentage of births attended by skilled health personnel (doctor, nurse or midwife)				Maternal mortality ratio (per 100,000 live births)	
	Survey year	Percentage	Survey year	Percentage	Reported 1990–2004[a]	World Bank estimate, 2005
Low-income						
Commonwealth countries						
Gambia, The	2000	55	2006	57	730	690
Papua New Guinea	2000	41			370	470
Solomon Islands	1999	85			550	220
Other countries						
Central African Republic	2000	44	2006	53	1,100	980
Comoros	2000	62				
Guinea-Bissau	2000	35	2006	39	910	1100
Liberia	1999–2000	51	2007	46	580	1200
Mauritania	2000–2001	57	2007	61	750	820
São Tomé & Principe	2003	76	2006	81	–	–
Middle-income						
Commonwealth countries						
Belize	1999	83	2006	96	140	52
Botswana	2000	94			330	380
Dominica	2004	100	2005	99	67	–
Fiji Islands	2000	99			38	210
Grenada	2000	100	2005	100	1	–
Guyana	2003	94	2006	83	120	470
Jamaica	2003	97	2005	97	110	170
Kiribati	1998	85			56	–
Lesotho	2000	60	2004	55	760	960
Maldives	2001	70	2004	84	140	120
Mauritius	2003	98			22	15
Namibia	2000	76	2006	81	270	210
Nauru	–	–			–	–
St Kitts & Nevis	2000	99	2005	100	250	–
St Lucia	2000	100	2005	100	35	–
St Vincent & Grenadines	2001	100	2005	100	93	–
Samoa	1998	100			–	
Seychelles	–	–			57	–
Swaziland	2002	74	2007	69	230	390
Tonga	2000	95			–	–
Tuvalu	2002	100			–	–
Vanuatu	1999	88			68	–
Other countries						
Albania			2005	100		92
Armenia			2005	98		76
Bahrain	1995	98			46	32
Bhutan	2003	56			260	440
Bosnia-Herzegovina			2005–06	100		3
Cape Verde	1998	89	2005	78	76	210

Table 49. Births delivered by skilled health personnel and maternal mortality (continued)

Group/country	Percentage of births attended by skilled health personnel (doctor, nurse or midwife)				Maternal mortality ratio (per 100,000 live births)	
	Survey year	Percentage	Survey year	Percentage	Reported 1990–2004[a]	World Bank estimate, 2005
Middle-income (contin.)						
Other countries						
Congo Republic	–	–	2005	83	–	740
Costa Rica	2001	98	2004	99	36	30
Djibouti	2003	61			74	650
Estonia	2002	100	2006	100	8	25
Gabon	2000	86			520	520
Georgia			2005	98		66
Latvia			2006	100		10
Lebanon			1994–96	98		150
Lithuania			2006	100		11
Macedonia FYR			2006	99		
Moldova			2005	100		22
Mongolia			2005–06	99		46
Montenegro			2005	99		
Panama	2003	93	2006	91	40	130
Suriname	2000	85	2006	90	150	72
Timor-Leste	2003	18			–	380
Turkmenistan			2006	100		
Uruguay	1999	100			26	20
High-income						
Commonwealth countries						
Antigua & Barbuda	2005	100	2006	100	65	–
Bahamas, The	2000	99	2006	99	–	16
Barbados	2000	98	2004	100	0	16
Brunei Darussalam	1999	99			0	13
Cyprus		100			0	10
Malta	1993	98			–	8
New Zealand	1995	100			15	9
Singapore	1998	100			6	14
Trinidad & Tobago	2000	96	2006	98	45	45
Other countries						
Croatia			2005	100		7
Equatorial Guinea	2000	65			–	680
Iceland	–	–			–	4
Ireland	2003	100			6	1
Kuwait	1996	98			5	4
Luxembourg	2003	100			0	12
Norway	1988	100			6	7
Oman	2000	95	2006	98	23	64
Qatar	1998	99			10	12
Slovenia			2006	100		6
United Arab Emirates	1995	99			3	37

Notes: – = data not available; [a]Data refer to the most recent year available during the period specified in the column heading.

Source: UNICEF, Childinfo.org, available at http://childinfo.org/; UNICEF, *The State of the World's Children 2007, New York*

Table 50. Prevalence of underweight children

Group/country	Prevalence of underweight children under five years of age				Prevalence of underweight children under five years of age			
	Year	Age (months)	Moderate and severe	Severe	Year	Age (months)	Moderate and severe	Severe
			(per cent)	(per cent)			(per cent)	(per cent)
Low-income								
Commonwealth countries								
Gambia, The	2000	0–59	17.0	4.0	2006	0–59	20.3	3.9
Papua New Guinea	–	–	–	–	–	–	–	–
Solomon Islands	–	–	–	–	–	–	–	–
Other countries								
Central African Republic	2000	0–59	24.0	6.0	2006	0–59	28.5	8.3
Comoros	2001	0–59	25.0	9.0	2004	0–59	24.9	–
Guinea-Bissau	2000	0–59	25.0	7.0	2006	0–59	19.4	4.0
Liberia	1999–2000	0–59	26.4	7.9	2007	0–59	24.0	6.0
Mauritania	2000–2001	0–59	31.8	9.8	2007	0–59	30.0	7.0
São Tomé & Principe	2000	0–59	13.0	2.0	2006	0–59	9.2	1.2
Middle-income								
Commonwealth countries								
Belize	2002	0–59	1.0	0.1	2006	0–59	6.0	1.0
Botswana	2000	0–59	12.5	2.4	–	–	–	–
Dominica	–	–	–	–	–	–	–	–
Fiji Islands	–	–	–	–	–	–	–	–
Grenada	–	–	–	–	–	–	–	–
Guyana	2000	0–59	13.6	3.0	2006	0–59	12.0	2.0
Jamaica	2002	0–59	4.0	–	2004	0–59	4.0	–
Kiribati	–	–	–	–	1999	0–59	13.0	–
Lesotho	2004	0–59	19.8	3.6	2007	0–59	–	–
Maldives	2001	0–59	30.4	7.2	–	–	–	–
Mauritius	1995	0–59	14.9	2.0	–	–	–	–
Namibia	2000	0–59	24.0	5.4	2006–07	0–59	–	–
Nauru	–	–	–	–	–	–	–	–
St Kitts & Nevis	–	–	–	–	–	–	–	–
St Lucia	–	–	–	–	–	–	–	–
St Vincent & Grenadines	–	–	–	–	–	–	–	–
Samoa	–	–	–	–	–	–	–	–
Seychelles	–	–	–	–	–	–	–	–
Swaziland	2000	0–59	10.3	2.2	2006–07	0–59	7.0	–
Tonga	–	–	–	–	–	–	–	–
Tuvalu	–	–	–	–	–	–	–	–
Vanuatu	–	–	–	–	–	–	–	–
Other countries								
Albania					2005	0–59	8.0	1.0
Armenia					2005	0–59	4.0	0.0
Bahrain	1995	0–59	8.7	1.8	–	–	–	–
Bhutan	1999	6–59	18.7	3.1	–	–	–	–
Bosnia-Herzegovina					2005	0–59	2.0	0.0
Cape Verde	–	–	–	–	–	–	–	–
Congo Republic	1998-99	0–71	14.0	3.0	2005	0–59	14.4	2.7

Table 50. Prevalence of underweight children (continued)

Group/country	Prevalence of underweight children under five years of age				Prevalence of underweight children under five years of age			
	Year	Age (months)	Moderate and severe (per cent)	Severe (per cent)	Year	Age (months)	Moderate and severe (per cent)	Severe (per cent)
Middle-income (contin.)								
Other countries								
Costa Rica	1996	0–71	5.1	0.4	–	–	–	–
Djibouti	1996	0–59	18.0	6.0	2006	0–59	28.9	10.3
Estonia	–	–	–	–	–	–	–	–
Gabon	2000	0–59	11.9	2.1	–	–	–	–
Georgia					2005	0–59	2.0	0.0
Latvia								
Lebanon					2004	0–59	4.0	–
Lithuania								
Macedonia FYR					2006	0–59	2.0	0.0
Moldova					2005	0–59	4.0	1.0
Mongolia					2005	0–59	6.0	1.0
Montenegro					2005	0–59	3.0	1.0
Panama	1997	0–59	8.1	1.2	–	–	–	–
Suriname	2000	0–59	13.3	2.1	2006	0–59	10.0	1.0
Timor-Leste	2003	0–59	45.8	14.9	2007	0–59	49.0	15.0
Turkmenistan					2005	0–59	11.0	2.0
Uruguay	1994-95	0–59	4.9	0.8	2002	0–59	5.0	1.0
High-income								
Commonwealth countries								
Antigua & Barbuda	–	–	–	–	–	–	–	–
Bahamas, The	–	–	–	–	–	–	–	–
Barbados	–	–	–	–	–	–	–	–
Brunei Darussalam	–	–	–	–	–	–	–	–
Cyprus	–	–	–	–	–	–	–	–
Malta	–	–	–	–	–	–	–	–
New Zealand	–	–	–	–	–	–	–	–
Singapore	2000	0–59	3.4	0.2	–	–	–	–
Trinidad & Tobago	2000	0–59	5.9	0.5	–	–	–	–
Other countries								
Croatia					1995–96	1–6	1.0	–
Equatorial Guinea	2000	0–59	18.6	4.3	–	–	–	–
Iceland	–	–	–	–	–	–	–	–
Ireland	–	–	–	–	–	–	–	–
Kuwait	1996	0–59	9.8	2.9	–	–	–	–
Luxembourg	–	–	–	–	–	–	–	–
Norway	–	–	–	–	–	–	–	–
Oman	1998	0–59	17.8	1.3	–	–	–	–
Qatar	1995	0–71	5.5	–	–	–	–	–
Slovenia					–	–	–	–
United Arab Emirates	1995	0–59	14.4	3.2	–	–	–	–

Source: UNICEF, Childinfo.org, available at http://childinfo.org/

Table 51. Under fives mortality rate

Group/country	Under fives mortality rate					
	1995	2000	2004	2005	2006	2007
	(per '000)					
Low-income						
Commonwealth countries						
Gambia, The	146	142	122	137	113	109
Papua New Guinea	87	80	93	74	73	65
Solomon Islands	35	32	56	29	73	70
Other countries						
Central African Republic	180	193	193	193	175	172
Comoros	101	84	70	71	68	66
Guinea-Bissau	235	215	203	200	200	198
Liberia	235	235	235	235	235	133
Mauritania	127	125	125	125	125	119
São Tomé & Principe	118	118	118	118	96	99
Middle-income						
Commonwealth countries						
Belize	32	23	39	17	16	25
Botswana	66	101	116	120	124	40
Dominica	15	14	14	15	15	11
Fiji Islands	19	18	20	18	18	18
Grenada	33	26	21	21	20	19
Guyana	79	70	64	63	62	60
Jamaica	20	20	20	20	31	31
Kiribati	77	70	65	65	64	63
Lesotho	91	108	82	132	132	84
Maldives	86	60	46	42	30	30
Mauritius	21	18	15	15	14	15
Namibia	77	69	63	62	61	68
Nauru	30	30	30	30	30	30
St Kitts & Nevis	30	25	21	20	19	18
St Lucia	21	16	14	14	14	18
St Vincent & Grenadines	22	22	22	20	20	19
Samoa	41	34	30	29	28	27
Seychelles	16	15	14	13	13	13
Swaziland	110	142	156	160	164	91
Tonga	29	26	25	24	24	23
Tuvalu	48	43	51	38	38	37
Vanuatu	50	48	40	38	36	34
Other countries						
Albania	34	24		17		15
Armenia	48	36		27		24
Bahrain	16	12	11	11	10	10
Bhutan	133	100	80	75	70	84
Bosnia-Herzegovina	19	17		15		14
Cape Verde	50	42	36	35	34	32
Congo Republic	108	108	108	108	126	125
Costa Rica	16	14	13	12	12	12
Djibouti	161	147	126	133	130	127
Estonia	19	11	8	7	7	6
Gabon	91	91	91	91	91	91

Table 51. Under fives mortality rate (continued)

Group/country	Under fives mortality rate					
	1995	2000	2004	2005	2006	2007
	(per '000)					
Middle-income (contin.)						
Other countries						
Georgia	40	35		32		30
Latvia	19	15		10		9
Lebanon	34	32		30		29
Lithuania	15	11		9		8
Macedonia FYR	26	16		17		17
Moldova	30	24		20		18
Mongolia	82	63		48		43
Montenegro	15	14		11		10
Panama	30	26	24	24	23	23
Suriname	44	41	39	39	39	29
Timor-Leste	154	107	80	61	55	97
Turkmenistan	87	71		55		50
Uruguay	20	15	17	15	12	14
High-income						
Commonwealth countries						
Antigua & Barbuda	21	15	12	12	11	11
Bahamas, The	24	19	13	15	14	13
Barbados	15	13	12	12	12	12
Brunei Darussalam	9	9	9	9	9	9
Cyprus	9	6	5	5	4	5
Malta	11	7	6	6	6	5
New Zealand	9	8	6	6	6	6
Singapore	5	4	3	3	3	3
Trinidad & Tobago	28	23	20	19	38	35
Other countries						
Croatia	10	8		7		6
Equatorial Guinea	187	200	204	205	206	206
Iceland	6	3	3	3	3	3
Ireland	8	7	6	6	5	4
Kuwait	14	11	12	11	11	11
Luxembourg	5	5	6	5	4	3
Norway	5	5	4	4	4	4
Oman	19	15	13	12	12	12
Qatar	24	23	21	21	21	15
Slovenia	7	5		4		4
United Arab Emirates	12	10	8	9	8	8

Source: UNICEF, Childinfo.org, available at http://childinfo.org/

Table 52. Summary statistics of HIV/AIDS, malaria and tuberculosis

Group/country	Estimate of the total number of people living with HIV/AIDS		Estimated prevalence: adult (15–49) rate		Estimated total deaths in adults and children		Deaths of children under 5 years from malaria	Estimated TB deaths, TB mortality, all forms (per year) > total			
	2005	2007	2005	2007	2005	2007	2000	2004	2005	2006	2007
			(%)				(%)				
Low-income											
Commonwealth countries											
Gambia, The	20,000	8,200	2.4	0.9	1,300	–	29.4	648	699	887	936
Papua New Guinea	60,000	54,000	1.8	1.5	3,300	<1000	0.8	2,698	2,725	3,006	3,817
Solomon Islands	–	–	–	–	–	–	0.1	119	112	111	105
Other countries											
Central African Republic	250,000	160,000	10.7	6.3	24,000	11,000	18.5	4,214	3,666	3,394	4,330
Comoros	<500	<200	<0.1	0.1	<100	–	19.4	57	54	54	54
Guinea-Bissau	32,000	16,000	3.8	1.8	2,700	1,100	21	592	640	655	747
Liberia	–	35,000	–	1.7	–	2,300	18.9	2,106	2,292	2,493	2,325
Mauritania	12,000	14,000	0.7	0.8	<1,000	<1000	12.2	1,831	2,115	2,156	2,353
São Tomé & Principe	–	–	–	–	–	–	0.6	42	42	40	42
Middle-income											
Commonwealth countries											
Belize	3,700	3,600	0.3	2.1	<100	<200	0	21	14	17	20
Botswana	270,000	300,000	24.1	23.9	18,000	11,000	0	1,555	1,547	1,696	3,649
Dominica	–	–	–	–	–	–	0	2	2	1	1
Fiji Islands	<1,000	–	0.1	0.1	<100	–	0	32	31	25	29
Grenada	–	–	–	–	–	–	0	1	1	1	1
Guyana	12,000	13,000	2.4	2.5	1,200	<1000	0.7	181	191	213	174
Jamaica	25,000	27,000	1.5	1.6	1,300	1,500	0	27	29	35	30
Kiribati	–	–	–	–	–	–	0.7	50	49	42	46
Lesotho	270,000	270,000	23.2	23.2	23,000	18,000	0	1,553	1,926	1,764	5.282
Maldives	–	–	–	0.1	–	–	0.6	14	11	12	12
Mauritius	4,100	13,000	0.6	1.7	<100	–	0	139	141	46	48
Namibia	230,000	200,000	19.6	15.3	17,000	5,100	0	1,555	1,561	1,956	2,124
Nauru	–	–	–	–	–	–	0	3	2	2	0
St Kitts & Nevis	–	–	–	–	–	–	0	1	1	1	1
St Lucia	–	–	–	–	–	–	0	3	3	3	3
St Vincent & the Grenadines	–	–	–	–	–	–	0	6	5	6	6
Samoa	–	–	–	–	–	–	0.1	5	6	5	5
Seychelles	–	–	–	–	–	–	0	3	4	4	4
Swaziland	220,000	190,000	33.4	26.1	16,000	10,000	0.2	2,761	3,137	3,157	3.619
Tonga	–	–	–	–	–	–	1.3	4	3	3	2
Tuvalu	–	–	–	–	–	–	0	6	6	6	2
Vanuatu	–	–	–	–	–	–	0.6	11	21	17	27
Other countries											
Albania	–	–	–	–	–	–	0.4	117	114	107	98
Armenia	2,900		0.1		<500	–	0.5	331	306	308	313
Bahrain	<1,000	<1000	–	–	–	–	0	30	29	30	35
Bhutan	<500	<500	<0.1	0	<100	–	0.8	422	412	45	288
Bosnia-Herzegovina	<500	–	<0.1		–	–	0	264	298	296	293
Cape Verde	–	–	–	–	–	–	4.3	224	189	189	166
Congo Republic	120,000	79,000	5.3	3.5	11,000	6,400	25.7	2,652	2,747	2,946	3,405
Costa Rica	7,400	9,700	0.3	0.4	<100	<200	0	54	60	60	39

Table 52: Summary statistics of HIV/AIDS, malaria and tuberculosis
(continued)

Group/country	Estimate of the total number of people living with HIV/AIDS		Estimated prevalence: adult (15–49) rate		Estimated total deaths in adults and children		Deaths of children under 5 years from malaria	Estimated TB deaths, TB mortality, all forms (per year) > total			
	2005	2007	2005	2007	2005	2007	2000	2003	2004	2005	2006
			(%)				(%)				
Middle-income (continued)											
Other countries											
Djibouti	15,000	16,000	3.1	3.1	1,200	1,100	0.8	982	1,012	1,136	1,304
Estonia	10,000	9,900	1.3	1.3	–	<500	0	94	84	84	81
Gabon	60,000	49,000	7.9	5.9	4,700	2,300	28.3	800	903	902	1.011
Georgia	5,600		0.2		<500		0.3	598	498	409	408
Latvia	10,000		0.8		<500		0	233	213	197	179
Lebanon	2,900		0.1		<100		0	72	72	77	82
Lithuania	3,300		0.2		<100		0	317	270	246	295
Macedonia FYR	<500		<0.1		<100		0	106	105	104	103
Moldova	29,000		1.1		1,400			732	730	726	722
Mongolia	<500		<0.1		<100		1	737	722	559	762
Montenegro											
Panama	17,000	20,000	0.9	1.0	<1,000	<1000	0.2	110	113	122	139
Suriname	5,200	6,800	1.9	2.4	<500	–	2.4	60	59	60	131
Timor-Leste	–	–	–	–	–	–	0.4	756	835	1,093	544
Turkmenistan	<500		<0.1	–	–	–	0.9	520	492	494	460
Uruguay	9,600	10,000	0.5	0.6	<500	<500	0	105	104	108	84
High-income											
Commonwealth countries											
Antigua & Barbuda	–	–	–	–	–	–	0	1	1	1	1
Bahamas, The	6,800	6,200	3.3	3.0	<500	<200	0	20	20	25	30
Barbados	2,700	2,200	1.5	1.2	<500	<100	0	4	4	6	1
Brunei Darussalam	<100	–	<0.1	–	<100	–	0	19	19	43	27
Cyprus	<500	<500	–	–	–	–	0	4	4	4	4
Malta	<500	<500	0.1	0.1	<100	–	0	3	3	3	3
New Zealand	1,400	1,400	0.1	0.1	–	–	0	37	36	35	30
Singapore	5,500	4,200	0.3	0.2	<100	<200	0	146	109	98	122
Trinidad & Tobago	27,000	14,000	2.6	1.5	1,900	–	0	19	18	21	26
Other countries											
Croatia	<500		<0.1				0	304	298	296	293
Equatorial Guinea	8,900	11,000	3.2	3.4	<1,000	–	24	233	238	267	442
Iceland	<500	<500	0.2	0.2	<100	–	0	1	1	1	1
Ireland	5,000	5,500	0.2	0.2	<100	<100	0	52	52	58	59
Kuwait	<1,000	<1000	–		–	–	0	72	66	59	68
Luxembourg	<1,000	–	0.2	0.2	<100	–	0	6	5	6	6
Norway	2,500	3,000	0.1	0.1	<100	–	0	25	24	26	26
Oman	–	–	–		–	–	0.1	24	22	29	30
Qatar	–	–	–	–	–	–	0	49	47	56	61
Slovenia	<500		<0.1		<0.1	–	0	45	40	39	37
United Arab Emirates	–	–	–	–	–	–	0	83	82	79	80

Note: – = not available.

Source: Malaria – World Health Organisation Statistical Information System (WHOSIS), available at http://www3.who.int/whosis/core/core_select_process.cfm; Tuberculosis – World Health Organisation, available at http://www.who.int/globalatlas/

Table 53. Environment

Group/country	CO^2 emissions			Forest annual change rate				Slum dwelling			
								Urban dwellers living in slums	Slum population	Urban dwellers living in slums	Slum population
	2003	2004	2005	1990–2000		2000–2005		2001	2001	2005	2005
	(metric tonnes per capita)			(1000 ha/yr)	(%)	(1000 ha/yr)	(%)	(%)	('000)	(%)	('000)
Low-income											
Commonwealth countries											
Gambia, The	0.2	0.2	0.2	2	0.4	2	0.4	67.0	280	45.4	371
Papua New Guinea	0.4	0.4	0.7	–139	–0.5	–139	–0.5	–	–	–	–
Solomon Islands	0.4	0.3	0.4	–40	–1.5	–40	–1.7	–	–	–	–
Other countries											
Central African Republic	0.1	0.1	0.1	–30	–0.1	–30	–0.1	92.4	1455	94.1	1446
Comoros	0.2	0.1	0.1	n.s.	–4	–1	–7.4	61.2	151	68.9	204
Guinea-Bissau	0.2	0.2	0.2	–10	–0.4	–10	–0.5	93.4	371	83.1	390
Liberia	0.1	–	0.1	–60	–1.6	–60	–1.8	55.7	788	–	–
Mauritania	0.6	0.8	0.6	–10	–2.7	–10	–3.4	94.3	1531	–	–
São Tomé & Principe	0.6	0.5	0.7	0	0	0	0	2.0	1	–	–
Middle-income											
Commonwealth countries											
Belize	2.9	2.9	2.8	0	0	0	0	62.0	69	47.3	61
Botswana	2.3	2.4	2.5	–118	–0.9	–118	–1	60.7	466	–	–
Dominica	2.0	1.5	1.6	n.s.	–0.5	n.s.	–0.6	14.0	7	–	–
Fiji Islands	1.3	1.2	2	2	0.2	0	0	–	–	–	–
Grenada	2.1	2.7	2.2	n.s.	n.s.	0	0	6.9	2	6.0	2
Guyana	2.2	1.9	2	n.s.	n.s.	0	0	4.9	14	33.7	72
Jamaica	4.1	4.0	3.8	n.s.	–0.1	n.s.	–0.1	35.7	525	60.5	852
Kiribati	0.3	–	0.3	0	0	0	0	–	–	–	–
Lesotho	–	–	–	n.s.	3.4	n.s.	2.7	57.0	337	35.1	118
Maldives	1.4	2.5	2.4	0	0	0	0	0.0	–	–	–
Mauritius	2.6	2.6	2.7	n.s.	–0.3	n.s.	–0.5	–	–	–	–
Namibia	1.2	1.2	1.3	–73	–0.9	–74	–0.9	37.9	213	33.9	242
Nauru				0	–	0	–	–	–	–	–
St Kitts & Nevis	2.7	3.2	2.8	0	0	0	0	5.0	1	–	–
St Lucia	2.0	2.2	2.2	0	0	0	0	11.9	7	11.9	6
St Vincent & the Grenadines	1.7	1.7	1.6	n.s.	0.8	n.s.	0.8	5.0	3	–	–
Samoa	0.8	0.8	0.8	4	2.8	0	0	–	–	–	–
Seychelles	6.6	6.7	7	0	0	0	0	2.0	1	–	–
Swaziland	0.9	0.8	0.8	5	0.9	5	0.9	–	–	–	–
Tonga	1.1	1.1	1.2	0	0	0	0	–	–	–	–
Trinidad & Tobago	22.1	24.9	24.7	0	0	0	0	32.0	310	24.7	247
Tuvalu	–	–	–	–1	–0.3	n.s.	–0.2	–	–	–	–
Vanuatu	0.4	0.4	0.4	0	0	0	0	–	–	–	–
Other countries											
Albania	1.0	1.2	1.1								
Armenia	1.2	1.2	1.4								
Bahrain	31.0	23.9	27.1	n.s.	5.6	n.s.	3.8	2.0	12	–	–
Bhutan	0.6	0.2	0.6	11	0.3	11	0.3	44.1	70	–	49
Bosnia-Herzegovina	6.2	6.5	6.9								

Table 53. Environment (continued)

Group/country	CO^2 emissions			Forest annual change rate				Slum dwelling			
								Urban dwellers living in slums	Slum population	Urban dwellers living in slums	Slum population
	2003	2004	2005	1990–2000		2000–2005		2001	2001	2005	2005
	(metric tonnes per capita)			(1000 ha/yr)	(%)	(1000 ha/yr)	(%)	(%)	('000)	(%)	('000)
Middle-income (continued)											
Other countries											
Cape Verde	0.3	0.7	0.6	8	0.4	8	0.4	69.6	193	–	–
Congo Republic	0.4	1.0	0.6	–17	–0.1	–17	–0.1	90.1	1,852	53.4	1,285
Costa Rica	1.5	1.5	1.7	2	3.6	n.s.	0.4	12.8	313	10.9	290
Djibouti	0.5	0.5	0.5	–19	–0.8	3	0.1	–	–	–	–
Estonia	13.5	14.0	13.5	0	0	0	0	–	–	–	–
Gabon	0.9	1.0	1.2	–10	n.s.	–10	n.s.	66.2	688	38.7	447
Georgia	0.8	0.9	1.1								
Latvia	2.9	2.8	2.8								
Lebanon	4.8	4.1	4.2								
Lithuania	3.6	3.9	4.1								
Macedonia FYR	5.1	5.1	5.1								
Moldova	1.8	2.0	2.1								
Mongolia	3.2	3.4	3.4								
Montenegro	–	–	–								
Panama	1.9	1.8	1.8	–7	–0.2	–3	–0.1	30.8	505	23.0	430
Suriname	5.0	5.2	5.2	0	0	0	0	6.9	22	3.9	13
Timor-Leste	0.2	0.2	0.2	–11	–1.2	–11	–1.3	12.0	7	–	–
Turkmenistan	9.2	8.3	8.6								
Uruguay	1.3	1.6	1.7	50	4.5	19	1.3	2.0	62	–	–
High-income											
Commonwealth countries											
Antigua & Barbuda	5.0	6.0	5.1	0	0	0	0	6.9	2	4.8	1
Bahamas, The	5.9	6.7	6.5	0	0	0	0	2.0	5	–	–
Barbados	4.4	4.7	4.5	0	0	0	0	1.0	1	–	–
Brunei Darussalam	12.7	24.0	15.8	–2	–0.8	–2	–0.7	2.0	5	–	–
Cyprus	10.1	9.2	8.4	1	0.7	n.s.	0.2	–	–	–	–
Malta	6.2	6.1	6.3	0	0	0	0	–	–	–	–
New Zealand	8.7	7.7	7.2	51	0.6	17	0.2	–	–	–	–
Singapore	11.4	12.3	13.2	0	0	0	0	0.0	–	–	–
Other countries											
Croatia	5.4	5.2	5.2								
Equatorial Guinea	0.3	10.5	9.0	–15	–0.8	–15	–0.9	86.5	201	66.3	130
Iceland	7.6	7.6	7.4	1	4.3	2	3.9	–	–	–	–
Ireland	10.4	10.5	10.2	17	3.3	12	1.9	–	–	–	–
Kuwait	32.7	37.1	36.9	n.s.	3.5	n.s.	2.7	3.0	56	–	–
Luxembourg	22.1	25.0	24.8	n.s.	0.1	0	0	–	–	–	–
Norway	9.9	19.1	11.4	17	0.2	17	0.2	–	–	–	–
Oman	12.8	13.6	12.5	0	0	0	0	60.5	1,214	–	1,461
Qatar	63.0	79.3	62.6	0	0	0	0	2	8	2.0	11
Slovenia	7.4	7.4	7.4								
United Arab Emirates	33.4	34.1	30.1	6	2.4	n.s.	0.1	2.0	46	–	–

Source: World Bank data, available at http://devdata.worldbank.org/data/; Food and Agriculture Organisation, available at http://www.fao.org/forestry/foris/webview/forestry2/index.jsp?siteId=6833&sitetreeId=32038&langId=1&geoId=0; UNHABITAT, *State of the World's Cities 2006/7,* Nairobi, Kenya

Table 54. Main indicators of communications

Group/country	Internet users (per 1000 people)				Mobile phones (per 100 inhabitants)			
	2005	2006	2007	2008	2005	2006	2007	2008
Low-income								
Commonwealth countries								
Gambia, The	–	52.9	58.7	68.8	16.31	25.99	46.84	70.24
Papua New Guinea	22.93	18.3	18.3	17.9	0.44	1.67	4.74	4.67
Solomon Islands	8.37	16.3	16.3	18.1	1.26	1.43	2.2	2.19
Other countries								
Central African Republic	2.72	3.2	3.2	4.4	1.53	2.69	2.99	3.55
Comoros	33.31	25.6	25.6	34.2	2.01	4.5	4.77	6.2
Guinea-Bissau	19.54	22.6	22.6	23.5	5.01	9.63	17.48	31.75
Liberia	–	0.3	5.3	5.5	4.87	8.34	15.01	19.3
Mauritania	6.52	9.5	9.5	14.3	20.04	33.57	41.62	65.07
São Tomé & Principe	–	137.4	145.9	154.8	7.64	11.51	19.09	30.59
Middle-income								
Commonwealth countries								
Belize	130.23	109.1	111.2	108.6	34.48	44.05	41.12	53.23
Botswana	34.0	45.5	53.1	41.6	46.63	46.78	75.84	77.34
Dominica	361.11	372.2	372.2	394.0	58.68	53.27	53.27	132.76
Fiji Islands	76.68	93.6	93.6	109.0	16.79	33.32	63.2	71.09
Grenada	–	212.4	217.7	222.9	42.05	44.59	44.59	57.97
Guyana	212.99	232.7	257.5	248.7	33.29	37.45	37.45	36.84
Jamaica	–	488.1	552.7	568.8	101.85	93.74	93.74	100.58
Lesotho	–	33.5	34.9	35.8	13.65	19.99	22.71	28.35
Kiribati	20.2	21.5	–	21.0	0.72	0.75	0.75	0.79
Maldives	–	89.7	108.0	235.2	46.77	90.7	102.61	142.82
Mauritius	–	254.8	269.5	296.9	57.29	61.5	73.6	80.74
Namibia	–	43.9	48.7	53.3	24.37	29.67	38.58	49.39
Nauru								
St Kitts & Nevis	–	–	–	297.5	20.0	–	–	146.78
St Lucia	–	616.9	667.0	586.8	62.0	65.72	65.72	99.53
St Vincent & the Grenadines	84	294.1	473.4	604.9	59.34	73.64	91.77	119.23
Samoa	32.44	44.6	44.6	47.5	12.97	25.39	45.98	48.06
Seychelles	248.54	356.7	369.5	381.7	70.37	86.52	89.23	101.78
Swaziland	–	40.8	40.8	41.3	19.36	24.29	33.29	39.13
Tonga	29.32	30.2	83.7	81.1	16.43	29.29	46.37	48.73
Tuvalu	–	–	–	406.3	–	–	–	18.28
Vanuatu	37.85	60.4	75.2	74.6	5.82	6.96	11.5	11.4
Other countries								
Albania	59.61	148.6	–	–	48.52	59.90	72.30	–
Armenia	53.35	57.4	–	–	10.54	41.86	62.36	–
Bahrain	213.32	284.4	332.2	519.5	102.99	122.88	148.28	180.51
Bhutan	39.27	35.7	46	58.2	4.85	9.77	17.18	36.55
Bosnia-Herzegovina	155.43	213.3	251.51	279.62	42.16	49.98	64.95	–
Cape Verde	49.33	63.6	69.8	206.1	16.12	20.99	27.9	55.68
Congo Republic	12.5	17.0	17	42.9	12.25	22.29	34.17	49.98
Costa Rica	254.2	276.1	335.7	323.1	25.45	32.82	33.76	41.75
Djibouti	12.61	13.6	13.6	13.4	5.07	5.55	5.55	5.47
Estonia	512.59	551.0	584.1	636.4	108.75	125.19	148.42	188.2
Gabon	48.42	54.5	61.6	62.1	46.95	63.86	87.86	89.77

Table 54. Main indicators of communications (continued)

Group/country	Internet users (per 1000 people)				Mobile phones (per 100 inhabitants)			
	2005	2006	2007	2008	2005	2006	2007	2008
Middle-income (continued)								
Other countries								
Georgia	60.67	74.9	81.84	–	26.25	38.44	59.1	–
Latvia	421.18	501.6	550.23	–	581.36	95.44	97.4	–
Lebanon	174.53	234.3	383.2	–	24.77	27.28	30.75	–
Lithuania	341.67	422.9	492.08	–	127.51	139.01	145.78	–
Macedonia FYR	230.05	250.1	272.96	–	62.02	69.59	95.57	–
Moldova	141.87	189.9	184.03	–	28.11	35.44	49.5	–
Mongolia	105.05	119.9	122.68	–	21.82	29.99	–	–
Montenegro	399.69	442.6	467.44	–	89.35	107.1	–	–
Panama	63.8	173.5	222.9	229.1	41.88	66.14	90.05	111.94
Suriname	71.23	84.1	96.1	86.2	51.85	70.8	70.8	63.33
Timor-Leste	–	1.2	1.2	1.4	–	4.88	6.77	7.35
Turkmenistan	9.99	13.2	14.1	–	2.17	4.43	7	–
Uruguay	192.89	243.9	289.8	400.1	18.51	66.83	89.96	104.73
High-income								
Commonwealth countries								
Antigua & Barbuda	350.3	642.4	722.9	750.3	70.13	133.55	133.55	157.67
Bahamas, The	318.82	336.0	362.2	420.5	58.68	77.27	112.9	106.04
Barbados	593.57	593.6	593.6	738.6	73.85	87.76	87.76	132.00
Brunei Darussalam	–	416.9	416.9	488.2	56.26	78.92	78.92	90.66
Cyprus	430.19	422.2	444.6	380.4	86.09	102.75	115.64	117.89
Malta	315.36	337.1	388.6	491.4	80.79	85.96	91.38	94.64
New Zealand	671.89	541.5	545.6	697.6	87.61	93.59	101.74	109.22
Singapore	–	596.1	699.9	692.4	101.38	109.34	133.55	138.15
Trinidad & Tobago	–	151.6	159.6	160.2	61.26	116.02	113.24	113.67
Other countries								
Croatia	331.5	379.41	447.44	–	82.16	98.99	113.49	–
Equatorial Guinea	13.9	15.5	15.5	18.2	19.26	27.18	43.35	52.49
Iceland	869.42	653.0	672.0	656.4	103.4	101.62	108.85	106.33
Ireland	275.71	342.3	397.1	637.9	101.49	112.59	115.86	113.77
Kuwait	276.09	289.3	315.7	315.7	88.57	91.49	97.28	97.28
Luxembourg	689.72	720.1	739.5	766.1	138.17	116.82	129.5	147.11
Norway	735.41	816.8	808.8	846.0	102.89	107.87	110.5	109.98
Oman	111.03	122.2	131.0	168.4	51.94	69.59	96.33	115.58
Qatar	269.43	345.5	417.5	340.4	92.15	109.6	150.41	131.39
Slovenia	462.09	499.6	525.64	–	87.94	90.67	95.55	–
United Arab Emirates	308.22	366.9	515.9	651.5	100.86	118.51	176.5	208.65

Source: International Telecommunications Union, Free Statistics, available at http://www.itu.int/ITU-D/ict/statistics/; World Bank, World Development Indicators, Data Query website, available at http://devdata.worldbank.org/data-query/

Small States Economic Review and Basic Statistics

List of Articles and Reviews Vol. 1 (1995) to Vol. 13 (2008)

1 Development Issues for Small States

How Small is Small? Vol. 1 (1995)
Major Characteristics of Small States Vol. 1 (1995)
Major Development Problems of Small States Vol. 1 (1995)
Major Development Concerns of Small States Vol. 2 (1996)
Progress Towards Achieving the Millennium Development Goals in the Small States of the Commonwealth, *Andrew S. Downes* Vol. 10 (2005)
The Macroeconomic and Growth Dynamics of Small States, *Gordon Cordina* Vol. 12 (2007)

2 Environmentally Sustainable Development

Role of Insurance in Covering Losses from Natural Disasters Vol. 2 (1996)
Small Island States in the Face of Climatic Change: The End of the Line in International Environmental Responsibility, *Alexander Gillespie* Vol. 8 (2003)
Sustainable Development of Small Island Developing States: The Challenge of Finance and Capacity Building, *Janet Strachan* Vol. 9 (2004)
Culture as the Fourth Pillar of Sustainable Development, *Keith Nurse* Vol. 11 (2006)
Renewable Energy and Energy Efficiency, *David Barrett* Vol. 12 (2007)

3 International Trade

Commonwealth Small States and the International Trading System Vol. 3 (1997)
WTO Issues for Small Vulnerable States, *Roman Grynberg* Vol. 5 (2000)
Small States in the Lomé Convention and in the New ACP-EU Partnership Agreement: A Commentary, *Pierre Berthelot* Vol. 6 (2001)
Small States in World Export Trade, *Mohammad A. Razzaque* Vol. 7 (2002)
Small Vulnerable Economy Issues and the WTO, *Roman Grynberg* and *Jan Yves Remy* Vol. 8 (2003)
Small Economies and Special and Differential Treatment: Strengthening The Evidence, Countering the Fallacies, *Virginia Horscroft* Vol. 10 (2005)

4 Competitiveness

Manufacturing Competitiveness with Special Reference to Small States Vol. 3 (1997)
Enhancing Small States' Competitiveness in the Global Economy, *Monique Pollard* Vol. 11 (2006)

5 Vulnerability and Resilience

An Overview of Vulnerability Issues Vol. 4 (1998)
Small States and Development: A Composite Index of Vulnerability Vol. 4 (1998)
Commonwealth Secretariat/World Bank Joint Task Force on Small States Vol. 5 (2000)
The Graduation issue for Small States, *Carlyle Mitchell* and *Eliawony J. Kisanga* Vol. 7 (2002)
Economic Vulnerability and Resilience: Concepts and Measurements, *Professor Lino Briguglio* Vol. 9 (2004)

6 Financial Sector

OECD Curbs on Offshore Financial Centres: Bullying Small States into Submission, *Professor Bishnodat Persaud* Vol. 6 (2001)

7 Small and Medium-sized Enterprises

Strengthening Supply Chains for Micro-, Small and Medium-sized Enterprises in Namibia, *Watipaso Mkandawire* — Vol. 13 (2008)

Experiences in MSME Networking Across Small States in the Commonwealth, *Ram Venuprasad* — Vol. 13 (2008)

MSME Development: Lessons from Small States, *David Ashiagbor* — Vol. 13 (2008)

Small-scale Activities and the Productivity Divide, *Naren Prasad* — Vol. 13 (2008)

Small States: Economic Review and Basic Statistics

Availability of previous volumes (at date of publication of Volume 14)

Vol. 1	1995	(no ISBN)	out of print
Vol. 2	1996	(no ISBN)	out of print
Vol. 3	1997	(978-0-85092-532-6)	out of print
Vol. 4	1998	(978-0-85092-610-1)	out of print
Vol. 5	2000	(978-0-85092-643-9)	out of print
Vol. 6	2001	(978-0-85092-683-5)	out of print
Vol. 7	2002	(978-0-85092-746-7)	out of print
Vol. 8	2003	(978-0-85092-794-8)	£12.50
Vol. 9	2004	(978-0-85092-816-7)	£12.50
Vol. 10	2005	(978-0-85092-831-0)	£25.00
Vol. 11	2006	(978-0-85092-848-8)	£25.00
Vol. 12	2007	(978-0-85092-863-1)	£25.00
Vol. 13	2008	(978-0-85092-893-8)	£25.00

Readership Survey

In order to improve the quality and relevance of *Small States: Economic Review and Basic Statistics*, we would like to have the views of readers about this publication.

It would therefore be greatly appreciated if you could complete the questionnaire below by **30 October 2010**.

The questionnaire can be completed online at: *http://www.thecommonwealth.org/economics*

If you wish this questionnaire to be sent to you via email, please send an email request to *a.armitage@commonwealth.int*

Alternatively, this form can be completed and faxed to +44 (0)207 7747 6235 or scanned and emailed to *a.armitage@commonwealth.int*

QUESTIONNAIRE

Introduction

1. Which of the following best describes your area of work? (please tick as appropriate)

Government ministry
Public enterprise
Private enterprise
Academic or research institution
International organisation
Media
Not-for-profit organisation
Other (specify)

2. How useful is *Small States: Economic Review and Basic Statistics* to your work?

1 (excellent)	2	3 (of some use)	4	5 (poor)

3. **Please give an example of how you have used, or plan to use, *Small States: Economic Review and Basic Statistics* in your work.**

Content

4. **Please indicate up to three things you like about *Small States: Economic Review and Basic Statistics.***

1.
2.
3.

5. **Please indicate up to three things you like least about *Small States: Economic Review and Basic Statistics.***

1.
2.
3.

6. **Please give one suggestion for an improvement to *Small States: Economic Review and Basic Statistics.***

7. What is your overall assessment of *Small States: Economic Review and Basic Statistics*?

1 (excellent)	2	3 (of some use)	4	5 (poor)
Further comments:				

8. *Small States: Economic Review and Basic Statistics* currently includes selected research papers in each issue. What should be the focus of the research papers? (please tick as appropriate)

Commonwealth Secretariat projects of relevance to small states
Case studies from small states
Research on issues of importance to small states
Other (please specify)

9. How can the statistical information presented in *Small States: Economic Review and Basic Statistics* be made more useful to you?

10. Did you find the chapter on recent economic developments in small states useful?

Yes ☐

No ☐

Please state reasons for your answer

Dissemination

11. Do you receive *Small States: Economic Review and Basic Statistics* each year? (please tick as appropriate)

Yes, and continue to send me copies (please confirm your name and address below).
Yes, but I do not wish to continue to receive copies (please confirm your name and address below).
No, and I do not wish to receive copies in the future.
No, but I would like to receive copies each year in the future (please confirm your name and address below).
Name
Address

12. Are there other persons and/or organisations in your country and region who you think would benefit from receiving a copy of each issue of this publication? If so, please provide their name, email address and postal address.

13. The statistics from the publication will soon be available online. How would you prefer the data to be available in the future? (please tick as appropriate)

Published online only
Published online and in print
Other
Please state reasons for your answer

14. **Please give the names of any other international annual economic dataset, review or publication that you currently make use of.**

15. **How does *Small States: Economic Review and Basic Statistics* compare with other publications and online sources**

Small states website

16. **How useful would you find web pages devoted to information on small states?**

1 (very useful)	2	3 (of some use)	4	5 (irrelevant)

Please state reasons for your answer:

17. **What do you think should be included on the web pages?**

Small states newsletter

18. How useful would you find a newsletter on small states?

1 (very useful)	2	3 (of some use)	4	5 (irrelevant) (please skip to question 21)
Please state reasons for your answer:				

Answer questions 19–20 if you would find a newsletter on small states very useful or of some use.

19. How often should the newsletter be issued? (please tick as appropriate)

Monthly
Quarterly
Other (please specify)

20. What do you think should be included in the newsletter? (please tick as appropriate)

Developments in small states which affect their vulnerability
Discussion/research on issues of importance to small states
Outcomes of international fora that affect small states, e.g. WTO, G20, World Bank
Articles relevant to small states from academic journals
Notices of upcoming meeting
Notices of recent publications
Feature articles written by small states' officials
Feature articles written by experts and staff of the Commonwealth Secretariat and other international organisations
Book reviews
Other (please specify)

Contact

21. Your name, organisation and email address (optional)